景观设计学（中英文）
LANDSCAPE ARCHITECTURE FRONTIERS

主管 中华人民共和国教育部
主办 高等教育出版社有限公司　北京大学
承办 北京大学建筑与景观设计学院
出版 高等教育出版社有限公司

SUPERVISOR Ministry of Education of the People's Republic of China
ADMINISTRATORS Higher Education Press Limited Company　Peking University
ORGANIZER College of Architecture and Landscape, Peking University
PUBLISHER Higher Education Press Limited Company

049 VOLUME 9 ISSUE 1
2021. 02
CN 10-1467/TU　ISSN 2096-336X
NATIONAL CIRCULATION CODE 80-985

目录

主编寄语

论文

观点与评论

主题实践

探索与过程

出版社 / **责任编辑** 张雪丽 / **地址** 北京市朝阳区惠新东街4号富盛大厦15层（100029）/ **网址** journal.hep.com.cn / **电话** 0086-10-5855 6534 / **编辑部** / **本期学术召集人** 袁嘉 / **编辑部主任** 佘依爽 / **责任编辑** 田乐 / **编辑** 王颖（兼本期内容编辑）、冉玲于、崔婧沄、张健（兼）/ **探索与过程专栏编辑** 陆小璇、蔡哲铭 / **美术指导** 王江 / **美术编辑** 陈丽丽 / **海外编辑** 姜斌 / **地址** 北京市海淀区中关村北大街127-1号北大科技园501室（100080）/ **电话** 0086-10-6274 7821 / **电子邮箱** lafrontiers@foxmail.com / **网站** www. lafrontiers.com @景观设计学LAFrontiers / **支持机构** 中国城市科学研究会景观学与美丽中国建设专业委员会 景观中国网站 www.landscape.cn @景观中国网 / **运营** 佘依爽、王秀丽 / **运营咨询** 0086-10-6274 5785 / **订阅咨询** 0086-10-6274 7841 / **广告经营许可证号** 京西工商广字第0430号 / **印刷** 北京雅昌艺术印刷有限公司 / **国内发行** 北京怡然置业装饰设计书店 / **国际发行** 中国国际图书贸易总公司 / **邮发代号** 80-985 / **定价** RMB 68.00 HKD 100.00 TWD 450.00 USD 40.00 EUR 35.00

目标与范围

《景观设计学》定位于景观设计的学术研究与设计实践的交叉领域，探讨如何通过景观设计学途径，探索解决中国和世界生态与环境问题的新观念、新理论和新方法；通过介绍和推广前沿景观设计实践，倡导有助于实现美丽中国与美丽地球的新美学和新文化；架设研究与社会需求之间的桥梁、科学与艺术之间的桥梁，引领当代景观设计学科的发展。读者群为相关领域的科研人员和专业实践群体、院校师生、决策者和广大城乡环境的建设者。

Aims and Scope

Landscape Architecture Frontiers puts its focus on the intersecting spheres of academic research and design practice in landscape architecture, discussing new opinions, theories, and approaches to address environmental and ecological issues through landscape architecture; advocating new aesthetics and new culture which benefit the beauty of China and the world by introducing and promoting most recent practice of landscape architecture. It acts as a bridge connecting research and social needs, science and art, leading the development of the discipline. Our audience includes researchers and professional architects, faculties and students, policy makers in related fields, and people who work on the environmental constructions in both urban and rural areas.

CONTENTS

EDITORIAL

PAPERS

VIEWS & CRITICISMS

THEMATIC PRACTICES

EXPERIMENTS & PROCESSES

PUBLISHER | EXECUTIVE EDITOR ZHANG Xueli ADD 4 Huixin Dongjie, Beijing 100029, China WEBSITE journal.hep.com.cn TEL 0086-10-5855 6534 **EDITORIAL OFFICE** | GUEST EDITOR OF THIS ISSUE YUAN Jia EDITORIAL DIRECTOR SHE Yishuang EXECUTIVE EDITOR Tina TIAN EDITORS WANG Ying (Editor-in-charge of this issue), RAN Lingyu, CUI Jingyun, Angus ZHANG COLUMN HOST OF EXPERIMENTS AND PROCESSES LU Xiaoxuan, Taro Zheming CAI ART DIRECTOR WANG Jiang GRAPHIC DESIGNER Lily CHEN OVERSEAS EDITOR JIANG Bin ADD Rm. 501, Peking University Science Park, 127-1 Zhongguancun North Street, Haidian District, Beijing (100080) TEL 0086-10-6274 7821 EMAIL lafrontiers@foxmail.com WEBSITE www.lafrontiers.com **SUPPORTING ORGANIZATIONS** | The Committee of Landscape Architecture, Chinese Society for Urban Studies (CLA) www.landscape.cn **OPERATION TEAM** | SHE Yishuang, WANG Xiuli **BUSINESS INQUIRIES** | 0086-10-6274 5785 **SUBSCRIPTION INQUIRIES** | 0086-10-6274 7841 **PRINTED BY** | Beijing Artron Colour Printing Co., Ltd. **GENERAL AGENCY IN CHINA** | Beijing Yiran Bookshop **GENERAL AGENCY ABROAD** | China International Book Trading Corporation **PRICE** | RMB 68.00 HKD 100.00 TWD 450.00 USD 40.00 EUR 35.00

理事单位
Council Members

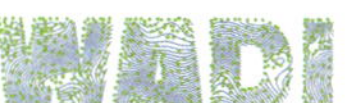

L&A 奥雅®

副理事长单位
Deputy Council Directors

时间 2005年4月7日
地点 圆明园遗址公园
拍摄 俞孔坚

圆明园遗址公园中正在消失的城市荒野。为迎接2008年北京奥运会，大规模的“美化运动”轰轰烈烈地开展起来。城市中的河流、湿地被硬化或渠化，湖底被铺上防渗膜，自生的乡土植物被视为杂草杂木彻底清除，代之以光鲜的观赏园艺花木，城市荒野被一扫而光。与此同时，一场捍卫城市荒野的行动也在生态学者和环保主义者的带领下声势浩大地进行着，2005年4月有关“圆明园环境整治工程环境影响”的全国性舆论即为其中一个焦点。正如梭罗所言，野性是有别于我们自身文明的另一种文明。因此，消灭或是捍卫城市荒野也是两种文明之间的斗争。

Date April 7, 2005
Location Yuan-ming Yuan
Photographer Yu Kongjian

The urban wildness that was disappearing in Yuan-ming Yuan: To prepare for the 2008 Summer Olympics, an aggressive beautification movement took place across the whole city of Beijing, where rivers and wetlands were channelized, lakebeds covered with anti-seepage geotextile, and spontaneous native plants weeded and replaced by ornamental flowers and trees. Ecologists and environmentalists soon launched a series of actions to resist the beautification movement that swept away urban wildness, among which the debate on the environmental impact of Yuanmingyuan Park Environmental Remediation Project in April 2005 was in the spotlight. Just like what Henry David Thoreau said, "What we call wildness is a civilization other than our own," wiping out or defending urban wildness is in essence a conflict between civilizations.

城市荒野：另一种文明
Urban Wildness as Another Civilization

俞孔坚
北京大学建筑与景观设计学院教授；美国艺术与科学院院士

YU Kongjian
Professor of College of Architecture and Landscape, Peking University; Member of the American Academy of Arts and Sciences

摘要

自折下树枝、打磨石块作为武器和工具、烧制黏土作为容器起，人类便开始走向背离荒野的文明之路——城市、农田和园林在化石能源和机械力的推动下，不断取代原生的自然，自然的野性被日益驯化。失去野性的人类变得寂寥而萎靡；于是，野性和荒野如今被重新提起。城市荒野既包括荒野景观，也包括保留了野性的、不受人工干预的自然过程和生物。作为一种自然生态系统，它依照自然规律做功，并以其自身逻辑建立起深邃的秩序，是保障城市生态系统健康和可持续性的要素。同时，城市荒野服务于人的审美启智，让人类探索未知的天性得以释放。不论是儿时记忆中的风水林和宅院中的水塘，还是圆明园遗址公园中的废墟，都是笔者难以忘怀的荒野。如今我们所经历的生态文明正是一种崇尚野性的新的文明，而捍卫城市荒野则是人类走向更高层次文明的必经之路。

关键词

城市荒野；野性；生态学；文化；生态文明

ABSTRACT

Ever since humans used branches and polished stones as weapons and tools, and made containers with clay, they had begun to get civilized apart from the wildness. With fossil energy and mechanical technology, cities, farmlands, and gardens have been constantly displacing the nature, and the wildness is disappearing. Human beings lost their instinct of wildness, lonely and dispirited. Nowadays, it is time to call for the return toward wildness. Urban wildness exists both in wildscapes and the human-intervention-free natural process or wild creatures. It is key to sustaining a healthy urban ecosystem as it can work with the laws of nature and the internal deep order as a natural ecosystem. Inspired by the aesthetics of urban wildness, humans explore the unknown world by their instinct. For me, the Fengshui forest and courtyard pond in my childhood and the relics in Yuan-ming Yuan were all unforgettable wildness. Today's ecological civilization enters a new era that embraces wildness, and defending urban wildness is the only way for humans to move toward a higher level of civilization.

KEYWORDS

Urban Wildness; Wildness; Ecology; Culture; Ecological Civilization

翻译 | 田乐、王颖
TRANSLATED BY | Tina TIAN, WANG Ying

城市中的荒野是工业文明桎梏下的野性遗漏，是由金属与玻璃构建的寂寥城市的凄美回眸和慰藉。好奇与探索的天性让人类文明在发展的道路上一往无前：从非洲草原走向亚洲丛林、欧洲冻原、美洲荒漠……于是，粗糙的矿石被打磨成光滑的玉器，黏土变作了洁白的瓷具，燧石的火星烧去了原野的荒芜，殖民地中的野花经过培育成为了贵族花园中的奇葩，自由流淌的溪流被改造为光滑的河渠，沼泽被开垦为田园和城镇……这是一条逐渐背离荒野的文明之路，城市、农田和园林在化石能源和机械力的推动下，不断取代原生的自然；自然的野性被日益驯化。“光滑”“精致”“高雅”和“温顺”等渐渐成为当代文明的重要特征。现代城市是当前最高层次文明的载体和象征，却已被演绎为用塑料、金属和玻璃搭建的宫殿——光鲜亮丽、不着尘埃，野草和昆虫失去容身之所，自然和野性只存在于电子屏幕和声光电的感官刺激之中。失去野性的人类，正如豢养在拉斯维加斯五星级酒店玻璃房中的老虎，寂寥而萎靡。于是，野性和荒野被重新提起。

城市荒野之于人类文明和城市化，恰如困兽囚笼中的一棵绿树、一丛野草或一条溪流。从发生学意义上讲，部分城市荒野作为原生自然的遗存斑块或廊道得以在城市中幸存，如残存的湿地（哈尔滨群力湿地公园等）；此外更多的是挣脱了文明约束的次生自然，如在荒废的灰色基础设施中恣意繁衍的自然（纽约高线公园的前身等）。城市荒野并不局限于荒野景观（wildscape或wilderness），还包含保留了野性（wildness）的、不受人工干预的自然过程和生物——从自由流淌的径流、未被改造的土壤和栖息其中的微生物、自由繁衍的乡土植物，到从水泥地中挣扎而出的野草和排水沟石壁上顽强生长的灌丛、随季节而生长凋落的树叶、能够感知天时的鸡鸣和蛙声……

从生态学意义上讲，城市荒野作为自然生态系统，依照自然规律做功，并以其自身逻辑建立起深邃的秩序，是保障城市生态系统健康和可持续性的要素。它为人类社会提供了不可或缺的生态系统服务，诸如净化空气和水、调节城市微气候、维持乡土生物多样性等。

从文化和心理学意义上讲，城市荒野的审美启智功能让人类探索未知的天性得以释放——这正是推动文明进步的原动力。于我看来，东西方哲人的深邃思考和智慧大多来源于荒野：如释迦摩尼的菩提树、穆罕默德的希拉山洞、王阳明的龙场山洞，以及梭罗的瓦尔登湖等。生态心理学认为，人与自然的日益分离将有损人类健康，而人类的健康源于地球的健康，疗愈人类身心疾病有赖于人与自然关系的修复，以及自然生态系统的修复[1]。景观感知的相关研究表明，景观的复杂性和可探索性决定了自然环境的美感[2]。相较而言，园艺化的景观（如修剪整齐的草坪）显得索然无味——它们纵然代表着文明进步、能令人获得须臾的喜悦和激动，却唤不起人类的探索欲望和冲动，也难以传达诗情画意的美感。

https://doi.org/10.15302/J-LAF-1-010012
收稿时间 RECEIVED DATE | 2021-01-06

中图分类号 | TU984
文献标识码 | C

谈及“荒野”，我的思绪不由地回到了儿时的两处秘境——一处是村子最南边的风水林，那里葬着祖先的遗骨，林冠蔽日、蘑菇遍地、野花隐约，时而有野兽出没；另一处是我家半亩宅院里的水塘，杂草丛生、鱼鳖藏匿，萤火虫和着各种虫鸣翻飞——它们时刻吸引着我去探寻并收获惊喜，就像鲁迅的百草园。拥有这样的荒野秘境，是我不幸童年的最大幸事。遗憾的是，它们都在我告别童年后相继消失了。先是风水林被园田化的水渠和机耕路切割开，随后林中的树木被砍伐殆尽，黄土深处的蛇洞被挖开，整整一窝赤链蛇（*Lycodon rufozonatus*）曝尸路面，原先见过的许多鸟兽也从此绝迹；而后，我宅院中的水塘逐渐干涸，最终被填平并盖上了房子。好在这两处荒野秘境尚能偶尔出现在梦境之中，给我带来无限的欢愉。

来到北京求学后，我也曾迷恋过一处荒野，那就是圆明园遗址公园中的废墟。几乎在整个20世纪80年代，这里都是我的最爱，也是我恋爱时流连忘返的去处。深浅不一的坑塘与土丘交错分布，乱石散落其间，零星的精美石雕露出水面，水岸边被芦苇（*Phragmites australis*）、野慈姑（*Sagittaria trifolia*）和香蒲（*Typha orientalis*）等植被覆盖，走近时会有鱼蛙受惊，搅动起“啪啦”的水声。早春时节，遍地的苦荬菜（*Ixeris polycephala*）、毛地黄（*Digitalis purpurea*）、诸葛菜（*Orychophragmus violaceus*）、点地梅（*Androsace umbellata*）和紫花地丁（*Viola philippica*）给枯黄的土地铺上绚烂的彩色；此后，山桃（*Prunus davidiana*）、毛樱桃（*Prunus tomentosa*）、鼠李（*Rhamnus davurica*）、黄刺玫（*Rosa xanthina*）等相继开花。夏天的荫凉来自杨、柳、榆、槐、椿等乡土乔木，每一种乔木都因地势之高低和土地的不同湿度而统治着各自的群落，喜鹊（*Pica pica*）、灰喜鹊（*Cyaponica cyanus*）、乌鸦（*Corvus* sp.）和各种啄木鸟（Picidae spp.）栖息其间。秋天则被黄栌（*Cotiuns coggygria*）、山杏（*Prunus sibirica*）、银杏（*Ginkgo biloba*）和芦苇抢了风头，饱含野性的花青素让树叶红得热烈。我尤其喜爱冬天里的漫步——听冰裂的回声，看乌鸦在白杨树梢盘旋、苇穗在寒风中颤动，细赏残雪下的碑刻和悄悄觅食的麻雀。

但就在2008年北京奥运会举办前夕，为了向世界展示北京的文明和城市化水平，在“高雅化”和“美化”的名义下，这处举世无双的遗迹和最具北京特色的城市荒野，几乎在一夜之间被铲除：湖底铺上了防渗膜；荒野不再，取而代之的是光鲜的草坪与牡丹（*Paeonia suffruticosa*）、月季花（*Rosa chinensis*）等各色园艺花木，以及喜庆的灯笼。

为此，全国学界掀起了一场具有历史意义的捍卫圆明园废墟荒野的“抗争”运动[3]。而这场由生态学者和环保人士发起、全国大部分媒体参与其中的大讨论，赋予了圆明园注解文明与荒野的标本意义：这里最早是天然山前沼泽湿地，后来被开垦为稻田，形成素有北方“江南”之美誉的农业文明景观；继而为康熙、乾隆所钟爱，仿江南文人山水构筑起象征帝国大一统和富华的皇家园林；而后又被西方列强所焚毁，成为西方工业文明之崛起和中华农业文明之衰弱的标志；接着被撂荒，自然恢复其统治地位，百年的风霜雨雪和生物群落之演替，使圆明园遗址变成了拥有丰富文化与自然遗产的城市荒野。

值得一提的是，当代表中华造园艺术巅峰的圆明园被付之一炬之时，西方的先哲们已经在思考荒野的意义：“我们所说的野性是有别于我们自身文明的另一种文明”[4]。显然，梭罗所说的“自身文明”是当时西方社会为之狂热的工业文明。近150年后，当圆明园废墟被高雅化和城市化的力量所主导时，一场维护城市荒野的抗争也正在中国悄然发生……这场抗争，正是过程曲折而生动的“两种文明的斗争”[5]。如今，一种崇尚野性的新的文明——生态文明——正在崛起。

29年前，我曾独自沿瓦尔登湖漫步，沉浸在启迪哲人思考的荒野之中，脑中回荡着他的妙句——“世界保存于荒野之中”“最有活力的人是最具野性的人”[4]，这亦是我对于城市荒野的理解。这里的“人”不仅代表人类个体，也可指某个群体、城市、民族、国家，乃至整个人类物种及人类的文明社会。因而，捍卫城市荒野是人类走向更高层次文明的必经之路。**LAF**

Urban wildness has become the lost pearl in the industrialized city built with metal and glass. Human civilization continuously advances due to humans' instincts of curiosity and exploration—from African savannahs to Asian jungles, European tundra, and to American deserts.... Gradually, the rough ores were polished into jades and clay was made into porcelains; the sparks lighted by firestones burned away wild plains; wildflowers were cultivated into horticultural flowers in aristocratic gardens; free-running rivers turned into canals; marshes occupied for urban and rural developments.... With fossil energy and mechanical technology, cities, farmlands, and gardens have been constantly displacing the nature, and the wildness is disappearing. Henceforth, "smooth," "exquisite," "elegant," and "docile" now become "synonyms" of modern civilization. Modern cities magnifying the advance of civilization have evolved into a bright, beautiful, and clean palace built with plastic, metal, and glass, where however weed and insect habitats are increasingly eliminated; the nature and wildness, instead, only exists as virtual reality presented by electronic devices. Human beings lost their instinct of wildness, as lonely and dispirited tigers living in the glass cages of fancy hotels. It is time to call for the wildness.

Urban wildness is encroached in civilization and urbanization processes, exactly like the trees, clumps of weeds, or streams in the tiger cages. In a phylogenetic sense, urban wildness exists as primary nature in forms of debris of natural patches or corridors, such as remained wetlands (e.g., Harbin Qunli Stormwater Park), and as secondary nature which is free from human intervention, such as the natural vegetation growing in the abandoned gray infrastructure (e.g., the previous site of the High Line in New York). In addition to such wildscapes, urban wildness also includes the natural process or creatures (such as the natural runoffs, soils and microbes, spontaneous plants, weeds in concrete cracks, shrubs growing tenaciously on the stone walls of drains, leaves growing and falling seasonally, and cocks and frogs singing in different weathers) that are free from human intervention.

Ecologically, urban wildness is key to sustaining a healthy urban ecosystem as it can work with the laws of nature and the internal deep order as a natural ecosystem, which provides ecosystem services critical to human society, including air and water purification, microclimate regulation, and the maintenance of local biodiversity.

Urban wildness is also of cultural and psychological significance. Inspired by the aesthetics of urban wildness, humans explore the unknown world by their instinct, which is the motivity to civilization advancing. The wildness is also considered inspiration source of both eastern and western philosophers, such as the Bodhi tree for Sakyamuni Buddha, the Cave of Hira for Muhammad, the Longchang Cave for Wang Yangming, and the Walden Pond for Henry David Thoreau. Ecological psychology believes that human beings separated from the nature may suffer from health problems, which could be alleviated by re-establishing the human–nature harmony and restoring the natural ecosystem[1]. Research on landscape perception also proves that complex and explorable landscapes contribute to creating beautiful natural environments[2]. Their horticultural counterparts (such as well-manicured lawns) are dull—no matter how civilized or pleasant they are, they can neither attract humans to explore, nor convey a poetic aesthetic sense.

Speaking of "wildness," I could not help but reminisce about two fairylands in my childhood—one was the Fengshui forest in the south of my village, where the ancestors' remains were entombed, with mushrooms growing under the trees, and scattered wildflowers and wild animals around; the other was the pond in my courtyard, which covered an area of about 300 m^2 and homed fish and turtles, with overgrown weeds and dancing fireflies with other insects. For me, they were as attractive and explorative as the Baicao Garden for Lu Xun, which dispelled the gloom in my childhood. Unfortunately, they all disappeared years later: the Fengshui forest was substituted by farmlands with channels and roads, trees cut down, snake holes excavated and dead *Lycodon rufozonatus* saw everywhere, and native birds and beasts vanishing; soon after, the courtyard pond dried up and was eventually filled up to build a house. Till now, I could still dream about these fairylands of wildness, bringing me much pleasure.

When studying in Beijing, I was fascinated by the ruins and wildness of Yuan-ming Yuan, which was the dreamland in my twenties, as well as a dating place with my beloved. Ponds, mounds, and rocks scattered on the site, and exquisite stone carvings stood in the lake. *Phragmites australis*, *Sagittaria trifolia*, and *Typha orientalis* grew on the lakesides; When approached by people, fish and frogs splashed in the water. In early spring, *Ixeris polycephala*, *Digitalis purpurea*, *Orychophragmus violaceus*, *Androsace umbellate*, and *Viola philippica* brought colors and vibrancy to the land; since then, *Prunus davidiana*, *Prunus tomentosa*, *Rhamnus davurica*, and *Rosa xanthina* bloomed one after another. Native dominant trees with leafy shade in summer, such as poplars, willows, elms, locust trees, and trees of heaven, formed vegetation communities with varied terrain and moisture conditions, where *Pica pica*, *Cyaponica cyanus*, *Corvus* sp., and several Picidae species inhabited. Colored-leaf trees such as *Cotiuns coggygria*, *Prunus sibirica*, and *Ginkgo biloba*, as well as *Phragmites australis*, together created an alluring autumn wildscape. In winter, I loved walking on the frozen river surface, enjoying echoes of ice cracking, watching crows hovering over the poplar trees and reeds trembling in the wind, and appreciating the inscription covered by snow and the quietly foraging sparrows.

Sadly, on the eve of the 2008 Summer Olympics in Beijing, the world-level stunning heritage of urban wildness manifesting historic characteristics of Beijing was almost eliminated in the name of beautification. The lakebeds were covered with anti-seepage geotextile; wild plants were removed and replaced with *Paeonia suffruticosa*, *Rosa chinensis*, and other colorful horticultural species, ornamented with festive lanterns.

At the same time, scholars all over the country set off a "protest" movement to defend the relics and the wildness of Yuan-ming Yuan[3]. This nationwide debate, initiated by ecologists and environmentalists and supported by public media, highlighted Yuan-ming Yuan's symbolic significance in human civilization and urban wildness. The original site of the park was a natural marsh in front of mountain, and then reclaimed as a rice field, forming a landscape of agricultural civilization reputed as the "Watertown of North China"; during the reigns of Kangxi and Qianlong from the 17th to 18th century, the park was expanded into an imperial grand garden that imitated the remarkable poetic landscapes in lower reaches of Yangtze River; afterwards, the park was destroyed by the war between the rising western industrial civilization and the collapsing Chinese agricultural civilization; over the past century, natural succession dominated the site again and made the park an urban wildness with rich cultural and natural heritage.

It is worth mentioning that when Yuan-ming Yuan—the pearl of Chinese gardening art—was ruined, western philosophers were exploring the implications of wildness: "What we call wildness is a civilization other than our own."[4] The "civilization of our own" mentioned by Thoreau here undoubtedly referred to the industrial civilization fanatically pursued by the western world. However, nearly 150 years later, the fight against the prevalent beautification and urbanization happened. This defense of urban wildness is exactly a "conflict between two civilizations."[5] Today, a new civilization that embraces wildness—ecological civilization—is rising.

I still remember the days when I walked alone along the Walden Pond 29 years ago. During my immersing in the wildness, the ideas of Thoreau echoed in my head—"In wildness is the preservation of the world," "the most alive is the wildest."[4] It is exactly my understanding of urban wildness. For me, "the most alive" here can not only refer to a person per se, but also to a certain group, city, nation, country, and even the entire human race and human civilization. Therefore, defending urban wildness is the only way for humans to move toward a higher level of civilization. **LAF**

REFERENCES

[1] Roszak, T. (2001). *The Voice of the Earth: An Exploration of Ecopsychology*. Newburyport, MA: Red Wheel / Weiser.

[2] Kaplan, R., & Kaplan, S. (1989). *The Experience of Nature: A Psychological Perspective*. Cambridge, England: Cambridge University Press.

[3] Yu, K. (2003). Be Kind to the Ruins of Yuan-ming Yuan—Speech at the Symposium of "Restorative Planning for Yuan-ming Yuan". *Beijing Planning Review*, Supplement, 53-55.

[4] Thoreau, H. D. (1906). *The Writings of Henry D. Thoreau*. Boston, MA: Houghton Mifflin and Company.

[5] Yu, K. (2020). The Conflict between Two Civilizations: On Nature-Based Solutions. *Landscape Architecture Frontiers*, 8(3), 4-9.

城市荒野：夹缝中的自然与机遇

Urban Wilderness: Nature and the Potential in the Urban Cracks

袁嘉

重庆大学建筑城规学院副教授、博士生导师，山地城镇建设与新技术教育部重点实验室固定研究人员；中国科学院山地生态恢复与生物资源利用重点实验室生态恢复与生物多样性保育四川省重点实验室中国科学院成都生物研究所合作研究人员；《景观设计学》期刊"城市荒野与植物设计"主题学术召集人

YUAN Jia

Associate Professor and PhD Supervisor of the School of Architecture and Urban Planning, Research Fellow at the Key Laboratory of New Technology for Construction of Cities in Mountain Area, Chongqing University; Cooperative Research Fellow of the CAS Key Laboratory of Mountain Ecological Restoration and Bioresource Utilization & Ecological Restoration and Biodiversity Conservation Key Laboratory of Sichuan Province, Chengdu Institute of Biology, Chinese Academy of Sciences; Guest Editor of the Issue Themed on Urban Wilderness and Planting Design, *Landscape Architecture Frontiers* Journal

摘要

城市荒野是普遍存在于城市系统夹缝中的自然，可提供野生动植物生境及自然游憩地等，蕴藏着提升城市生态韧性的重要机遇。一方面，前所未有的城市化进程和公众的负面假设造成了城市荒野的不断缩减；另一方面，自然过程重新主导因工业衰退和城市收缩而产生的闲置土地，再野化理念与技术也逐步发展，突显了重建和激活城市荒野景观的巨大潜力。随着生态文明建设、"山-水-林-田-湖-草"生命共同体统筹协调，以及"基于自然的解决方案"在中国的不断推进，当前正是我们深入认知城市荒野、辨识其内涵与价值、构建认同并开展保护与修复实践的最佳时机。

关键词

城市荒野；生态机遇；生态文明；再野化；基于自然的解决方案

ABSTRACT

Urban wilderness is the remnant nature existing within the cracks of urban context, which can provide habitats for wildlife and natural recreation areas, with significance in optimizing urban ecological resilience. On the one hand, the unprecedented urbanization processes and the public's negative hypotheses on the concept have caused continuous reduction of urban wilderness; on the other hand, opportunities are seen in reconstructing and activating urban wilderness when natural processes return to dominate the idle lands resulting from industrial recession and urban shrinkage, and the rewilding concept and techniques develop gradually. With ecological civilization construction, the initiative of a systematic management of the mountains, waters, forests, farmlands, lakes, and grasslands, and the advance of adopting Nature-Based Solutions in China, it is the best time to acknowledge urban wilderness in depth, identify its connotations and values, construct identity recognition, and carry out practices of conservation and restoration.

KEYWORDS

Urban Wilderness; Ecological Opportunity; Ecological Civilization; Rewilding; Nature-Based Solutions

翻译 | 嵇扬、王颖、田乐
TRANSLATED BY | Victor JI, WANG Ying, Tina TIAN

过去数十年，城市的不断扩张导致了大量自然景观的丧失；同时，城市内部空间结构的变化造成了建筑密度的快速增加和土地利用集约化，使城市居民身边的自然空间不断收缩。长期缺乏自然体验导致的自然缺失症正成为一场不可忽视的社会危机，既威胁着人们的身心健康，也造成了人们对自然的敬畏心与保护意识的缺席[1]。在日常生活中，城市绿地为居民提供了接触自然的唯一途径。然而，受限于过度的人工干扰和偏狭的审美意识，城市绿地往往植物种类贫乏且景观结构单一，既无法展现真正的自然野趣，也难以提供足够的生物多样性来有效维持生态系统服务，部分人工痕迹浓厚的城市绿地更是被批判为"绿色荒漠"[2]。

如今，人们更加清晰地认识到，城市的可持续发展离不开基于自然的解决方案[3]，即保护、修复和可持续管理自然资源，在适应社会变革与环境变化的同时提供人类福祉，特别是生物多样性的效益[4]。事实上，人类的生态福祉根植于自然荒野，无论是关乎身心灵的全人健康，还是大气、水体与生物多样性的修复，都依赖于荒野[5]-[7]。无论是当今中国生态文明建设强调的统筹"山—水—林—田—湖—草"系统治理，还是全球范围内"自然需要一半"（Nature Needs Half）等生态运动的兴起[8]，都反映出人们对荒野不可替代价值的重视。

在高度人工化的城市中，依然残存着片段化的荒野景观。它们可能是被城市化吞没、但尚未开发的原生性荒野地，亦可是动植物种群自发迁入并自然演替而产生的次生荒野[9]。以笔者生活的重庆主城为例，在坡、坎、崖、槽谷、沟壑、平坝中的孤立高地、长江河道里的孤立岛屿、老旧工厂、废弃铁路等寻常可见的城市夹缝场景中，大量分布着以自然过程为主导的城市荒野片段，具有弥足珍贵的生态价值：丰富多样的乡土植物恣意生长，蛙鸣虫叫不绝于耳，黑冠鹃隼（*Aviceda leuphotes*）和短耳鸮（*Asio flammeus*）等猛禽时常可见，可为居民提供无需远行就能体验的自然野性；为野生动植物提供了栖息地与迁徙踏脚石，增加了城市绿地网络的生态连通性，从而维持城市生态系统的整体健康[10]；此外，有助于公众认识到人类与其他生物共享城市空间这一事实，开拓人们看待城市的不同视角[11]。

https://doi.org/10.15302/J-LAF-1-010013
收稿时间 RECEIVED DATE | 2021-04-03

中图分类号 | TU984
文献标识码 | C

然而，说服人们接受城市荒野这一概念，并意识到其自然资源属性和蕴藏的生态价值，是一项艰巨的挑战。人们习惯于欣赏模式化的人工造景，往往漠视城市荒野中富有野性的生命活力，忽视它们的生态效益，甚至可能因为其“无序”的视觉感受而对其加以清理或改造。美国荒野保护先驱奥尔多·利奥波德就曾批判城市居民（尤其是管理者）对城市景观中荒野要素的负面假设，认为城市荒野的价值能够、也应当在任何城市林地、公园甚至私家花园中得到体现[12]。而与此同时，我们正迎来重构城市荒野系统的机遇——无论是工业转型遗留下的棕地，还是因虚拟空间兴起和城市收缩而产生的闲置土地，亦或是退化的城市园林绿地，都具有再度转化成为城市荒野的潜力。此外，逐渐兴起的“再野化”（rewilding）理念鼓励减少人类活动干扰，借助自然力量修复生态系统和生态过程，从而增强城市景观的野性特征，提供了将“夹缝中的自然”转化为荒野斑块甚至复杂生境网络的可能。

时至今日，城市荒野的存在和价值依然存在争议。在本期中，我们为进一步厘清城市荒野的概念、内涵与价值而展开争鸣。万斯·G·马丁基于城市荒野与自然荒野的显著差别，提出将“城市荒野”概念表达为“城市野境”的学术思考；英戈·科瓦里克肯定了荒野片段在城市空间中的实际存在，并提出“古老”与“新生”两种主要城市荒野类型及分类标准。两位学者在城市荒野对于城市生态保护与绿色基础设施发展等方面的价值、机遇和挑战达成了共识。邵钰涵等人剖析了城市荒野概念的发展与演化，并对城市荒野价值认同的构建逻辑展开深入讨论，意图为城市居民和管理者发现、体验和可持续管理城市荒野提供科学依据。

本期亦汇集了一系列针对城市荒野保护、修复与管理的实践案例及相关思考。袁嘉等人基于主动利用景观生态流，模拟荒野植物群落结构、动态与过程，以及最小限度干预理念，提出城市植物景观再野化的技术框架，并结合重庆本土实践阐述了重建兼具生态调控和野态审美城市荒野景观的技术范式。沃尔特·科姆等人回顾了加拿大多伦多市汤米—汤普森公园在自然做功主导下，逐渐从建筑废料填埋场演变为自然保护区的历史过程，探讨了自然修复与设计干预之间的动态平衡，以及随时间推移而彼此和谐相融的理想状态与实现可能。托马斯·雷纳结合Phyto工作室在美国华盛顿特区的实践经验，介绍了拟自然植物群落设计的具体途径，提供了“后荒野”时代进行生态种植、突破当前人工植栽功能局限的积极策略。尹豪等人关注城市闲置地中自生植物所提供的生态自我修复机遇，基于实地观测，分析了闲置地自生植被的时空特征、植物群落特征及其环境因子和种源条件等。郭陶然等人结合上海乡土生态科普示范基地项目，从乡土生物引种、生物群落构建及后期效益评估等角度，记录了以生物多样性提升为目标的城市荒野生境营建实践过程。张子豪等人则探讨了将人工智能应用于解译和营建野地的可能性与理论框架，试图为利用全新景观策略培育新型野地提供一种发展技术多样性的潜在路径。

充分发挥城市荒野所提供的自然补偿功能，对实现城市韧性与优化城市系统的“自然—人工”二元驱动结构具有关键意义。希望本期内容能为广大国土空间规划、景观设计与生态领域从业者及相关决策制定者提供认识城市荒野的多元视角，共同探索城市荒野保护修复理论与技术，让城市重归文明与野性相融的乐土。**LAF**

In the past decades, the continuing urban sprawl leads to the huge loss of natural landscapes. Worse, the already limited natural spaces for citizens are undergoing shrinkage due to the rapid increase of building density and intensive land use brought about by the changes of the city's spatial structure. The long-term lack of opportunities for nature experience leads to the nature-deficit disorder, a non-negligible social crisis, not only threatening people's physical and mental health, but also resulting in the absence of veneration or conservation awareness of nature[1]. Nowadays, citizens' urgent need of urban green spaces for connecting with nature is hardly met due to the poor plant richness and homogeneous landscape structures. Excessive human interventions and the public's negative aesthetic awareness undermine the values of urban wilderness, decrease urban biodiversity that is vital to sustaining ecosystem services, and aggravate the creation of urban green spaces that require high maintenance as “green deserts”[2].

By now, an unparalleled emphasis has been put on Nature-Based Solutions[3] in keeping the sustainable development of cities, i.e. conserving, restoring, and sustainably managing natural resources to attune to social and environmental changes and guarantee human well-beings, especially the biodiversity benefits[4]. The natural wilderness is exactly where the ecological benefits rooted, supporting the holistic health of humans, the improvement of air and water quality, and the restoration of biodiversity[5]~[7]. Nowadays no matter at home or abroad—such as the initiative of the sustainable management of territorial ecosystems of mountains, rivers, forests, farmlands, lakes, and grasslands emphasized in China's ecological civilization construction, and the rise of ecological movements like "Nature Needs Half" worldwide[8]—people begin to recognize the irreplaceable values of wilderness.

In highly artificialized cities, fragments of wilderness exist as well, including the undeveloped original wilderness encompassed by urbanization, and the secondary wilderness shaped by the spontaneous migration of wildlife and succession in natural communities[9]. In the center of Chongqing, for instance, these urban wilderness fragments based on a robust self-regulation of ecosystem processes are ubiquitously seen in the cracks in the city, from slopes, banks, cliffs, trough valleys, ravines to isolated highlands in intermountain basin, isolated islands in the river course, derelict factories, and abandoned railways. They are of rich ecological values: various native plants grow wildly with singing frogs and insects, and raptors such as *Aviceda leuphotes* and *Asio flammeus* are commonly observed, providing citizens with opportunities embracing nature without a long journey. Serving as the habitats and stepping stones for wildlife migration, wilderness fragments can also enhance the ecological connectivity of urban green networks to maintain a holistic health of urban ecosystems[10]. Furthermore, the wilderness fosters citizens' awareness that they are sharing urban spaces with other creatures, inspiring them to consider the city from a new perspective[11].

However, it remains a challenge to enhance the public's acceptance to urban wilderness and recognition of its core ecological values as natural resources. Ubiquitous man-made formal landscapes have overshadowed the wild vitality and ecological benefits of urban wilderness, for which the latter might be eliminated or transformed due to their disorder in appearance. Aldo Leopold, the American pioneer in wilderness preservation, criticized the negative hypotheses on wilderness by urban residents (especially the administrators), holding that the values of urban wilderness could and should be embodied in every urban forest, park or private garden[12]. Fortunately, opportunities are seen in reconstructing the urban wilderness system—leftover brownfields, idle lands due to advance of virtual space technology or urban shrinkage, and degraded urban green spaces all have the potential to be restored towards urban wilderness. In addition, the gradually accepted concept of rewilding encourages replacing human interventions with the natural restoration of ecosystems and ecological processes to strengthen the wildness of urban landscapes, illustrating the feasibility to transform "nature in the urban cracks" into wilderness patches or even more complex habitat networks.

Today, controversies over the existence and values of urban wilderness continue. This issue gathers scholars' insights that contribute to the understanding of the concept, connotation, and values of urban wilderness. Vance G. Martin presented a rationale for using the term of "urban wildness" to replace "urban wilderness" based on the significant differences between urban wilderness and natural wildness. Ingo Kowarik highlighted the existence of wilderness fragments in urban spaces and categorizes urban wilderness into "ancient wilderness" and "novel wilderness." Martin and Kowarik reached a consensus on the values, opportunities, and challenges of urban wilderness in practices of urban ecological conservation and green infrastructure development. Shao Yuhan et al. analyzed the conceptual development and evolution of urban wilderness and propose a value recognition framework, providing scientific guidelines for urban residents and governors to discover, experience, and sustainably manage urban wilderness.

This issue also presents a series of practical cases and thoughts on the conservation, restoration, and management of urban wilderness. Yuan Jia et al. established a technical framework of urban vegetation rewilding by leveraging ecological flows, stimulating natural plant communities, and designing with minimum human interventions. With a case study in Chongqing, they amplified the key procedure of rebuilding urban wilderness on both ecological and aesthetic values. Reviewing the history of the Tommy Thompson Park in Toronto, Canada which spontaneously evolved from rubble into a natural refuge, Walter Kehm et al. probed into the dynamic balance and harmony between natural restoration and design interventions over time. Thomas Rainer shared the practical experience of Phyto Studio in Washington D.C., the USA and the approaches to quasi-natural plant community design, providing feasible strategies for ecological planting in the "post-wilderness" era, offering an alternative to current planting design. Yin Hao et al. focused on opportunities for ecological self-restoration provided by spontaneous plants in urban idle lands, analyzed the characteristics in its early stage, the growth of plant communities and related environmental factors, and inventoried the potential seed sources of the site. In the project of Shanghai Urban Biodiversity Education Base, Guo Taoran et al. expounded the design process of urban wilderness establishment that improves local biodiversity through native species introduction, community construction, ecological benefit assessment, etc. Zhang Zihao et al. explored the potential and theoretical framework to apply Artificial Intelligence in interpreting and constructing wildness, providing new opportunities for landscape strategies to cultivate new forms of wild places via technodiversity.

The natural compensation function of urban wilderness is significant to sustain urban resilience and optimize the natural–constructed ecosystem in the city. This issue hopes to provide multiple perspectives for practitioners and decision makers in territorial spatial planning, landscape architecture, and ecology. By collecting the latest theoretical and technical efforts in urban wilderness conservation and restoration, this issue is expected to inspire thoughts that make cities the Promised Land integrating with civilization and wildness. **LAF**

REFERENCES

[1] "Ming" Kuo, F. E. (2013). Nature-deficit disorder: Evidence, dosage, and treatment. *Journal of Policy Research in Tourism, Leisure and Events*, 5(2), 172-186. https://doi.org/10.1080/19407963.2013.793520

[2] Ignatieva, M., & Ahrné, K. (2013). Biodiverse green infrastructure for the 21st century: From "green desert" of lawns to biophilic cities. *Journal of Architecture and Urbanism*, 37(1), 1-9. https://doi.org/10.3846/20297955.2013.786284

[3] Vujcic, M., Tomicevic-Dubljevic, J., Grbic, M., Lecic-Tosevski, D., Vukovic, O., & Toskovic, O. (2017). Nature based solution for improving mental health and well-being in urban areas. *Environmental Research*, (158), 385-392. https://doi.org/10.1016/j.envres.2017.06.030

[4] Faivre, N., Fritz, M., Freitas, T., de Boissezon, B., & Vandewoestijne, S. (2017). Nature-Based Solutions in the EU: Innovating with nature to address social, economic and environmental challenges. *Environmental research*, (159), 509-518. https://doi.org/10.1016/j.envres.2017.08.032

[5] Davis-Berman, J., & Berman, D. S. (1994). *Wilderness Therapy: Foundations, Theory and Research*. Dubuque, IA: Kendall Hunt Publishing Company.

[6] Mittermeier, R. A., Mittermeier, C. G., Brooks, T. M., Pilgrim, J. D., Konstant, W. R., da Fonseca, G. A., & Kormos, C. (2003). Wilderness and biodiversity conservation. *Proceedings of the National Academy of Sciences*, 100(18), 10309-10313. https://doi.org/10.1073/pnas.1732458100

[7] Vannini, P., & Vannini, A. (2016). *Wilderness*. Abingdon, England: Routledge, Taylor & Francis Group.

[8] Kopnina, H., Washington, H., Gray, J., & Taylor, B. (2018). The 'future of conservation' debate: Defending ecocentrism and the Nature Needs Half movement. *Biological Conservation*, (217), 140-148. https://doi.org/10.1016/j.biocon.2017.10.016

[9] Kowarik, I. (2011). Novel urban ecosystems, biodiversity, and conservation. *Environmental Pollution*, 159(8-9), 1974-1983. https://doi.org/10.1016/j.envpol.2011.02.022

[10] Trzyna, T. (2005). Urban dwellers and protected areas: Natural allies. In J. A. McNeely (Ed.), *Friends for Life: New partners in support of protected areas*. Gland, Switzerland: The International Union for Conservation of Nature. https://doi.org/10.2305/IUCN.CH.2005.4.en

[11] Jorgensen, A., & Keenan, R. (Eds.). (2011). *Urban wildscapes*. Abingdon, England: Routledge, Taylor & Francis Group.

[12] Leopold, A. (1942). Wilderness values. *The Living Wilderness*, (7), 24-25.

城市荒野景观：内涵与价值审视
The Intension and Values of Urban Wildscapes

邵钰涵
同济大学建筑与城市规划学院景观学系副教授、硕士生导师，上海市城市更新及其空间优化技术重点实验室成员；英国谢菲尔德大学社会空间城市主义研究中心成员

徐欣瑜
同济大学建筑与城市规划学院景观学系硕士研究生

袁嘉*
重庆大学建筑城规学院副教授、博士生导师，山地城镇建设与新技术教育部重点实验室固定研究人员；中国科学院山地生态恢复与生物资源利用重点实验室生态恢复与生物多样性保育四川省重点实验室中国科学院成都生物研究所合作研究人员

SHAO Yuhan
Associate Professor and Master Supervisor at the Landscape Department, College of Architecture and Urban Planning, and Member of Shanghai Key Laboratory of Urban Renewal and Spatial Optimization Technology, Tongji University; Member of Socio-spatial Urbanism Unit (SsUU), University of Sheffield

XU Xinyu
Master Student at the Landscape Department, College of Architecture and Urban Planning, Tongji University

YUAN Jia
Associate Professor and PhD Supervisor of the School of Architecture and Urban Planning, Research Fellow at the Key Laboratory of New Technology for Construction of Cities in Mountain Area, Chongqing University; Cooperative Research Fellow of the CAS Key Laboratory of Mountain Ecological Restoration and Bioresource Utilization & Ecological Restoration and Biodiversity Conservation Key Laboratory of Sichuan Province, Chengdu Institute of Biology, Chinese Academy of Sciences

*通讯作者
地址：重庆市沙坪坝区沙坪坝正街174号
邮编：400044
邮箱：jyuan523@vip.163.com

编辑 | 田乐
翻译 | 徐欣瑜、朱亦婷、田乐
EDITED BY | Tina TIAN
TRANSLATED BY | XU Xinyu, ZHU Yiting, Tina TIAN

摘要

城市的扩张、转型和收缩等进程为城市荒野景观的产生与发展创造了可能。在物理范畴上，城市荒野景观指生态过程基本维持以自然为主导，且具备类似自然荒野野性表征与功能类型的城市空间。隐含在城市中的荒野景观片段，其存在与持续得益于有限程度的人工管理和对自然做功的最小干预。由于自然过程与社会过程的共同作用与相互抗衡，城市荒野景观往往呈现出不同的“荒野度”。这类景观具有独特和不可替代的生态、人文、审美、经济及健康价值，引发了多学科关注和广泛认同。本文对城市荒野景观概念进行界定，梳理其内涵的构建与衍生历程，并在价值认同研究的基础上分析城市荒野景观的复合效益。内涵辨析与价值审视能够为城市荒野景观的实证研究打下重要的认知基础，为城市居民、规划设计者和管理者发现、欣赏、体验与可持续管理城市自然资源和生态网络提供科学支持，对中国城市的生态化发展具有现实的指导意义。

关键词
荒野；城市；城市自然；城市荒野景观；再野化

ABSTRACT

The process of urban sprawl, restructure, and shrinkage provides the possibility for the formation and evolution of urban wildscapes. Physically, urban wildscapes refer to the urban spaces where the ecology is basically dominated by natural processes and similar to the natural wilderness in appearance and functions. The existence and persistence of wilderness fragments in cities often result from the reduction of human management and with minimal intervention on the nature. Due to the different interactions and confrontations between natural processes and social processes, the wildness of urban wildscapes varies. The unique and irreplaceable values of urban widlscapes in ecology, culture, aesthetics, economy, and well-being have gained multi-disciplinary attention and been widely recognized. This paper defines the concept of urban wildscapes, reviews the conceptual development of its connotation, and analyzes the multiple benefits of urban wildscapes on the basis of value recognition research. It hopes to provide a value recognition framework for empirical studies, helping urban residents, planning designers, and managers identify, appreciate, experience, and sustainably manage natural resources and urban ecological network, and providing scientific guidelines for ecological urban development.

KEYWORDS
Wilderness; City; Urban Nature; Urban Wildscapes; Rewilding

基金项目
国家自然科学基金青年科学基金项目“城市自然景观视觉舒适度感应机理研究”（编号：51808393）
国家自然科学基金青年科学基金项目“山地城市水敏性区域草本植物群落适应性设计研究”（编号：51808065）
上海市城市更新及其空间优化技术重点实验室“城市街道视觉疗愈与经济活力平衡调控系统研究”（编号：2020010201）

RESEARCH FUNDS
Research on the Visual Comfort Mechanism of Urban Natural Landscapes, Young Scientists Fund of National Natural Science Foundation of China (No. 51808393)
Research on the Adaptive Design for Herbaceous Communities of the Water Sensitive Urban Area in Mountainous Cities, Young Scientists Fund of the National Natural Science Foundation of China (No. 51808065)
Research on the Balance Regulation System of Visual Restoration and Economic Vitality in Urban Streets, Shanghai Key Laboratory of Urban Renewal and Spatial Optimization Technology (No. 2020010201)

https://doi.org/10.15302/J-LAF-1-020039
收稿时间 RECEIVED DATE | 2021-02-09

中图分类号 | TU986
文献标识码 | A

1 引言

全球城市化与城市环境的高度人工化引发了城市生态系统的结构与功能缺失、城市居民自然体验的极度匮乏等一系列生态环境与人类健康的复杂问题[1]。保存、利用城市自然资源并借助自然之力塑造城市的生态韧性，成为人类回应自身维持与发展诉求的必要途径[2]。城市荒野景观作为城市自然的重要组成部分，其概念内涵与独特价值逐渐引发生态学[3]、社会学[4]、城乡规划与景观设计学[5][6]等诸多学科的密切关注。

"城市荒野景观"（urban wildscape）的概念具有矛盾性与复杂性：传统观念中，象征文明与安全的"城市"与象征野蛮与未知的"荒野"是两种严格对立的意象[7]，而"景观"一词是人–地关系的体现；"城市荒野景观"一词显示出对既有"自然–文明"矛盾关系的否定，以及对"回归自然"的重新思考和再度构建。实际上，城市荒野景观片段化地隐藏于城市之中，是生态过程基本维持以自然为主导，且具备类似自然荒野野性表征与保育生物多样性、提供游憩体验等功能的城市空间[8]。目前，城市荒野景观概念已不局限于描述城市中的自然碎片，安娜·乔根森等人[9]在《城市荒野景观》一书中将城市荒野景观理解为城市空间中自然主导与人工管理拉锯关系的映射，将这一概念延伸为一种体现人地关系变革的城市自然空间新认知方式。

对城市荒野景观的内涵与价值进行深入辨识，能够进一步为城市荒野景观的实证研究提供关键认知基础，为城市居民、规划设计师和管理者发现、欣赏、体验与可持续地管理城市自然资源和生态网络提供科学引导。本文分析了城市荒野景观的产生、动态和概念发展，从而归纳、辨析其内涵；基于多学科交叉研究，分析城市荒野景观的多重价值与效益；并从当前价值认同研究出发，尝试构建城市荒野景观的价值认同路径框架。

2 城市荒野景观的产生、动态与概念发展

2.1 产生和动态

城市荒野景观具有两个重要特征：1）动植物群落演替及变化由自然过程主导，具有类似自然荒野无序和野性的表征，极富景观生命力；2）具有野生动植物种群保育功能、能够提供城市中稀缺的自然体验，但仍然容易受到人类活动影响。这些特征决定了城市荒野景观的产生、维持、退化和再生等动态。城市荒野景观的产生与城市的扩张、转型和收缩等进程紧密关联。在城市横向扩张阶段，人工建设区逐渐扩大并纳入周边的乡村与未开发的原野[10]。由于地形复杂、植被保护、开发资金流转不畅等因素，一些自然荒野区域得以保存，成为城市荒野景观斑块。随着城市扩张导致市区拥挤、用地紧张，中心区工业外迁成为城市产业和空间转型的必由之路[11]。城市转型阶段腾挪出的后工业用地，包括亟需治理的棕地或有待再开发的用地，经历少则数年、多则数十年的闲置，被自生植被占据，因次生演替而形成城市荒野[12]。在城市收缩阶段，经济萎缩等原因导致公共资金匮乏和人工管理不足，一些城市空间重新由自然过程主导，逐步重归荒野[13]–[15]。此外，通过"善意忽视"

1 Introduction

The global issues on complex ecological crisis and human health and well-beings, such as the structural and functional defects of urban ecosystems and the extreme lack of opportunities for natural experience, result from urbanization and the aggressive urban construction[1]. The conversation and utilization of urban natural resources, and the enhancement of urban resilience through the power of nature are essential to human beings' survival and long-term development[2]. As an important part of urban nature, urban wildscapes, as well as their intension and unique values, have attracted great attention in the fields of ecology[3], sociology[4], urban planning and landscape architecture[5][6].

The concept of "urban wildscape" is contradictorily complex and traditionally dichotomous—"urban," the symbol of civilization and safe haven; "wilderness," the symbol of frightening and unknowable world[7]; and "landscape," manifesting the human–land relationship. This term denies the existing contradiction between nature and civilization, and suggests the re-thinking and re-construction of the return to nature. In fact, urban wildscape existing in the city as fragments is urban space dominated by natural processes, with similar forms as natural wilderness and functions such as preserving biodiversity and providing recreational opportunities[8]. As Anna Jorgensen et al.[9] argued in *Urban Wildscapes*, they are urban spaces of a continuum ranging from "wilderness" to apparently ordered spaces, rather than the natural fragments in cities, which extended this concept to a new cognition of urban nature that reflects the revolution of human–land relationship.

An in-depth exploring on the intension and values of urban wildscape may provide an important cognitive lens for related empirical studies, and provide scientific guidelines for urban residents, planners, and governors to discover, appreciate, experience, and sustainably manage natural resources and ecological network in cities. This paper reviews the emergence, evolution, and conceptual development of urban wildscape to summarize and characterize its intension. Based on literature review of multidisciplinary studies, the paper also highlights the multiple values and benefits of urban wildscape, and then develops a value recognition framework to promote the academic and public understanding of urban wildscape.

2 The Emergence, Evolution, and Conceptual Development of Urban Wildscape

2.1 The Emergence and Evolution of Urban Wildscape

An urban wildscape is characterized by 1) the evolution and changes of the flora and fauna communities, which are dominated by the nature and similar to the disordered wild forms of natural wilderness, with high landscape vitality; and 2) its services in preserving wildlife communities and providing natural experience that is scarce in cities but vulnerable to human disturbance. These characteristics define the emergence, maintenance, degradation, and regeneration of urban wildscape.

或主动保护自生植被与引入野生动物关键种等再野化手段，自然机能退化的城市景观有望实现再野化[16]。城市荒野景观通常具有暂时性和变化性[17]，既可能随着地块开发而变成人工化的城市空间——退化，其后也可能由于闲置而重新回归荒野——再生。

2.2 概念发展

城市荒野景观独特的物理感知、空间特性、审美形式与生态特征，引发了生态学[3]、社会学[4]、规划设计学科[5][6]、心理学[18]及文学[19]等学科的广泛关注。一方面，多学科的概念研究为深入揭示城市荒野景观的特性和多重价值提供了基础；另一方面，基于不同学科视角的研究提出了多种与"城市荒野景观"类似或有所交叠的术语，一定程度上导致了概念的混淆及术语的泛滥（表1）。

城市荒野景观的概念建立在"荒野"一词所建构的空间与文化语境上。"荒野"最初的语义具有排他性，即地球表面的无人涉足之地[52]。在东西方的传统认识中，荒野都被看作是未知、危险、难以抵达的境与地，这种自然与人二元对立的刻板认识形成了荒野概念的原始"排斥"阶段[53][54]。随着技术发展，尤其是枪械和交通工具的飞跃式突破，荒野的危险、未知和不可达已不符合当代语境[7]。自20世纪60年代起，现代环保主义运动和生态学的蓬勃发展使荒野生态系统的价值不断被证实并逐渐引发广泛关注[55]。由此，人们意识到荒野是一种城市化浪潮下重要而濒危的资源，荒野概念进入"接纳"的阶段，并逐渐被浪漫化为美好、富饶和自由的存在，生态批评文学作品常予以颂扬[19][56]。当代，城市生物多样性锐减、生态系统服务缺失和食物产能下降等严峻挑战凸显出荒野景观作为栖息地资源、支撑城市人居环境与生态系统健康稳定的宝贵性与重要性[6]。随着人与自然的关系进入崭新的协同互惠阶段，荒野概念开始在城市空间语境下被人辨识、讨论，与人共存的荒野景观也在城市语境下被更加频繁地索求[57]。

城市荒野景观概念的认知也经历了由刻板到灵活的过程。起初，城市荒野景观常指完整保留了片段化自然荒野的区域（如城区扩张过程中纳入的荒野地块或荒野公园[58]），或者是在城市中模拟自然荒野（如动物园中还原的荒野环境[59]）。这种刻板认知将城市荒野景观看作是城市发展过程中的偶发现象，直到1988年费伊·达夫恩等人[23]对德国柏林萨基兰德调车站荒地展开论述，指明城市荒野景观形成于自然主导和干预缺席。目前，由自生植被占据的城市非正式绿地空间（如闲置的棕地、街道边缘和铁轨等）都被认为是城市荒野景观的组成部分[60]。实际上，当下城市荒野景观概念的适用范畴较为宽泛，既包括城市中未受开发干扰的自然地块，也包括由于忽视管理而发生自然演替或通过再野化方法建立的次生演替的荒野。城市荒野景观的尺度可大可小——从城市中保留的大片自然公园，到路缘缝隙因缺乏管理而产生的"自生植被—动物"种团——与城市居民的日常生活紧密相关。

由于城市荒野景观是一种介于高度人工化和自然之间的阈限状态[60]，较难以某一标准界定。乔根森等人将城市荒野景观视作自然与社会过程的拉锯，强调了城市荒野景观的本质[9]。基于此，考察人工管理与自然力量的对抗程度（以城市空间的"荒野度"衡量），是从城市自然空间

The emergence of urban wildscapes is highly involved with the processes of urban sprawl, transformation, and shrinkage. During the "explosion of the city," artificially built areas gradually enclose peripheral rural and wild lands[10]. Some natural areas are preserved as urban wildscape patches due to reasons such as terrain complexity, the needs for vegetation conservation, or development funding shortage. Due to the congestion and tight land use resulting from urban sprawl, the relocation of industrial land-use from central urban areas is often necessitated in the urban industrial and spatial restructure and transition[11]. A large number of "left-over" post-industrial lands, including the brownfields to be restored and the lands to be redeveloped, would be occupied by spontaneous vegetation after being void or derelict for several years to decades, resulting in urban wildscapes under secondary succession[12]. When a city shrinks, economic crisis and other reasons often lead to the disinvestment and the insufficiency of urban space management. Some urban spaces would then be dominated by natural processes again, transforming towards the wilderness[13]-[15]. In addition, degraded urban landscapes may be rewilded by means of benign neglect or by conserving spontaneous vegetation and introducing keystone wildlife species[16]. Urban wildscape is usually temporary and changing[17], since they may either be reclaimed for urban development (degradation of wildscape), or return to wildscapes after being void (regeneration of wildscape).

2.2 The Conceptual Development

The unique physical perception, spatial features, aesthetic forms, and ecological characteristics of urban wildscapes have become the research interests to many disciplines such as ecology[3], sociology[4], planning and design[5][6], psychology[18] and literature[19]. On the one hand, the multidisciplinary theoretical studies have laid a foundation for revealing the characteristics and multiple values of urban wildscapes; On the other hand, a variety of terms similar to "urban wildscape" proposed from various disciplinary perspectives has caused the conceptual confusion (Table 1).

The concept of urban wildscape derives from the spatial and cultural implications of "wilderness." Originally, wilderness exclusively refers to a place on the earth that no one had reached[52]. In both eastern and western traditional cultures, wilderness was considered unknown, dangerous, and inaccessible, as a rigid dichotomy against human settlements[53][54]. However, with the advance of modern technology, especially the leaps in firearms and transportation, the danger, ambiguity, and inaccessibility of wilderness is not true anymore[7]. The modern environmentalism movement and vigorous developments in ecology since the 1960s have brought a broader recognition on wilderness ecosystems[55] as an important and endangered resource under urbanization. Wilderness was widely accepted as a romantic idea of beauty, abundance, and freedom, and often celebrated in eco-critical literature[19][56]. Contemporary cities are faced with severe challenges such as biodiversity loss, defect in delivering ecosystem services, and declining food productivity. Wildscapes have been unprecedentedly important

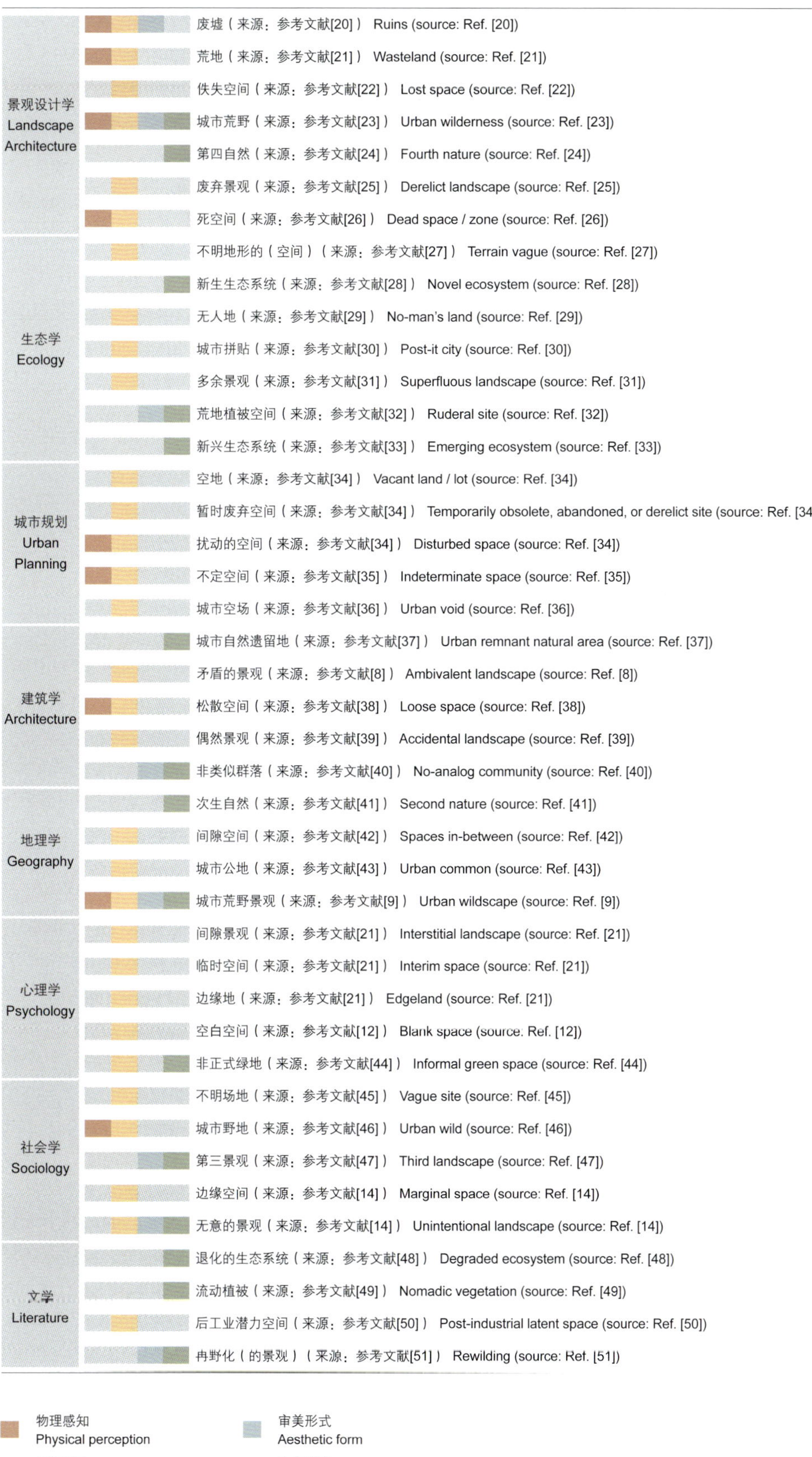

表1：不同学科视角下的城市荒野景观相关术语
Table 1: Related terms about "urban wildscape" from different disciplinary perspectives

学科 Discipline	术语 Term
景观设计学 Landscape Architecture	废墟（来源：参考文献[20]） Ruins (source: Ref. [20])
	荒地（来源：参考文献[21]） Wasteland (source: Ref. [21])
	佚失空间（来源：参考文献[22]） Lost space (source: Ref. [22])
	城市荒野（来源：参考文献[23]） Urban wilderness (source: Ref. [23])
	第四自然（来源：参考文献[24]） Fourth nature (source: Ref. [24])
	废弃景观（来源：参考文献[25]） Derelict landscape (source: Ref. [25])
	死空间（来源：参考文献[26]） Dead space / zone (source: Ref. [26])
生态学 Ecology	不明地形的（空间）（来源：参考文献[27]） Terrain vague (source: Ref. [27])
	新生生态系统（来源：参考文献[28]） Novel ecosystem (source: Ref. [28])
	无人地（来源：参考文献[29]） No-man's land (source: Ref. [29])
	城市拼贴（来源：参考文献[30]） Post-it city (source: Ref. [30])
	多余景观（来源：参考文献[31]） Superfluous landscape (source: Ref. [31])
	荒地植被空间（来源：参考文献[32]） Ruderal site (source: Ref. [32])
	新兴生态系统（来源：参考文献[33]） Emerging ecosystem (source: Ref. [33])
城市规划 Urban Planning	空地（来源：参考文献[34]） Vacant land / lot (source: Ref. [34])
	暂时废弃空间（来源：参考文献[34]） Temporarily obsolete, abandoned, or derelict site (source: Ref. [34])
	扰动的空间（来源：参考文献[34]） Disturbed space (source: Ref. [34])
	不定空间（来源：参考文献[35]） Indeterminate space (source: Ref. [35])
	城市空场（来源：参考文献[36]） Urban void (source: Ref. [36])
建筑学 Architecture	城市自然遗留地（来源：参考文献[37]） Urban remnant natural area (source: Ref. [37])
	矛盾的景观（来源：参考文献[8]） Ambivalent landscape (source: Ref. [8])
	松散空间（来源：参考文献[38]） Loose space (source: Ref. [38])
	偶然景观（来源：参考文献[39]） Accidental landscape (source: Ref. [39])
	非类似群落（来源：参考文献[40]） No-analog community (source: Ref. [40])
地理学 Geography	次生自然（来源：参考文献[41]） Second nature (source: Ref. [41])
	间隙空间（来源：参考文献[42]） Spaces in-between (source: Ref. [42])
	城市公地（来源：参考文献[43]） Urban common (source: Ref. [43])
	城市荒野景观（来源：参考文献[9]） Urban wildscape (source: Ref. [9])
心理学 Psychology	间隙景观（来源：参考文献[21]） Interstitial landscape (source: Ref. [21])
	临时空间（来源：参考文献[21]） Interim space (source: Ref. [21])
	边缘地（来源：参考文献[21]） Edgeland (source: Ref. [21])
	空白空间（来源：参考文献[12]） Blank space (source: Ref. [12])
	非正式绿地（来源：参考文献[44]） Informal green space (source: Ref. [44])
社会学 Sociology	不明场地（来源：参考文献[45]） Vague site (source: Ref. [45])
	城市野地（来源：参考文献[46]） Urban wild (source: Ref. [46])
	第三景观（来源：参考文献[47]） Third landscape (source: Ref. [47])
	边缘空间（来源：参考文献[14]） Marginal space (source: Ref. [14])
	无意的景观（来源：参考文献[14]） Unintentional landscape (source: Ref. [14])
文学 Literature	退化的生态系统（来源：参考文献[48]） Degraded ecosystem (source: Ref. [48])
	流动植被（来源：参考文献[49]） Nomadic vegetation (source: Ref. [49])
	后工业潜力空间（来源：参考文献[50]） Post-industrial latent space (source: Ref. [50])
	再野化（的景观）（来源：参考文献[51]） Rewilding (source: Ref. [51])

as habitats and assets to the health and stability of urban living environments and ecosystems[6]. As the human-nature relationship is entering an era of synergy, wilderness is increasingly identified and widely discussed, and the wildscapes co-existing with human beings are also frequently sought in urban settings[57].

Similarly, the concept of "urban wildscapes" initially referred to areas that remain intact fragments of natural wilderness (e.g., wild plots and wilderness parks incorporated in urban sprawl[58]), or that simulate natural wilderness in cities (e.g., wilderness-like landscapes in zoos[59]). Urban wildscape was stereotyped as occasional enclaves between the urban development, until the study on the wasteland of Südgelände in Berlin, Germany, in 1988 by Fay Duffner et al.[23], which suggested that urban wildscapes were the results of the natural dominance and the absence of artificial interventions. Urban informal green spaces occupied by spontaneous vegetation (e.g. brownfield, street verges, and rail tracks) are considered parts of urban wildscapes[60]. In fact, currently the term of urban wildscape refers to a wider variety that ranges from the natural plots away from the impact of urban development to the wilderness under natural processes due to human neglect or through rewilding. The scale of urban wildscapes varies—from large natural parks in cities to the "spontaneous-vegetation–animal" guilds at street verges due to the absence of management. Urban wildscapes are part of urban residents' daily life.

However, it is difficult to identify urban wildscape due to its liminality and betweenness of the highly artificial and nature[60]. Jorgensen et al.[9] considered the essence of urban wildscapes a continuum between natural and social processes. The degree of confrontation between human interventions and natural forces of an urban space can be measured by its wildness level, which is an effective way to identify urban wildscapes from urban nature (Fig. 1). Anke Müller et al.[61] proposed 4 indicators to quantify wildness: 1) perceived naturalness of land cover; 2) challenging terrain; 3) remoteness (which can be measured by the level of traffic noise); and 4) visibility of built modern artefacts.

3 Recognition of the Multiple Values of Urban Wildscapes

3.1 Multiple Values of Urban Wildscapes

3.1.1 Multi-disciplinary Research on Urban Wildscapes

Existing studies regard urban wildscape as an irreplaceable part of the urban ecosystems, explore its ecological and recreational values that are different from the manicured

1. 城市自然空间荒野度量表
1. The wildness gradient of urban natural spaces

中识别城市荒野景观的有效方式（图1）。安克·穆勒等人[61]提出了量化荒野度的4项指标：1）地表覆盖植被的自然程度；2）是否具有特殊地形；3）偏远程度（可以借由城市交通噪声水平衡量）；4）人工构筑的可见度。

3 城市荒野景观的多重价值及其认同

3.1 城市荒野景观的多重价值

3.1.1 多学科研究进展

大量既有研究将城市荒野景观视为城市生态系统中不可替代的组成部分，探索城市荒野景观有别于修剪整齐的景观的生态与游憩价值，并基于“自然—社会”的相互作用机制思考可持续发展的路径，意图充分发挥城市荒野景观的多重价值。例如，国内外景观设计学科近年来逐渐发展的新自然主义种植设计，包含了以荒野景观植被为模板进行再野化的理念，这些场地具有更高的物种丰富度与群落结构多样性，表现效果更具野趣，生物多样性保育价值高[62][63]。

生态学者针对城市荒野景观中野生动植物的分布情况、多样性、生存状况等基础信息展开调查，并在此基础上讨论了城市野生动物栖息地的生态价值及其营造、保护、管理的方式[3][64]-[66]。其中，最具代表性的是英戈·科瓦里克等人针对城市新生森林斑块的生态学研究，在其编著的《城市野生林地：城市森林新视野》一书中讨论了次生森林生态系统

landscapes, and examine new paths of sustainability under the mechanism of natural–social interactions to maximize the multiple values of urban wildscape. For example, new naturalistic planting design that adopts the rewilding concept has been promoted in the field of landscape architecture in recent years; these rewilded sites have a higher diversity of species and community structures, richer wild forms, and a greater performance in biodiversity conservation[62][63].

Ecologists investigated the distribution, diversity, and status of wildlife in urban wildscapes to identify the ecological values of urban wildlife habitats and the approaches of construction, protection, and management[3][64]-[66]. A representative ecological finding on novel forest patches in city is the book *Wild Urban Woodlands: New Perspectives for Urban Forestry* edited by Ingo Kowarik et al., which argued the ecological role of secondary woodlands in providing habitats for species and connecting urban ecological networks[67]. There are also some studies that compared the different values between the secondary and primary ecosystems, and between the managed and unmanaged ecosystems. For example, a survey on unmanaged forested areas in Singapore by Hwang Yun Hye highlighted the joint importance of biodiversity, environmental function, and aesthetics of urban wildscapes[68]. Animal ecology focuses on the keystone species that conflict with human activities are beneficial to urban ecosystems, such as boars in urban wildscapes[69][70], and bees and other pollinators[71][72]. Studies have also demonstrated the role of urban wildscapes as important wildlife habitats, which improve the functions of urban ecosystem.

Medical and psychological studies have proven the restorative benefits of various urban natural spaces and the relatively high effect in urban wildscapes. For example, in her interdisciplinary publication, *Wildness and Wellbeing: Nature, Neuroscience, and Urban Design*, Zoë Myers discussed the benefits of roadside vegetation and verges on mental health upon the interaction between urban residents and nature[18]. The metaphor of “city” as ”wilderness” has been traced

在提供物种栖息地、构建城市生态网络等方面的作用[67]。还有一些研究对比了次生与原生、人工管理与未管理的生态系统的价值差异，如黄云惠等人通过对新加坡未管理林地的研究，证明了其在生物多样性、环境功能和美学形式方面的价值[68]。动物生态学则侧重探讨与人类活动存在冲突或对城市生态系统有益的关键物种，如城市荒野中的野猪[69][70]、蜜蜂等传粉动物种群[71][72]，大量相关研究揭示了城市荒野景观作为野生动物栖息地对提升城市生态系统功能的重要性。

医学与心理学研究了城市中各种自然空间的疗愈效能，认为城市荒野景观具有较高的疗愈价值。其典型论述见于苏伊·迈尔斯的跨学科著作《野性与健康：自然、神经科学与城市设计》，该书从城市居民与自然的互动关系出发，探讨了街道边缘绿化等城市荒野对心理健康的益处[18]。生态主义批评文学很早就对“荒野”作为“城市”的隐喻展开了溯源和逻辑辩论[73][74]，拓展了荒野的文化内涵，肯定了城市与荒野的并置并非无中生有。文化社会学研究则挖掘了城市与荒野两种意象的文化内涵和关系演变，为城市荒野这类“表面无用之物”的人文价值挖掘提供了依据[21]。此外，人类学领域对城市荒野中的城市探索[75]、游击园艺[76]、城市觅食[4]等特殊行为进行了研究，也肯定了城市荒野景观在承载社会与文化要素方面的价值。

在中国，城市荒野景观是近5年来的新兴议题，一些学者针对城市荒野景观的理论及保育利用的可能性开展了研究。例如，王晞月等人回顾了城市荒野的概念发展，以江洋畈公园为实证案例阐释了城市荒野景观的价值和发展潜力[57]；曹越等人界定了“城市野境”概念并提出营造城市野境的4种途径[6]；谢梦云对比了中外荒野观的差异，讨论了荒野审美在中国再兴起的必然性[77]。

3.1.2 城市荒野景观的多重价值

本文根据城市荒野景观在城市生态系统及人居环境所发挥的功能类型，将其价值归纳为5种类型（图2），分别为：1）生态价值，包括提供生物栖息地、调整微气候、涵养水源、保育城市内野生动植物种群等；2）人文价值，提供重新联系人与自然的物质与精神场所，提供多功能游憩空间，发挥在地生态科普的宣教功能；3）审美价值，提供多感官刺激，具有“乱中有序”的生态伦理审美形式；4）健康价值，促进使用者放松压力和心理恢复；5）经济价值，提供低投入、粗管护、高收益的绿色基础设施。

城市荒野景观的生态价值和人文价值在自然—人工影响下的城市空间中体现得最为明显。一方面，自然过程主导的群落演替为乡土野生动植物提供了更加适宜、异质性更高的栖息地与“踏脚石”[83][84]。而人类干预的减少使城市荒野景观的生物多样性明显高于精细管护的人工绿地[78][79]。良好的生物多样性和自我维持能力为城市荒野景观能够持续提供生产食物和药物[81]的供给服务、荒野体验[83]的文化服务，以及促进城市环境适应气候变化[5][83]的调节服务等多样生态系统服务打下基础。另一方面，自然做功形成的野性景观表征与内部群落结构使城市荒野景观具有密集管理式绿地所不能提供的自然体验和与自然要素发生更多互动的可能性[51]。

and logically debated in the ecological criticism for a long time[73][74], expanding cultural intension of wildscapes and recognizing the juxtaposition of city and wilderness. Studies in cultural sociology have explored cultural intension of the city and the wilderness, as well as the evolution of their interactions, proving the cultural values of urban wilderness as the “intrinsic worth of the ostensibly useless”[21]. In addition, anthropological scholars have recognized the social and cultural significance of urban wildscapes by studying the behaviors observed within such as urban exploration[75], guerrilla gardening[76], and urban foraging[4].

In China, urban wildscape has been an emerging research topic in the past 5 years. Scholars have been concentrating on the theory and the possibilities of conservation and utilization. For instance, Wang Xiyue et al.[57] reviewed the conceptual development of urban wildscapes, illustrating the values and development trends of urban wildscape with the case of Jiangyangfan Eco-Park; Cao Yue et al.[6] defined the concept of “urban wildness” and proposed 4 approaches to its protection and construction; Xie Mengyun compared the views on wilderness between China and the West, and reasoned the inevitable revival of wilderness aesthetics in China[77].

3.1.2 Multiple Values of Urban Wildscapes

According to the varied functions in urban ecosystems and human settlements, the authors summarize the values of urban wildscapes into 5 types (Fig. 2): 1) ecological values, including providing habitats, regulating microclimate, conserving water sources, and wild flora and fauna in the city, etc.; 2) cultural values, by serving as physical and spiritual places re-connecting humans and nature, and providing multi-functional spaces for recreation and on-site ecological education; 3) aesthetic values, by providing sensory stimuli in the “order in chaos” form of ecological ethics; 4) value of health and well-being, by facilitating stress release and mental health restoration; and 5) economic value, by providing green infrastructure with low investment, minimal management, and high yield.

The ecological and cultural values of urban wildscape are mostly manifested in the urban spaces influenced by the natural–social processes. On the one hand, community succession dominated by natural processes provides suitable and heterogeneous habitats and stepping stones for native wildlife[83][84]. The reduction of human interventions makes the biodiversity of urban wildscapes significantly higher than carefully managed green spaces[78][79]. The high biodiversity and self-sustainability of urban wildscapes make them capable to continuously provide various ecosystem services, including provision services (e.g., food and medicine source[81]), cultural services (e.g., urban wild nature experience[83]), and regulatory services (e.g., promoting the adaptation to climate change of urban environments[5][83]). On the other hand, the wilderness-like appearance and internal community structure shaped by natural processes lead to more possibilities of natural experience and more connections with natural elements that the intensively managed green spaces cannot provide[51].

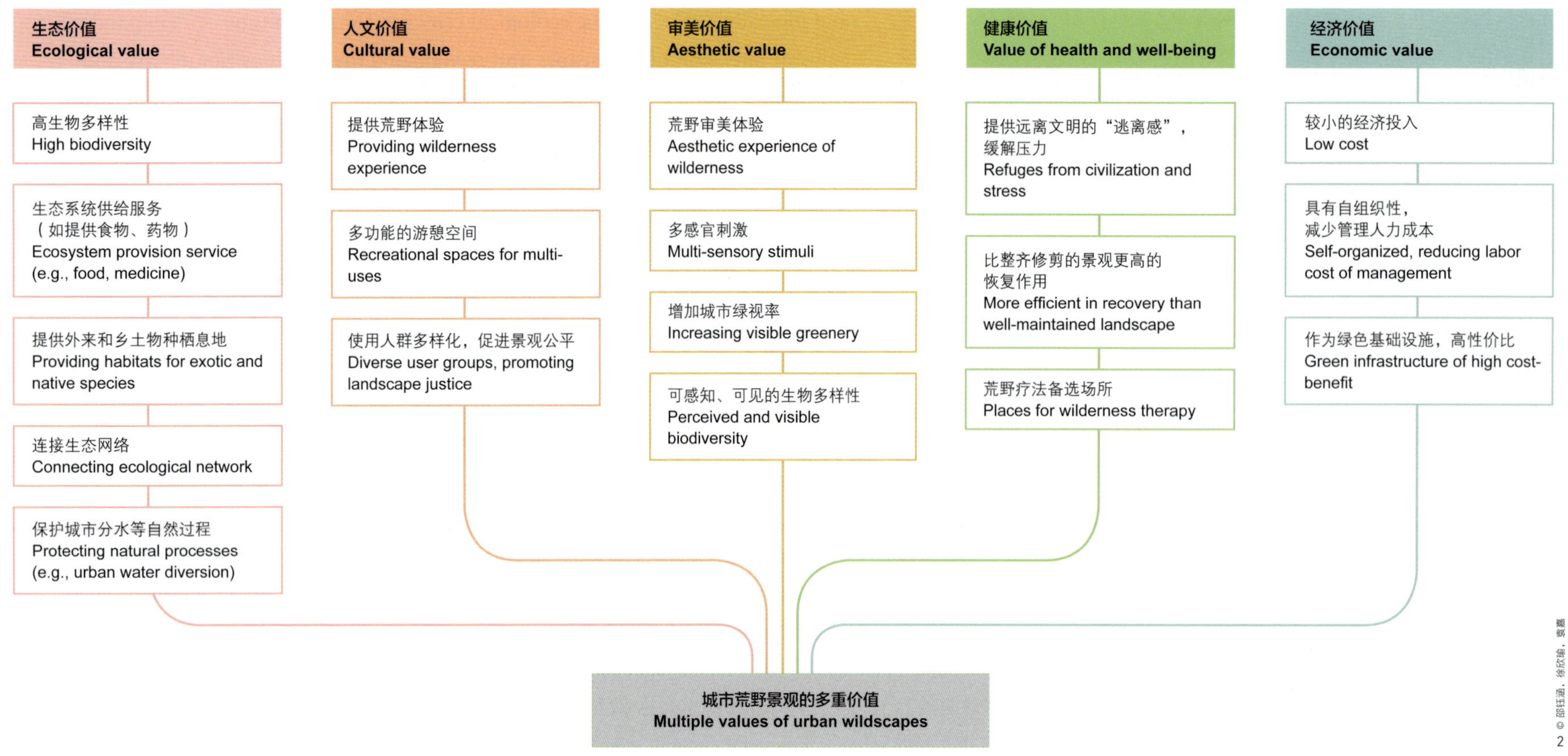

2.　城市荒野景观的多重价值内涵图示（来源：参考文献[5][51][62][78]~[89]）
2.　The multiple values of urban wildscapes (Source: Refs. [5][51][62][78]~[89])

除此之外，城市荒野景观的特殊审美价值，也往往依赖于其生态价值，这是生态主义价值观得到广泛公众认同的结果。生态审美观使人们更关注“能感知到的”生物多样性[68]：在城市荒野景观中，视觉、听觉和嗅觉所引发的一系列刺激强化了人们对生物多样性的感知[88]，并形成了较为独特的自然野性审美体验。与此同时，城市荒野景观还承担着补充公园绿地、增加城市绿视率、提高城市景观视觉舒适度的作用[44]，对城市景观的多样性有重要贡献。

与野生动植物等自然要素进行互动，能缓解人们的压力，因而城市荒野景观能够显著地作用于人类身心恢复[18]，促进正面情绪的产生，提高幸福感。目前，“荒野疗法”已成为城市荒野景观的潜在功能——该疗法的机理是患者通过荒野中的多感官感知达到疗愈目的[90]，多项循证研究为这一健康价值提供了支撑依据。

另外，由于具有的良好自组织与自我维持能力，城市荒野景观主要的经济价值体现在其维护所需的资金或人力成本很低[5]。而且城市荒野

In addition, the special aesthetic values of urban wildscapes are usually closed to their ecological value, due to the broader recognition of ecologism. Ecological aesthetics make people pay more attention to the “perceived biodiversity”[68]: In urban wildscapes, the array of sensory stimuli (e.g. the sights, sounds, and smells) strengthens people’s perception of biodiversity[88], which brings about a unique aesthetic experience of wilderness. At the same time, urban wildscapes also contribute to the increase of green spaces and visible greenness[44], creating urban landscapes of visual pleasure, and the diversity of urban landscape.

Since the interaction with wildlife and other natural elements helps relieve stress, urban wildscapes can significantly affect human physical and mental recovery[18], promoting positive emotions so as to improve human well-beings. At present, urban wildscapes also see a potential of “wilderness therapy,” which allows patients to get recovered through multisensory experience in the wilderness, has developed a potential function of urban wildscapes[90]. A number of evidence-based studies proved the value of health and well-beings delivered by urban wildscapes.

Economically, urban wildscape allows for low maintenance cost due to its capacity of self-organization and self-maintenance[5]. Moreover, urban wildscape can provide recreational spaces for various daily uses of different

景观可以提供多功能、具有可塑性的游憩空间，满足不同社会群体的日常使用需求[84][86]，一定程度上可避免城市自然空间的士绅化，有利于城市的景观公平。

3.2 城市荒野景观价值认同构建研究

城市荒野景观多重价值的循证研究为其得到广泛利用提供了有力的证据支持。然而，价值利用的基础是价值评估，价值评估的基础是价值认同。只有深入了解真正利益相关者的价值认同，才能引导他们的意识发展，从而优化更新城市荒野景观的利用途径，充分发挥其多重价值。价值认同研究的主要目标是了解使用者对城市荒野景观的感知方式、审美偏好和使用意愿，其过程和结果受到不同群体社会属性的影响。一般的基础调查通常先利用社会学方法收集使用者感受，然后进行研究区域的跨尺度整合，从而在城市或区域尺度形成总体认同评价。这一评价标准及评价结果能够为城市荒野景观的多重价值和复合效益提供利用方式参考。

早期由于对荒野的负面印象，部分研究先入为主地低估甚至否定了城市居民对城市荒野景观的利用，并产生了几种典型的错误认知：1）公众并不能区分城市荒野景观与有意设计的景观的差异；2）城市荒野景观是消极空间，不具备游憩价值；3）低收入人群等弱势群体不接受或不使用城市荒野景观[84]。这些观念往往是由主观臆断或缺乏科学性与系统性的调查取证和统计分析所导致。

类似的误区被当前逐渐深化的循证研究不断纠正，明晰了学界及公众对城市荒野景观的认识。越来越多的研究表明，公众不仅能够区分城市荒野景观与更正式设计的景观[87]，并且在满足最低限度的游憩和可达性等诉求的基础上，对荒野景观抱有较高的认可与好感度。其中，人文价值往往是主导公众偏好的关键因素，而非城市荒野景观的外在表现形式[91][92]。城市荒野景观的人文价值广受认可，尤其是自然野趣且多样化的游憩体验，相较精细管护的城市公园更受青睐[93]。对城市荒野景观的游憩利用也逐渐普遍（图3），如在后工业闲置场地中进行探险活动和涂鸦创作[94]、在城市自然林地中进行艺术展览和宣教活动[95]等。游憩活动偏好也因社会群体及自然观而异[96]，例如，景观设计学或生态学研究及实践从业者往往比一般城市居民更偏爱可达性低、物种丰富度高的自然区域[92]；老人、儿童等弱势群体往往更受益于城市荒野景观，对其认同感更高[86]；西方学者也发现不同种族群体（如白人与非白人群体）对城市荒野景观的使用情况存在差异[13]。城市荒野景观可满足不同群体的游憩需求，已成为城市中具有很高潜力的多元文化载体。

social groups[84][86]. It avoids the gentrification of urban natural spaces, which is conducive to the justice of urban landscape.

3.2 The Value Recognition Framework

Evidence-based research on the multiple values of urban wildscapes can promote the application of related findings. However, the application depends on its evaluation, which is defined by its value recognition. Only by deeply understanding the value recognition of real stakeholders, their consciousness and awareness could be developed, so as to improve urban wildscape and maximize the multiple values. The main goal of value recognition studies is to reveal users' perception mechanism, as well as their aesthetic preferences and willingness to use. The perception process and results are affected by the social attributes of different groups. General surveys usually collect users' experience at first, and then integrate across-scaled studies to support city- or region-scale evaluation. The evaluation standards and results can provide a reference for the application of multiple values and overall benefits of urban wildscapes.

Some early studies had underestimated or denied the use of urban wildscapes by urban residents. Typical misunderstandings included that 1) the public are not able to distinguish the difference between urban wildscapes and formal landscapes; 2) urban wildscapes are negative spaces with poor recreational value; 3) the disadvantaged such as low-income people do not appreciate or support urban wildscapes[84]. These arguments often came from scholars' negative preconception of the wilderness, or unscientific even incorrect investigations or statistical analyses.

These misunderstandings have been continuously eliminated by evidence-based studies, and the academic's and the public's awareness of urban wildscapes has increasingly reshaped. More and more studies have proved that the public can distinguish urban wildscapes from formal landscapes[87], and have an obvious recognition and preference of wildscapes if their primary needs for recreation and accessibility are met. Instead of aesthetics, cultural values wherein influence the users' preferences of urban wildscapes the most[91][92]. Compared with manicured park settings, the cultural values of urban wildscapes are widely recognized, especially for the wild and multiple recreational experiences[93]. The recreational uses of urban wildscapes are increasingly recognized (Fig. 3), such as exploration and graffiti in post-industrial derelict sites[94], and art exhibition and ecological education in urban natural woodland[95]. Preferences for recreational activities vary by social groups and their views to nature[96]. For example, scholars and practitioners in Landscape Architecture and Ecology tend to prefer natural areas with low accessibility and high species richness, compared with ordinary urban residents[92]. Disadvantaged groups such as the elderly and children are often benefited more from urban wildscapes, therefore seeing a greater recognition[86]. Western scholars have also found that different ethnics (such as white and non-white groups) varied in the ways to use urban wildscapes[13]. Urban wildscapes become multi-cultural spaces that can meet the diverse recreational needs of different groups.

除先入之见外，跨地域差异是城市荒野景观价值认同研究的另一大难点。近年来的研究结果显示，英国谢菲尔德[87]、中国北京[97]、新加坡[91]、澳大利亚布里斯班和日本札幌[96]等地区的城市居民普遍表达了对城市荒野景观的承认和接受。然而，在德国4座不同城市进行的两项研究则呈现出相对立的观点：柏林和科隆的居民对路边的自生植物有很高的接受度，认为其生态价值和经济功能比整齐的视觉观感更为重要[98]；而德累斯顿和莱比锡的居民则倾向于取缔城市棕地上自发生长的植被，建造整洁的公园景观，因为这样更符合他们的“有序观念”[99]。上述研究表明了一些地区居民对城市荒野景观的认知态度，但对于更广泛和系统性的公众认同研究还有所欠缺。因此，需要针对不同地域、不同文化背景和社会属性人群进行针对性研究，以解决现有研究中不同社会背景的样本类型和数量不足的问题。

至于中国城市居民对城市荒野景观的价值认同，以及与西方国家的差异，由于目前中国学者针对城市荒野景观的循证研究极少，对其分布状况、使用情况、公众偏好等的基础调查严重缺乏，尚无法得出可靠结论。因此，当务之急是针对国内不同发展状况的城市进行城市荒野景观识别和价值认同调查，为相关价值评价及公众意识引导提供必要支持。

综上，城市荒野景观丰富的游憩利用价值是其吸引多种不同社会群体的关键，而不同的地域、文化背景和城市荒野景观的状态等也导致使用者偏好和使用意愿上的差异，为城市荒野景观的认识和价值判别的研究发展带来了瓶颈。只有从研究者、使用者的价值认同意识调查出发，利用科学手段充分而全面地判别城市荒野景观的价值与人们的偏好，才有可能得到明晰的认识、中肯的评价，进而受到合理的利用与保护。因此，本文从城市荒野景观的价值及其利用过程出发，提出相应的价值认同体系构建路径（图4），意为公众教育和未来研究发展提供指引。

In addition, cross-regional differences pose another challenge to the research on the value recognition of urban wildscapes. Studies in recent years shown urban residents in Sheffield, UK[87], Beijing, China[97], Singapore[91], Brisbane, Australia, and Sapporo, Japan[96] have witnessed a general value recognition and acceptance of urban wildscapes. While two studies from 4 cities in Germany showed opposing findings: residents of Berlin and Cologne had a high acceptance of spontaneous vegetation by roadside and considered the vegetation's ecological and economic values greater than orderly visual aesthetic[98]; residents of Dresden and Leipzig tended to uproot spontaneous vegetation on urban brownfields and prefer park-like landscapes due to their "ideas of orderliness"[99]. Studies above show the disparity of local residents' awareness of urban wildscapes, yet there is still a lack of systematic research on the recognition of a broader public. It is necessary to conduct targeted surveys for people in different regions and with varied social-cultural contexts to enrich the research samples.

Regarding the value recognition of urban wildscapes by Chinese urban residents and the difference from Western countries, few evidence-based studies have conducted by Chinese scholars, and surveys on the distribution, usage, public preference of urban wildscape are extremely insufficient, barely supporting the reliability of findings. Urban wildscape identification and value recognition surveys in Chinese cities with specific development status are expected to provide necessary support and guidance for the related value evaluation and the promotion of public awareness.

In summary, the rich recreational opportunities by urban wildscapes are key to attracting a variety of social groups. The disparity of the regional and cultural contexts of urban wildscape leads to various use preferences and willingness, and also results in bottlenecks to the research on the recognition and evaluation of urban wildscapes. Only by investigating the value recognition of researchers and users and using scientific methods to comprehend the value and people's preferences of urban wildscapes, can they be clearly and scientifically understood, and then be appropriately used and conserved. This paper reviews the values and utilization process of urban wildscapes, and proposes a value recognition framework (Fig. 4) to guide public education and support further research.

3-1. 重庆市合川区森楷路棕地再野化景观
3-2. 重庆长江干流九龙外滩段江岸景观

3-1. The rewilded landscape on the Senkai Road of Hechuan District in Chongqing
3-2. The rewilded landscape along the Yangtze River in the Jiulong Waitan section of Chongqing

© 邵钰涵，徐欣瑜，袁嘉
3-1

© 邵钰涵，徐欣瑜，袁嘉
3-2

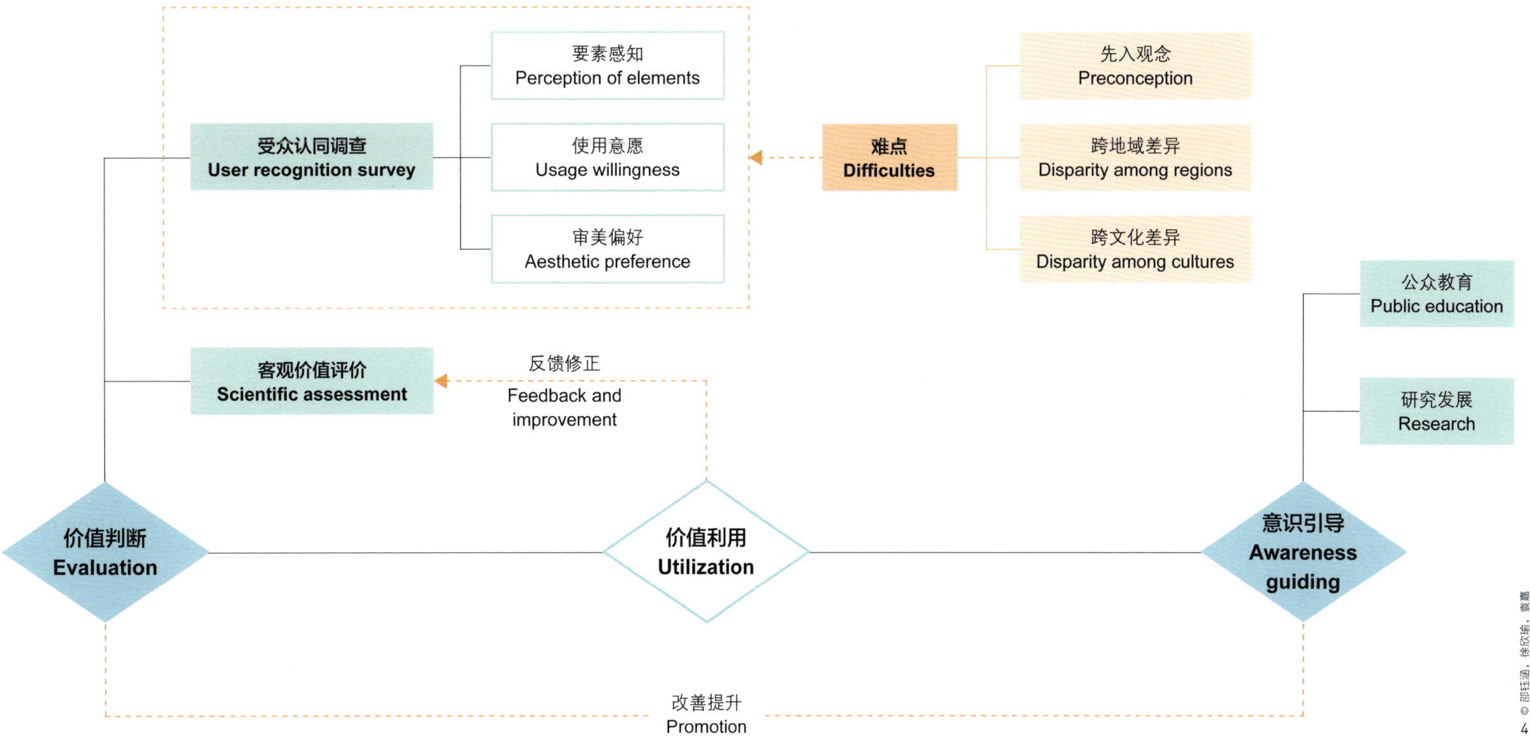

4. 城市荒野景观价值认同体系构建路径图示
4. The value recognition framework of urban wildscape

4 结语

城市扩张以及对自然资源的无序开发，加剧了城市居民与自然的隔阂。城市荒野景观是珍稀且濒危的城市自然，作为荒野在城市空间的一种延续，是城市居民与自然联系的重要窗口。城市荒野景观的保护、重构与利用尚处在理论与技术探索阶段，方兴未艾。在今后的研究与实践中需要进一步结合先进技术（如图像语义分割、深度学习等）进行系统性的城市荒野空间识别，利用条件估值等货币化方法尝试量化城市荒野景观的多重价值并深入探讨其认同构建机制；需要自下而上地引导城市居民与管理者重新思考城市中的自然，展开城市荒野景观的在地科普，鼓励欣赏其美学形式，主动拥抱城市荒野景观所带来的社会关系及文化观念的转变，令人类切实受益于城市荒野景观所提供的生态、人文、审美、健康与经济价值。在倡议国土空间生态修复与基于自然的解决方案的时代背景下，对城市荒野景观的重视、深入认知与有效利用对中国城市的生态文明建设具有现实指导意义，促进创造和谐宜居的城市人居环境，以及文明与自然的融合共生。**LAF**

4 Conclusion

Urban sprawl and disordered exploitation of natural resources have intensified the disconnection between urban residents and nature, where urban wildscapes have become a rare and endangered natural resource in cities, fragments of wilderness in urban settings, and an important channel for urban residents to interact with nature. The conservation, reconstruction, and utilization of urban wildscapes still need burgeoning development in theory and practice, including integrating advanced methods (such as semantic image segmentation and deep learning) into the systematic identification of urban wilderness, and valuation methods (such as contingent valuation method) to quantify their multiple values and to explore the mechanism of value recognition. It needs necessary bottom-up guidance for urban residents and governors to rethink of the urban nature and promote on-site public education of urban wildscape, appreciate the unique aesthetic forms, and embrace the changes in social awareness and cultural perception by urban wildscape, so as to make people truly benefit from the ecological, cultural, aesthetic, health, and economic values. Along the development of territorial ecological restoration and nature-based solutions, the awareness promotion, in-depth cognition, and effective utilization of urban wildscape would propel the ecological civilization construction in Chinese cities, helping create a more livable urban living environment and the harmony between human civilization and nature. **LAF**

REFERENCES

[1] Liu, Y., Li, R., & Song, X. (2005). Grey Associative Analysis of Regional Urbanization and Eco-evironment Coupling in China. *Acta Geographica Sinica*, 60(2), 237-247.

[2] Masnavi, M. R., Gharai, F., & Hajibandeh, M. (2019). Exploring urban resilience thinking for its application in urban planning: A review of literature. *International Journal of Environmental Science and Technology*, 16(1), 567-582. doi:10.1007/s13762-018-1860-2

[3] Madre, F., Vergnes, A., Machon, N., & Clergeau, P. (2014). Green roofs as habitats for wild plant species in urban landscapes: First insights from a large-scale sampling. *Landscape and Urban Planning*, (122), 100-107. doi:10.1016/J.LANDURBPLAN.2013.11.012

[4] Williams, D. R. (2020). Urban Wild Foraging–Walk with Me, a One-Mile Radius. In J. B. Pontius, M. P. Mueller, & D. Greenwood (Eds.), *Place-Based Learning for the Plate* (pp. 11-24). Berlin, Germany: Springer.

[5] Kitha, J., & Lyth, A. (2011). Urban wildscapes and green spaces in Mombasa and their potential contribution to climate change adaptation and mitigation. *Environment and Urbanization*, (23), 251-265. doi:10.1177/0956247810396054

[6] Cao, Y., Martin, V. G., & Yang, R. (2019). Urban Wildness: Protection and Creation of Wild Nature in Urban Areas. *Landscape Architecture*, 26(8), 20-24.

[7] Avery, B. (2017). Fragments of Wilderness City: An Extract from a Book by Bryan Avery with the Same Title. *Urban Design*, (2), 6-33.

[8] Jorgensen, A., & Tylecote, M. (2007). Ambivalent landscapes—wilderness in the urban interstices. *Landscape Research*, 32(4), 443-462. doi:10.1080/01426390701449802

[9] Jorgensen, A., & Keenan, R. (2012). *Urban Wildscapes*. Abingdon, England: Routledge.

[10] Di Tommaso, A. (2014). *The wildëor downtown: Exploring wilderness remnants in urban America* (Doctoral dissertation). Polytechnic University of Catalonia, Barcelona.

[11] Several Measures to Control the Size of the City in Tokyo, London, Paris. (1978). *City Planning Review*, (4), 11-15.

[12] Unt, A. -L., Travlou, P., & Bell, S. (2014). Blank Space: Exploring the Sublime Qualities of Urban Wilderness at the Former Fishing Harbour in Tallinn, Estonia. *Landscape Research*, 39(3), 267-286. doi:10.1080/01426397.2012.742046

[13] Danford, R. S., Strohbach, M. W., Warren, P. S., & Ryan, R. L. (2017). Active Greening or Rewilding the city: How does the intention behind small pockets of urban green affect use?. *Urban Forestry and Urban Greening*, (29), 377-383. doi:10.1016/J.UFUG.2017.11.014

[14] Gandy, M. (2016). Unintentional landscapes. *Landscape Research*, (41), 1-8. doi:10.1080/01426397.2016.1156069

[15] Rink, D. (2009). Wilderness: The Nature of Urban Shrinkage? The Debate on Urban Restructuring and Restoration in Eastern Germany. *Nature and Culture*, 4(3), 275-292. doi:10.3167/NC.2009.040304

[16] Wang, X. (2019). Wilderness in the City. *Landscape Architecture*, 26(8), 4-5.

[17] Sheridan, D. (2012). Disordering public space: urban wildscape processes in practice: Dougal Sheridan. In A. Jorgensen, & R. Keenan (Eds.), *Urban Wildscapes* (pp. 201-220). Abingdon, England: Routledge.

[18] Myers, Z. (2019). *Wildness and Wellbeing: Nature, Neuroscience, and Urban Design*. Singapore: Springer.

[19] Zantingh, M. (2018). Wildness and Windsor: Di Brandt's "Zone: ←le Détroit→," Environmental Praxis, and Urban Nature. *Interdisciplinary Studies in Literature and Environment*, 25(2), 396-411. doi:10.1093/ISLE/ISY048

[20] Han, L. (2008). *Study on the Continuation of Ruins Landscape and City Memory* (Master's thesis). Retrieved from Wanfang database.

[21] Gandy, M. (2013). Marginalia: Aesthetics, Ecology, and Urban Wastelands. *Annals of the Association of American Geographers*, 103(6), 1301-1316. doi:10.1080/00045608.2013.832105

[22] Trancik, R. (1986). *Finding Lost Space: Theories of Urban Design*. New York, NY: Wiley.

[23] Duffner, F., & Wathern, P. (1988). Building an Urban Wilderness. *Environment*, 30(2), 12-34. doi:10.1080/00139157.1988.9930874

[24] Kowarik, I. (1991). Unkraut oder Urwald? Natur der vierten Art auf dem Gleisdreieck [Weeds or jungle? Nature of the fourth kind on the Gleisdreieck]. *Dokumentation Gleisdreieck Morgen. Sechs Ideen für einen Park, Berlin* [Documentation Gleisdreieck Tomorrow. Six ideas for a Park in Berlin] (pp. 45-55). Retrieved from https://umweltzoneberlin.de/wp-content/uploads/2019/08/Kowarik_1991_Unkraut_Urwald_Natur_derviertenArt_Gleisdreieck.pdf.

[25] Jakle, J. A., & Wilson, D. (1992). *Derelict Landscapes: The Wasting of America's Built Environment*. Savage, MD: Rowman & Littlefield.

[26] Coleman, A. (1982). Dead space in the dying inner city. *International Journal of Environmental Studies*, 19(2), 103-107. doi:10.1080/00207238208709976

[27] Mével, Y. (2001). Beckett and the wasteland of melancholy. *Samuel Beckett Today—Aujourd'hui*, 11(1), 469-477. doi:10.1163/18757405-01101054

[28] Chapin, F. S., & Starfield, A. M. (1997). Time lags and novel ecosystems in response to transient climatic change in arctic Alaska. *Climatic Change*, 35(4), 449-461. doi:10.1023/A:1005337705025

[29] Doron, G. M. (2000). The Dead Zone and the Architecture of Transgression. *City*, (4), 247-263. doi:10.1080/13604810050147857

[30] Varra, G. I. (2001). POST-IT CITY: The Other European Public Spaces. Retrieved from http://subsol.c3.hu/subsol_2/contributors0/lavarratext.html

[31] Nielsen, T. (2002). The Return of the Excessive: Superfluous Landscapes. *Space and Culture*, 5(1), 53-62. doi:10.1177/1206331202005001006

[32] Frund, H. C., Sontgen, M., Schulte, W., & Ruszkowski, B. (1988). Studies on the biology of urban soil. 1. Conception of the Bonn-Bad Godesborg research project and first overall results. *Verhandlungen—Gesellschaft fur Okologie*, (18), 167-174.

[33] Milton, S. J. (2003). 'Emerging ecosystems'—A washing-stone for ecologists, economists and sociologists?. *South African Journal of Science*, 99(9-10), 404-406.

[34] Bowman, A. O. M., & Pagano, M. A. (2004). *Terra Incognita: Vacant Land and Urban Strategies*. Washington, DC: Georgetown University Press.

[35] Groth, J., & Corijn, E. (2005). Reclaiming urbanity: Indeterminate spaces, informal actors and urban agenda setting. *Urban Studies*, 42(3), 503-526. doi:10.1080/00420980500035436

[36] Armstrong, H. (2006). Time, Dereliction and Beauty: An Argument for 'Landscapes of Contempt. Paper presented at the IFLA Eastern Region Conference, Sydney, Australia.

[37] Gong, B., & Che, S. (2007). Discussion on the Concept and Classification of Urban Remnant Natural Area. *Journal of Shanghai Jiaotong University* (Agricultural Science), (3), 223-227, 231.

[38] Franck, K. A., & Stevens, Q. (Eds.). (2006). *Loose Space: Possibility and Diversity in Urban Life*. London, England: Routledge

[39] Beckenstein, J. (2014). April gornik: Accidental landscapes. *Woman's Art Journal*, 35(2), 3-10.

[40] Williams, J. W., & Jackson, S. T. (2007). Novel climates, no-analog communities, and ecological surprises. *Frontiers in Ecology and the Environment*, 5(9), 475-482. doi:10.1890/070037

[41] Geuze, A. (2010). Second Nature: New Territories of Wilderness for Unknown Future Colonization. *Topos: European Landscape Magazine*, (71), 40-42.

[42] Kamvasinou, K. (2011). The public value of vacant urban land. *Municipal Engineer*, 164(ME3), 157-166. doi:10.1680/MUEN.9.00020

[43] Gilbert, O. L. (1991). *The Ecology of Urban Habitats*. London, England: Chapman and Hal.

[44] Rupprecht, C., & Byrne, J. A. (2014). Informal urban green-space: Comparison of quantity and characteristics in Brisbane, Australia and Sapporo, Japan. *PloS One*, 9(6), 1-17. doi:10.1371/JOURNAL.PONE.0099784

[45] Kullmann, K. (2014). The usefulness of uselessness: Towards a landscape framework for un-activated urban public space. *Architectural Theory Review*, 19(2), 154-173. doi:10.1080/13264826.2014.967330

[46] Jorgensen, A. (2003). Living in the urban wild woods: A case study of the ecological woodland approach to landscape planning and design at Birchwood, Warrington New Town (Doctoral dissertation). University of Sheffield, Sheffield.

[47] Clément, G., Tiberghien, G., & Morris, S. (2015). *"The Planetary Garden" and Other Writings*. Philadelphia, PA: University of Pennsylvania Press.

[48] Mascaro, J., Harris, J. A., Lach, L., Thompson, A., Perring, M. P., Richardson, D. M., & Ellis, E. C. (2013). Origins of the Novel Ecosystems Concept. In R. J. Hobbs, E. S. Higgs, & C. M. Hall (Eds.), *Novel Ecosystems: Intervening in the New Ecological World Order* (pp. 45-57). Oxford, England: John Wiley & Sons, Ltd.

[49] Vuscan, I. S., & Feng, S. (2018). Civilized enclaves of wilderness: Substitutes for an alienated urban nature. Paper presented at the *3rd China-Romania Science and Technology Seminar*, Brasov, Romania.

[50] Vosloo, P. (2018). Post-industrial urban quarries as places of recreation and the new wilderness – A South African perspective. *Town and Regional Planning*, 72(1), 43-57. doi:10.18820/2415-0495/TRP72I1.4

[51] Kaae, B. C., Holm, J., Caspersen, O. H., & Gulsrud, N. M. (2019). Nature Park Amager—Examining the transition from urban wasteland to a rewilded ecotourism destination. *Journal of Ecotourism*, 18(4), 348-367. doi:10.1080/14724049.2019.1601729

[52] Gao, K. (2019). The Changing of the Wilderness Idea and the Origin of the U.S. National Parks. *American Studies Quarterly*, 33(3), 142-160.

[53] Wang, X. (2017). Urban Interstitial Space: Strategic Research on the Planning of Wildscape in the Context of Living Environment. *Urban Development Studies*, 24(7), 11-16, 24.

[54] Chen, W., Hao, P., & Qi, J. (2016). Wilderness and Landscape-The Thinking of Conceptualizing Ecological Landscape-ism. *Chinese Landscape Architecture*, 32(10), 50-53.

[55] Ma, T. (2018). A New Vision of Western Ecocriticism: A Review of Urban Ecocriticism. *Journal of Poyang Lake*, (6), 108-116, 128.

[56] Light, A. (1995). From Classical to Urban Wilderness. *Trumpeter*, 12(1), 19-21.

[57] Wang, X., & Wang, X. (2017). Urban Wilderness Based on the View of Landscape Architecture. *Chinese Landscape Architecture*, 33(8), 40-47.

[58] Rust, S. P. (1995). The urban wilderness park: an oxymoron?. Paper presented at the the *Second Symposium on Social Aspects and Recreation Research*, San Diego, California.

[59] Kooij, P. (2010). The tiger and the tram. Zoos as an urban wilderness. *Town and Countryside in a Dutch Perspective* (pp. 221-245). Groningen, The Netherlands: NAHI.

[60] Rupprecht, C. D. D., Byrne, J. A., Garden, J. G., & Hero, J. -M. (2015). Informal urban green space: A trilingual systematic

review of its role for biodiversity and trends in the literature. *Urban Forestry and Urban Greening*, 14(4), 883-908. doi:10.1016/J.UFUG.2015.08.009
[61] Müller, A., Bøcher, P. K., Fischer, C., & Svenning, J. -C. (2018). 'Wild' in the city context: Do relative wild areas offer opportunities for urban biodiversity?. *Landscape and Urban Planning*, (170), 256-265. doi:10.1016/J.LANDURBPLAN.2017.09.027
[62] Hang, Y. (2017). Development and Application of Herbaceous Vegetation in New Naturalistic Ecological Planting Design. *Landscape Architecture*, (5), 16-21.
[63] Yuan, J., & Du, C. (2017). The Application and Design of the New Naturalistic Herbaceous Planting in Urban Rain Gardens. *Landscape Architecture*, (5), 22-27.
[64] Taylor, B., Andrews, D., & Fraser, G. S. (2011). Double-crested cormorants and urban wilderness: conflicts and management. *Urban Ecosystems*, 14(3), 377-394. doi:10.1007/S11252-011-0165-8
[65] Ikeda, T., Kuninaga, N., Suzuki, T., Ikushima, S., & Suzuki, M. (2019). Tourist-wild boar (Sus scrofa) interactions in urban wildlife management. *Global Ecology and Conservation*, (18), e00617. doi:10.1016/J.GECCO.2019.E00617
[66] Wastian, L., Betz, O., & Unterweger, P. (2016). Influence of the reduction of urban lawn mowing on wild bee diversity (Hymenoptera, Apoidea). *Journal of Hymenoptera Research*, (49), 51-63. doi:10.15496/PUBLIKATION-17707
[67] Kowarik, I., & Körner, S. (2005). Wild Urban Woodlands: New Perspectives for Urban Forestry. Berlin, Germany: Springer.
[68] Hwang, Y. H., & Roscoe, C. J. (2017). Preference for site conservation in relation to on-site biodiversity and perceived site attributes: An on-site survey of unmanaged urban greenery in a tropical city. *Urban Forestry and Urban Greening*, (28), 12-20. doi:10.1016/J.UFUG.2017.09.011
[69] Stillfried, M., Fickel, J., Börner, K., Wittstatt, U., Heddergott, M., Ortmann, S., ... Frantz, A. C. (2017). Do cities represent sources, sinks or isolated islands for urban wild boar population structure?. *Journal of Applied Ecology*, 54(1), 272-281. doi:10.1111/1365-2664.12756
[70] Castillo-Contreras, R., Carvalho, J., Serrano, E., Mentaberre, G., Fernández-Aguilar, X., Colom, A., ... López-Olvera, J. R. (2018). Urban wild boars prefer fragmented areas with food resources near natural corridors. *Science of the Total Environment*, (615), 282-288. doi:10.1016/J.SCITOTENV.2017.09.277
[71] Buchholz, S., & Egerer, M. H. (2020). Functional ecology of wild bees in cities: Towards a better understanding of trait-urbanization relationships. *Biodiversity and Conservation*, 29(9), 2779-2801. doi:10.1007/S10531-020-02003-8
[72] Egerer, M., Cecala, J. M., & Cohen, H. (2019). Wild Bee Conservation within Urban Gardens and Nurseries: Effects of Local and Landscape Management. *Sustainability*, 12(1). doi:10.3390/SU12010293
[73] Vicenzotti, V., & Trepl, L. (2009). City as Wilderness: The Wilderness Metaphor from Wilhelm Heinrich Riehl to Contemporary Urban Designers. *Landscape Research*, 34(4), 379-396. doi:10.1080/01426390903019041
[74] Te, A. B. (2012). Wild City: On the Metaphor Experience. *Journal of Jiangnan University (Humanities & Social Sciences)*, 11(3), 86-90.
[75] Bunting, B. S. (2015). An Alternative Wilderness: How Urban Exploration Brings Wildness to the City. *Interdisciplinary Studies in Literature and Environment*, 22(3), 602-622. doi:10.1093/ISLE/ISU093
[76] Adams, D., & Hardman, M. (2014). Observing Guerrillas in the Wild: Reinterpreting Practices of Urban Guerrilla Gardening. *Urban Studies*, 51(6), 1103-1119. doi:10.1177/0042098013497410
[77] Xie, M. (2019). Pursuing Wilderness Aesthetics in Contemporary Chinese Cities. *Landscape Architecture*, 26(8), 35-38.
[78] Filibeck, G., Petrella, P., & Cornelini, P. (2016). All ecosystems look messy, but some more so than others: A case-study on the management and acceptance of Mediterranean urban grasslands. *Urban Forestry and Urban Greening*, (15), 32-39. doi:10.1016/J.UFUG.2015.11.005
[79] Aurora, A. L., Simpson, T. R., Small, M. F., & Bender, K. C. (2009). Toward increasing avian diversity: Urban wildscapes programs. *Urban Ecosystems*, 12(3), 347-358. doi:10.1007/S11252-009-0084-0
[80] Kowarik, I., Buchholz, S., von der Lippe, M., & Seitz, B. (2016). Biodiversity functions of urban cemeteries: Evidence from one of the largest Jewish cemeteries in Europe. *Urban Forestry and Urban Greening*, (19), 68-78. doi:10.1016/J.UFUG.2016.06.023
[81] Mollee, E., Pouliot, M., & McDonald, M. A. (2017). Into the urban wild: Collection of wild urban plants for food and medicine in Kampala, Uganda. *Land Use Policy*, (63), 67-77. doi:10.1016/J.LANDUSEPOL.2017.01.020
[82] McLain, R. J., Poe, M., Hurley, P. T., Lecompte-Mastenbrook, J., & Emery, M. R. (2012). Producing edible landscapes in Seattle's urban forest. *Urban Forestry and Urban Greening*, 11(2), 187-194. doi:10.1016/J.UFUG.2011.12.002
[83] Kowarik, I., Hiller, A., Planchuelo, G., Seitz, B., von der Lippe, M., & Buchholz, S. (2019). Emerging Urban Forests: Opportunities for Promoting the Wild Side of the Urban Green Infrastructure. *Sustainability*, 11(22). doi:10.3390/SU11226318
[84] Hester, R. T., Blazej, N. J., & Moore, I. S. (1999). Whose Wild? Resolving Cultural and Biological Diversity Conflicts in Urban Wilderness. *Landscape Journal*, 18(2), 137-146. doi:10.3368/LJ.18.2.137
[85] Cheesbrough, A. E., Garvin, T., & Nykiforuk, C. I. J. (2019). Everyday wild: Urban natural areas, health, and well-being. *Health and Place*, (56), 43-52. doi:10.1016/J.HEALTHPLACE.2019.01.005
[86] Sikorska, D., Łaszkiewicz, E., Krauze, K., & Sikorski, P. (2020). The role of informal green spaces in reducing inequalities in urban green space availability to children and seniors. *Environmental Science and Policy*, (108), 144-154. doi:10.1016/J.ENVSCI.2020.03.007
[87] Özgüner, H., & Kendle, A. D. (2006). Public attitudes towards naturalistic versus designed landscapes in the city of Sheffield (UK). *Landscape and Urban Planning*, 74(2), 139-157. doi:10.1016/J.LANDURBPLAN.2004.10.003
[88] Colley, K., Brown, C., & Montarzino, A. (2016). Restorative wildscapes at work: An investigation of the wellbeing benefits of greenspace at urban fringe business sites using 'go-along' interviews. *Landscape Research*, 41(6), 598-615. doi:10.1080/01426397.2016.1197191
[89] Cameron, R. W. F., Brindley, P., Mears, M., McEwan, K., Ferguson, F., Sheffield, D., ... Richardson, M. (2020). Where the wild things are! Do urban green spaces with greater avian biodiversity promote more positive emotions in humans?. *Urban Ecosystems*, 23(2), 301-317. doi:10.1007/S11252-020-00929-Z
[90] Rutko, E., & Gillespie, J. (2013). Where's the Wilderness in Wilderness Therapy? *Journal of Experiential Education*, (36), 218-232. doi:10.1177/1053825913489107
[91] Hwang, Y. H., Yue, Z. E. J., Ling, S. K., & Tan, H. H. V. (2019). It's ok to be wilder: Preference for natural growth in urban green spaces in a tropical city. *Urban Forestry and Urban Greening*, (38), 165-176. doi:10.1016/J.UFUG.2018.12.005
[92] Hofmann, M., Westermann, J. R., Kowarik, I., & van der Meer, E. (2012). Perceptions of parks and urban derelict land by landscape planners and residents. *Urban Forestry and Urban Greening*, 11(3), 303-312. doi:10.1016/J.UFUG.2012.04.001
[93] Paul H. (2012). Appreciating urban wildscapes: Towards a natural history of unnatural places. In A. Jorgensen, & R. Keenan (Eds.), *Urban Wildscapes* (pp. 33-48). Abingdon, England: Routledge.
[94] Edensor, T., Evans, B., Holloway, J., Millington, S., & Binnie, J. (2012). Playing in industrial ruins: Interrogating teleological understandings of play in spaces of material alterity and low surveillance. In A. Jorgensen & R. Keenan (Eds.), *Urban Wildscapes* (pp. 65-79). Abingdon, England: Routledge.
[95] Palmer, H. M. (2012). Upstaging nature: Art in Sydenham Hill Wood. In A. Jorgensen, & R. Keenan (Eds.), *Urban Wildscapes* (pp. 160-169). Abingdon, England: Routledge.
[96] Rupprecht, C. D. D., Byrne, J. A., Ueda, H., & Lo, A. Y. (2015). 'It's real, not fake like a park': Residents' perception and use of informal urban green-space in Brisbane, Australia and Sapporo, Japan. *Landscape and Urban Planning*, (143), 205-218. doi:10.1016/J.LANDURBPLAN.2015.07.003
[97] Jiang, Y., & Yuan, T. (2017). Public perceptions and preferences for wildflower meadows in Beijing, China. *Urban Forestry and Urban Greening*, (27), 324-331. doi:10.1016/J.UFUG.2017.07.004
[98] Weber, F., Kowarik, I., & Säumel, I. (2014). A walk on the wild side: Perceptions of roadside vegetation beyond trees. *Urban Forestry and Urban Greening*, 13(2), 205-212. doi:10.1016/J.UFUG.2013.10.010
[99] Mathey, J., Arndt, T., Banse, J., & Rink, D. (2016). Public perception of spontaneous vegetation on brownfields in urban areas—Results from surveys in Dresden and Leipzig (Germany). *Urban Forestry and Urban Greening*, (29), 384-392. doi:10.1016/J.UFUG.2016.10.007

基于植被再野化的城市荒野生境重建
——以野花草甸为例

Reconstruction of Urban Wilderness Habitats Based on Vegetation Rewilding: Taking Wildflower Meadows as an Example

袁嘉*
重庆大学建筑城规学院副教授、博士生导师，山地城镇建设与新技术教育部重点实验室固定研究人员；中国科学院山地生态恢复与生物资源利用重点实验室生态恢复与生物多样性保育四川省重点实验室中国科学院成都生物研究所合作研究人员

游奉溢
重庆千洲生态环境工程有限公司工程师

侯春丽
重庆大学建筑城规学院博士研究生

欧桦杰
重庆大学建筑城规学院硕士研究生

尹渊
重庆千洲生态环境工程有限公司工程师

YUAN Jia
Associate Professor and PhD Supervisor of the School of Architecture and Urban Planning, Research Fellow at the Key Laboratory of New Technology for Construction of Cities in Mountain Area, Chongqing University; Cooperative Research Fellow of the CAS Key Laboratory of Mountain Ecological Restoration and Bioresource Utilization & Ecological Restoration and Biodiversity Conservation Key Laboratory of Sichuan Province, Chengdu Institute of Biology, Chinese Academy of Sciences

YOU Fengyi
Engineer at Chongqing Qianzhou Ecological Environment Engineering Co., Ltd.

HOU Chunli
PhD Student of the School of Architecture and Urban Planning, Chongqing University

OU Huajie
Master Student of the School of Architecture and Urban Planning, Chongqing University

YIN Yuan
Engineer at Chongqing Qianzhou Ecological Environment Engineering Co., Ltd.

地址：重庆市沙坪坝区沙正街174号
邮编：400030
邮箱：jyuan523@vip.163.com

编辑 | 田乐、崔婧沄
翻译 | 袁嘉、田乐
EDITED BY | Tina TIAN, CUI Jingyun
TRANSLATED BY | YUAN Jia, Tian TIAN

摘要

城市环境中残存着一些以自然过程为主导的荒野生境片段，在生物多样性保育、维持城市生态过程、连接人与自然等方面具有不可替代的作用。植被再野化提供了重建城市荒野生境的重要途径，旨在恢复严重退化的城市植物群落的物种组成、结构及功能，使其逐渐野化并达到自然过程基本不受人类干扰的程度。本文以野花草甸景观为例，提出了主动利用景观生态流、拟自然设计与最小限度干预进行城市植被再野化的技术框架；从自我设计、微地形设计、拟自然群落设计、植物－动物关键种协同共生设计，以及自然柔性材料运用等5个方面详细探讨并提供科学参考。同时，以重庆市梁平区双桂湖湖岸公园绿地为例，阐述了在“自然－人工”斑块复杂镶嵌的城市景观中进行植被再野化与荒野生境重建的实践原则与应用范式。

关键词

城市荒野；城市植物景观；再野化；生境；草本植物群落；野花草甸

ABSTRACT

Fragments of wilderness dominated by natural succession exist in urban environments, and play a critical role in protecting biodiversity, supporting urban ecological processes, and connecting human beings with nature. Urban vegetation rewilding is a key approach to restricting urban wilderness by restoring the species composition, community structure and functions, eventually towards a self-maintained vegetation community. This paper, taking wildflower meadows as a reference, establishes a technical framework of urban vegetation rewilding by leveraging ecological flows and adopting quasi-nature design with minimum interventions. The framework covers 5 aspects, namely self-design, micro-topographic design, quasi-nature design, collaborative symbiosis design between plant community and keystone animal species, and design with natural materials. Studying the green space along the northwest lakeside of the Shuangguihu National Wetland Park in Liangping District, Chongqing, this paper provides a scientific guidance and technical paradigm for vegetation rewilding and urban wilderness restoration in the complex context of natural-artificial urban landscapes.

KEYWORDS

Urban Wilderness; Urban Plant Landscape; Rewilding; Habitat; Herbaceous Communities; Wildflower Meadow

基金项目

国家自然科学基金青年科学基金项目“山地城市水敏性区域草本植物群落适应性设计研究”（编号：51808065）
中央高校基本科研业务费项目“山地城市江岸景观的植物群落适应性设计研究”（编号：2020CDJQY-A010）
中国科学院山地生态恢复与生物资源利用重点实验室及生态恢复与生物多样性保育四川省重点实验室开放课题“川西地区野花草甸种质资源调查及应用设计研究”（编号：KXYSWS2001）

RESEARCH FUNDS

Adaptive Design for the Herbaceous Community of the Water Sensitive Urban Area in Mountainous Cities, Young Scientists Fund of the National Natural Science Foundation of China (No. 51808065)
Research on Adaptive Design of Plant Community in Riverside Landscape of Mountainous City, Fundamental Research Funds for the Central Universities (No. 2020CDJQY-A010)
Germplasm Resources of Wildflower Meadow in Western Sichuan and Application in Landscape, Open Project of the CAS Key Laboratory of Mountain Ecological Restoration and Bioresource Utilization & Ecological Restoration and Biodiversity Conservation Key Laboratory of Sichuan Province, Chengdu Institute of Biology, Chinese Academy of Sciences (No. KXYSWS2001)

https://doi.org/10.15302/J-LAF-1-020041
收稿时间 RECEIVED DATE | 2020-11-19

中图分类号 | TU986
文献标识码 | A

1 城市荒野及再野化

"荒野"（wilderness）是指地球表面尚未因受人类活动影响而发生明显改变、由自然生态过程主导的大片区域。荒野在生物多样性保护、自然遗产保护等方面发挥着不可替代的作用[1][2]，且基本无需额外的人工投入来维持其生态系统与生态系统服务[3]。荒野景观使人类与野性保持联系，凭借自由生长及生机勃勃的特性，成为了文化、道德与宗教中的重要元素[4][5]。尽管荒野景观可带来广泛的生态、经济和社会效益，但农耕、伐木、采矿与城镇化等高强度人类活动正导致荒野迅速退化甚至消失[6][7]。

高度人工化的城市环境中残存着片段化的荒野生境。城市荒野是存在于人工系统夹缝中的自然本底，通常位于城市内或城郊人迹难至的高地或沟谷，或是闲置、废弃的水体、林地、农田、工业用地（包括废弃矿坑）等，其生物群落的形成与自然演替在一定时间内基本不受人工干扰[8]。相较于需要精心养护的人工景观，城市荒野景观往往有利于空气、水体与土壤净化，更有利于促进人类身心健康[9]；城市荒野景观在城市绿地系统中的镶嵌分布提升了城市生态基础设施网络的连续性和有效性。然而，城市化造成土地开发需求不断增加，针对城市荒野生境保护、管控与补偿的政策措施仍不完善；在过度追求整洁秩序的审美意识下，人类对于荒野景观仍存在负面认知[10]。这些问题导致城市荒野生境日渐衰退与稀缺。

城市绿地中的植被在长期高强度的管理和维护下，往往存在景观单调、物种贫乏、结构单一、生态功能低下、资源消耗严重等问题。在此背景下，"再野化"（rewilding）理念被提出：再野化旨在终止人为干预并实施有效的修复设计，使退化的生物群落的物种组成、结构及功能恢复至接近自然荒野的状态[11]。城市植被再野化正是重建城市荒野生境，修复完善"荒野生境—人工绿地"复杂镶嵌的城市生态网络，实现低维持、可持续、高韧性城市景观系统的关键途径。

自20世纪90年代以来，西欧与北美地区开始启动城市植被再野化的相关研究与应用，城市植被再野化的关注焦点逐渐转向自生植物的管理及应用。琼·艾弗森·纳索尔于1995年发表《无序系统，有序框架》一文，认可了在城市中自然定居的自生植物群落的重要生态功能与美学价值[12]。诺伯特·库恩进一步提出了利用自生植被优化城市景观的

1 Urban Wilderness and Rewilding

Wilderness refers to a large area of unmodified or slightly modified earth surface retaining its natural character and ecological processes. Wilderness plays a critical role in the conservation of biodiversity and natural heritages[1][2], and no additional or minimum human-made investment is needed to sustain its ecosystem and ecosystem services[3]. Wilderness connects human beings with wildness, and is a significant element in culture, morality, and religion for its spontaneity and vitality[4][5]. Wilderness brings considerable ecological, economic, and social benefits, but is undergoing rapid degradation or even disappears due to intensive human activities like farming, logging, mining, and urbanization[6][7].

Fragments of wilderness exist in highly artificialized urban environment as well. Urban wilderness, manifesting the nature scattering among constructed systems, includes the highlands or valleys in the cities or suburbs with poor accessibility, or the idle or abandoned water bodies, forestlands, farmlands, and industrial lands (including wasted mining pits). The composition and natural succession of the biotic communities in the wilderness are free from human intervention for a certain length of time[8]. Compared to well-maintained landscapes, urban wilderness landscape provides better ecosystem services such as purifying air, water, and soil, and delivering more benefits for human health[9]. The scattering pattern of urban wilderness enhances the continuity and efficacy of urban ecological infrastructure. However, as the land is growingly developed during the urbanization, policies and measures on wilderness protection, regulation, and compensation are inadequate, and the public's aesthetics that admire cleanness and order remains negative about wilderness[10]. As a result, urban wilderness increasingly degrades and disappears.

Under long-term intensive management and maintenance, urban green spaces often appear homogenous, with low biodiversity, poor structures and ecological services, as well as high resource consumption. In such a context, the concept "rewilding" was proposed which advocates replacing human intervention with natural restoration on degraded communities so as to reconstruct the species composition, structure, and functions of them[11]. Urban vegetation rewilding is a key approach to restoring urban wilderness, improving urban ecological networks of wilderness–artificial green spaces, and building sustainable landscape systems that require little maintenance and perform stronger sustainability and resilience.

Since the 1990s, scholars from West Europe and North America started the studies on urban vegetation rewilding, which have shifted its focus to the management and application of spontaneous vegetation. In 1995, Joan Iverson Nassauer published the paper "Messy Ecosystems, Orderly Frames," which recognizes the ecological functions and aesthetic values of urban spontaneous plant communities[12]. Norbert Kühn came up with the design strategy that

设计策略[13]。这一策略在德国北杜伊斯堡景观公园和卡尔－亚历山大矿山公园、美国高线公园、中国江洋畈生态公园等项目中均有运用。

然而，以限制人类干扰和利用自生植物为主的植被再野化措施存在群落演替方向不确定、演替时间长、过程中植被结构及功能稳定性较差，以及景观表现力欠佳等问题[13]。定向、高效且更加美观地建立野化植物群落现已成为城市植被再野化的新需求。近年来，模拟自然野花草甸群落设计营建植物景观的案例逐渐增多[14]；其中，荒野野花草甸具有稳定的群落结构、丰富的观赏效果与多种生态服务功能[15]，是城市植被再野化良好的参考对象。基于此，本文以野花草甸为例，提出以最小限度干预措施重建城市荒野生境、利用景观生态流和拟自然设计制定城市植被定向再野化的技术框架。同时，以重庆市梁平区双桂湖国家湿地公园西北侧湖岸绿地为例，探讨如何在“自然－人工斑块”复杂镶嵌的城市景观中构建可持续植被景观和重建荒野生境。

2 城市植被再野化技术框架——以野花草甸为例

基于自然荒野的景观与生态机制，城市植被再野化的基本技术目标为：通过分析荒野植物群落的物种组成、群落结构及生态功能，使其结构与功能接近荒野植物群落，最终实现在无人工或粗放管护条件下，借助自然演替和景观生态流的作用进行自我维持。本研究以野花草甸为例，提出城市植被再野化基本技术范式的关键流程（图1）：1）调控生态流，驱动植物群落的自我设计；2）充分利用微地形设计，创造风力与水力传播条件；3）模拟荒野野花草甸群落结构进行拟自然设计；4）植物群落－动物关键种协同共生设计；5）运用自然柔性材料（如残枝与块石等）进行设计。

2.1 自我设计

荒野生境的最佳管理方式之一是通过设置保护红线与制定“善意忽略策略”（benign neglect strategy）来减少人为干扰，以促进植被的自然演替[16][17]。为尽可能减少人工管护并适应自然管理做功，再野化的植被群落需要具备良好的自我设计能力以实现群落的自我维持。可从以下三个方面建立和发挥植物群落的自我设计能力：

optimizes urban landscapes with spontaneous vegetation[13]. This strategy has been applied in worldwide projects like Landscape Park Duisburg-Nord and Carl-Alexander Park in Germany, High Line Park in the United States, and Jiangyangfan Eco-Park, China.

However, vegetation rewilding approaches that minimize human interventions and use spontaneous plants see limitations such like uncertain and long-time succession of communities, poor stability of vegetation structure and functions, and low landscape attractiveness[13]. New approaches to urban vegetation rewilding are required to build appealing wild plant communities with a directed succession and in an efficient way. In recent years, more and more restoration design practices of urban rewilded landscapes stimulate natural wildflower meadows[14] which have stable community structures, visual attractiveness, and diverse ecosystem services[15]. On this basis, this paper, taking wildflower meadows as a reference, proposes the methods to rebuild urban wilderness with minimum interventions, and establishes a technical framework of urban vegetation rewilding by leveraging ecological flows and adopting quasi-nature design. Studying the green space along the northwest lakeside of the Shuangguihu National Wetland Park in Liangping District, Chongqing, this paper provides a scientific guidance and technical paradigm for vegetation rewilding and urban wilderness restoration in the complex context of natural–artificial urban landscapes.

2 A Technical Framework of Urban Vegetation Rewilding: Wildflower Meadow Restoration

Based on the landscape and ecological mechanism of the wilderness, the primary technical objective of urban vegetation rewilding is to analyze the species composition, structure, and ecological functions of wild plant communities, imitating their structures and functions to achieve a self-maintained urban vegetation community along natural succession and ecological flows. Illustrating with a case of wildflower meadow restoration, this paper comes up with the key procedures of urban vegetation rewilding (Fig. 1): 1) regulating ecological flows to drive the self-design of plant communities; 2) using micro-topographic design to improve habitat heterogeneity, as well as the wind and hydrological seed dispersal; 3) mimicking the community structure of wildflower meadows; 4) establishing the collaborative symbiosis between plant community and keystone animal species; and 5) combining the design with natural soft materials, e.g., woody debris and rocks.

2.1 Self-design

One of the best management practices of the wilderness is to identify the protection boundary and develop benign neglect strategies so as to reduce human management and promote natural succession[16][17]. Rewilded plant community can be designed to improve its self-design capacity for self-maintenance in the following ways:

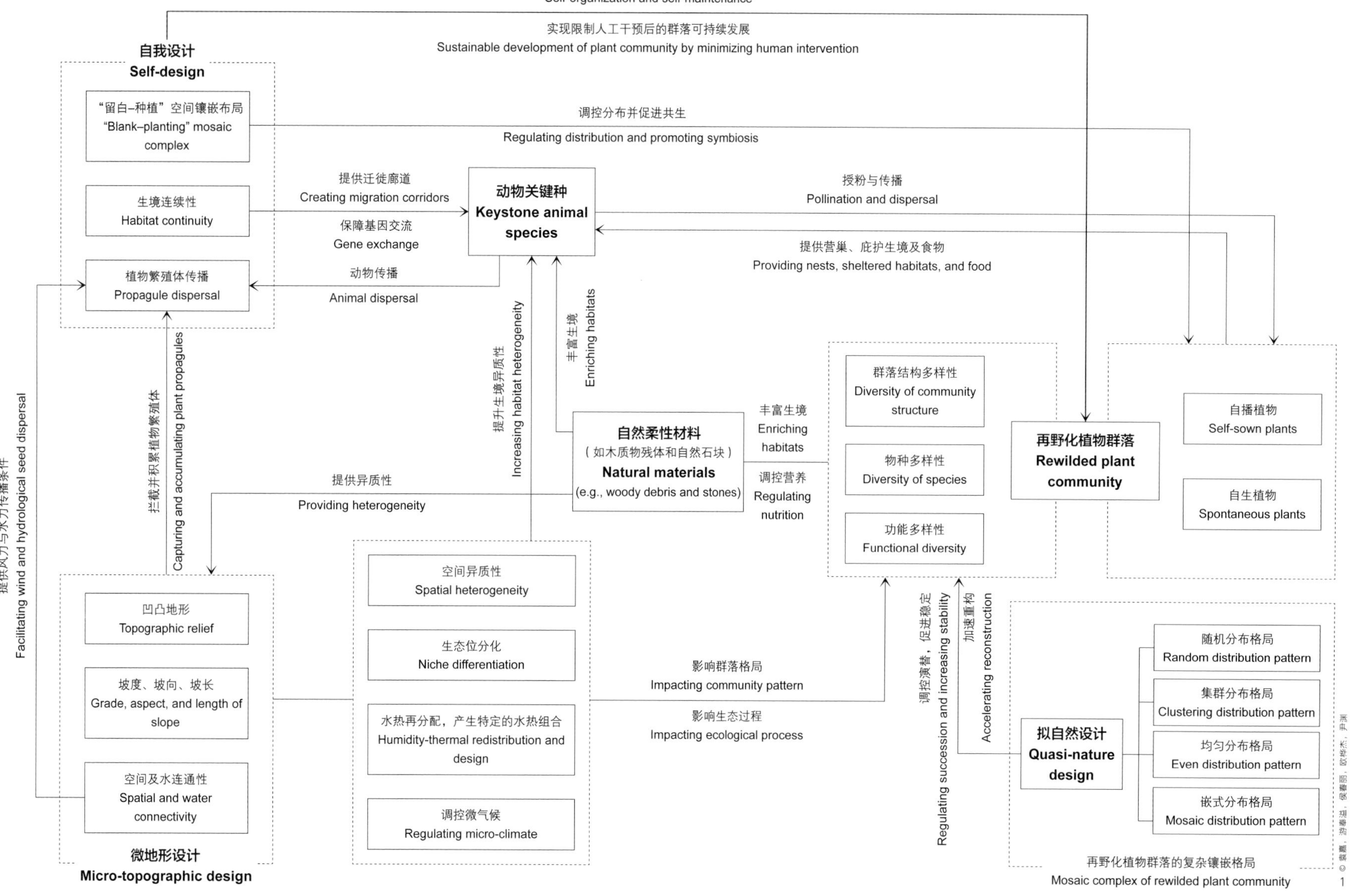

1. 城市植被再野化技术框架
1. The technical framework of urban vegetation rewilding

1）选用可自播繁衍的植物物种：难以自播或自播后无法完成生活史的植物物种在缺少替换与补植等人工干预的城市荒野生境中会被迅速淘汰。可自播繁衍的草本植物种类能够通过播种占据空间与资源，建立对入侵物种的竞争优势，维持群落组成与结构的稳定。可自播繁衍的植物是城市植被再野化的重要种源。种子能够长期存活于地表以下，并在自然灾害或次生灾害发生后重塑地表植被；种子随风、水与动物传播，在林地、湿地、阳台与屋顶、人行道或石墙缝隙等城市环境中萌发，完成野花草甸的迁移与复制。

1) Selecting self-sown species: Species that can hardly plant or establish itself would be eliminated soon in urban wilderness when human intervention is minimized. Self-sown herbaceous species can be dominant in space and resources, maintaining the stability of community composition and structure against invasive species. Self-sown species can provide important germplasm for urban vegetation rewilding. Their seeds survive as parts of soil seed bank that restructures the ground vegetation after natural disasters or secondary disasters. Via wind, water or animals, these seeds can disperse to other urban habitats such as forests, wetlands, terraces or rooftops, sidewalks, and cracks of stone walls, resulting in the migration and colonies of rewilded meadows.

2）为自生植物预留空间：自生植物是城市生物多样性的重要组成部分，对城市环境具有良好适应能力，是城市荒野生境形成的关键要素。再野化野花草甸设计应创建种植空间和留白空间的嵌套生境格局，不仅可以促进土壤种子库中自生植物的萌发生长，也为借助风、水及动物传播的自生植物提供了生长空间，进而可建立丰富多样的自生植物群落。

3）提高生境连续性：提高生境连续性有利于保障物种在生境斑块间的扩散与基因交流[18]，能够保证野花草甸的遗传多样性；通过拆除物理边界来保持设计地块的开放性；基于更大尺度的城市景观格局，以风廊、水廊及生物走廊连通场地与其他景观斑块；以及设计不同演替阶段的群落镶嵌分布。

2.2 微地形设计

地形变化是形成空间异质性的重要原因，宏观地形起伏对生物多样性的演变和分布具有调控作用[19]，而微地形的变化则是塑造植物生境的关键。荒野野花草甸景观因内部微地形变化（图2）而产生的特定水热条件将影响微气候并形成生态位分化，从而对植物群落的格局和生态过程产生深刻影响[20]~[22]。

微地形因素（包括坡度、坡向、坡长与起伏程度等）决定了土壤与水分的留存能力，以及温度和光照分布，从而影响植物群落的组成结构、数量分布及生长发育状况[23][24]。超过30° 的大斜率坡面土壤含量较低且利于排水，适于耐瘠薄与耐旱植物生长[22]；平缓的坡面湿度适中，且水湿变化较为丰富，设计营建缓坡并增加坡长能有效增加坡面面积，有利于增加植物群落的物种丰富度[25]；南向坡地利于聚热采光，有助于提升物种多样性并促进植物生长[26]。凹凸地形及其组合能通过制造地表的小微起伏缓冲或拦截水流以获取随水传播的植物繁殖体，从而建立自生植被群落。浅洼地与沟槽等浅凹地形可保持较高的土壤水分；池、塘、渠等深凹地形能够拦截并蓄滞地表径流，是形成小微湿地的地形要素，有利于构建湿地植物群落，并为周边生境提供良好水源、降低环境温度。小丘等凸地形能够形成遮荫，在为喜荫植物提供适宜生长条件的同时，可形成抵挡冷风的屏障或引导风向形成微型风廊。增加连续的凹凸地形变化有助于创造多样化的空间生态位，为不同植物种群的生长提供条件[27]。

2) Reserving room for spontaneous plants: Spontaneous plants are robust in urban environments, and play an important role in urban biodiversity and urban rewilding. Establishing a mosaic pattern of rewilded meadow, which both considers planting space and reverses blank space for the growth of spontaneous species in the soil seed bank and for the colony of seeds dispersed by wind, water, and animals. In this way, a diverse community of spontaneous plants can be established.

3) Enhancing habitat patch continuity: Enhancing the continuity among habitat patches facilitates species spread and gene flows[18], ensuring the genetic diversity of rewilded meadows. The physical boundaries between the habitat patches shall be removed. Connecting the restoration site with other habitat patches with ecological corridors for natural dispersal. Besides, adopting a mosaic distribution of plant communities at different succession stages is also encouraged.

2.2 Micro-topographic Design

Topographic change is the main causality to spatial heterogeneity. The macro-scale terrain design would help regulate the evolution and distribution of biodiversity[19], while the micro-topography defines the plant species habitats. The humidity-thermal condition resulting from micro-topographic variation within natural meadows (Fig. 2) would impact the micro-climate and differentiate niche, which will then profoundly impact the pattern and ecological processes of plant communities[20]~[22].

Micro-topographic factors (including the grade, aspect, and length of slope; and the topography) define the preservation capacity of soil and water, and the solar and thermal distribution, which will then determine the composition, quantity, distribution, and growth of the plant communities[23][24]. For example, a steep slope of over 30° is often covered by thin soil layer, and has relatively good drainage condition that is suitable for drought-tolerant plant species[22]. Since gentle slopes would have a mesic moisture with a richer moisture gradient, the increase of the length of slope will enrich the plant species that grow in different moisture regimes[25]. South-faced slopes have better light and thermal conditions, which is conducive to enhancing the species diversity and facilitating plant growth[26]. Through the design of topographic relief, buffers can be created to gather the plant propagules via water dispersal, then establishing spontaneous plant communities. Shallow depressions and swales can keep soil moisture, while deep concave terrain such as ponds and canals can retain runoffs. These landform design measures are often used in constructing micro and seasonal wetlands, to provide water source for nearby habitats and adjust microclimate. Small hills can provide shade and suitable growth conditions for shade-requiring species, and form shelters against cold wind or guide the wind to form micro-wind-corridors. Enriching the topographic relief helps create diverse niches, providing suitable growth conditions for various plant communities[27].

2. 中国四姑娘山地区高山野花草甸及其内部微地形变化
3. 荒野野花草甸群落的水平分布格局示意图（改绘自参考文献[29]）

2. Wildflower meadows on the Mount Siguniang in China and the micro-topographical changes
3. Diagrams of the horizontal distribution of the wildflower meadow community (Adaptation source: Ref. [29])

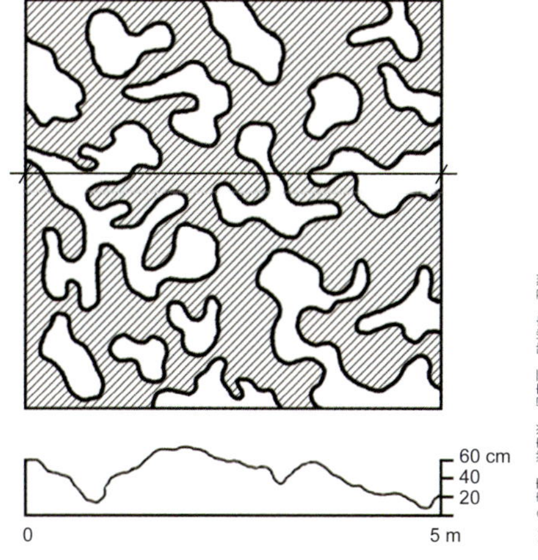

© 袁嘉，游苯溢，侯春丽，欧桦杰，尹渊

2

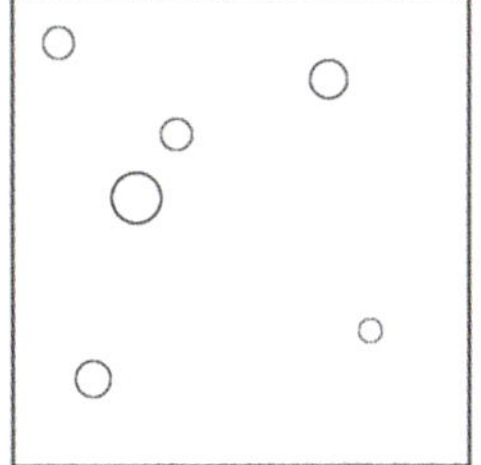

随机分布格局
Random distribution

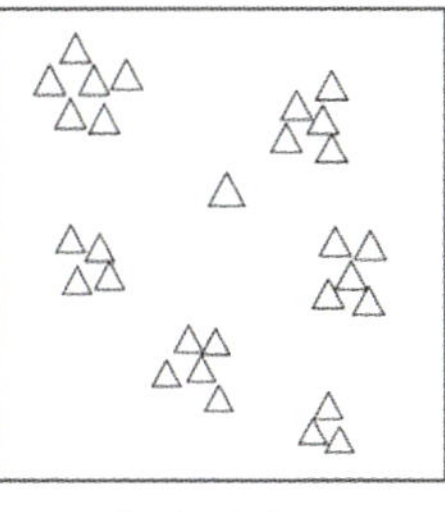

集群分布格局
Clustering distribution

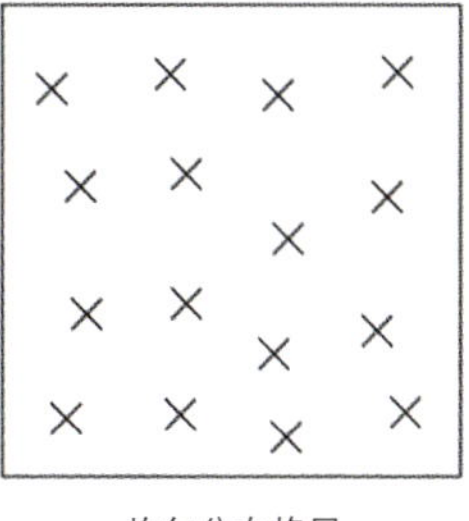

均匀分布格局
Even distribution

嵌式分布格局
Mosaic distribution

3

2.3 拟自然设计

荒野野花草甸群落具备复杂的水平结构，包含三种基本分布格局（图3）：

1）随机分布，指植物个体在水平空间中偶然出现，个体间的位置没有必然联系；

2）集群分布，指植物个体成群成簇地密集分布；

3）均匀分布，指植物个体按一定间距分布[28]，当种群个体簇生集合成许多集群且集群间呈规则分布，则将形成一种特殊的集群分布形式——嵌式分布[29]。

基于荒野群落的形成机制进行拟自然设计是合理调控再野化野花草甸的演替过程、形成稳定群落结构的关键。植物被引入新地块时，往往依种子的散布而随机分布。设计应建立“留白—种植”空间的复合嵌套格局，不仅有利于群落自我设计，也可限制迁入物种的生长空间，促进自生植物形成集群格局。将环境适应能力良好并能提供重要生物多样性保育与环境调节功能的植物（如蜜粉源植物、寄主植物和净水植物）进行集群种植，形成优势种群，有利于抵御外来物种入侵。自播植物的种子一般落在母株附近萌发，能够较好地保持种群的集群分布格局，并随

2.3 Quasi-Nature Design

Natural meadows can be horizontally structured as in three patterns (Fig. 3):

1) Random distribution: plants haphazardly distribute horizontally, and each individual plant has no spatial relation with others;

2) Clustering distribution: plants densely distribute in clusters;

And 3) even distribution: plants distribute by certain distances[28], and when a number of individual clusters form a particular pattern, a mosaic distribution comes into being[29].

The aim of quasi-nature design is to regulate the succession of rewilded meadows and maintain their community structures by learning from sustainable communities in wilderness. For a randomized species assemblage of naturally colonized plants, the “blank–planting” mosaic complex not only facilitates self-design of the spontaneous communities, but also limits the growth of introduced plant species, fostering the establishment of the clusters of spontaneous plants which can have a better environmental adaptability, provide ecological benefits (e.g., nectar and pollen source, hosting, and water purification), grow into the dominant populations, and resist the invasion of exotic species. The seeds of self-sown plants often sprout near the maternal plants, which maintain the clustering pattern of mixed species and generally result in an even distribution over time[29]. A mixed-species meadow in an evenly distributing pattern often has a richer color combination and a higher attractiveness to wildlife and human beings[30][31].

时间趋向于均匀分布[29]。均匀分布格局往往有利于形成更为丰富的色彩组合，进而增强对野生动物的吸引力及景观观赏体验[30][31]。混播是营建均匀分布格局的良好方式，同时也能够极大降低成本投入与环境影响[32]。播种时要避免使用生长迅速、结种量过大、匍匐茎或根状茎过于发达的植物种类，避免形成单优群落。

2.4 植物群落—动物关键种协同共生设计

传粉昆虫维持着植物群落的有性繁殖与遗传活力，食用并携带植物繁殖体的小型鸟类与兽类则扮演着传播植物的关键角色[33]。这些物种对城市景观的植物分布和多样性具有重要调控作用，是“动物关键种”（keystone animal species）[34]，其种群生存繁衍情况与荒野生境的比例和面积密切相关[35]。引入动物关键种、促成“植物群落—动物关键种”的协同共生是城市植被再野化的核心目标和重要实现途径。

通过提供“踏脚石”、食物来源与营巢条件，可以吸引并保育动物关键种。城市野花草甸的选址应介于人工绿地斑块之间，以形成有效的“踏脚石”，并尽量形成廊道格局引导动物关键种的迁移，促进基因流[36]。选择蜜粉源丰富的乡土植物作为建群种可以为传粉昆虫提供充足的食物；增加蜜粉源植物的种类多样性能够有效增强传粉昆虫和植物的“取食—传粉”共生结构的复杂嵌套，从而提高野花草甸群落的结构稳定性和传粉昆虫的种群增长率[37][38]；将蜜粉源植物进行集群配置有助于传粉昆虫发现和搜集蜜粉[33]。野花草甸群落的地上亚层与地下分层可为动物关键种的栖息、完成生活史和繁衍提供多样化的生态位和巢穴空间。疏松土壤或卵石堆、块石堆提供的孔穴空间能够为部分不具备筑巢能力的传粉昆虫和小型兽类提供庇护空间；由木材、砖块或聚氯乙烯管等废弃材料建造的多孔穴小型设施也能够成为良好的巢穴空间[39]。

Mixture sowing can help establish an even distribution and reduce the cost and environmental impact significantly[32]; however, the use of species with rhizomes, a greater plant size or seed quantity should be avoided.

2.4 Collaborative Symbiosis Design Between Plant Community and Keystone Animal Species

Pollinator insects are vital to sustaining the sexual reproduction and genetic heredity of plant communities. Small birds and mammals that feed on and carry plant propagules play a key role to the propagule dispersal[33]. These species, as keystone animal species, regulate the plant distribution and diversity of urban landscapes[34]. The survival and reproduction of these species is largely impacted by the proportion and area of the wilderness[35]. Thus, one of the primary objectives of urban vegetation rewilding is to introduce the keystone animal species and encourage their collaborative symbiosis with plant communities.

Creating favorable stepping-stones, food sources, and nestling conditions can attract and conserve keystone animal species. Rewilded meadows should be located among artificial patches to form effective stepping-stones and corridors that could guide the migration of keystone animal species and enhance gene flows[36]. Native nectariferous plants provide sufficient food sources for pollinators. Increased diversity of nectariferous plant species enhances the mosaic complexity of the feeding–pollinating symbiosis structure, thus strengthening the stability of rewilded meadow and increasing the population of pollinators[37][38]. Clustering nectariferous plants can promote pollinators' nectar collection[33]. Increasing the number of aboveground and underground layers of the rewilded meadows can diversify niches and nestling spaces for the inhabitation, completion of life history, and reproduction

4 © 袁嘉，游春溢，侯春丽，欧桦杰，尹澜

4. 中国川西荒野中的野花草甸及其内部分布的木质物残体与自然石块

4. Wildflower meadow in western Sichuan, and the woody debris and natural stones within.

5. 研究场地区位图及实施修复前航拍照片

5. Site location and aerial photo before restoration

2.5 自然柔性材料的设计运用

荒野野花草甸内部往往大量分布着自然柔性材料，例如腐烂的树桩、倒木、枯枝等木质物残体，以及砾石、片石、卵石等自然石块（图4）。自然柔性材料附近分布的植物群落往往具有更丰富的物种多样性与群落结构复杂性，能够有效支撑生态系统的结构与组成异质性[40]。木质物残体在分解过程中能够释放氮、磷等营养元素，为周边生境提供营养；木质物残体和自然石块粗糙、龟裂的表面有利于土壤积存和植物种子附着，是良好的自生植物苗床；木质物残体和自然石块不仅能够为喜光植物提供更高的生长平台，还能够形成小范围的遮荫与潮湿空间，为耐荫植物和苔藓植物提供良好的生长条件，借此促进土壤碳平衡与水分涵养[41][42]。同时，木质物残体和自然石块既是鸟类与传粉昆虫的良好落脚点，又能够为喜阴湿环境的无脊椎动物提供生境，进而吸引鸟类停留取食。因此，主动置入与利用自然柔性材料应成为城市野花草甸再野化与荒野生境重建的重要设计措施。

3 设计案例：重庆双桂湖国家湿地公园植被再野化实践

3.1 研究场地与设计目标

研究场地位于重庆市梁平区中心地带，是双桂湖国家湿地公园湖区西北侧滨水空间内的公园绿地。场地面积约3.72hm^2，整体地势自北向南平缓降低，北侧紧邻梁平区新建开发区（图5）。实施修复前，研究区域原地势平缓，含有大面积的均质生境，难以促进生物多样性提

of keystone species. Loose soils, gravels or rocks, and small-sized porous spaces built with woody debris, bricks or PVC pipes can also provide ideal habitats for pollinators and small wild animals[39].

2.5 Design With Natural Materials

There are often massive natural materials within the natural meadow itself, including rotten stumps, logs, deadwood, gravels, rubbles, and pebbles (Fig. 4). The plant communities nearby such materials often see a richer biodiversity and greater structure complexity, supporting the heterogeneity of ecosystem structure and composition[40]. Woody debris would release nitrogen and phosphorus during decomposition, increasing the nutrient level of nearby habitats. The rough surfaces of woody debris and natural stones help with soil gathering and provide seed beds for spontaneous plants. These materials not only provide higher growth beds for photophilous plants, but also create micro-scale shading and moist habitats for shade-tolerant species and mosses which help adjust the carbon balance and water conservation of soil[41][42]. Also, woody debris and natural stones act as footholds for birds and pollinators, and provide habitats for invertebrates that favor shade and humid environment. Therefore, the use of natural materials shall be emphasized in the rewilding of urban meadow and urban wilderness rehabilitation.

3 Case Study: Vegetation Rewilding in Shuangguihu National Wetland Park, Chongqing

3.1 Study Site and Design Objectives

The paper studies the green space on the northwest lakeside of Shuangguihu National Wetland Park, which sits in the central area of Liangping District, Chongqing City. Covering an area of 3.72 hm^2, the site is high in the north and low in the south in elevation, and neighbors a newly developed zone in the north (Fig. 5). Before

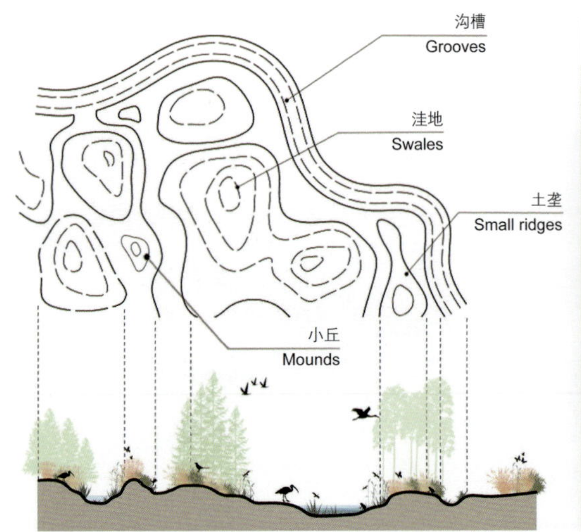

6 © 袁嘉，游幸滋，侯春丽，欧桦杰，尹渊

6. 研究场地微地形营造与生境设计示意图与现场照片（摄于2020年4月）

6. Micro-topography creation and habitat design (taken in April 2020)

升，有害生物的入侵与扩散较为明显，影响景观的生态可持续性。场地内植物种类贫乏，以狗牙根（*Cynodon dactylon*）、结缕草（*Zoysia japonica*）等草坪草为群落优势种，鬼针草（*Bidens pilosa*）、喜旱莲子草（*Alternanthera philoxeroides*）、小蓬草（*Erigeron canadensis*）等入侵植物较多；草坪退化严重、景观品质差，生态系统服务低下。

研究区域是城市建成环境与双桂湖水体之间的重要生态屏障，需要提供生态缓冲和生物多样性保育等生态系统服务，并以最小化建设与管控成本实现景观的可持续性。自2018年起，研究团队（即本文作者）通过实施植被再野化进行生境修复，以期实现荒野意象与功能的回归，重建自然—人工复合系统的生态平衡。

3.2 微地形营造与生境设计

研究遵循并强调浅水区—湖岸带—过渡坡地—高地空间梯度上的生境变化与连续性，构建了宽度、深度、坡度变化丰富的洼地、沟槽、小丘、土垄等凹凸地形组合，提供多种多样的基面并产生多样化的水热条件，从而提升景观的生境异质性。设计增加了洼地与土垄结构中南向缓坡的占比与坡长，有利于温度累积和丰富水湿梯度变化，同时保障了高坡—湖体之间的自然径流过程与竖向生态交换的基本连续性。设计营建了由“塘—坑—沟—渠—湖”结构复杂水平镶嵌而成的小微湿地群（图6），重建了多景观层次、多生态序列的荒野生境。复杂性与连续性并

the restoration, the study area's terrain was flat and homed a large area of homogeneous habitat, which resulted in a poor biodiversity and the invasion of harmful organisms, severely impacting the site's ecological sustainability. The site was predominated by a few of grass species including *Cynodon dactylon* and *Zoysia japonica*, and invasive ruderals including *Bidens pilosa*, *Alternanthera philoxeroides*, and *Erigeron Canadensis*. The existing lawn was severely degraded and deteriorated in ecosystem services.

The site is one of the important ecological buffers between the built environment and water bodies in the city. It is required to provide ecosystem services such as ecological buffer and biodiversity conservation, and to ensure the landscape sustainability while minimizing construction and maintenance cost. Since 2018, the research team (the authors) have worked on habitat restoration via vegetation rewilding, facilitating the return of the wilderness in image and function, and rebuilding the eco-balance of artificial ecosystems with nature.

3.2 Micro-topography Creation and Habitat Design

In line with the habitat gradient and continuity from shallow water, lakefront, buffer slope to upland, the design created micro-topography such as swales, grooves, mounds, small ridges with dynamic changes in width, height, and slope. The combination of concave and convex microstructures can enrich the site's contour and diversify humidity-thermal conditions, resulting in an increase of habitat heterogeneity. The design increased the amount and length of south-facing slope in swales and ridges to facilitate thermal accumulation and dynamic moisture content, and guarantee the continuity of natural runoffs and vertical ecological exchanges between the slopes and the lake. The design created clusters of small and micro wetland groups formed by mosaic complex of "pond–pit–swale–ditch–lake" (Fig. 6), thereby established the urban wilderness with multiple functional layers and multiple ecological sequences. With emphasis on the complexity and continuity of micro-topography creation, the design promotes the

表1：研究场地内新引入的植物物种

Table 1: The newly introduced plant species to the study site

阔叶草花集群（密集混栽成苗） The assembly of broad-leaf flower species (mixed seedlings densely planted)	高草集群（密集混栽成苗） The mixture of tall grass species (mixed seedlings densely planted)	均匀式种子混播组合 The seed mixture for evenly planting
大花萱草 *Hemerocallis hybridus*	斑叶芒 *Miscanthus sinensis* 'Zebrinus'	雏菊 *Bellis perennis*
钓钟柳 *Penstemon campanulatus*	灯心草 *Juncus effusus*	大滨菊 *Leucanthemum maximum*
佛甲草 *Sedum lineare*	黑心菊 *Rudbeckia hirta*	黑心菊 *Rudbeckia hirta*
黄金菊 *Euryops pectinatus*	节节草 *Equisetum ramosissimum*	金鸡菊 *Coreopsis basalis*
藿香蓟 *Ageratum conyzoides*	蓝羊茅 *Festuca glauca*	美女樱 *Glandularia × hybrida*
假龙头花 *Physostegia virginiana*	墨西哥鼠尾草 *Salvia leucantha*	蓍 *Achillea millefolium*
柳叶马鞭草 *Verbena bonariensis*	千屈菜 *Lythrum salicaria*	松果菊 *Echinacea purpurea*
毛地黄 *Digitalis purpurea*	细叶芒 *Miscanthus sinensis* 'Gracillimus'	天人菊 *Gaillardia pulchella*
鼠尾草 *Salvia japonica*		天竺葵 *Pelargonium hortorum*
千屈菜 *Lythrum salicaria*		黄花鸢尾 *Iris wilsonii*
山桃草 *Gaura lindheimeri*		
土人参 *Talinum paniculatum*		
玉簪 *Hosta plantaginea*		
八宝 *Hylotelephium erythrostictum*		

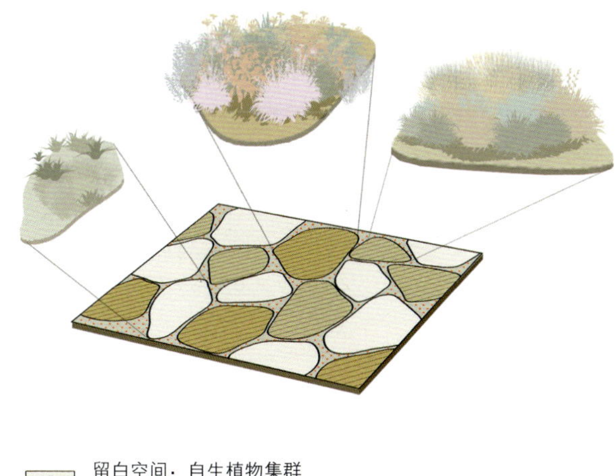

7 © 袁嘉，游菶溢，侯春丽，欧桦杰，尹渊

7. 留白空间－种植空间嵌套格局与集群分布布局

7. The blank-planting mosaic pattern and the clustering distribution of planting design

重的微地形设计有利于引导植物借助水流及动物媒介在场地内外扩繁，形成自我设计与维持的再野化植被。

3.3 植物选择与空间布局

设计在场地内引入了30余种具有良好自播能力的多年生草本植物（表1），在水平空间布局上采用"留白—种植"的空间嵌套格局（图7）。为控制成本投入，种植空间仅占场地面积的40%左右。场地自北向南平缓降低的地势变化，以及重庆地区秋冬季盛行偏北风，使成熟种子随自然径流和风传播的基本方向一致；鸟类与小型哺乳动物进入场地寻觅水源的行动方向也与风力、水力传播方向接近。因此，设计主动调控了提供重要种源群落的种植空间的分布，使种植空间的数量与面积占比从北至南、由高到低逐渐递减，借助场地内生态流（水、风和动物）传播植物，实现低干预的植被再野化。此外，为保护双桂湖水体与土壤种子库，再野化实施期间不施用任何化学除草剂，仅人工拔除恶性杂草（如鬼针草和喜旱莲子草）。

natural dispersal in and out of the site via flows and animals, ensuring the self-design and self-maintenance of rewilded vegetation.

3.3 Plant Species Selection and Planting Design

Over 30 perennial species with excellent self-sown capacity were introduced to the site (Table 1), and the blank–planting mosaic complex was used horizontally (Fig. 7). For considerations on project cost, the planting space only covers 40% of the site area. The site gently sloped from north to south, coupled with the prevailing north winds in Chongqing in autumn and winter, resulting in a same basic direction of seed dispersal by natural runoffs and wind, which is also the same as the direction that birds and small mammals enter the site to collect water. Therefore, the design regulates the distribution of planting space, so that the number and area of planting space gradually decrease from north to south along the slope. In this way, ecological flows (e.g., water, wind, and animal) leverages plant spread, ensuring the low-intervention vegetation rewilding. In addition, to environmental protection reasons, no chemical herbicide was used during the entire rewilding process. Weeds (e.g. *Bidens pilosa* and *Alternanthera philoxeroides*) were suppressed manually.

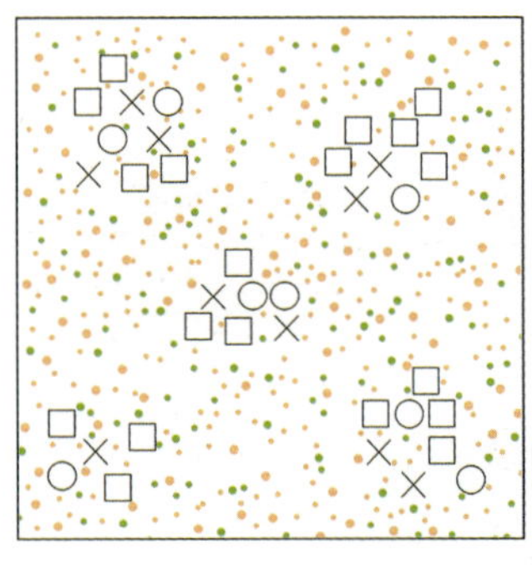

8 © 袁嘉，游荃溢，侯春丽，欧桦杰，尹渊

自然界中植物群落的镶嵌格局十分复杂，本研究采用嵌式分布与均匀分布格局，形成易操作、可控性好的水平种植格局图式（图8）。密集混栽具有重要生态功能的植物物种，形成小集群；这些小集群之间可形成规则的嵌式分布格局，以便施工人员定点种植；集群种植也有利于隔离具有直接竞争关系的植物物种。同时，选择种子萌发能力强、开花时间交错的植物物种，形成种子混播组合，均匀撒播以尽可能形成均匀分布格局。依据不同植物的种子千粒重与种子萌发率计算该物种种子在组合中所占的重量比例，使每个物种所占数量接近；在小集群之间的空隙播种混种组合，播种量约为5g/m^2。

3.4 动物关键种保育设计

研究设计的三种小集群模式分别对应了三种“植物群落—动物关键种”组团模式：

1）阔叶草花—传粉昆虫组团：以总状花序较大、色彩鲜明且蜜粉源丰富的阔叶草本植物为优势种，吸引并保育传粉昆虫种群；

2）高草—小型鸟类组团：以植株较大的观赏禾草为优势种，为小型鸟类提供庇护生境；

3）自生植物—土壤动物组团：随着自生植物在留白空间的富集逐渐形成集群，为依赖自生乡土草本植物的线虫、蚯蚓、甲虫、蜘蛛等土壤动物提供生存条件，进而借助土壤动物改善土壤结构与质量。

In nature, the mosaic pattern of plant communities is complicated. In the Shuangguihu case, the design horizontally adopted a combination of the mosaic complex and even distribution, which can be easily built and managed (Fig. 8). Plant species with important ecological functions (e.g., nectariferous plants and host plants) were densely mixed to form small clusters. The combination of small clusters can form a regular mosaic layout that allows for convenient fixed-point transplanting; and the cluster planting would separate competing species, helping maintain a diversified plant community. Mixed seeding was adopted by selecting the species with excellent germination capacity and different flowering seasons. Seed mixtures were evenly spread to form an even distribution pattern as much as possible; in the mixture, the proportion of each species was decided by seed TKW (thousand kernel weight) and germination rate, with the seeding rate being 5 g/m^2.

3.4 Conservation Design for Keystone Animal Species

Three small-clusters planting modes were employed respectively for three functional groups of plant–animal mutualism:

1) Broad-leaf herbs and pollinators, dominated by broad-leaf nectariferous herbs with large racemes and bright flowers which attract and facilitate the conservation of pollinators;

2) Tall grass and small birds, dominated by tall ornamental grass, providing shelters for small birds;

And 3) spontaneous plants and soil animals, native spontaneous plants survive and grow in the blank space, creating living conditions for soil animals (e.g., nematodes, earthworms, beetles, and spiders) and then improving the soil structure and quality.

These functional groups ensure the conservation of keystone animal species.

In terms of habitat creation, porous structures were introduced within the wildflower meadows, providing shelters for pollinators and small mammals that cannot build nests by themselves. Gentle slopes in small and micro wetlands

9 © 袁嘉，游荃溢，侯春丽，欧桦杰，尹渊

10 © 袁嘉，游荃溢，侯春丽，欧桦杰，尹渊

8. 嵌式分布与均匀分布交错的水平种植格局示意图
9. “多孔穴小型构筑物—野花草甸—小微湿地—倒木”复合生物生境
10. 结合倒木、块石等自然柔性材料形成的不同尺寸、深度（即湿度）的连续微地形设计。

8. Mosaic planting and evenly distributing planting
9. A compound habitat is established by integrating small porous elements with wildflower meadows, small and micro wetlands, and downed logs.
10. Continuous micro-terrain design of different sizes and water depths combined with natural materials like logs and stones

11

© 袁嘉，游孝溢，侯春丽，欧桦杰，尹渊

11. 再野化野花草甸景观
11. Rewilded wildflower meadow

这三个组团之间的相互嵌套也进一步保障了动物关键种保育的稳定性。

在生境营建方面，设计在野花草甸群落内部构建了多孔穴的小型构筑物，为无法自主筑巢的传粉昆虫与小型哺乳动物提供了庇护；洼地等小微湿地的边缘缓坡与留白空间组合，为蝴蝶等昆虫提供了啜饮泥浆的安全环境；小微湿地网络中放置了倒木和石块，为鸟类与昆虫提供了可短暂停留的落脚点；具有高度连续性的微地形既是青蛙等两栖动物的庇护空间，又不妨碍它们的自由运动；常年积水的深塘及水生植物群落为青蛙和昆虫若虫提供了水下栖息环境；灯心草（*Juncus effusus*）、千屈菜（*Lythrum salicaria*）等挺水植物和倒木则为昆虫提供了驻足和产卵空间（图9，10）。

3.5 绩效评估

良好的生境连续性保障了种植植物与自生植物在场地内的传播，使其不断扩繁并以走廊或网络形式分布。研究场地内的植被覆盖率、物种丰富度与结构多样性随时间推移而不断增加，展现了良好的群落自我设计与维持能力。2020年10月，研究团队在研究场地内开展调查统计，共记录草本植物116种，其中自生植物共83种。相较2018年项目实施前的调查（共记录草本植物63种），草本植物群落的物种数量增加了84.1%，自生植物物种占新增物种总数量的43.4%；自生植物与种植植物优势种群交混分布，良好共生。再野化的野花草甸群落形成了层次丰富、季相鲜明的植被景观（图11）；生境连续性、群落多样性及物种团复合镶嵌格局的复杂程度不断提高，保障了动物关键种的基因流与多样性，形成了稳定的野花草甸生态系统。修复后研究区域内动物关键种种类增长明显；其中，观测到的蝴蝶及草丛鸟种类增加最为明显。

(e.g. swales, pits, and ponds) were combined with the blank spaces, so that insects can safely sip water from damp patches for hydration. Logs and stones were placed in small and micro wetlands to provide footholds for birds and insects. The highly continuous micro-terrains provide shelters for amphibians (e.g. frogs) without impeding their free movement. Deep ponds and aquatic vegetation provide underwater habitats for frogs and nymphs; emergent plants (e.g. *Juncus effuses* and *Lythrum salicaria*) and woody debris provide halting and oviposition spaces for insects (Fig. 9, 10).

3.5 Performance Evaluation

A high habitat continuity ensures the spread of the planted and spontaneous species on the site in forms of corridors and networks. The vegetation coverage, species richness, and structure diversity increase over time, demonstrating the self-design and -maintenance capacity as expected. The research team carried out field investigation in October 2020 and found 116 herbaceous species, 83 of which are spontaneous. Compared to the survey results in 2018 before the rewilding, the number of herbaceous species increased by 84.1%; spontaneous plants accounted for 43.4% of all the newly increased species and well co-existed with the dominant plants. The rewilded meadow shows a vegetation with rich layers and distinctive seasonal changes (Fig. 11). The improvement of habitat continuity, community diversity, and mosaic pattern of functional groups guarantees gene flows and diversity of keystone species, and forms a stable wildflower meadow ecosystem. After the rewilding, the amount of keystone animal species, particularly butterflies and grassland birds, on the site increases remarkably.

除了为环境科学与生命科学的相关研究提供样本外，目前研究场地已成为重庆地区向公众传播生态文明建设与生物多样性保育知识的重要科普基地。在再野化野花草甸景观中，人们开展漫步探索，进行动植物识别与观测等在地自然教育行动（图12），传播了以“尊重、顺应、回归大自然”为核心的城市荒野认知。

4 结语

本文以荒野野花草甸为城市植被再野化及荒野生境重建的模板，从主动利用生态流、拟自然设计和最小限度干预等角度提出技术框架与应用范式，形成了一种应对城市动植物生境与整体生态系统退化的解决图景，对城市公共绿地、非林地乡村区域，以及林缘区域的再野化均有良好的参考价值。当前，来自土地开发与公众审美的挑战使得植被再野化的方法尚未在城市荒野保护与管理中广泛应用。未来，学者及行业人士需要以远见超越未知，不断揭示自然及城市荒野的形成与维持机制，改进公众对城市荒野景观的评估与认知；注重对再野化设计的定量探索，例如“留白—种植”嵌套格局中的适宜空间比例、入侵植物的防治与生态缓冲带结构组成，以及在不同空间尺度上建立多功能荒野生境的有效镶嵌与复合格局等；通过在退化绿地、闲置土地、孤立岛屿或林地等城市环境中应用自然荒野所呈现的生命智慧，逐步积累城市植被再野化与荒野生境重建的科学原则与技术方法，并为自上而下的政策和法规制定以及自下而上的实践探索提供科学依据。**LAF**

In addition to functioning as samples for the research on environmental science and life science, the site also provides opportunities for place-based ecological educational programs, which promotes the public's knowledge about ecological civilization construction and biodiversity conservation. The rewilded meadow allows visitors to carry out walks and explorations, as well as the identification and observation of animals and plants (Fig. 12), promoting public awareness of urban wilderness and fostering the ideas that respects, adapts to, and return to nature.

4 Conclusion

With wildflower meadow as the restoration target for urban vegetation rewilding and wilderness reconstruction, this paper comes up with a technical framework and design paradigm that leverages ecological flows, quasi-nature design, and minimal intervention in urban rewilding. It offers a solution to the degradation of animal and plant habitats and urban ecosystems, which is of reference value to the rewilding of urban public green spaces, non-forest countryside areas, and forest edges. Challenged by urban development and public aesthetics, vegetation rewilding has not been widely applied in practices of urban wilderness protection and management. In future, scholars and professionals are expected to explore the mechanism of the formation and maintenance of natural and urban wilderness, improve public awareness of urban wilderness. Quantitative studies on rewilding design are needed to fully understand the appropriate-ranked proportion of the blank versus planting area, the control of invasive plants and structure of ecological buffer zone, as well as the solutions to optimizing the mosaic complex of multiple-purpose wilderness habitats on varied scales. The ecological wisdom represented by natural wilderness can also be applied in responding to the degradation of green spaces, idle lands, isolated islands or woods, so as to enhance scientific studies on the principles and technical methods associated with urban vegetation rewilding and wilderness restoration, and inform the formulation of top-down policies and bottom-up approaches to urban rewilding. **LAF**

12. 在再野化野花草甸中进行的自然教育行动
12. Public education programs in the rewilded wildflower meadow

12 © 袁嘉，游泰溢，侯春丽，欧梓杰，尹渊

REFERENCES

[1] Mittermeier, R. A., Mittermeier, C. G., Brooks, T. M., Pilgrim, J. D., Konstant, W. R., da Fonseca, G. A. B., & Kormos, C. (2003). Wilderness and biodiversity conservation. *Proceedings of the National Academy of Sciences*, 100(18), 10309-10313. https://doi.org/10.1073/pnas.1732458100

[2] Daily, G. C. (1997). *Nature's services: Societal dependence on natural ecosystems*. Washington, DC: Island Press.

[3] Pimm, S. L., Ayres, M., Balmford, A., Branch, G., Brandon, K., Brooks, T., ... Wilcove, D. (2001). Can we defy nature's end? *Science*, 293(5538), 2207. doi:10.1126/science.1061626

[4] Cronon, W. (1996). *Uncommon ground: Rethinking the human place in nature*. New York, NY: W.W. Norton & Company.

[5] Botkin, D. B. (2001). *No man's garden: Thoreau and a new vision for civilization and nature*. Washington, DC: Island Press.

[6] Allan, J. R., Venter, O., & Watson, J. E. M. (2017). Temporally inter-comparable maps of terrestrial wilderness and the last of the wild. *Scientific Data*, 4(1), 170-187. doi:10.1038/sdata.2017.187

[7] Watson, J. E. M., Shanahan, D. F., Di Marco, M., Allan, J., Laurance, W. F., Sanderson, E.W., ... Venter, O. (2016). Catastrophic declines in wilderness areas undermine global environment targets. *Current Biology*, 26(21), 2929-2934. doi:10.1016/j.cub.2016.08.049

[8] Jorgensen, A., & Tylecote, M. (2007). Ambivalent landscapes—Wilderness in the urban interstices. *Landscape Research*, 32(4), 443-462. doi:10.1080/01426390701449802

[9] Page, J. (2016). *Tidy or tangled: How people perceive landscapes*. University of Maryland, Partnership for Action Learning in Sustainability. https://doi.org/10.13016/M2HH6C69B

[10] Kowarik, I., Hiller, A., Planchuelo, G., Seitz, B., von der Lippe, M., & Buchholz, S. (2019). Emerging urban forests: opportunities for promoting the wild side of the urban green infrastructure. *Sustainability*, 11(22), 6318. https://doi.org/10.3390/su11226318

[11] Kowarik, I. (2018). Urban wilderness: Supply, demand, and access. *Urban Forestry & Urban Greening*, (29), 336-347. https://doi.org/10.1016/j.ufug.2017.05.017

[12] Nassauer, J. I. (1995). Messy ecosystems, orderly frames. *Landscape Journal*, 14(2), 161-170. doi:10.3368/lj.14.2.161

[13] Kühn, N. (2006). Intentions for the unintentional. *Journal of Landscape Architecture*, 1(2), 46-53. doi:10.1080/18626033.2006.9723372

[14] Hoyle, H., Jorgensen, A., Warren, P., Dunnett, N., & Evans, K. (2017). "Not in their front yard"—The opportunities and challenges of introducing perennial urban meadows: A local authority stakeholder perspective. *Urban Forestry & Urban Greening*, (25), 139-149. https://doi.org/10.1016/j.ufug.2017.05.009

[15] Gibbons, B. (2014). *Wildflower wonders: The 50 best wildflower sites in the world*. London, England: A&C Black.

[16] Bernes, C., Jonsson, B. G., Junninen, K., Lõhmus, A., Macdonald, E., Müller, J., & Sandström, J. (2015). What is the impact of active management on biodiversity in boreal and temperate forests set aside for conservation or restoration? A systematic map. *Environmental Evidence*, 4(1), 25. https://doi.org/10.1186/s13750-015-0050-7

[17] Müller, A., Bøcher, P. K., Fischer, C., & Svenning, J. -C. (2018). 'Wild' in the city context: Do relative wild areas offer opportunities for urban biodiversity? *Landscape and Urban Planning*, (170), 256-265. https://doi.org/10.1016/j.landurbplan.2017.09.027

[18] Bollmann, K., & Braunisch, V. (2013). To integrate or to segregate: balancing commodity production and biodiversity conservation in European forests. In D. Kraus, & F. Krumm (Eds.), *Integrative approaches as an opportunity for the conversation of forest biodiversity* (pp. 18-31). Joensuu, Finland: European Forest Institute.

[19] Antonelli, A., Kissling, W. D., Flantua, S. G. A., Bermúdez, M. A., Mulch, A., Muellner-Riehl, A. N., ... Hoorn, C. (2018). Geological and climatic influences on mountain biodiversity. *Nature Geoscience*, 11(10), 718-725. https://doi.org/10.5281/zenodo.1341999

[20] Ivanov, V. Y., Bras, R. L., & Vivoni, E. R. (2008). Vegetation-hydrology dynamics in complex terrain of semiarid areas: 2. Energy-water controls of vegetation spatiotemporal dynamics and topographic niches of favorability. *Water Resources Research*, 44(3), W03430. https://doi.org/10.1029/2006WR005595

[21] Denney, D. A., Jameel, M. I., Bemmels, J. B., Rochford, M. E., & Anderson, J. T. (2020). Small spaces, big impacts: contributions of micro-environmental variation to population persistence under climate change. *AoB PLANTS*, 12(2), plaa005. https://doi.org/10.1093/aobpla/plaa005

[22] Hais, M., Chytrý, M., & Horsák, M. (2016). Exposure-related forest-steppe: A diverse landscape type determined by topography and climate. *Journal of Arid Environments*, (135), 75-84. https://doi.org/10.1016/j.jaridenv.2016.08.011

[23] Pereira, A. (2016). Plant abiotic stress challenges from the changing environment. *Frontiers in Plant Science*, (7), 1123. https://doi.org/10.3389/fpls.2016.01123

[24] Li, X., Fan, S., Guan, J., Zhao, F., & Dong, L. (2019). Diversity and influencing factors on spontaneous plant distribution in Beijing Olympic Forest Park. *Landscape and Urban Planning*, (181), 157-168. https://doi.org/10.1016/j.landurbplan.2018.09.018

[25] Yuan, J., & Dunnett, N. (2018). Plant selection for rain gardens: Response to simulated cyclical flooding of 15 perennial species. *Urban Forestry & Urban Greening*, (35), 57-65. https://doi.org/10.1016/j.ufug.2018.08.005

[26] Nadal-Romero, E., Petrlic, K., Verachtert, E., Bochet, E., & Poesen, J. (2014). Effects of slope angle and aspect on plant cover and species richness in a humid Mediterranean badland. *Earth Surface Processes and Landforms*, 39(13), 1705-1716. https://doi.org/10.1002/esp.3549

[27] Silvertown, J. (2004). Plant coexistence and the niche. *Trends in Ecology & Evolution*, 19(11), 605-611. https://doi.org/10.1016/j.tree.2004.09.003

[28] Niu, C., Lou, A., Sun, R., & Li, Q. (2015). *Foundations in ecology* (3rd ed.). Beijing, China: Higher Education Press.

[29] Song, Y. (2017). *Vegetation ecology*. Beijing, China: Higher Education Press.

[30] Dunnett, N. (2004). The dynamic nature of plant communities - pattern and process in designed plant communities. In D. Nigel, & J. Hitchmough (Eds.), *The dynamic landscape*. (pp. 97-114). London, England: Spon Press.

[31] Hoyle, H., Norton, B., Dunnett, N., Richart, J. P., Russell, J. M., & Warren, P. (2018). Plant species or flower colour diversity? Identifying the drivers of public and invertebrate response to designed annual meadows. *Landscape and Urban Planning*, (180), 103-113. https://doi.org/10.1016/j.landurbplan.2018.08.017

[32] Hitchmough, J., & Dunnett, N. (2004). Introduction to naturalistic planting in urban landscapes. In D. Nigel, & J. Hitchmough (Eds.), *The dynamic landscape* (pp. 1-32). London, England: Spon Press.

[33] Yuan, J. & Du, C. (2020). Design framework of collaborative symbiosis between urban plant landscape and keystone species: Taking wildflower meadows and pollinators as a case study. *Landscape Architecture*, 27(4), 50-55. doi:10.14085/j.fjyl.2020.04.0050.06

[34] Paine, R. T. (1969). A note on trophic complexity and community stability. *The American Naturalist*, 103(929), 91-93. https://doi.org/10.1086/282586

[35] Senapathi, D., Goddard, M. A., Kunin, W. E., & Baldock, K. C. R. (2017). Landscape impacts on pollinator communities in temperate systems: Evidence and knowledge gaps. *Functional Ecology*, 31(1), 26-37. https://doi.org/10.1111/1365-2435.12809

[36] Jha, S., & Kremen, C. (2013). Urban land use limits regional bumble bee gene flow. *Molecular Ecology*, 22(9), 2483-2495. doi:10.1111/mec.12275

[37] Menz, M. H. M., Phillips, R. D., Winfree, R., Kremen, C., Aizen, M. A., Johnson, S. D., & Dixon, K. W. (2011). Reconnecting plants and pollinators: Challenges in the restoration of pollination mutualisms. *Trends in Plant Science*, 16(1), 4-12. https://doi.org/10.1016/j.tplants.2010.09.006

[38] Rohr, R. P., Saavedra, S., & Bascompte, J. (2014). On the structural stability of mutualistic systems. *Science*, 345(6195), 416-425. doi:10.1126/science.1253497

[39] MacIvor, J. S., & Packer, L. (2015). 'Bee Hotels' as tools for native pollinator conservation: A premature verdict? *PLoS ONE*, 10(3), e0122126. https://doi.org/10.1371/journal.pone.0122126

[40] Seibold, S., Bässler, C., Brandl, R., Gossner, M. M., Thorn, S., Ulyshen, M. D., & Müller, J. (2015). Experimental studies of dead-wood biodiversity—A review identifying global gaps in knowledge. *Biological Conservation*, (191), 139-149. https://doi.org/10.1016/j.biocon.2015.06.006

[41] Silvan, N., Jokinen, K., Näkkilä, J., & Tahvonen, R. (2017). Swift recovery of Sphagnum carpet and carbon sequestration after shallow Sphagnum biomass harvesting. *Mires and Peat*, (20), 1-11. https://doi.org/10.19189/MaP.2015.OMB.198

[42] Slate, M. L., Sullivan, B. W., & Callaway, R. M. (2019). Desiccation and rehydration of mosses greatly increases resource fluxes that alter soil carbon and nitrogen cycling. *Journal of Ecology*, 107(4), 1767-1778. https://doi.org/10.1111/1365-2745.13162

城市闲置地块的生态自我修复特征研究——以北京林业大学校园为例

The Characteristics of Ecological Self-restoration in Urban Idle Lands: A Case Study of Beijing Forestry University

尹豪*
北京林业大学教授，城乡生态环境北京实验室

罗婧
北京林业大学风景园林专业硕士研究生

宁雅萱
北京林业大学风景园林专业硕士研究生

刘芳妮
北京林业大学风景园林专业硕士研究生

YIN Hao
Professor at Beijing Forestry University, Beijing Laboratory of Urban and Rural Ecological Environment

LUO Jing
Master student of Landscape Architecture at School of Landscape Architecture, Beijing Forestry University

NING Yaxuan
Master student of Landscape Architecture at School of Landscape Architecture, Beijing Forestry University

LIU Fangni
Master student of Landscape Architecture at School of Landscape Architecture, Beijing Forestry University

*通讯作者
地址：北京市海淀区清华东路35号北京林业大学学研中心A1311
邮编：100083
邮箱：yinhaonet@163.com

摘要

疏于人工管理的城市闲置用地会自发生长出一些植物，混杂无序的生长状态形成荒野自然景观。在荒野状态下自然生长的植被特征最能反映生态自我修复发生的特征。本文对北京林业大学校园一处闲置用地内的自生植被进行了研究，调查分析其生成变化特征、植物种类、优势植物群落、生长条件及周边同种成株的情况，探讨了城市闲置地生态自我修复的初始特征。结果表明，闲置场地封闭管理后，自生植物很快出现，3年后自生植被覆盖了场地近1/3的面积；自生植物绝大多数为乡土植物，草本植物种类多于木本植物；在优势植物群落的构成中木本植物群落和草本植物群落数量相差不大；场地日照充分的情况下，土壤条件的差异对草本植物和木本植物的分布有着明显的影响。研究认为，即便是在生长条件极差的城市环境中，只要停止或降低人为干扰，且具备植物生长的最基本条件（光照、土壤、种源），生态自我修复的现象就能迅速发生；在生态自我修复的初始阶段，乡土植物种类具有明显优势；迅速出现的以乡土乔木为建群种的木本植物群落，提示了城市环境中乡土木本植物的自生现象值得关注和深入研究。

关键词

生态修复；自生植物；荒野景观；城市闲置地；乡土植物

ABSTRACT

Natural plants would see a free growth in an idle land after an absence of management, leading to spontaneous biological processes that form the wildscape. Such vegetation demonstrates the characteristics of the ecological self-restoration. This paper studies the spontaneous species found on a site in Beijing Forestry University, inventories and analyzes the species, site conditions, possible maternal plants of them, and discusses the changes and characteristics of the community in its early establishment. The results show that several spontaneous plants sprout early, and cover nearly 1/3 of the site 3 years later. Most of spontaneous plant species are native, more of which are herbaceous, while little difference is found between the number of woody communities and that of herbaceous communities. Their distribution is obviously affected by soil conditions when the light is sufficient. This paper concludes that once the human disturbances are stopped or reduced, ecological self-restoration can occur rapidly with essential conditions for growth (light, soils, and seed sources), even poor as urban environment. At the early stage of ecological self-restoration, native plant species dominate obviously. It is worthy of attention to and further study on the spontaneous native woody communities as they emerge rapidly.

KEYWORDS

Ecological Restoration; Spontaneous Plant; Wildscape; Urban Idle Land; Native Plants

基金项目
北京市共建项目（编号：2019GJ-03）
国家重点研发计划项目“乡村生态景观营造关键技术研究”（编号：2019YFD1100400）

RESEARCH FUNDS
Special Fund for Beijing Common Construction Project (No. 2019GJ-03)
Research on Key Technologies of Rural Ecological Landscape Construction, National Key R&D Program of China (No. 2019YFD1100400)

编辑 | 崔婧沄、田乐
翻译 | 肖杰、崔婧沄、田乐
EDITED BY | CUI Jingyun, Tina TIAN
TRANSLATED BY | XIAO Jie, CUI Jingyun, Tina TIAN

https://doi.org/10.15302/J-LAF-1-020042
收稿时间 RECEIVED DATE | 2020-12-10

中图分类号 | TU986, S731.2
文献标识码 | A

1 引言

荒野不仅在西方有着深厚的历史文化内涵，也与中国传统的“天人合一”的自然观密切相关[1][2]，规划设计领域对于“荒野之美”的肯定之声越来越高[3][4]。因其在维护城市栖息地和丰富城市生物多样性方面具有重要作用，荒野对于城市生态系统提升具有积极意义[5][6]。场地由于闲置而长期无人管理会呈现出自然动植物混杂无序生长状态，出现自发的生物活动和演替过程[7]，这种生态自我修复会形成荒野自然景观。

在城市建设过程中，土地闲置现象时有发生，在闲置地块中会自发生长出一些植物。这些自生植物在景观管理上常被认为是杂草，不仅有损城市环境品质，也为景观养护管理带来了诸多问题。但近年来的研究推动了公众对自生植物的观念改变：自生植物的养护管理需求较低，且能够提供野生动物栖息地、提升城市景观的生态系统服务[8][9]，对于建设资源节约型城市、维持城市可持续发展有着重要意义。越来越多的研究开始关注各种城市环境条件下自生植物的物种组成[10]~[14]、观赏特征[11][12]、生长规律[12]和设计实践的可能性[10][12][14]。自生植物的多样性水平在不同绿地类型间存在差异，防护绿地和荒废地中的自生草本植物多样性要高于附属绿地和公园绿地[15]。这表明人类管理行为与自生植物的生长有着直接关系。而城市闲置地常由于缺乏管理会被自发生长出的植物覆盖，以较高的植物多样性水平在保护生物多样性方面发挥积极的作用[16]。但是，目前对于城市闲置地中自生植物生长的状态和基本规律，特别是对于没有人类管理行为的情况下发生的生态自我修复机制研究不足。本文以北京林业大学校园内的一处闲置地块为研究对象，调查其中的自生植物种类、生长条件和周边同种成株植物，分析植被生成的时空特征、植物群落特征及环境因子和种源条件的影响，以期深入了解闲置地中生态自我修复发生的初始现象和特征，为相关研究提供参考。

2 研究对象和方法

2.1 研究对象

研究场地位于北京林业大学校园内，属于待建设用地，计划用于建设教学办公建筑。在进行了场地清理后，由于建设计划搁置，场地暂时处于无人管理的闲置状态。在此期间，场地在无人类扰动的状态下很快发生了生态自我修复现象，出现了众多自生植物。因此选择该地块作为研究对象，研究城市闲置地块的生态自我修复发生的初始现象和特征。

1 Introduction

Wilderness is not only a profound cultural notion in the western world but also a correlate of the “harmony of man with nature” in Chinese traditional ideology[1][2], and the beauty of wilderness has been increasingly recognized in the field of planning and design[3][4]. Due to the important role it plays in maintaining urban habitats and enhancing urban biodiversity, wilderness is of positive significance to the improvement of urban ecosystems[5][6]. Natural plant and animal communities would see a free growth in an idle land after a long-time absence of management, leading to spontaneous biological processes and natural succession[7]. Such an ecological self-restoration will form the wildscape.

Idle lands are commonly found during urban construction, where plants sprout spontaneously. Such plants are often regarded as weeds unfavorable to both urban environmental management and landscape maintenance. However, recent studies on spontaneous plants have helped change the public’s view: They are an asset to sustainable city construction and development due to the low demand in maintenance and management and the delivered ecosystem services such as providing wildlife habitats and improving urban landscapes[8][9]. There are studies on the species composition[10]~[14], landscape characteristics[11][12], growth pattern[12], and design feasibility[10][12][14] of spontaneous plants under different urban environmental conditions. The richness of spontaneous plants varies between land uses (e.g., that in green buffers and wastelands is higher than in attached green spaces and parks[15]), revealing the direct influence of human management on the growth of spontaneous plants. Due to the absence of human management, the high plant diversity in urban idle lands contributes to the city’s biodiversity conservation[16]. However, research on the growth condition and pattern of spontaneous plants, especially the mechanism of ecological self-restoration without human interventions, is not yet sufficient. This paper attempts to inventory the species, site conditions, and possible maternal plants of the spontaneous plants found on a site in Beijing Forestry University, and analyze the changes and characteristics of the community in its early establishment, as well as the influence of abiotic factors and seed sources, hoping to enrich the case studies of associated research.

2 Study Area and Research Methods

2.1 Study Area

The study area, located in the campus of Beijing Forestry University, is to be constructed for a building for teaching and administration. Due to the halt of the construction, the site was temporarily idle without any management after demolition, when ecological self-restoration quickly occurred and spontaneous plants diversely appeared. It was therefore chosen as a sample where the characteristics of the early stage of ecological self-restoration in urban idle lands are studied.

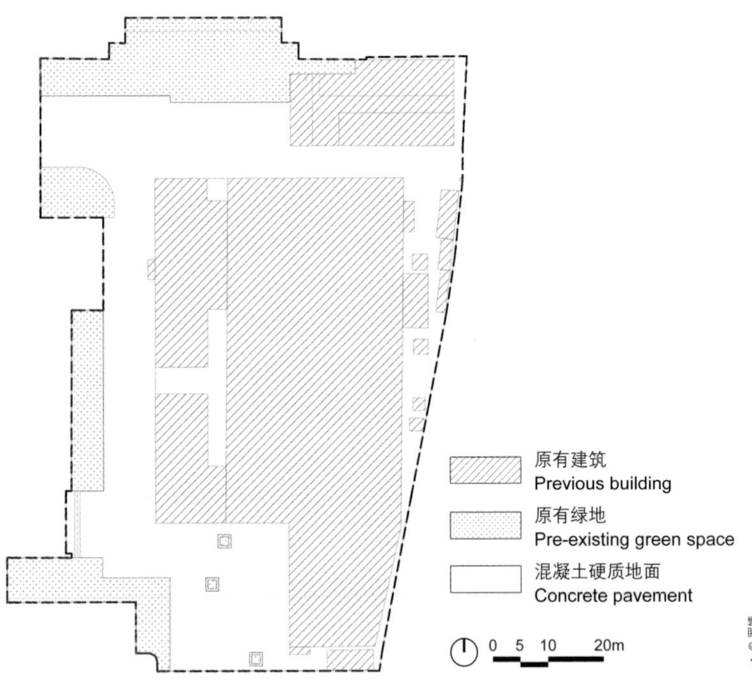

表1：卫星影像资料
Table 1: Information of satellite images

影像采集日期 Acquisition date	图像分辨率 Spatial resolution
2017年8月23日 August 23, 2017	0.23 m × 0.23 m
2018年6月1日 June 1, 2018	0.11 m × 0.11 m
2018年8月23日 August 23, 2018	0.11 m × 0.11 m
2019年6月14日 June 14, 2019	0.11 m × 0.11 m
2019年9月22日 September 22, 2019	0.11 m × 0.11 m
2020年8月28日 August 28, 2020	0.11 m × 0.11 m

1. 场地平面图
2. 场地历年卫星影像图（来源：Google Earth）
3. 场地植被分布示意图

1. Site plan
2. Satellite images of the site in different years (Source: Google Earth)
3. Vegetation distribution on the site

场地总面积7 657.3m^2，其中混凝土硬质地面面积约2 774.6m^2；场地上原来建有临时建筑作为学生餐厅使用（占地面积3 696.4m^2），其地上建筑部分于2017年8月拆除，依然留有地面铺装（室内地板砖），透水透气性差，只在建筑墙体破拆处和混凝土地面间隙处存有土壤；绿地面积仅1 186.3m^2，土壤条件较好，适于植被生长。场地自拆建之日起建起围墙实行封闭管理，截至2021年3月底一直闲置，没有实施新的建设活动，场地内除堆积杂物外无任何养护管理行为发生（图1）。

2.2 研究方法

2.2.1 卫星影像分析

研究采用卫星影像分析场地植被分布及生长变化特征。卫星影像采用Google Earth全色历史卫星影像，使用BIGEMAP地图下载器下载，具体参数如表1所示。

2.2.2 现场踏查

研究采用现场踏查的方法于2020年9月至11月间对场地内的植被生长条件、植物种类及场地内外的种源植物情况进行了6次全面调查。研究对植物物种进行人工辨识，并逐株测量木本植物的胸径、地径、树高、冠幅和具体位置等信息，勘察记录场地内存有土壤的位置的宽度及深度；研究以场地为中心，调查自生木本植物在场地内外同种成株的分布和距离情况。

The site covers a total area of 7,657.3 m^2, of which about 2,774.6 m^2 is concrete pavement. A 3,696.4-square-meter temporary structure as a student canteen was demolished in August 2017 where the interior paving of floor tiles were remained with poor permeability, and thin soils exist in the gaps between the demolished walls and the concreate pavement. The pre-existing green spaces on the site, 1,186.3 m^2, have deep and fertile soils for vegetation growth. Since the demolition, the site has been enclosed and idle, without any construction or maintenance activities on the site except for piling building debris (Fig. 1) till the end of March 2021 (when the study began).

2.2 Research Methods

2.2.1 Satellite Image Analysis

To analyze the characteristics of vegetation distribution and growth on the site, the research adopted the full-color historical satellite images from Google Earth downloaded with BIGEMAP. The parameters of the images are listed in Table 1.

2.2.2 Site Inventory

From September to November 2020, 6 full site inventories were conducted covering the growth conditions, species, and possible maternal plants in- and outside the site. The plant inventory included species identification and the measurement of the diameter at breast height (DBH), basal diameter, height, crown diameter, location, and the width and depth of soils. The distribution of mature woody species, the possible maternal plants, in and outside the site were mapped.

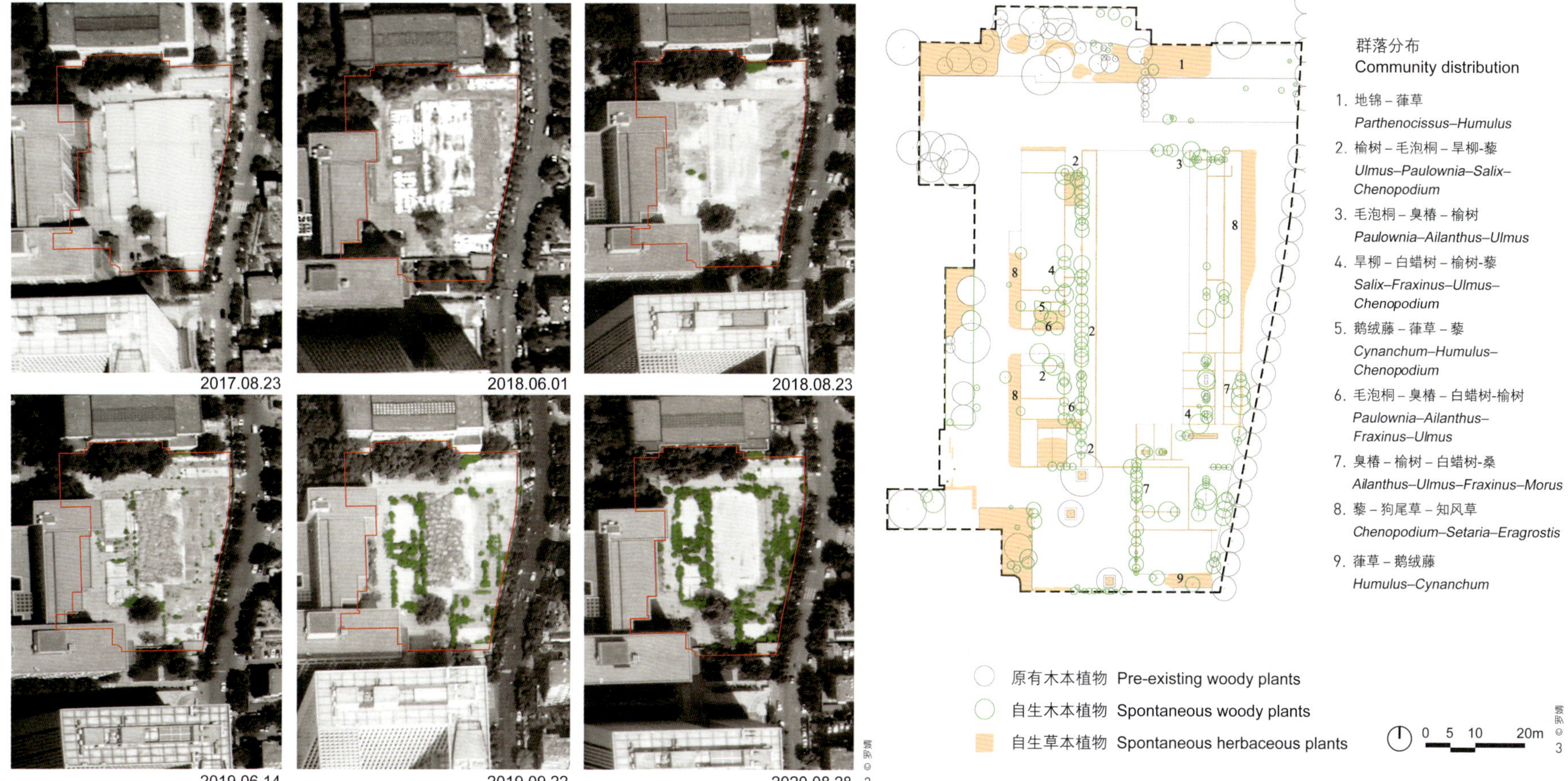

2.2.3 光环境数字模拟分析

对北京市生态绿廊植物景观的研究发现，较强光照条件会引起草本植物多样性水平和均匀度指数降低，而这些草本植物具有较高的自发性[23]。受此启发，本研究分析了场地的光照条件差异对自生植物生长分布可能产生的影响。参考徐毅等人的研究[24]，以日照时数为测算因子对场地的光照条件进行数字模拟分析。根据不同自然光光环境模拟软件自身的特点及适用范围[17]~[19]，选择Ecotect Analysis软件对场地进行光环境数字模拟，分析场地的日照时数多少和分布情况。参考北京及河北地区草本植物物候观测数据[20]~[22]，选取5个与植物生长相关联的标志性时间节点分析场地的日照情况，对应设定数字模拟分析的时间节点为春分（3月21日）、清明（4月5日）、立夏（5月6日）、小暑（7月7日）、霜降（10月24日）。使用Ecotect Analysis软件设置北京地区气象参数并进行日照模拟计算。

2.2.3 Digital Simulation Analysis of Light

Existing study on the plant landscape of Beijing Ecological Green Corridor reveals that strong lights may lead to lower richness and evenness of herbaceous species of high spontaneity[23]. In this research, the impact of light conditions of the site on the growth and distribution of spontaneous plants was studied. Referring to the research by Xu Yi et al.[24], the sunshine duration was simulated; and according to the application advantages and scopes of different digital stimulation softwares[17]~[19], Ecotect Analysis was selected for sunlight duration analysis and distribution of the site. Referring to existing phenological research findings of herbaceous plants in Beijing and Hebei[20]~[22], 5 days of representative solar terms impacting plant growth, namely Vernal Equinox (March 21), Qingming Festival (April 5), Summer's Begin (May 6), Slight Heat (July 7), and Frost's Descent (October 24), were selected to analyze the on-site light patterns.

3 研究结果与分析

3 Results and Analyses

3.1 植被生成的时空特征

2017年8月的卫星影像显示了建筑拆除前的场地情况（绿地面积仅

3.1 Characteristics of the Early Establishment of Spontaneous Plant Community

The satellite image taken in August 2017 showed that the vegetation coverage of

占15.5%）。拆除后，2018年6月的影像中尚未出现清晰可辨的植物痕迹；2018年8月出现了明显的植物影像；从2019年6月的影像中可以清晰辨认出零散的树冠形态，几乎全部生长于硬质铺装的间隙；2019年9月，植被呈现出条带状及团块状的分布趋势；2020年8月，植被条带状及团块状的分布态势更加显著，局部已呈成片分布，植被覆盖度增长到30.7%，树木覆盖面积多于草本覆盖面积，两者的比例为1:0.65（图2，3）。

虽然硬质铺装地面对于植物生长极为不利，但临时建筑拆除一年后场地内就出现了明显的自生植物生长痕迹，此后植被生长发展特征显著。虽然自生植物起初只是在硬质铺装间隙处生长，但其生长扩展的速度很快，在三年后植被覆盖场地裸露区域接近1/3。

3.2 植被特征

3.2.1 自生植物种类

调查结果显示，场地中的原生植物有17种，自生植物35种（表2）。自生植物中有落叶乔木8种，为臭椿（*Ailanthus altissima*）、构树（*Broussonetia papyrifera*）、白蜡树（*Fraxinus chinensis*）等；落叶灌木1种，为荆条（*Vitex negundo* var. *heterophylla*）；一年生草本11种，包括某蒿（*Artemisia* sp.）、藜（*Chenopodium album*）、虎尾草（*Chloris virgata*）等；多年生草本10种，包括天名精（*Carpesium abrotanoides*）、积雪草（*Centella asiatica*）、野菊（*Chrysanthemum indicum*）等；木质藤本1种，为地锦（*Parthenocissus tricuspidata*）；一年生草质藤本1种，为牵牛（*Ipomoea nil*）；多年生草质藤本3种，为鹅绒藤（*Cynanchum chinense*）、葎草（*Humulus scandens*）、萝藦（*Metaplexis japonica*）。在所有科属中，禾本科植物和菊科植物居多，且草本植物种类明显多于木本植物。35种植物中仅有小蓬草（*Erigeron canadensis*）1种非乡土植物。

3.2.2 优势植物群落

调查结果显示，场地内自生植物分布情况存在局部差异，存在9种优势植物群落（图3），分别为：1）地锦—葎草；2）榆树—毛泡桐—旱柳—藜；3）毛泡桐—臭椿—榆树；4）旱柳—白蜡树—榆树—藜；5）鹅绒藤—葎草—藜；6）毛泡桐—臭椿—白蜡树—榆树；7）臭椿—榆树—白蜡树—桑；8）藜—狗尾草—知风草；以及9）葎草—鹅绒藤。

3.3 环境因子对自生植物的影响

3.3.1 土壤条件对自生植物生长分布的影响

调查发现，场地内的自生植物出现在原有绿地、角隅和建筑墙体破拆面三种土壤条件中（图4）。除了原有绿地土层深厚，角隅和建筑墙体破拆面处土层浅薄，主要是一些混杂建筑碎屑的土壤积存，没有特意进行土壤覆盖和改良。场地没有进行过施肥、灌溉等绿地养护管理行

the site was 15.5% before the demolition. After then, in June 2018, no identifiable vegetation was found; but 2 months later, vegetation can be identified in the image. Since June 2019, the scattered crowns could be clearly identified inbetween the pavement, and the image of September 2019 showed a strip and clump distribution of vegetation, which became more obvious and connected in August 2020, with the vegetation coverage increasing to 30.7% and the tree-herb ratio of the vegetated area was 1:0.65 (Fig. 2, 3).

Although concrete or tile paving surfaces are detrimental to plant growth, the growth pattern of the spontaneous plants observed on the site is increasingly obvious only after one year of being idle. They grew along with the gaps between paving at the beginning, however, covering an area nearly 1/3 of the bare area of the site only after 3 years.

3.2 Vegetation Characteristics

3.2.1 Spontaneous Plant Species

The inventories show that there were previously 17 plant species and later 35 species sprouted spontaneously (Table 2), and the latter ones include 8 deciduous trees (*Ailanthus altissima*, *Broussonetia papyrifera*, *Fraxinus chinensis*, etc.); 1 deciduous shrub (*Vitex negundo* var. *heterophylla*); 11 annual herbs (*Artemisia* sp., *Chenopodium album*, *Chloris virgata*, etc.); 10 perennial herbs (*Carpesium abrotanoides*, *Centella asiatica*, *Chrysanthemum indicum*, etc.); 1 woody vine (*Parthenocissus tricuspidate*); 1 annual vine (*Ipomoea nil*); and 3 perennial vines (*Cynanchum chinense*, *Humulus scandens*, and *Metaplexis japonica*). Poaceae and Asteraceae species are the majority, and herbaceous species significantly more than woody ones. Except *Erigeron canadensis*, all species are native.

3.2.2 Dominant Plant Communities

The inventories show the variation of vegetation distribution on the site: there are 9 plant communities (Fig. 3) respectively dominated by 1) *Parthenocissus–Humulus*; 2) *Ulmus–Paulownia–Salix–Chenopodium*; 3) *Paulownia–Ailanthus–Ulmus*; 4) *Salix–Fraxinus–Ulmus–Chenopodium*; 5) *Cynanchum–Humulus–Chenopodium*; 6) *Paulownia–Ailanthus–Fraxinus–Ulmus*; 7) *Ailanthus–Ulmus–Fraxinus–Morus*; 8) *Chenopodium–Setaria–Eragrostis*; and 9) *Humulus–Cynanchum*.

3.3 Influence of Environmental Factors on the Spontaneous Plants

3.3.1 Influence of Soil Conditions on the Growth and Distribution of Spontaneous Plants

The spontaneous plants are only found in the pre-existing green spaces, corners, and the gaps between the demolished walls (Fig. 4). Except for the pre-existing green spaces, the soils at the corners and the gaps are thin and mixed with building debris, without soil supplementing or cultivating. None fertilization, irrigation or other maintenance activities were conducted to the site. The overall terrain of the site is flat that ensures rainwater drainage, no waterlogging being found.

表2：研究场地内植物名录
Table 2: Plant list of the study site

类型 Life form	物种名称 Species	科 Family	原有或自生 Pre-existing or spontaneous
常绿乔木 Evergreen tree	圆柏 *Juniperus chinensis*	柏科 Cupressaceae	原有 Pre-existing
	白皮松 *Pinus bungeana*	松科 Pinaceae	原有 Pre-existing
	侧柏 *Platycladus orientalis*	柏科 Cupressaceae	原有 Pre-existing
落叶乔木 Deciduous tree	元宝槭 *Acer truncatum*	无患子科 Sapindaceae	原有 Pre-existing
	臭椿 *Ailanthus altissima*	苦木科 Simaroubaceae	二者均有 Both
	构树 *Broussonetia papyrifera*	桑科 Moraceae	二者均有 Both
	白杜 *Euonymus maackii*	卫矛科 Celastraceae	原有 Pre-existing
	白蜡树 *Fraxinus chinensis*	木犀科 Oleaceae	自生 Spontaneous
	胡桃 *Juglans regia*	胡桃科 Juglandaceae	原有 Pre-existing
	桑 *Morus alba*	桑科 Moraceae	自生 Spontaneous
	毛泡桐 *Paulownia tomentosa*	泡桐科 Paulowniaceae	二者均有 Both
	小叶杨 *Populus simonii*	杨柳科 Salicaceae	自生 Spontaneous
	旱柳 *Salix matsudana*	杨柳科 Salicaceae	二者均有 Both
	榆树 *Ulmus pumila*	榆科 Ulmaceae	自生 Spontaneous
落叶灌木 Deciduous shrub	平枝栒子 *Cotoneaster horizontalis*	蔷薇科 Rosaceae	原有 Pre-existing
	连翘 *Forsythia suspensa*	木犀科 Oleaceae	原有 Pre-existing
	女贞 *Ligustrum lucidum*	木犀科 Oleaceae	原有 Pre-existing
	绣线菊 *Spiraea salicifolia*	蔷薇科 Rosaceae	原有 Pre-existing
	欧洲荚蒾 *Viburnum opulus*	五福花科 Adoxaceae	原有 Pre-existing
	荆条 *Vitex negundo* var. *heterophylla*	马鞭草科 Verbenaceae	自生 Spontaneous
一年生草本 Annual	某蒿 *Artemisia* sp.	菊科 Asteraceae	自生 Spontaneous
	藜 *Chenopodium album*	苋科 Amaranthaceae	自生 Spontaneous
	虎尾草 *Chloris virgate*	禾本科 Poaceae	自生 Spontaneous
	牛筋草 *Eleusine indica*	禾本科 Poaceae	自生 Spontaneous
	小蓬草 *Erigeron canadensis*	菊科 Asteraceae	自生 Spontaneous
	某蓼 *Persicaria* sp.	蓼科 Polygonaceae	自生 Spontaneous
	马齿苋 *Portulaca oleracea*	马齿苋科 Portulacaceae	自生 Spontaneous
	朝天委陵菜 *Potentilla supina*	蔷薇科 Rosaceae	自生 Spontaneous
	狗尾草 *Setaria viridis*	禾本科 Poaceae	自生 Spontaneous
	龙葵 *Solanum nigrum*	茄科 Solanaceae	自生 Spontaneous
	苦苣菜 *Sonchus oleraceus*	菊科 Asteraceae	自生 Spontaneous
多年生草本 Perennial	天名精 *Carpesium abrotanoides*	菊科 Asteraceae	自生 Spontaneous
	积雪草 *Centella asiatica*	伞形科 Apiaceae	自生 Spontaneous
	野菊 *Chrysanthemum indicum*	菊科 Asteraceae	自生 Spontaneous
	刺儿菜 *Cirsium arvense* var. *integrifolium*	菊科 Asteraceae	自生 Spontaneous
	狗牙根 *Cynodon dactylon*	禾本科 Poaceae	自生 Spontaneous
	香附子 *Cyperus rotundus*	莎草科 Cyperaceae	自生 Spontaneous
	知风草 *Eragrostis ferruginea*	禾本科 Poaceae	自生 Spontaneous
	麦冬 *Ophiopogon japonicus*	天门冬科 Asparagaceae	原有 Pre-existing
	芦苇 *Phragmites australis*	禾本科 Poaceae	自生 Spontaneous
	地黄 *Rehmannia glutinosa*	列当科 Orobanchaceae	自生 Spontaneous
	蒲公英 *Taraxacum mongolicum*	菊科 Asteraceae	自生 Spontaneous
竹类 Bamboo	早园竹 *Phyllostachys propinqua*	禾本科 Poaceae	原有 Pre-existing
木质藤本 Woody vine	地锦 *Parthenocissus tricuspidata*	葡萄科 Vitaceae	自生 Spontaneous
一年生草质藤本 Annual vine	牵牛 *Ipomoea nil*	旋花科 Convolvulaceae	自生 Spontaneous
多年生草质藤本 Perennial vine	鹅绒藤 *Cynanchum chinense*	夹竹桃科 Apocynaceae	自生 Spontaneous
	葎草 *Humulus scandens*	大麻科 Cannabaceae	自生 Spontaneous
	萝藦 *Metaplexis japonica*	夹竹桃科 Apocynaceae	自生 Spontaneous

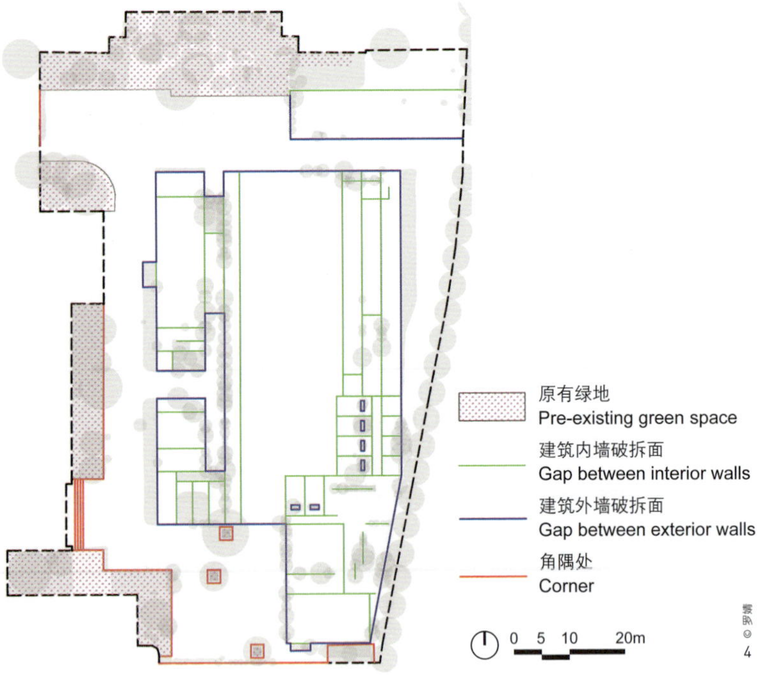

4. 场地土壤条件示意图
5. 建筑内墙破拆面实景照片。自生植物在建筑内墙破拆面上旺盛地生长着。
6. 全年场地日照分布与自生植物覆盖情况
7. 通过5个标志性节点呈现的植物生长期内场地日照变化情况

4. Soil conditions on the site
5. Real photo of gap between interior walls where spontaneous plants thrive.
6. Annual sunshine duration contour map and spontaneous plant coverage
7. Sunshine variation on the site during the vegetation growing seasons represented by 5 solar terms

为，且场地整体地势平整，雨水可以自然排出场地，未发现雨水积存现象。

原有绿地中主要栽有乔灌木（表2），场地闲置后萌发自生植物20种，其中草本植物9种，木本植物7种，藤本植物4种。

花坛（原有绿地的一部分）、台阶与混凝土地面相夹的角隅空间极为狭窄，宽度为0.5~8cm，土壤厚度仅1~2cm。此处萌发自生植物18种，其中草本植物10种，木本植物6种，藤本植物2种，以藜为代表的草本植物占据优势。

场地内现有两类建筑墙体破拆面：一种为建筑内墙破拆面，宽约30cm，其中蓄积了厚约3cm的土壤，掺杂有大量建筑材料碎屑；此处萌发植物22种，其中草本15种，木本植物6种，藤本植物1种，优势种为藜、狗尾草等草本植物（图5）。另一种为建筑外墙破拆面，宽约12cm，与地基层的缝隙相连，蓄积土壤厚度约20cm；萌发自生植物17种，其中草本植物8种，木本植物7种，藤本植物2种，毛泡桐、臭椿、榆树等木本植物占据生长优势。

调查结果显示，场地中土壤条件对自生植物的种类和分布影响明显。角隅处和建筑墙体破拆处的土壤较薄，萌发的草本植物较多；建筑外墙破拆处的土壤较厚，那里的自生木本植物长势明显优于建筑内墙破拆处和角隅处。原有绿地里的土壤条件明显优于角隅和建筑墙体破拆

Existing shrub and tree species in the pre-existing green spaces are listed in Table 2. In total, there are 20 spontaneous plant species observed, of which 9 are herbaceous, 7 are woody, and 4 are vines, after the site was idle.

The corners and gaps between flowerbeds (as part of pre-existing green spaces), steps, and the concrete pavement are extremely narrow, where the soil is in a width of 0.5 to 8 cm and a thickness of 1 to 2 cm. 18 spontaneous species are found there, including 10 herbaceous plants (dominant and represented by *Chenopodium album*), 6 woody plants, and 2 vines.

Two types of gaps are found between the demolished walls: 1) the 30-centimeter-wide gaps between the interior walls, where the soil is 3-centimeter thick and mixed with building debris. 22 spontaneous species are found there, including 15 herbaceous plants, 6 woody plants, and a vine, among which herbs like *Chenopodium album* and *Setaria viridis* dominate (Fig. 5); and 2) the 12-centimeter-wide gaps between the exterior walls, connected to the building foundation, where the soil is about 20-centimeter thick. There, 17 species sprout, including 8 herbaceous plants, 7 woody plants, and 2 vines, with woody plants such as *Paulownia tomentosa*, *Ailanthus altissima*, and *Ulmus pumila* being dominate.

The inventories show that the soil conditions significantly influence the species and distribution of spontaneous plants on the site. Soils at the corners and gaps are thinner, and more herbaceous plants sprout; the soil in the gaps between exterior walls are thicker, where spontaneous woody species grow better than those grow at the corners and the gaps between interior walls. Pre-existing green spaces have sound soil conditions, however, species there are not richer than

处，但出现的自生植物种类并没有明显多于其他区域，这一现象是否受到原有绿地中已栽植植被的遮荫影响尚待进一步探究。由于原有绿地之外的区域没有既有植被，无法进行相同遮荫条件下的比对研究。

3.3.2 场地的光照条件对自生植物总体分布的影响

场地年日照时数分布的梯度曲线图显示（图6），年日照时数自东北至西南逐渐减少，年日照时数最多的区域可达3 400小时以上；受到周围建筑和围墙的影响，沿东侧和南侧围墙的带状区域、西侧建筑凹入的区域年日照时数明显低于场地东北部，最低的区域是场地西南角围墙和建筑包围处，年日照时数低于200小时。5个标志性的植物生长时间节点的日照分析显示，场地内绝大部分区域日照时数的分布相对均匀，光照条件充足；场地北部区域的光照条件更好，而南部和西部边缘受建筑和围墙影响严重，尤其是角落和靠近围墙的区域在春分和霜降时节的日照时数显著减少（图7）。

通过将光照分析结果与自生植被覆盖场地情况进行比对研究，发现自生植被沿土壤存在的区域呈清晰的线形分布；较大的自生植物团块集中于原有绿地中；在贴近场地东边、南边围墙和西边建筑的区域，年日

other places. The impact of other possible factors (e.g. the shades of the existing vegetation) needs to be verified by further research—Since pre-existing plants only grow in pre-existing green spaces, comparative studies on the shades on the site is hard to conduct in this research.

3.3.2 Impact of Light Conditions on the General Distribution of Spontaneous Plants

According to the annual sunshine duration contour map of the site (Fig. 6), the total sunshine duration decreases from northeast to southwest, with the maximum exceeding 3,400 hours. Subject to the shades from nearby buildings and fences, the sunshine duration drops down in the belt zone along the south and east fences and within the narrow corner adjacent to the building in the west, southwest of which has the minimum of fewer than 200 hours. The analysis of the light conditions on the 5 representative solar days suggests that the sunshine duration is sufficient and roughly even across most parts of the site. The north part has relatively better light conditions, while those along the fences in the south and the building in the west are the worst, particularly on Vernal Equinox and Frost's Descent (Fig. 7).

The overlapping analysis between the light contour map and spontaneous plant distribution reveals that the spontaneous plants were found in linear patterns and larger clusters of spontaneous plants found in the pre-existing green

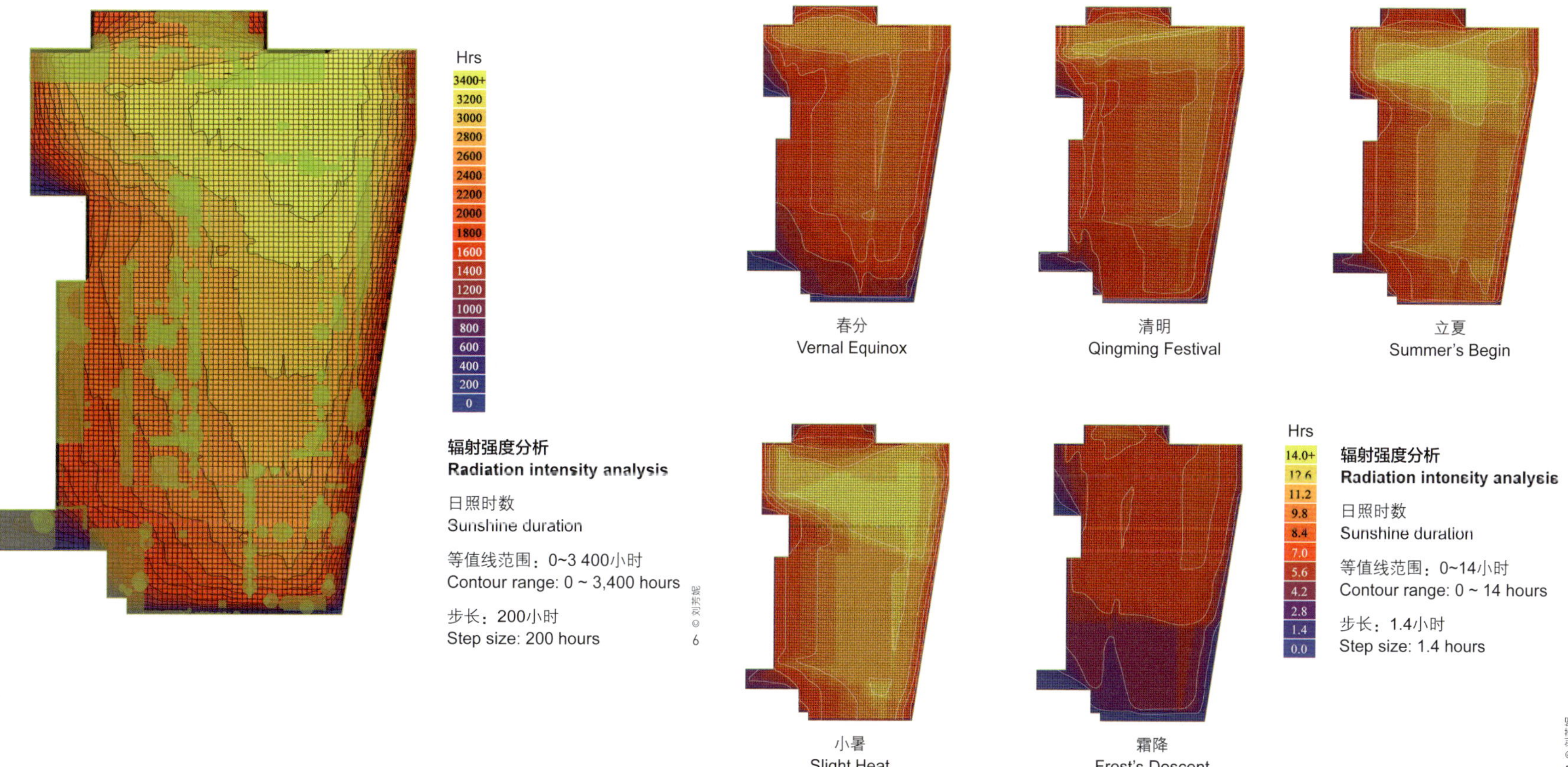

照时数明显较少，但依然生长了不少自生植物。总体而言，自生植被分布的状态没有表现出与日照分布梯度曲线对应的迹象。

通过将光照分析结果与植物种类分布进行比对研究，未发现自生植物种类的分布与日照时数的分布变化有明显关联。以榆树—毛泡桐—旱柳—藜的木本植物群落为例，该群落沿直线南北分布，分布地年日照时数自2 400小时跨越至3 200小时；藜—狗尾草—知风草的草本植物群落散布于东部和西部的多个年日照时数不同的区域，也未表现出与日照时数分布变化相关联。

场地光照条件对自生植物总体分布的影响不显著，虽然场地上的全年日照时数分布有差异，但在植物主要生长期（春分至霜降）内场地基本光照均匀、充足。这可以解释自生植被覆盖区域和自生植物种类的分布都未表现出与光照时数分布变化有关联的原因，也说明光照条件不是影响该场地自生植被发展的主要因素。

3.3.3 自生植物种源调查及自生能力分析

除光照和土壤条件因素外，场地内自生植物的出现及分布情况还取决于植物的种源环境。植物以风力、水力、火力、生物携带及通过种子或其载体本身产生的机械力完成种子的传播和散布[25]，分析自生植物的种源环境可以更好地了解生态自我修复发生的条件。由于研究场地位于校园内，场地周边区域的人工养护管理程度均较高，自生草本植物的种源调查存在难度，而木本植物同种成株的调查具有可行性。在10种木本植物中乔木类居多（乔木8种，灌木1种，藤本1种），并且乔木树种主导了多个植物群落，因此研究针对乔木树种的同种成株情况在场地内外进行了调查。结果显示，毛泡桐、臭椿、构树和旱柳在场地内有存在，场地外白蜡树、小叶杨和榆树3种树木距离较近，只有桑距离场地最远，达154m（表3，图8）。

从木本自生植物的萌发量来看，毛泡桐、臭椿和榆树的数量最多，其次是白蜡树、旱柳和桑。通过比较植株的冠幅、树高等参数，生长优势明显的树木有毛泡桐、臭椿、榆树和旱柳。毛泡桐和榆树种源母株数量少，但场地内的幼苗萌发量却最多，且冠幅、株高较大；臭椿在场地内外种源母株数量众多，萌发量大，冠幅、株高大；场地外白蜡树的母株较多、距离较近，但幼苗萌发量和冠幅株高明显小于臭椿等；旱柳虽然母株数量少，幼苗萌发量却仅次于白蜡树，冠幅、株高大；桑的母株

spaces. Although the annual sunshine duration is short in the areas adjacent to the fences and buildings, quite a few spontaneous plants grow. To sum up, the distribution pattern of the spontaneous plants is not consistently related with the annual sunshine duration contour map.

The overlapping analysis between the light contour map and the species distribution reveals no significant correlation: The *Ulmus–Paulownia–Salix–Chenopodium* community distributes from south to north in a linear pattern, with the annual sunshine duration ranging from 2,400 to 3,200 hours; The *Chenopodium–Setaria–Eragrostis* community scatters in east and west of the site with different sunshine duration contours, and the distribution does not correspond to sunshine duration.

The light conditions have no significant impact on the general distribution of the spontaneous plants. Despite the differences in the annual sunshine duration of the site, the sunshine duration during the growing season (from Vernal Equinox to Frost's Descent) is sufficient and roughly even generally in the site. This explains why the distribution and species of the spontaneous plants are not correlated to the sunlight duration. In other words, light conditions are not the major factor that affects the growth of the spontaneous plants on the site.

3.3.3 Maternal Plant Investigation and Viability Analysis

In addition to the light and soil factors, the presence and distribution of spontaneous plants depend on the maternal plants as well. Seeds are dispersed via wind, water, fire, and other creatures, or by the mechanical force of the fruits[25]. The analysis of possible maternal plants of spontaneous plants helps reveal the environmental conditions for ecological self-restoration. As the study site is located in a university campus that is intensively maintained, it is more feasible to trace the maternal plants of spontaneous woody plants, compared with herbaceous species. On the study site, most of the spontaneous woody plants are trees (8 tree species, 1 shrub, and 1 woody vine), dominating many communities. The survey results of the possible maternal plants in and outside the site show that mature *Paulownia tomentosa*, *Ailanthus altissima*, *Broussonetia papyrifera*, and *Salix matsudana* exist on the site; mature *Fraxinus chinensis*, *Populus simonii*, and *Ulmus pumila* are close to the site; and the nearest mature *Morus alba* is 154 m away from the site (Table 3, Fig. 8).

In terms of quantity, *Paulownia tomentosa*, *Ailanthus altissima*, and *Ulmus pumila* rank the top, followed by *Fraxinus chinensis*, *Salix matsudana*, and *Morus alba*. Comparing the crown diameter and height, *Paulownia tomentosa*, *Ailanthus altissima*, *Ulmus pumila*, and *Salix matsudana* are dominant species. *Paulownia tomentosa* and *Ulmus pumila* have the fewest maternal plants, yet they sprout the most seedlings, with larger crowns and heights. The quantity of the outside maternal plants of both *Ailanthus altissima* and *Fraxinus chinensis* are large, while the seedling quantity, crown diameter, and height of the former are all obviously larger than those of the latter. Despite the small amount of the maternal plants, the seedling amount of *Salix matsudana* is second to *Fraxinus*

表3：自生植物种源分布调查表

Table 3: Possible maternal plant distribution of spontaneous plants

树种 Tree species	自生幼株 Spontaneous seedling and sapling		场地内外同种成株 Possible maternal plants inside and outside the site	
	萌发量（株） Quantity of germination	冠幅（m） Crown width (m)	场地内数量（株） Quantity observed inside	场地外可能种源的最近距离（m） Distance to the nearest possible maternal plant outside (m)
毛泡桐 *Paulownia tomentosa*	53	1.0 ~ 4.0	1	94.7
构树 *Broussonetia papyrifera*	7	1.6 ~ 3.6	4	220.3
旱柳 *Salix matsudana*	19	1.0 ~ 4.2	1	98.7
臭椿 *Ailanthus altissima*	50	0.8 ~ 4.0	8	19.0
白蜡树 *Fraxinus chinensis*	23	0.6 ~ 2.5	–	1.0
小叶杨 *Populus simonii*	2	0.3 ~ 0.4	–	1.3
榆树 *Ulmus pumila*	50	0.6 ~ 4.0	–	0.5
桑 *Morus alba*	16	0.5 ~ 3.0	–	154.0

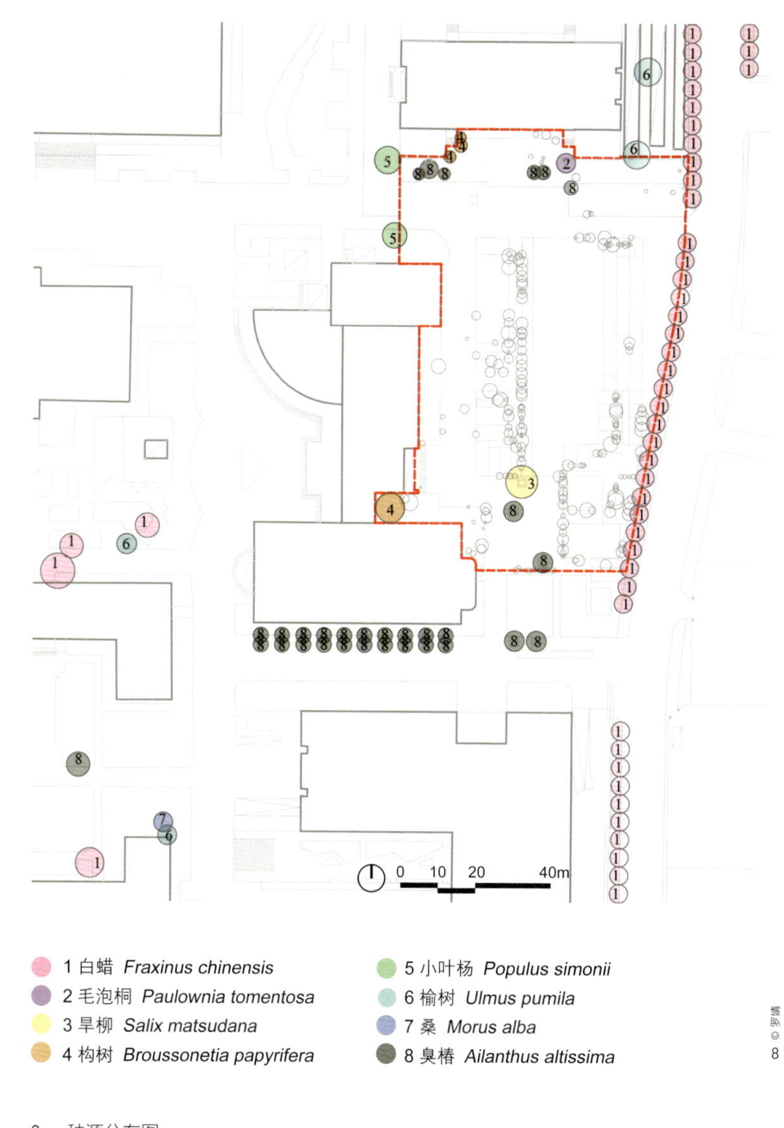

8. 种源分布图

8. Possible maternal plant distribution

距离远，幼苗萌发量次于旱柳，但冠幅、株高较小；小叶杨无论是萌发量还是冠幅株高都处于相对较弱的水平。综合考量，在8种乔木树种中，除了小叶杨和构树，其余6种树木都有着很强的自生优势，其中毛泡桐、臭椿和榆树的优势更为明显。

4 结论与讨论

4.1 生态修复与人为干扰

本研究对大学校园内一处闲置场地的植被自生情况进行了分析，在土壤条件极为苛刻的情况下，场地闲置封闭管理后一年即观察到植被自生现象，并且植被覆盖区域发展迅速，三年后自生植被覆盖场地的裸露区域接近1/3。这说明，当人类行为的扰动程度降低（建设行为和管护行为均终止）时，城市闲置地块中便会迅速发生生态修复现象。英戈·科瓦里克和安德烈斯·朗格尔对德国一处废弃的火车站的研究发现，废

chinensis, with larger crowns and taller heights. *Morus alba* has a distant possible maternal plant, though its seedling amount follows *Salix matsudana*, its crowns and heights are relatively small. *Populus simonii* is of low competitiveness among all indicators. In conclusion, except *Populus simonii* and *Broussonetia papyrifera*, the other 6 tree species have stronger viability, especially *Paulownia tomentosa*, *Ailanthus altissima*, and *Ulmus pumila*.

4 Conclusions and Discussions

4.1 Ecological Restoration and Human Intervention

This study analyzes the spontaneous vegetation in an idle site on a university campus in Beijing. Despite the harsh soil conditions, plants sprout spontaneously only after one year the site being idle and enclosed. The vegetation grows fast and has covered nearly 1/3 of the bare land in 3 years. This suggests that ecological

弃30年后场地上草地和林地混杂，草地面积较大，而之后10年林地面积扩展了近一倍，两者面积占比发生了反转[26]。本研究在演替初期场地中就有多个自生的木本群落和草本植物群落出现，场地封闭闲置3年后前者覆盖面积超过了后者开始占据主导地位，经历时间较短。两项研究结果虽然相似，但演替时间却相差甚远，自生植被演替过程中木本植被扩展的速度和影响因素值得进一步研究。

自然界中的火灾、风灾、洪水和入侵物种等都可能损害自然植被、破坏生态系统[27]，但往往人为扰动具有更大的破坏力，甚至可能完全破坏生态自我修复的能力[28]。要实现生态系统修复，一方面可停止或减少人为扰动，激发生态系统自我修复；另一方面，在了解影响生态系统自我修复过程及影响机制的基础上，借助人工措施改变限制因素可以促进植被发展，推动生态修复的进程。本研究中，在场地光照条件充分的情况下，自生植物的生长发展受到土壤条件的直接影响。如果土壤条件得到改善（如增加土壤厚度、降低硬质铺装的面积），本研究场地上物种构成和植被覆盖会发生很大改变。

4.2 植物自生现象与乡土植物

有研究对北京39个公园内的自生植物进行了调查，记录到242种植物，且大部分为乡土物种[29]。本研究场地内仅发现自生植物35种，较低的物种丰富度与场地面积小、场地内硬质铺装地面比例大的生境条件有关。场地内仅发现了一种非乡土植物（小蓬草），说明在城市闲置地块生态自我修复的初始阶段，乡土植物占有物种优势。但是，这也引发了作者关于入侵植物问题的思考：入侵植物或是具有入侵特性的植物容易形成绝对优势种群，进而影响生物多样性[13][15]。这一现象需要引起业内学者高度关注，生命力强健的外来入侵植物在疏于管理的情况下可能会迅速蔓延生长，对生态系统的稳定性产生威胁。

本研究调查记录的自生植物中有10种木本植物，物种多样性主要受草本植物种类影响。但是，与北京市公园绿地自生植物的调查结果相比（在242种植物中，灌木15种，木质藤本9种）[29]，本研究中木本植物种类占有更高的比例。有研究在杭州市建成区范围内进行了自生植物调查，记录到的木本植物种类的比例超过40%[11]。另外，本研究的植物群落构成分析结果显示，木本植物群落的数量和草本植物群落的数量相近。通过对8种乔木的种源条件及自生能力进行研究发现，多数木本乡土树种在萌发数量和长势上都表现出显著的自生优势，其中一些种类优

restoration occurs rapidly in urban idle lands when human interventions like construction or maintenance reduce. Studying an abandoned railway station in Germany, Ingo Kowarik and Andreas Langer found that the site was covered with grass (dominant) and trees after being abandoned for 30 years; another 10 years later, tree coverage doubled, exceeding that of grass[26]. In this study, several spontaneous woody and herbaceous communities were found at the early stage of the ecological self-restoration; 3 years later, the former covered a larger area than the latter, becoming obviously dominant. Although the research findings are similar, the time diverges from those observed by Kowarik and Langer. It requires further studies to explore the growth speed and impact factors of woody spontaneous species during the natural succession.

Natural hazards, e.g. fires, windstorms, floods, and species invasions, may damage natural vegetation and ecosystems[27]. Yet human interventions are often destructive that can damage their self-restoration capacity[28]. It is suggested to stop or reduce human interventions, and / or to facilitate vegetation development and ecological restoration based on the understanding of the self-restoration mechanism. In this study, with sufficient light, the soil conditions are what directly impact the growth of spontaneous plants—If the soils are improved by increasing the depth or decreasing paving, the species composition and vegetation coverage might change significantly.

4.2 Spontaneous Plants and Native Plants

A study investigating the spontaneous plants in 39 parks in Beijing recorded 242 spontaneous plant species, mostly native[29]. Only 35 spontaneous plant species were found on this study site, which may be limited by the small site area and the large ratio of hard paving on the site. Only one non-native species (*Erigeron canadensis*) was found on the site, suggesting a dominance of native species at the early stage of ecological self-restoration. However, this arouses a concern that invasive plants can easily form absolutely dominant populations, thus suppressing biodiversity[13][15]. This asks scholars to alert that robust invasive plants can spread rapidly in the absence of management, threatening the stability of ecosystems.

Among the spontaneous plant species observed on the study site, 10 are woody. The species diversity is thus mainly depended on the richness of herbaceous species. Yet compared with inventories of urban parks in Beijing (15 shrub species and 9 woody vines among 242 plants)[29], the woody plants in this study accounted for a larger share. An inventory of the spontaneous plants in the built-up areas in Hangzhou shows a woody proportion of over 40%[11]. Besides, the number of woody communities and herbaceous communities is close. The possible maternal plants and viability analyses of 8 tree species indicate that most native woody plants have a stronger germination and growth vigor, especially *Paulownia tomentosa*, *Ailanthus altissima*, and *Ulmus pumila*. Trees species spreading via wind dispersal see a shortest distance of possible maternal plants of nearly 100 m (94.7 m for *Paulownia tomentosa* and 98.7 m

势更为突出（毛泡桐、臭椿和榆树）；风力传播的树木最近可能种源距离接近100m（毛泡桐94.7m、旱柳98.7m），而动物传播的树木最近可能种源距离更远（桑154m）。这些结果都表明在城市环境中，乡土木本植物的自生优势值得引起关注和深入研究，尤其是生态自我修复初期阶段木本植物的生长规律，其研究结果将会为城市生态系统修复实践的物种选择提供借鉴。**LAF**

for *Salix matsudana*), and the species via animal dispersal see a larger distance (154 m for *Morus alba*). The findings suggest that the strong spontaneity and vigor of native woody plant species are worthy of future research efforts, particularly the growth pattern at the early stage of ecological self-restoration, which would offer references to the species selection for similar cases of urban ecosystem restoration. **LAF**

REFERENCES

[1] Li, J., & Meng, X. (2016). Wilderness Landscape in Cities. *Huazhong Architecture*, 34(12), 37-40. doi:10.13942/j.cnki.hzjz.2016.12.009

[2] Wang, X., & Wang, X. (2017). Urban Wilderness Based on the View of Landscape Architecture. *Chinese Landscape Architecture*, 33(8), 40-47.

[3] Xie, M. (2019). Pursuing Wilderness Aesthetics in Contemporary Chinese Cities. *Landscape Architecture*, 26(8), 35-38. doi:10.14085/j.fjyl.2019.08.0035.04

[4] Chen, W. (2019). How Does Urban Aesthetics Accommodate Wilderness?. *Journal of Zhengzhou University* (Philosophy and Social Sciences Edition), 52(4), 5-8, 158.

[5] Guo, G. (2019). Praise the wilderness—Discuss the Conservation of Urban Biodiversity. *China Environment*, (6), 30-33.

[6] Wang, X. (2019). Urban Wilderness and Urban Habitat. *Landscape Architecture*, 26(1), 4-5.

[7] Wang, X. (2017). Urban Interstitial Space: Strategic Research on the Planning of Wildscape in the Context of Living Environment. *Urban Development Studies*, 24(7), 11-16.

[8] Anderson, E. C., & Minor, E. S. (2018). Assessing social and biophysical drivers of spontaneous plant diversity and structure in urban vacant lots. *Science of the Total Environment*, (653), 1272-1281. doi:10.1016/j.scitotenv.2018.11.006

[9] Deng, H., & Jim, C. Y. (2017). Spontaneous plant colonization and bird visits of tropical extensive green roof. *Urban Ecosystems*, (20), 337-352.

[10] Xu, W. (2015). The investigation and study on self-growth plants in city proper—Take Hangzhou for example (Master's thesis). Zhejiang A&F University, Hangzhou.

[11] Xia, X. (2020). Investigation of Spontaneous Plants on Roads in Nanjing Old City. *Flowers*, (2), 119-120.

[12] Li, X., Dong, L., Guan, J., Zhao, F., & Wu, S. (2018). Temporal and spatial characteristics of spontaneous plant composition and diversity in a Beijing urban park. *Acta Ecologica Sinica*, 38(2), 581-594. doi:10.5846/stxb201610272193

[13] Chen, C. (2020). Forgotten urban habitats: Analysis of spontaneous vegetation on the urban walls of Chongqing City. *Acta Ecologica Sinica*, 40(2), 473-483. doi:10.5846/stxb201804130848

[14] Liu, R., Xu, X., & Yuan, L. (2020). Application of Urban Wall Autogenous Plants in Vertical Greening Based on New Naturalistic Ecological Planting Design. *Chinese Landscape Architecture*, 36(4), 111-116. doi:10.19775/j.cla.2020.04.0111

[15] Wang, K. (2014). Research on the Spontaneous Herbaceous Plants in Beijing Urban Area (Master's thesis). Beijing Forestry University, Beijing.

[16] Chen, J., Ji, D., Xiao, Y., & Shen, J. (2019). Micro-renewal Exploration of Urban Vacant Lots from the Perspective of Biodiversity—Taking Temporary Community Garden as the Example. *Chinese Landscape Architecture*, 32(12),28-33. doi:10.19775/j.cla.2019.12.0028

[17] Luo, T., Yan, D., Zhao, J., & Wang, S. (2011). Comparative Study on Simulation Softwares of Natural Light Environment. *Building Science*, 27(10), 1-6, 12. doi:10.3969/j.issn.1002-8528.2011.10.001

[18] Ayoub, M. (2020). A review on light transport algorithms and simulation tools to model daylighting inside buildings. *Solar Energy*, 198, 623–642. doi:10.1016/j.solener.2020.02.018

[19] Xie, X., Wu, M., & Yuan, R. (2015). Comparative study of Ecotect Analysis and Radiance natural lighting simulation. *Low Carbon World*, (1), 195-196.

[20] Ge, Q., Dai, J., Liu, H., Xu, Q., & Wang, H. (2014). Typical Plant Phenological Observation Dataset of Chinese Phenological Observation Network, Beijing (1963-2012). *Acta Geographica Sinica*, 69(s1), 95-97. doi:10.3974/geodb.2014.01.19.v1

[21] Wang, J., Chang, Q., & Liu D. (2014). The flowering phenophase response of early spring herb to the urbanization process in Beijing. *Acta Ecologica Sinica*, 34(22), 6701-6710. doi:10.5846/stxb201302200283

[22] Gao, Q., Chen, J., Yan, F., & Zhao, W.-L. (2012). Phenological characteristics of herbaceous plants in Hebei Province and their responses to climate warming. *Chinese Journal of Ecology*, 31(3), 600-605.

[23] Zhang, N. (2014). Study on the Plant Landscape of Urban Ecological Corridors in Beijing (Master's thesis). Beijing Forestry University, Beijing.

[24] Xu, Y., & Chang, G. (2010). Ecotype and Regional Division of Afforestation Plants in China. *Agricultural Science & Technology*, 11(1), 173-175, 185. doi:10.3969/j.issn.1009-4229-B.2010.01.050

[25] Guo, Y., Wang, S., Che, Z., Cao, J., Sun, H., & Lu, W. (2020). The Relationship of Seed Size Variation, Plant Life Forms and Distribution Types of 132 Species Plants. *Journal of Shihezi University (Natural Science)*, 38(1), 89-90. doi:10.13880/j.cnki.65-1174/n.2019.23.017

[26] Kowarik, I., & Langer, A. (2005). Natur-Park Südgelände: Linking Conservation and Recreation in an Abandoned Railyard in Berlin. In I. Kowarik, & S. Körnern (Eds), *Wild Urban Woodlands. New perspectives for Urban Forestry* (pp.287-299). Berlin, Germany: Springer.

[27] Lu, Y. (2016). Research on the Vegetation Succession and Restoration Mechanism of the Central Bars in Lijiang River (Doctoral dissertation). Beijing Forestry University, Beijing.

[28] Witmer, A. D., & Roelke, D. L. (2014). Human interference prevents recovery of infaunal beach communities from hurricane disturbance. *Ocean and Coastal Management*, (87), 52-60. doi:10.1016/j.ocecoaman.2013.11.005

[29] Li, X., & Dong, L. (2020). Species Composition and Community Types of Spontaneous Plants in Various Parks of Beijing. *Landscape Architecture*, 27(4), 42-49. doi:10.14085/j.fjyl.2020.04.0042.08

育野：技术多样性与机器中的“野”

Cultivated Wildness: Technodiversity and Wildness in Machines

张子豪
弗吉尼亚大学建筑学院构建环境博士候选人、景观系讲师

耿百利
弗吉尼亚大学建筑学院景观设计学系教授、系主任

ZHANG Zihao*
PhD Candidate in Constructed Environment and Lecturer in Landscape Architecture, School of Architecture, University of Virginia

Bradley CANTRELL
Professor and Chair, Department of Landscape Architecture, School of Architecture, University of Virginia

* Corresponding Author
Address: Campbell Hall, School of Architecture, 110 Bayly Dr, Charlottesville, VA 22903, USA
Email: zz3ub@virginia.edu

摘要

本文基于景观设计和人工智能的交叉领域探究了“育野”这一理念。当代景观实践应克服针对“荒野”概念可能存在的狭义理解，借鉴环境人文学、科学技术论、生态科学及景观设计学理念，探索用以培育新型野地的景观策略。通过剖析环境工程、计算机科学及景观设计案例，本文构想了利用智能机器营造“野地”的理论框架。该框架将机器视为具有能动性、能够参与合作生产的智能体，而非用来扩大人类对环境影响力的“数字基础设施”。近年来控制论技术发展迅速，传感网络、人工智能和网络物理系统等理念亦可为构建“育野”框架提供支持。该框架的核心是与“生物多样性”同等重要的“技术多样性”，以性能优化、追求效率为目标的技术发展单一愿景拘囿了人们的思想，剥夺了人们与环境相联系的其他可能。因此，育野的关键也在于认识机器的“野”。

关键词

人工智能；野性；景观设计；机器生态；技术多样性

ABSTRACT

This paper investigates the idea of cultivated wildness at the intersection of landscape design and artificial intelligence. The paper posits that contemporary landscape practices should overcome the potentially single understanding on wilderness, and instead explore landscape strategies to cultivate new forms of wild places via ideas and concerns in contemporary Environmental Humanities, Science and Technology Studies, Ecological Sciences, and Landscape Architecture. Drawing cases in environmental engineering, computer science, and landscape architecture research, this paper explores a framework to construct wild places with intelligent machines. In this framework, machines are not understood a layer of "digital infrastructure" that is used to extent localized human intelligence and agency. Rather machines are conceptualized as active agents who can participate in the intelligence of co-production. Recent developments in cybernetic technologies such as sensing networks, artificial intelligence, and cyberphysical systems can also contribute to establishing the framework. At the heart of this framework is "technodiversity," in parallel with biodiversity, since a singular vision on technological development driven by optimization and efficiency reinforces a monocultural approach that eliminates other possible relationships to construct with the environment. Thus, cultivated wildness is also about recognizing "wildness" in machines.

KEYWORDS

Artificial Intelligence; Wildness; Landscape Design; Machine Ecology; Technodiversity

编辑 | 田乐、王颖
翻译 | 张书瑞、张子豪、王颖
EDITED BY | Tina TIAN, WANG Ying
TRANSLATED BY | ZHANG Shurui, ZHANG Zihao, WANG Ying

https://doi.org/10.15302/J-LAF-1-020040
收稿时间 RECEIVED DATE | 2020-12-18

中图分类号 | TP18, TU98
文献标识码 | B

1 引言：从自然的社会建构到多元的“野”

除却环境问题层面针对荒野保护的科学探讨外，“荒野”（wilderness）概念一直颇具争议。在《荒野的困境》这一引发了众多讨论的评论文章中，环境历史学家威廉·克罗农从历史角度批判了荒野概念，并梳理了20世纪中叶以来美国在荒野保护工作中存在的问题。[1]收录了克罗农对现代环保主义辛辣批判的文集——《不同的立场：对自然的重构》——也已然成为环境人文学及其他交叉学科的重要论著。[2]该文集还收录了其他学者的观点，包括景观理论家安妮·惠斯顿·斯本、景观地理学家肯尼斯·奥维格、女性主义理论家唐娜·哈拉维和文学评论家N·凯瑟琳·海尔斯，他们当中的很多人如今都已成为人文社会科学和设计学科（包括景观设计学）翘楚。从该文集中可以窥见学者们在社会文化和历史语境下对“自然”和“荒野”等概念的质疑，这些“反叙事”的论述极大挑战了当时的主流认知。

上述学术探讨是“自然的社会建构”运动的重要组成[2]~[6]，该运动反映了20世纪下半叶至21世纪初各个学科对科学事实和真理的广泛反思[7]~[12]。此次思潮的主要论点是：自然和荒野等概念的形成离不开社会建构，它们承载着某些特定的社会文化价值观，但忽视了主流叙事之外的人类和非人类物种。[2][5][6][13]~[16]受此影响，当下逐渐形成了一种批判自然和荒野等概念的主要框架——通过情景化和地方性知识观来挖掘反叙事策略，向与人类及环境相关的主流观念发起挑战。[16][17]若不具备这种批判性视野，特定的荒野意象就会成为傀儡，任由各种环境实践中道德律令般的价值观肆意主导。某些特定文化的价值观不仅固化了对荒野的狭义认知，也加剧了长久以来的社会和政治冲突。例如近来有关美国阿拉斯加地区石油开采权的争论，再如工人阶级利益与环保主义者保护“原始自然”行动的冲突，又如原住民保卫家园和殖民者开拓“想象中的荒野”之间的长期纷争。[18]~[21]

当然，这些批判性思考绝不是要否定人们为环境保护做出的努力，而是要揭露那些可能削弱当代环境实践道德准则的价值观。不断发展的批判性观念正融入当代跨领域的环境正义运动中，积极推动设计师、环境工程师和环保主义人士反思其价值观并拓展对自然和荒野的认知。例如，美国山峦协会和荒野保护协会等环保组织已经拓宽对自然和荒野的定义，并致力于贯彻环境实践的包容性和公平性；近期

1 Introduction: From Social Construction of Nature to Plurality of Wildness

Outside the scientific environmentalist conservation and preservation discourse, “wilderness” has always been a contentious concept and a contested ground. In his (in)famous essay “The Trouble with Wilderness,” environmental historian William Cronon issued a critique of the notion of wilderness from a historical lens and teased out the problematic aspects of America’s wilderness preservation efforts since the mid-20th century.[1] Cronon’s provocative critique of modern environmentalism is the leading essay in an important anthology in and outside environmental humanities—*Uncommon Ground: Toward Reinventing Nature*.[2] Other authors include landscape theorist Anne Whiston Spirn, landscape geographer Kenneth Olwig, feminist theorist Donna Haraway, and literary critic N. Katherine Halyes. Many of them later became influential and widely cited scholars across humanities, social sciences, and design disciplines, including Landscape Architecture. The anthology contributors interrogated the conception of nature and related concepts, including wilderness, by situating the terms within socio-cultural and historical contexts, revealing the counter-narratives that challenge mainstream beliefs.

This body of scholarship can be situated in a movement known as “social construction of nature,”[2]~[6] which mirrors the broad-based reflection on scientific facts and truth across disciplines in the second half of the 20th century and early 21st century.[7]~[12] The major argument formed wherein was that concepts such as nature and wilderness are at least partly constructed by the society and laden with specific socio-cultural values, overlooking people and nonhuman species that are outside the mainstream narratives.[2][5][6][13]~[16] This becomes the major analytical framework of today’s critique on the conceptions of nature and related concepts including wilderness: unearthing counter-narratives with situated and localized knowledge to challenge the mainstream conceptualizations of human and the environment.[16][17] Without a critical lens, the image of a specific wild place could become a vessel into which the society pours all kinds of values that serve as moral imperatives for environmental practices. These culturally specific values reinforce a single vision of wild places, underpinning ongoing social and political conflicts, such as recent political debates on oil rights in Alaska, disputes between the working class and environmentalists’ effort to protect “pristine nature,” as well as long-term contentions rooted in indigenous people’s home and colonialists’ “wilderness imaginary.”[18]~[21]

Of course, these critical reflections are never meant to undermine environmental efforts but only reveal the underpinning values in contemporary environmental practices that may undercut moral imperatives. These critical arguments keep developing and feed into contemporary environmental justice movements across fields, impelling designers, environmental engineers, conservationists, and preservationists to reflect their values and conceptions about nature and wilderness. For example, many environmental groups, such as Sierra Club and the Wilderness Society, have been addressing their ongoing inclusion and equity efforts in preservation and conservation practices; Also, recent land acknowledgment

北美各种机构开展的领土权属确认运动也肯定了原住居民长久以来的土地管理者身份。

随着自然和荒野概念的拓展，不同领域的学者开始以多元化的视角来理解和定义“野地”。在人类世的背景下，生态学家和生物学家开始将研究重心转移到“新形式的野”（new wilds）和人类世生态系统（novel ecosystems）上。[22]~[25]近年来提出的环境策略也已不再强调维持或恢复历史生态格局，而鼓励通过促进生态系统过程、非人类物种和智能机器的自主性来实现“再野化”。[26]~[28]人文和科学技术论等领域的学者也不再批判自然和荒野，转而以“非人类能动性”（nonhuman agency）为概念框架来理解人类与非人类物种及机器之间的合作生产和共同进化过程，探究三者间不同的关联方式。[29]~[34]与此同时，景观设计师和规划师也不断吸纳新型生态系统、多物种相互作用、机器智能和非人类能动性等新兴思想，以期畅想更具开放型的设计项目。[35]~[39]

在承认荒野概念的核心在于自然的自主性（无或较少人工干预）的前提下，我们也需要认识到，机器在与其他自然过程和非人类物种的不断融合中，能够甚至已经发展出新颖有趣的荒野概念，并产生了重要的社会和生态影响。本文提出“育野”（cultivated wildness）概念，期望通过传感网络、人工智能和网络物理系统等前沿数字技术，探究有助于培育新型野地的全新景观策略，为有关荒野的讨论提供新思路。

通过剖析环境工程、计算机科学及景观设计和研究中的案例，本文认为，智能机器并非人类用以扩大自身（构想的）能动性或统治非人类物种的控制机制；它们作为多尺度的参与者，深深嵌入各种环境过程中，共同创造出超越人类认知范围的各种形式的“野”。换言之，景观设计师如今所需考虑的“环境”已经与过去大相径庭——它不再是可供设计师在其上尽情畅想各种景观动态变化的背景板或白纸，而是一种遍布各种智能的“反馈环境”。因此，“再野化”不再仅仅意味着利用有限的人类智能来恢复历史生态格局，或根据特定社会团体的标准来固化“荒野”意象。我们可以通过提升生态系统、非人类动植物物种和智能机器的自主性，精心培育新形式的野。当这些智能体发展出自己的路线、轨迹和变化过程后，便形成了真正开放、未知的荒野。

endeavors across North American institutions have recognized indigenous peoples as the longest-serving stewards of the land.

With the thickening of the conceptions of nature and wilderness, scholars across fields have begun to embrace a plurality in interpreting and conceptualizing wild places. Some ecologists and biologists have shifted their attention to “new wilds” and novel ecosystems in the face of Anthropocene.[22]~[25] Recent environmental strategies have surpassed maintaining or recovering historical ecological patterns and instead promote the autonomy of ecosystem processes, nonhuman species, and intelligent machines as strategies for “rewilding.”[26]~[28] Scholars in Humanities and Science and Technology Studies (STS) have also turned their attention away from critiquing “nature” and “wilderness,” and deployed “nonhuman agency” as a conceptual frame to understand the co-production and co-evolution between human and nonhuman species and machines, speculating different forms of associated relationships as well.[29]~[34] Landscape architects and planners also incorporate emerging ideas about novel ecosystems, multispecies interactions, machine intelligence, and nonhuman agency to envision a greater openness in their projects.[35]~[39]

Notwithstanding the essence of the wilderness concept as nature is “on its own” with little or no human guidance, there also is a sufficient need to understand how a convergence of machines with natural processes and nonhuman species can develop—and has already developed—new and interesting concepts of wildness with important socio-ecological ramifications. This paper contributes to this broad discourse about wilderness by proposing the idea of “cultivated wildness.” Focusing on recent developments in cybernetics technologies such as sensing networks, artificial intelligence (AI), and cyberphysical systems, this paper attempts to demonstrate that such technologies can provide new opportunities for landscape strategies to cultivate new forms of wild places.

With examples drawn from environmental engineering, computer science, and landscape design and research, this paper argues that intelligent machines are not a layer of control mechanism through which humans extend imagined agency and expand an illusory control regime. Instead, intelligent machines should be conceived as multi-scalar actors that are deeply embedded in all kinds of environmental processes and give rise to all kinds of wild conditions outside human comprehension. In other words, today the concept “environment” is fundamentally different from what landscape designers considered and conceived in the past—Environment no longer stands only for a passive background and a tabula rasa on which designers entertain landscape dynamics. Rather, landscape architects have to confront a “cybernetic environment” with different forms of distributed intelligence. This paper argues that “rewilding” is no longer only about using localized human intelligence to restore historical ecological patterns and reinforce an image of wild place based on certain social groups’ standards. Instead, “new wild” can be carefully cultivated by promoting the autonomy of ecological systems, nonhuman animals and plant species, and intelligent machines. In this way, by allowing the agents to take their courses, trajectories, and processes of becoming, wild places can be truly open-ended and indeterminate.

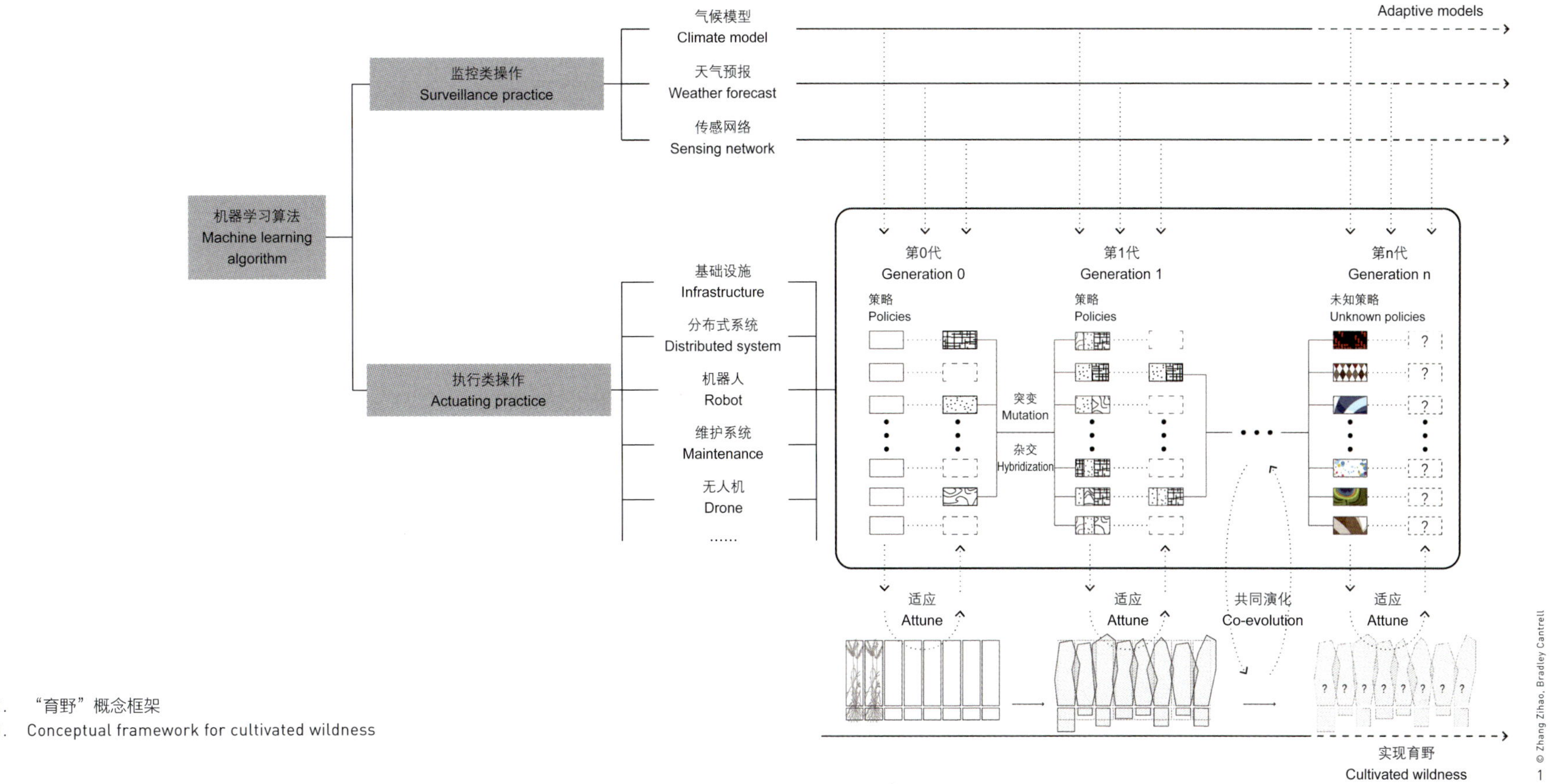

1. “育野”概念框架

1. Conceptual framework for cultivated wildness

本文提出一种“育野”概念框架（图1）：机器学习算法分布在不同的信息物理系统中——从环境监测系统（如气候模型、天气预报系统、传感网络等）到各种执行系统（如信息物理基础设施、机械装置、分布式机器人和无人机等）。这些智能体尺度各异，机械装置等小型执行器能够直接与植物相互作用，而加装了自动装置的水闸和溢洪道等大型执行器则可以通过改变土壤条件和水文格局来影响植物生境。机器学习智能体可通过持续学习和遗传算法来尝试各种不同策略，并通过迁移学习来彼此交换经验。机器学习技术还可以帮助建立更多的气候和天气适应性模型，这些模型的预报结果反过来又可用来训练分布式机器学习智能体。这些松散耦合的模型和智能体可以根据环境监测和过往经验来调整其策略；甚至随着时间的推移，提出超越人类理解范围的策略——即实现育野。通过开发与不同尺度的模型和系统相交互的界面，景观设计师可参与到这种新环境中。[40]此时，机器与其他非人类主体之间应当“相互依存”，而非“单向依赖”。在育野框架中，机器不仅是自动化工具，更是环境的共同创造者。正如

This paper maps out a conceptual framework to approach cultivated wildness (Fig. 1). Machine learning (ML) algorithms are distributed in cyberphysical systems from environmental surveillance practices such as climate models, weather forecasting systems, sensing networks to all kinds of actuating systems, including cyberphysical infrastructures, robotic armatures, distributed robots, and drones. These agents are multi-scalar, and some actuators (e.g. robotic armatures) can directly interact with the plants while the others (e.g. retrofitted flood gates and spillways) can impact plant habitats by modifying soil conditions and hydrological patterns. ML agents test out strategies through a framework based on continuous learning, genetic algorithms, and transfer learning. ML techniques also help build more adaptive climate and weather models, and the prediction results can feed into the training of the distributed ML agents. These loosely coupled models and agents could adjust their strategies, and, over time, would start developing unexpected strategies beyond human comprehension—cultivated wildness. Landscape architects can participate into it by developing different interfaces with these multi-scalar models and systems.[40] The relationship between machines and other nonhuman agents should be considered with the notion of interdependency rather than codependency. In this framework, machines are not tools for automation but have always been involved in and will play a preeminent role in the co-production of the environment. Eventually, constructing wild places with intelligent machines is about expanding landscape architects' understanding of the environment itself, just like

"阿尔法狗"拓展了棋手对围棋的理解一样，利用智能机器创造荒野的最终目的是加深人们对环境本身的理解。机器可以揭示和构建人类以往无法识别和诠释的环境格局。唯有如此，"培育的野"才能孕育人类当前无法想象的可能和未来。

提出上述育野框架的目的并非提供制造强效机器的技术蓝图，而是促进景观设计师理解和认识环境的复杂性，意识到除人类智能外还存在其他形式的智能。该框架源于上述生态学、景观设计学、环境人文学和科学技术论等学科中的技术和理论探索，要求设计师在本体论和认识论上进行根本性转变，将所谓的"环境"理解为不同框架、意图和目标函数互相作用后的混合体。不同的智能体——不论是人类或非人类，不论存活与否，不论是技术上的或生态的，不论是生物或非生物——都能相互调整、增强、抑制、利用与抵消。由此产生的环境融合了不同的视角，超越了每个个体的原始意图，无数的智能体精心培育着环境中的"野"。当代景观设计要不断拓展人们的审美体验范畴。[41][42]相应的景观策略也不应局限于保护和恢复层面，而需在如今与非人类领域如此疏远的文化中，孕育意料之外的机遇。因此，育野也意味着为当代城市居民培育一种新的审美观念，鼓励人们拥抱城市中的"野"并与之共生。

2 机器智能与构建的"野"

基于近年控制论技术的发展，我们可从三个方向探索上述育野框架：1）深度强化学习和机器策略；2）响应式景观和分布式智能；3）植物–机器交互。需要注意的是，育野的具体操作不能单独建立在以上任意一个方向上。诚然，这类育野实践的可行性仍待商榷，但下文示例从多视角对框架进行剖析，共同描绘了机器在景观策略中发挥重要作用的未来蓝图。

2.1 深度强化学习和机器策略

在过去几年中，人工智能研究突破不断，在深度强化学习（DRL）方面更是见证了众多变革，驱动了有关智能的更深层次的探索。就DRL而言，智能体可以观察环境状态并采取行动：如果某些行动被证明是有效的，那么智能体将得到奖励。近年来，科学家已经训练出了多个DRL智能体，其中包括"阿尔法狗"系列，它们精通围棋并击败了最高水平的人类棋手。[43]"阿尔法狗"的训练过程采用自对弈——除基本规则外，人工智能系统未曾学习任何人类棋手的对局方式；类似的应用也可见于对人工智能游戏选手AlphaStar的训练中。[44]这些DRL智能体超越了人类水平，探索出了人类未曾探知的全新策略。在某种程度上，它们基于机器对游戏的理解，提出具有"机器风格"的策略，从而扩大了人们对游戏本身的理解。

景观设计师和生态学家亦探究过机器学习在环境管理中的应用潜力。例如，在某项思维实验中，研究人员构想了一种基于DRL的人工智能系统——"荒野创造者"，该系统可自行制定策略并创建超越人类认知的野性空间。[29]实验挑战了人们对"荒野"的传统认知，为探

AlphaGo that has expanded players' understanding of the Go game. Machines may reveal and construct patterns in the environment that humans previously cannot recognize and translate. Only in this way cultivated wildness can become a reserve for possibilities and a future that we cannot think of now.

This framework is never a technical blueprint for building powerful machines, but a roadmap with which landscape architects can start to understand and appreciate the environment's complexity, recognizing different forms of intelligence other than human. It is deeply rooted in the aforementioned technical and theoretical explorations in Ecology, Landscape Architecture, Environmental Humanities, and STS. It challenges designers to take on an ontological and epistemological shift in understanding the environment as a mash-up of different frameworks, goals, and objective functions. Different agents—human or nonhuman, living or nonliving, technical or biological, biotic or abiotic—modify, amplify, depress, utilize, and cancel each other. Thus the resulting environment is always already a mash-up of different perspectives beyond every agent's original intention. Agents are carefully cultivating a sense of wildness in the environment. Contemporary landscape design should expand people's aesthetic categories.[41][42] Landscape strategies are no longer limited to preservation, conservation, and restoration but about promoting unexpected encounters in contemporary culture that is so alienated from nonhuman realms. Cultivated wildness entails cultivating a new sense of aesthetic among modern urban dwellers to embrace and learn to live with the wild in the city.

2 Machine Intelligence and Constructed Wildness

There are three venues to explore the framework of cultivated wildness regarding the recent development in cybernetic technologies: 1) deep reinforcement learning and machine strategies, 2) responsive landscapes and distributed intelligence, and 3) plant–machine interactions. It should be noted that none of these examples solely illustrate the kind of operation that can create wild places—In fact, it is doubtful that such a practice exists. However, examples in the following sections represent different aspects of the framework of constructed wildness, and together, they render a possible future where machines play an important part in the developing of landscape strategies.

2.1 Deep Reinforcement Learning and Machine Strategies

The past few years have seen breakthroughs in AI research, especially on deep reinforcement learning (DRL) which provides transformative cases for scholars to ask more profound questions about intelligence. In DRL, an agent can observe the state of the environment and then act: If the act turned out to be effective, then the agent would get rewarded. Over the past few years, scientists have trained many DLR agents, including the AlphaGo series that have mastered the Go game and beaten the best human Go players.[43] The training process used the self-play technique, which means that the AI system has played with itself based on basic

究机器在构建野性空间过程中的作用提供了新思路。在某种程度上，这些荒野的“野”正在于人类无法用既有模型来理解人类世生态系统。

上述思维实验在当年看起来或许离经叛道，但如今相关研究已相继展开。例如，美国弗吉尼亚大学Link实验室的科学家们即探索了训练DRL智能体来管理雨洪的方法。[45][46]实验根据弗吉尼亚州诺福克市的雨洪系统构建了一处模拟环境，系统中的两片汇水区分别与独立的蓄水池相连；蓄水池的出口处安装有可控阀门，可以灵活调节启闭程度（图2）。智能体通过调节两个阀门来控制蓄水池的水位，一方面可防止出现洪涝，另一方面可维持蓄水池的理想水位。

在每一个模拟周期中，DRL智能体都能够获取系统的最新状态，包括不同节点的水深及洪涝风险、未来24小时的降水预测和潮汐预报。根据这些数据，DRL智能体可通过相应策略调节阀门。模拟系统会依据不同的策略进行更新，如果策略有效，则智能体会得到奖励。该DRL智能体的奖励机制取决于它能否有效防止因潮汐和降雨产生的洪涝并维持理想水位。在整个实验过程中，科学家们利用真实的潮汐和降雨数据模拟出一系列雨洪事件来训练和测试DRL智能体。

DRL智能体不仅可以识别实时数据的细微变化，还能够实现实时控制，这是人类能力远达不到的。最重要的是，DRL智能体能够提出一些意想不到的策略：雨后蓄水池充盈，智能体会连续地打开或关闭阀门缓慢排水，以维持目标水位，此时下游或出现小型洪涝，但洪水总量仍在可控范围内。智能体的这一行为提醒着设计师，城市水系统管理往往只能优化个别变量，而智能体则能另辟蹊径，利用洪水的频率而非水量控制来管理雨洪，提出了基于信息物理系统的全新策略。由于从未接触过任何人类已掌握的雨洪系统知识，DRL智能体的学习

2. Link实验室的DRL实验示意图（改绘自参考文献[46]）
2. Schematic diagram for Link Lab's DRL experiment (Adaptation source: Ref. [46])

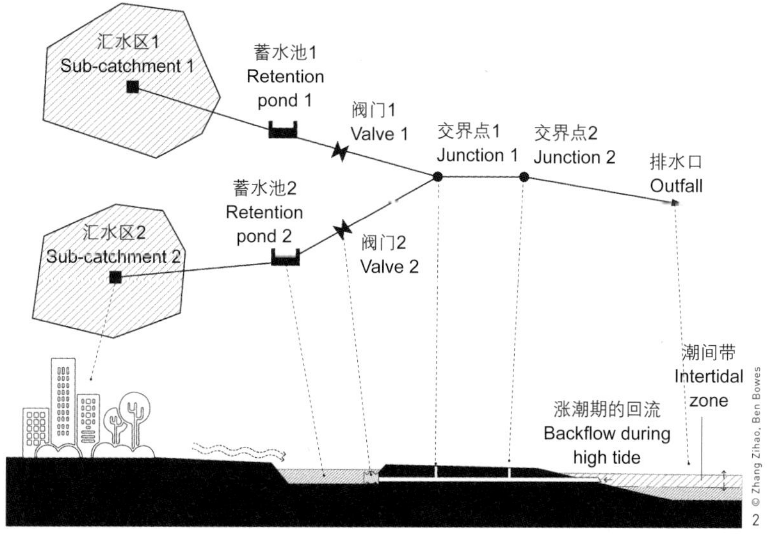

rules, without learning from any human knowledge. Similar applications can be found in video games, such as AlphaStar.[44] These DRL agents have not only outperformed humans but also came up with novel strategies that human players had never thought of. In a way, they developed a machine understanding of the games and came up with strategies in a "machine mindset," expanding human understanding of the games.

Landscape architects and ecologists have also speculated on the implications of ML in environmental management. In a thought experiment, the researchers imagined a DRL-based AI system called "wildness creator" that can devise its own strategies and create wild places beyond human comprehension.[29] This thought experiment questions the notion of wilderness and provides an alternative way to conceptualize machines' role in constructing wild places. The places constructed by the machines are wild in the sense that they are novel ecologies for which humans do not have a model to comprehend.

This thought experiment may sound outlandish, but there are, in fact, already related research efforts. Scientists from the Link Lab at the University of Virginia have explored training DRL agents to control stormwater systems.[45][46] The scientists constructed a simulated stormwater system inspired by a system located in Norfolk, Virginia, USA. It consists of two sub-catchments connected to two separate retention ponds. At the outlet of each pond is a controllable valve that can be closed or open to any degree (Fig. 2). The agent can control the two valves to adjust the water volume in the ponds. The goal is to, on the one hand, prevent overall flooding in the system, and, on the other hand, maintain a desired water level in the retention ponds.

In each step, the DRL agent can observe the current state of the system, including the water depths and flooding rate on each nodes, as well as rainfall and tide forecast in next 24 hours. Based on the data, the DRL agent can come up with a control policy to adjust valves. The policy would update the system, and the agent will be rewarded if the action is desirable. This DRL agent's reward function is defined by how well the agent could prevent overall flooding (both from tide and rainfall) and maintain certain water depths in the ponds. Scientists used real-world rainfall and tidal data to produce a range of flood events to train and test the DRL agent.

The agent can not only respond to the subtle changes of the real-time data, but also achieved a level of real-time control beyond human capacity. Most importantly, the agent has devised some unexpected strategies. When the pond is filled after a rain event, the agent would open / close the valves repeatedly and slightly discharge water to maintain the target water level. Though this would cause minor floods downstream, the agent can keep the overall volume under a threshold. This reminds designers that urban water systems are often optimized with a few parameters, and the agent's unexpected behaviors—for example, exploiting the frequency dimension of floods—offer a new range of potential strategies based on frequency rather than volume to manage urban stormwater with cyberphysical systems. Since no human knowledge of the stormwater system was given to the DRL agent, the machine

完全从零开始，它形成了自身对雨洪系统的了解，并独立提出了一套管理策略。

在上述案例中，训练智能体目的是防止雨洪。但雨洪对生态系统的重要性同样不容忽视，景观设计师大可构想某种智能体，使其在城市的特定区域策略性地制造小型洪涝，从而建立新的生态系统。此外，DRL智能体控制蓄水池特定水深的优势也可应用到湿地设计中以构建理想生境。

在最近的研究中，科学家们正在建立更复杂、可解决冲突目标（如需同时考虑水质）的算法。初步结果表明，DRL理论框架可以迅速训练出擅长达成不同目标（防洪或控制污染）的智能体，部分智能体兼具多种功能，能够提出复杂的管理策略。受此启发，景观设计师还可以设计由不同智能体管控的具有多个优先级的城市排水系统。不同智能体之间的相互反馈将带来前所未有的复杂局面：智能体提出的策略可促使雨洪系统形成新的水文格局；而在智能体的精心培育下亦会出现新的生态类型。一种“培育”的城市荒野由此形成，不同的智能体对其施以严格维护，而智能体的某些行为甚至可能超越人类的认知范畴。

2.2 响应式景观和分布式智能

设计师们往往容易忽略这样一个事实——智能机器早已广泛分布于环境中，并大范围参与了各种环境过程。以佛罗里达州适应性管理①的最佳实践“大沼泽地生态修复项目”为例，南佛罗里达州水域管理区成立于1949年，是一个地区性政府机构，管理着佛罗里达州南半部的水资源，其中就包括这个滋养了无数野生动植物的约6 000km^{2}的大沼泽地。[47]在城市居民眼中，这里绝对称得上是“荒野”；但看似野生的大沼泽地实际上却是高度维护的结果。南佛罗里达州的水体中随处可见监测站，实时生成的水文和水质数据被用于建立水文系统的模拟模型。其中，“南佛罗里达州水域管理模型”即为分析水文系统运行变化及形成合理管理决策的重要模型之一。此外，数千英里长的人工运河和管道遍布佛罗里达州，运河中战略性地设置了水道、溢洪道、堰门、水泵、水坝和闸门等管控设施（执行器）。整个系统中的执行器可以直接影响南佛罗里达州的水文格局（图3）。在某种程度上，得益于实时水文数据、天气预报、气候模型数据支持下的模拟模型，南佛罗里达州的水量和水文格局每时每刻都受到精确计量与管控。

大沼泽地生态修复项目只是利用信息物理系统管理环境过程的众多尝试之一。最近关于智慧城市的讨论激发了社会各界对智能自动化的构想。正如上述案例中的诺福克市一样，许多城市都在使用由致力于开发实时环境监测和实时控制方案的新兴公司（如Opti雨洪管理公司和Xylem水科技公司）提供的可控智能执行器来改造雨洪系统。[48][49]在一定程度上，智能机器遍布于城市环境中，有待设计师去开发利用。以下两个探索式景观设计研究项目及一系列机器人和机器学习案例或可为构建基于实时反馈和机器学习的适应性框架提供启示，促进人类与智能机器的相互沟通与协同设计。

在“走向感知”项目中，设计师雷夫·埃斯特拉达提议在洛杉矶河中分散设置智能机器和传感网络，用于调整水文模式与构建地形。

① 适应性管理可以理解为一种边做边学的决策方法，需通过严格的监控和执行来实现。

started from scratch and developed its own understanding of the system and came up with a set of strategies on its own.

In this example, the agent is trained to prevent floods. However, by understanding the importance of flood events to ecosystems, landscape architects can imagine a DRL agent trained to strategically promote flood events in certain areas in a city to create novel and emergent ecologies. Moreover, the DRL agent can actively maintain water depths in the retention ponds, which provide ideal conditions for wetland species.

More recently, scientists are looking to build more complex objective functions with multiple competing goals, such as water quality. Preliminary results suggest that the DRL framework can quickly build a diverse school of agents attending to different objectives (e.g. controlling flooding, managing pollutants), and there are many hybrid ones in the middle with complex behaviors. With this example, one can imagine multiple urban drainage systems managed by different agents with slightly different priorities. The feedback between these agents will give rise to complex phenomena beyond human imagination now. The agents' strategies would result in new hydrological patterns in the system; new ecological types would emerge through the DRL agents' careful cultivation. The result is a cultivated urban wild that is highly maintained by intelligent agents whose actions are sometimes beyond human comprehension.

2.2 Responsive Landscapes and Distributed Intelligence

Designers tend to ignore how deeply intelligent machines are already distributed in the environment, overlooking the scale at which they have participated in all kinds of environmental processes. For example, the Everglades restoration project in Florida is considered as an exemplar for adaptive management① framework and the best practice in environmental engineering. Established in 1949, the South Florida Water Management District is a regional governmental agency that manages the water resources in the southern half of Florida, including the Everglades, a 1.5 million-acre wetland sustaining numerous wildlife species.[47] This is the ultimate “wilderness” in the eyes of urban residents. However, the wild Everglades is, in fact, a highly maintained place. In South Florida, numerous sensing stations are installed across the water bodies generating real-time hydrological and water quality data used to build simulation models of the water system. The South Florida Water Management Model is one of the models to analyze operational changes to the water system and to inform management decision making. Moreover, thousands of miles of engineered canals and pipes are carved into Florida's landscape, and water control infrastructures such as water basins, spillways, weir gates, pumps, dams,

① Adaptive management can be understood as a decision-making method via learning by doing, which is achieved by intensely monitoring and actuating processes.

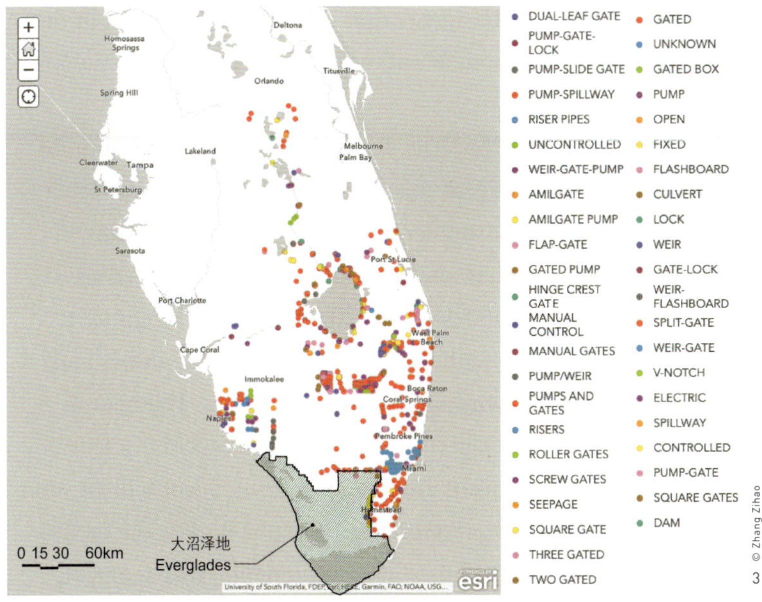

3. 南佛罗里达州水域管理系统（数据来源：Arc Hydro增强数据、在线ArcGIS数据）

3. South Florida Water Management System (Data source: Arc Hydro Enhanced Database and ArcGIS Online)

他利用哈佛大学设计研究生院响应环境与人工制品实验室的水文地貌模拟沙床测试了“感应—处理—制动”响应框架。沙床中沉积物和水流的输入由4个进料器和一个水泵进行控制，此外还配备了传感和监控设备来收集实时数据，包括工作台上方的微软体感设备Kinect和下游的超声波传感器。而后通过Grasshopper软件中的自定义插件将实时数据输入三维建模软件Rhinoceros 3D中。在一次设计实验中，埃斯特拉达提出了名为“调制器”的执行系统，它由一组连接在伺服电机上的亚克力管组成。每个亚克力管均由伺服电机单独驱动，亚克力管的底部插在沉积物中。转动的伺服电机驱动亚克力管上下移动，进而影响水流形态，在工作台的下游形成不同的地形。再通过传感器实时跟踪地形，并使用高程数据建立数字高程模型，便可在设计软件中识别出一系列高地和低地。上述信息可以为接下来的操作提供依据，例如要在高地上建造更多的土地就需要沉积更多的沙子，要侵蚀高地就需要引入更多的水。[50]埃斯特拉达表示，机器人系统展现出了超越人类水平的实时更新和反馈水平。[51]

埃斯特拉达的实验测试了基于“感应—处理—制动”反馈回路的响应式景观框架的可行性，以期利用环境中的传感器和执行器来提供实时景观策略。而遍布环境中的传感器和执行器也为机器学习算法的

and locks are strategically placed along the waterways. These actuators in the system can directly influence the hydrological patterns in South Florida (Fig. 3). In a way, the amount of water and the hydrological patterns are carefully calculated and controlled using simulation models based on real-time hydrological data, weather forecast, and climate modeling.

The Everglades restoration project is only one instance of numerous efforts to use cyberphysical systems to manage environmental processes. The recent discourse of smart cities has fueled cybernetic imaginaries across social sectors. Like Norfolk in the above example, many cities are retrofitting their stormwater systems with controllable and smart actuators provided by emerging companies such as Opti and Xylem that are specialized in live environmental monitoring and real-time control solutions.[48][49] To some extent, the environment is laden with intelligent machines to be mobilized by designers. Two speculative landscape design research projects and a range of robotic and ML examples shed light on an adaptive framework based on real-time feedback and ML, offering insights for communicating and designing with intelligent machines.

In the first project, Towards Sentience, designer Leif Estrada proposed distributing intelligent machines and sensing networks in the Los Angeles River to influence hydrological patterns and build landforms over time. He tested the sensing–processing–actuating responsive framework on a hydromorphology table at the Responsive Environments and Artifacts Lab in the Graduate School of Design, Harvard University. The sediments and water flow inputs were controlled with 4 material feeders and a water pump. The table was also equipped with sensing and monitoring devices to gather real-time data, including a Microsoft Kinect above the table and ultrasonic sensors downstream. Real-time data then fed into Rhinoceros 3D with Grasshopper plugins and customized interfaces. In one of the design experiments, Estrada proposed an actuating system called “attuner” that consists of a matrix of acrylic dowels connected to servo motors. Every dowel was separately driven by a servo motor, and the bottom portion of the dowel sticks into the sediments. When the servo motors turned on, they drove the dowels moving up and down to change the flow pattern, thus creating different landforms downstream of the table. The topography was then live tracked by sensors, and elevation data were used to build a digital elevation model so that a series of high grounds and low grounds can be identified. This information could inform operations such as building more land in a high ground by depositing more sand, and eroding the high ground away by directing more water.[50] Estrada reported that the cyborg system exhibits a level of live updates and feedback beyond human capacity.[51]

Estrada’s experiment tested sensing–processing–actuating feedback loop as a viable responsive landscape framework to utilize sensors and actuators in the environment for deploying real-time landscape strategies. Moreover, the environment laden with sensors and actuators sets the basis for applying ML algorithms. Designers can speculate a DRL agent that can test different policies with the “attuners” and adjust strategies according to real-time feedback.

应用奠定了基础。例如，设计师可以构想一种DRL智能体，利用“调制器”来测试不同的景观策略，并根据实时反馈进行调整；或将不同的DRL智能体嵌入环境中，随时间的推移与其他人类及非人类个体和系统共同演化。

要实现以上构想，需要解决两个问题。首先，只有在“持续学习”策略的支持下，才能促使智能机器与其他人类和非人类行为者在环境中共同演化。然而，大多数AI算法其实是“离线”的，这意味着在完成训练后，上传到网络物理系统中的是一个已经经过调试的模型（如深度学习中的神经网络）。训练过程实质上是通过将神经网络暴露在大量数据中来调整单个神经元的权重。训练完成后，神经网络将被校准到最佳状态，仅根据输入信息进行输出，而不会在运行时学习任何新知识。一旦应用到气候变化等动态环境中，这些智能体将会很快过时。因此，开发持续学习框架是将智能机器应用于环境治理过程中的一大挑战。其次，机器学习分为训练和测试环节。在实际应用智能体之前，科学家需要提供训练数据供行机器学习。在前文所述的DRL案例中，智能体能够在模拟环境（如电子游戏）中寻找策略，而这种环境是可以无限次重启的。但真实环境没有“重启键”，如果某个智能体无故造成了恶劣结果，那么将难以挽回。这也是利用人工智能来管理环境所不得不面对的伦理挑战。

另一个探索性研究项目和人工智能研究的最新进展或许可为这些困境提供新思路。来自麻省理工学院建筑学院的设计师里卡多・詹尼・冈萨雷斯在他的论文中提出了一种嵌于冰冻圈环境中的系统。该系统由一个中央“大脑”（可以理解为超级计算机单元）和分布各处的“身体”（改变物理环境的执行器）组成。在具体操作中，“大脑”首先对“身体”施加不同的执行策略，而后根据预测结果与实际差异来评估策略；再将更新后的新策略投放到“身体”中。产生最佳结果的策略将作为成功经验嵌入下一轮干预中。在这样的模式下，某一“身体”可以通过将知识转移给其他“身体”来彼此影响。经过不断迭代，该分布式系统可以逐渐适应冰冻圈环境并随环境一起演化。[52]

该项目的理论框架反映了一些被广泛使用的机器学习算法和技术，例如持续学习、遗传算法和迁移学习。值得注意的是，持续学习一直都是DRL理论的基础（常与DRL相类比的概念是人类的试错学习，而人类的学习过程需要终身且持续的努力）。实际上，有关人工智能的研究已经在探索如何使智能体边学习边衍变的策略，科学家们也在克服“灾难性遗忘”方面取得了可喜进展。“灾难性遗忘”是持续学习的主要障碍——智能体往往会在获取新知识后突然完全“忘记”之前学习过的信息。[53]在目前的人工智能应用中，理论层面的持

Designers can also speculate various DRL agents that are deeply embedded in the environment and co-evolve with other human and nonhuman agents and systems over time.

This kind of speculation raises two concerns. First, designers need continuous learning strategies to anticipate an intelligent machine that co-evolves with other human and nonhuman agents in the environment. Most of the AI algorithms are considered “offline,” which means that after training, what is uploaded to a cyberphysical system is a fine-tuned model—a neural network in the context of deep learning. The training process essentially tunes the weights in individual neurons by exposing a neural network with large amounts of data. The neural network is calibrated after training, and simply generates outputs without learning anything new when in operation. In terms of climate change, an agent will be soon out of date. Therefore, developing a continuous learning framework is the next challenge for incorporating intelligent machines in environmental management. Second, ML consists of training and testing sessions. Scientists need training data for machines to learn from before the agent can be applied in real-world situations. In the DRL case, an agent develops its strategies in a simulated environment (e.g. video game) which can be restarted for unlimited times. However, there is no “reset button” for the environment, and if an agent somehow causes an unwanted result, there is no way to go back. This also poses ethical challenges to applying AI agents in environmental management.

Another speculative research project and some recent advances in AI research provide insights into these predicaments. In an MIT architectural thesis research, designer Ricardo Jnani Gonzalez proposed a system deeply embedded in the cryosphere environment. The system consists of a central “mind,” which can be understood as a supercomputer unit, and distributed “bodies,” which are actuators that change the physical environment. In operation, the “mind” first casts a vast array of varied actuating policies across the “bodies.” Then the “mind” evaluates the policies based on the discrepancies between projected scenarios and actual outcomes. The “mind” then updates and casts the policies to the “bodies” again. If one policy yields the best outcome, the successful experience would be embedded within the next iteration of intervention. In this way, one “body” could influence other “bodies” by knowledge exchange, through which this distributed system can gradually attune to the cryosphere environment and evolve with it.[52]

This project’s framework mirrors some widely used ML algorithms and techniques such as continuous learning, genetic algorithms, and transfer learning. It should be recognized that continuous learning has always been a theoretical premise for deep reinforcement learning—DRL is often compared with human learning through trial and error which requires lifelong and continuous efforts. In fact, there are already efforts in the AI community to develop strategies that allow agents to learn and evolve. Scientists are making promising progress in overcoming “catastrophic forgetting,” which is the major obstacle to continuous learning—an agent tends to completely and abruptly “forget” previously learned information after acquiring new knowledge.[53] In current AI applications, this theoretical

续学习主要通过不断提高人工智能系统的更新频率来实现。可以预见，在不久的将来，更多的持续学习框架和自动更新机制将会被广泛运用。这就要求设计师相应提出具有足够灵活性和适应性的理论框架以支持这些技术的实践应用。

遗传算法的灵感来源于自然选择过程——将上一代的优秀基因遗传给下一代。与此相类似，在遗传算法的训练中，一系列随机策略中的最佳策略会被保留；在下一代的训练中，这些成功策略经过变异，更新为新一套策略进行应用。随着"选择—变异"过程的循环往复，算法的性能也不断提高。同样，在环境管理方面，设计师不应追求模型的复杂性，以期生成一劳永逸的策略；相反，可以尝试利用可单独实施渐进式干预的分布式智能体，使其共享知识、共同演进。当前已有众多相关研究案例：一款名为"Romu"的机器人可将联锁板桩打入地下来建造拦水坝，在防止水土流失的同时促进干旱地区的地下水补给[54]；另一款名为"RangerBot"的水下视觉式机器人可用于保护大堡礁，它可识别并杀死以珊瑚为食的海星，并监测珊瑚礁的健康状况和水质情况。这类机器人主要依赖机器学习和计算机视觉来识别水下环境中的有害海星[55]。上述机器人都是基于机器学习不断进化并发展策略的分布式"身体"。

冈萨雷斯所设想的系统可将某一"身体"的成功策略转移给其他"身体"，这与人工智能研究中的迁移学习异曲同工，即将从某个领域中获得的知识应用于另一领域。相关案例[56]~[58]可为设计师提供借鉴：一方面，机器在分散投放到环境中之前就可以预先接受一般性知识的训练，因而可以快速适应不同的条件；另一方面，成功经验可以通过迁移学习推广到不同的环境中。

2.3 植物—机器交互

景观设计师如何开发能与植物直接互动的工具以在城市环境中现实育野？他们或可从当前的农业实践和艺术创作两种模型中汲取经验。精准农业使用传感器来监控植物，并利用机械臂在单株植物尺度施肥、浇水和收获农产品。许多现代农场已将这些机器纳入日常作业中。随着传感技术和机器人技术的不断发展，诸如FarmBot等初创公司开始专注于构建小型自动化园艺系统。[59]精准农业的目标是通过控制植物生长来提高生产力。但这种单一变量系统仅优化了植物作为生命体的其中一个方面。在某种程度上，精准农业通过消除植物的"野性"来提高生产率，强调"植物为人所用"。

continuous learning process is substituted by updating the AI models with higher frequencies. It should be anticipated that more continuous learning architectures and automated updating mechanisms will be widely and shortly available. This requires designers to develop equivalent conceptual frameworks that are flexible and adaptive enough to incorporate these techniques in practice.

Genetic algorithms are inspired by the natural selection process, in which the best qualities of the parent generation are preserved in the child generation. When training with a genetic algorithm, the parent generation represents an array of random policies, and the most effective ones are preserved. In the next generation, mutations can be introduced to diversify the preserved strategies, and a new array of updated policies can be deployed. Repeating this selection-mutation process can increase the performance of the algorithms. For environmental management, one should not speculate on one complex model that does all the hard labors to compute one-shot policies. Instead, one can imagine many distributed agents making incremental interventions individually, and they can share knowledge and evolve together. There are many examples in related research. Romu, a robot designed to build check dams by driving interlocking sheet piles into the ground, can prevent erosion and promote groundwater recharge in arid regions.[54] RangerBot is a vision-based underwater robot that can identify and kill coral-eating starfish and monitor reef health and water quality, protecting the Great Barrier Reef. It relies on ML and computer vision to identify the unwanted starfish underwater.[55] These robots can act as distributed "bodies" for ML agents to evolve and develop strategies.

Gonzalez's speculation of one body transferring successful policies to other bodies requires a technique in AI research known as transfer learning—a machine learning framework that can transfer knowledge acquired from one domain to another. Related examples[56]~[58] are inspirational for designers: on the one hand, machines can be pre-trained with general knowledge about the system before being distributed in the environment. They can quickly attune to different conditions. On the other hand, successful experiences can be generalized and applied to another case.

2.3 Plant–Machine Interaction

How can landscape architects cultivate wildness by developing tools that directly interact with the plants in urban environments? There are two existing models: one in agriculture and the other in art. Precision farming uses sensors to monitor the plants and robotic arms to fertilize, water, and harvest at an individual plant level. Many modern farms have started to incorporate these machines into daily practice. With advances in sensing and robotic technologies, startup firms focus on small-scale robotic gardening systems, such as FarmBot.[59] The goal of precision farming is to manipulate plants for a greater productivity. It is a single variant system that only optimizes one aspect of plant life. In a way, precision farming increases productivity by eliminating "wildness" in plants; plants are exploited for human use.

在艺术创作方面，艺术家戴维·鲍温利用智能技术来创造装置艺术，进而探索机器与植物之间的关系。他于2007年建造的“植物生长描绘装置”建立了机器与植物之间的反馈系统。鲍温将豌豆苗置于一瓶水培营养液中，并将瓶子挂在垂直扫描仪器上，其他工具还包括一卷纸、喷墨打印机针头和日光灯。该装置为植物提供养分和光照，并通过扫描数据绘制图纸，记录植物生长。装置每24小时完成一次绘图，而后纸卷滚动，开启下一个绘图周期。正如鲍温所述，该艺术装置的绘图结果无法预先确定，因为它可能记录植物的生长，也可能记录植物的死亡和凋零。[60]基于类似原理，鲍温于2009年创作了“生长建模装置”，分别从三个不同的角度扫描植物，再利用3D打印技术每24小时打印植物的形态。新装置不再设纸卷，取而代之的是一条传送带，每次打印完成后传送带前进约45cm，开启下一个周期。[61]在2019年创作的另一个艺术装置“植物无人机”中，植物开始充当飞行员的角色：鲍温将一株植物安装在无人机中，叶片与电极相连，植物叶片发出的生物电控制无人机飞行方向。由植物“驾驶”的无人机在夜空中飞行，长时间曝光摄影技术将飞行轨迹记录了下来。[62]

人们通常认为艺术创作仅限人类所为。然而，在以上这些艺术装置中，最终生成的绘作、模型及照片并非完全由艺术家或机器决定，它们是机器和植物共同的作品。鲍温通过破解机器原理来制造全新的系统，让植物发挥能动性，实现植物的自我表达和艺术创作。

上述案例表明，智能系统的开发可以绕开“控制”和“优化”这两个概念。来自弗吉尼亚大学的设计师开发了一个名为“算法种植平台”的原型设计项目②，平台由机械装置、照明系统和种植槽组成（图4）。机械装置可配备传感器和自定义执行器来直接与植物互动（如修剪和浇水）。该项目的目标是构建机器与植物之间的松散耦合，而非利用机器来促进植物生长。研究团队期望观察植物如何对机器的算法管理做出反馈，而植物的反馈又如何推动机器适应和调整其

Another model is in art. Artist David Bowen used cybernetic technologies to create art projects that explore the relationship between machines and plant materials. Growth Rendering Device (2007) was such a feedback system: A pea plant was suspended in a hydroponic solution in a bottle attached to a vertical scanner, a roll of paper, an inkjet printer head, and a light. The system provided food and light to the plants and recorded their growth with drawings. A drawing was produced every 24 hours, and then the system scrolled the roll of paper and started the next drawing cycle. As Bowen suggested, this work's outcome was not predetermined because it might record growth, decay or demise of the plant.[60] Based on a similar principle, Growth Modeling Device (2009) scanned a plant from three different angles and 3D printed the plant every 24 hours. Instead of scrolling a paper roll, a conveyor belt advanced approximately 17 inches after each printing.[61] In the art project Plant Drone (2019), Bowen made a plant pilot: A drone was mounted with a plant whose leaves were attached to electrodes. Bioelectricity emitted from the plant leaves became the input to the drone's movements. The plant piloted the drone under the night sky, and the movements were captured with long-exposure photography.[62]

Art production is commonly assumed as human endeavors. Nevertheless, in these projects, the drawings, models or photographs were not completely determined by the artist or the machines; instead, they were co-produced results by machines and plants. Bowen hacked machines and built systems that allowed plants to express themselves and exercise their agency to produce art.

These examples show that it is possible to develop cybernetic systems that bypass control and optimization. Algorithmic Cultivation, a prototyping project developed by designers from the University of Virginia②, is a platform consisting of robotic armatures, lighting systems, and planters (Fig. 4). The robotic armatures can be equipped with sensors and customized actuators to directly interact with

② “算法种植平台”由耿百利、罗宾·德里普斯、露西亚·菲尼和张雯菁开发，该项目是弗吉尼亚大学人文信息实验室资助的智慧环境小组所开发的5个项目之一。

② Algorithmic Cultivation was developed by Bradley Cantrell, Robin Dripps, Lucia Phinney, and Emma Mendel. It is one of the 5 projects developed within the Smart Environment Group, which is funded by Humanities Informatics Lab, University of Virginia.

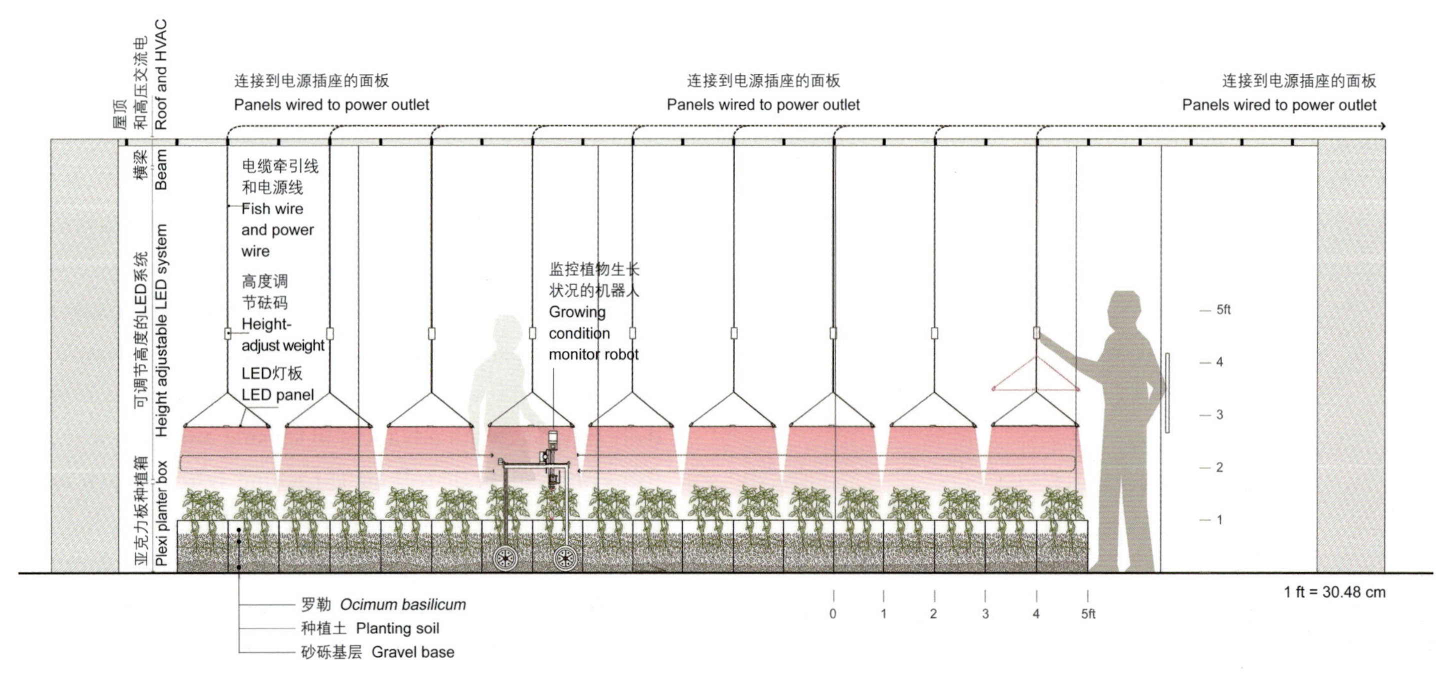

4-1

策略。机器和植物之间将形成正反馈回路，共同演生出离轨的行为。由此产生的结果可视为“高度培育的野”，因为其间的管理逻辑并非人类所熟知或易于理解的（图5）。

从概念上讲，算法种植平台介于工程手段（如精准农业）与艺术表达（如鲍文的艺术装置）之间。一方面，该项目并非可产品化的工业原型。当前市场上已有众多类似系统，尤其是在精准农业和机器人种植领域。另一方面，与概念化的艺术表达不同，算法种植平台是一个持续的探索过程，具有实用价值。该项目为师生们提供了一个聚焦于机器和植物之间相互作用的景观策略测试平台，它也值得设计师更进一步在艺术与科学间进行探索。我们可以将这一项目中应用的方法理解为“后原型开发”，它利用一种全新的框架来解读人们所熟知的主流实践，使其变得陌生，进而鼓励人们重新理解这些实践并探寻更多未知的领域。

3 结语：迈向技术多样性与机器的“野”

本文认识到荒野概念的多元性，鼓励设计师通过构建“新形式的野”来拓展对自然和荒野的认知。设计城市荒野并非要建造看起来“自然”和“野生”的风景或恢复历史生态格局。本文认为，应当探索不同于仅利用自然过程来实施再野化的育野策略：通过促进各种非人物种和智能机器的自主性，让它们也成为创造景观的积极协作者。基于该理念，本文探讨了智能机器如何能够大力推进城市环境中野地的构建，并基于科学、工程和景观研究实例，构想了在景观和环境实践中探讨机器智能的理论框架。

该框架的核心——“技术多样性”和“机器生态”也是哲学家许煜的关键思想，可以帮助我们反观本文所述案例。许煜认为，物种的多样性是生物间生态关系的基础，因而生态取决于生物多样性[63]。相

4-1. 算法种植平台装备示意图
4-2. 算法种植平台装备实景图

4-1. Schematic diagram of the Algorithmic Cultivation platform setup
4-2. Photo of the Algorithmic Cultivation platform setup

© Bradley Cantrell, Robin Dripps, Lucia Phinney, Emma Mendel
4-2

the plants, such as pruning and watering. Rather than using machines to optimize plant growth, this project aims to develop loose couplings between machines and plants. The team is interested in observing how plants are responding to algorithmic management and, in turn, how the machine starts to adapt and attune to the plants' growth. The machine and plants would form positive feedback loops that, together, produce spin-off and emergent behaviors. The outcome can be said as highly cultivated wildness, as the logic for management is foreign and not easily understood by human observers (Fig. 5).

Conceptually, Algorithmic Cultivation sits between engineering approaches such as the precision farming and artistic expressions such as Bowen's installations. On the one hand, the project is not an industrial prototype that can be monetized as a product. There are already a plenty of similar systems in the market, especially when considering precision farming and robotic agriculture. On the other hand, unlike artistic expressions that function at a conceptual level, Algorithmic Cultivation is an ongoing process with a sense of pragmatism. The project establishes a platform for faculties and students to test out landscape strategies that focus on the interactions between machines and plants. From this vantage, it merits further explorations between art and science. The technique used in this project can be conceptualized as *post-prototyping* because it denaturalizes mainstream practices and reframes them in a different discourse to cultivate alternative understandings and reveal unexplored territories.

3 Conclusion: Towards Technodiversity and Wildness in Machines

This paper recognizes the plurality in the wilderness concept and challenges designers to expand the conception of nature and wilderness by constructing "new wilds." Designing urban wilds is not about constructing sceneries that look "natural" and "wild" or restoring historical ecological patterns. Instead, this paper proposes an alternative framework for rewilding to what is practiced with natural processes alone. Cultivated wildness suggests a distinct new type of practices which is about promoting the autonomy of different nonhuman species along with machine agents which are all active co-conspirators in shaping the landscapes. With this conviction, the paper explores how intelligent machines can be important actors in constructing wild experiences in urban environments. Drawing examples from science, engineering, and landscape research, the paper maps out a framework to conceptualize machine intelligence in landscape and environmental design practices.

At the heart of this framework is a sense of "technodiversity" and "ecology of machines," which are two key concepts in philosopher Yuk Hui's thinking that can help us reflect on the cases presented in this paper. Hui's notion of ecology is based on biodiversity because the diversity in species is the fundament for ecological relations between beings.[63] Consequently, "ecology of machines" relies on technodiversity. The advance of one technique as a universal solution (e.g. precision farming becoming the go-to approach in agriculture) means the elimination of other cultural techniques: there was technodiversity before precision farming became the

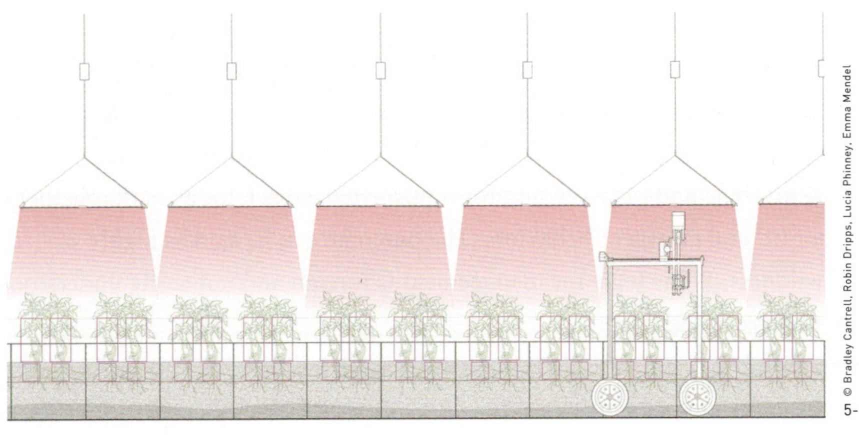

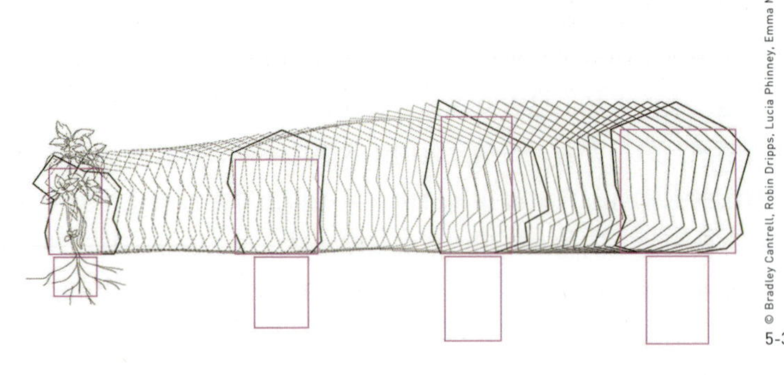

5. 概念图显示，随着时间的推移，不同植物个体对算法培育策略的反馈各有差异，且植物形态和株型也呈现出“野性”（紫色方框表示植物的地上及地下部分）。

5. Conceptual diagrams showing individual plants responding to algorithmic cultivation strategies differently over time and exhibiting wildness in terms of plant form and architecture (purple boxes in the diagram represent plant shoots and roots).

应的，所谓“机器生态”则取决于“技术多样性”。若将某种技术作为普世方法（如将精准农业作为农业实践的首选手段），便会抹杀其他“文化技术”：这意味着技术多样性仅存在于精准农业成为主流之前。在这里，技术多样性指通过不同的认知框架来理解同一个机器，而非同一个机器的不同使用方法。尽管当下机器种类繁多，但主流技术发展仍依赖单一的技术框架，即不断追求效率，扩大人类在环境中的影响力；这也意味着当前尚未形成“机器生态”。因此，本文通过案例分析，期望在主流技术畅想（实现更好的人为控制）之下唤起人们对技术多样性的思考。

在某种程度上，育野也意味着意识到机器的“野”（即不受控制）。技术是人类与其他物种和环境联系的媒介，但技术发展的单一愿景拘囿了人们的思想，剥夺了物种间本有可能形成的相互作用与联系途径。因此，本文认为，荒野的生物多样性保护离不开技术多样性的探索，我们应当通过多元的技术与框架来超越狭隘的愿景。**LAF**

mainstream solution. Technodiversity does not mean to use a machine in different ways, but to explore a machine with different epistemic frameworks. Even though there are different machines, contemporary mainstream technological development is still a monoculture with a single framework for the optimization of efficiency to extend human influence in the environment; nowadays there is no “ecology of machines.” The cases presented in this paper are efforts to cultivate a sense of technodiversity within the mainstream technological imagination built around human control.

To some extent, the notion of cultivated wildness also means recognizing the sense of wildness found in machines. Technologies are media through which humans connect with other species and the environment. But a singular vision on technological development promotes a monocultural approach that eliminates other possibilities that species could connect and interact with each other. Thus, one important aspect of preserving biodiversity in wild places is preserving technodiversity—different techniques and frameworks of using the tools beyond a singular vision. **LAF**

致谢

感谢审稿人及《景观设计学》编辑部在同行评议过程中给予本文的大力支持。

ACKNOWLEDGEMENTS

The authors thank the reviewers’ engagement and the support by editors of *Landscape Architecture Frontiers* journal in the exchange of ideas in the peer-review process.

REFERENCES

[1] Cronon, W. (1995). The trouble with wilderness; Or, getting back to the wrong nature. In W. Cronon (Ed.), *Uncommon Ground: Toward Reinventing Nature* (1st ed., pp. 69-90). New York, NY: W.W. Norton & Company.

[2] Cronon, W. (Ed.). (1995). *Uncommon Ground: Toward Reinventing Nature*. New York, NY: W.W. Norton & Company.

[3] Eder, K. (1996). *The Social Construction of Nature: A Sociology of Ecological Enlightenment*. Thousand Oaks, CA: SAGE Publications.

[4] Demeritt, D. (2002). What is the 'social construction of nature'? A typology and sympathetic critique. *Progress in Human Geography*, 26(6), 767-790. https://doi.org/10.1191/0309132502ph402oa

[5] Evernden, N. (1985). Constructing the natural: The darker side of the environmental movement. *The North American Review*, 270(1), 15-19.

[6] Smith, N. (2008). *Uneven Development: Nature, Capital, and the Production of Space* (3rd ed.). Athens, GA: University of Georgia Press.

[7] Kuhn, T. S. (2012). *The Structure of Scientific Revolutions*. Chicago, IL: University of Chicago Press.

[8] Bijker, W. E. (2010). How is technology made?—That is the question!. *Cambridge Journal of Economics*, 34(1), 63-76. https://doi.org/10.1093/cje/bep068

[9] Bijker, W. E., Hughes, T. P., & Pinch, T. (Eds.). (1987). *The Social Construction of Technological Systems: New Directions in the Sociology and History of Technology*. Cambridge, MA: The MIT Press.

[10] Latour, B. (1987). *Science in Action: How to Follow Scientists and Engineers Through Society*. Cambridge, MA: Harvard University Press.

[11] Daston, L., & Galison, P. (2007). *Objectivity*. New York, NY: Zone Books.

[12] Pinch, T. J., & Bijker, W. E. (1984). The Social construction of facts and artefacts: Or how the sociology of science and the sociology of technology might benefit each other. *Social Studies of Science*, 14(3), 399-441. https://doi.org/10.1177/030631284014003004

[13] Loftus, A. (2017). Production of nature. In D. Richardson, N. Castree, M. F. Goodchild, A. Kobayashi, W. Liu, & R. A. Marston (Eds.), *International Encyclopedia of Geography* (pp. 1-6). Hoboken, NJ: John Wiley & Sons. https://doi.org/10.1002/9781118786352.wbieg0289

[14] Nye, D. E. (1994). *American Technological Sublime*. Cambridge, MA: The MIT Press.

[15] Nye, D. E. (Ed.). (2000). *Technologies of Landscape: From Reaping to Recycling*. Amherst, MA: University of Massachusetts Press.

[16] Nye, D. E. (2003). *America as Second Creation: Technology and Narratives of New Beginnings*. Cambridge, MA: The MIT Press.

[17] Reuss, M., & Cutcliffe, S. H. (Eds.). (2010). *The Illusory Boundary: Environment and Technology in History*. Charlottesville, VA: University of Virginia Press.

[18] Bell, K. (2020). *Working-Class Environmentalism: An Agenda for a Just and Fair Transition to Sustainability*. London, England: Palgrave Macmillan.

[19] Hopson, M. (2011). The wilderness myth: How the failure of the American national park model threatens the survival of the lyaelima tribe and the bonobo chimpanzee. *Environmental and Earth Law Journal (EELJ)*, 1(1), 61-102. Retrieved from https://lawpublications.barry.edu/ejejj/vol1/iss1/4

[20] Freedman, E. (2002). When indigenous rights and wilderness collide: Prosecution of Native Americans for using motors in Minnesota's Boundary Waters Canoe Wilderness Area. *American Indian Quarterly*, 26(3), 378-392. doi:10.1353/aiq.2003.0037

[21] Rechciński, M., Tusznio, J., & Grodzińska-Jurczak, M. (2019). Protected area conflicts: A state-of-the-art review and a proposed integrated conceptual framework for reclaiming the role of geography. *Biodiversity and Conservation*, 28(10), 2463-2498. https://doi.org/10.1007/s10531-019-01790-z

[22] Ellis, E. C. (2015). Ecology in an anthropogenic biosphere. *Ecological Monographs*, 85(3), 287-331. https://doi.org/10.1890/14-2274.1

[23] Hobbs, R. J., Higgs, E. S., & Hall, C. (2013). *Novel Ecosystems: Intervening in the New Ecological World Order*. Hoboken, NJ: Wiley-Blackwell.

[24] Martin, L. J., Quinn, J. E., Ellis, E. C., Shaw, M. R., Dorning, M. A., Hallett, L. M., ... Wiederholt, R. (2014). Conservation opportunities across the world's anthromes. *Diversity and Distributions*, 20(7), 745-755. https://doi.org/10.1111/ddi.12220

[25] Ellis, E. C. (2019). To conserve nature in the Anthropocene, Half Earth is not nearly enough. *One Earth*, 1(2), 163-167. https://doi.org/10.1016/j.oneear.2019.10.009

[26] Corlett, R. T. (2016). Restoration, reintroduction, and Rewilding in a changing world. *Trends in Ecology & Evolution*, 31(6), 453-462. https://doi.org/10.1016/j.tree.2016.02.017

[27] Svenning, J. -C., Pedersen, P. B. M., Donlan, C. J., Ejrnæs, R., Faurby, S., Galetti, M., ... Vera, F. W. M. (2016). Science for a wilder Anthropocene: Synthesis and future directions for trophic rewilding research. *Proceedings of the National Academy of Sciences*, 113(4), 898-906. https://doi.org/10.1073/pnas.1502556112

[28] Cantrell, B., Martin, L. J., & Ellis, E. C. (2017). Designing autonomy: Opportunities for new wildness in the Anthropocene. *Trends in Ecology & Evolution*, 32(3), 156-166. https://doi.org/10.1016/j.tree.2016.12.004

[29] Harman, G. (2018). *Object-Oriented Ontology: A New Theory of Everything*. London, England: Penguin UK.

[30] Morton, T. (2007). *Ecology Without Nature: Rethinking Environmental Aesthetics*. Cambridge, MA: Harvard University Press.

[31] Morton, T. (2016). *Dark Ecology: For a logic of future coexistence*. New York, NY: Columbia University Press.

[32] Bryant, L. R. (2014). *Onto-Cartography: An Ontology of Machines and Media*. Edinburgh, United Kingdom: Edinburgh University Press.

[33] Haraway, D. (2010). When species meet: Staying with the trouble. *Environment and Planning D: Society and Space*, 28(1), 53-55. https://doi.org/10.1068/d2706wsh

[34] Bennett, J. (2010). *Vibrant Matter: A Political Ecology of Things*. Durham, NC: Duke University Press.

[35] Houston, D., Hillier, J., MacCallum, D., Steele, W., & Byrne, J. (2018). Make kin, not cities! Multispecies entanglements and 'becoming-world' in planning theory. *Planning Theory*, 17(2), 190-212. https://doi.org/10.1177/1473095216688042

[36] Prominski, M. (2014). Andscapes: Concepts of nature and culture for landscape architecture in the 'Anthropocene.' *Journal of Landscape Architecture*, 9(1), 6-19. https://doi.org/10.1080/18626033.2014.898819

[37] Cantrell, B., & Holtzman, J. (2016). *Responsive landscapes: Strategies for responsive technologies in landscape architecture*. Milton, United Kingdom: Routledge.

[38] Reed, C., & Lister, N. -M. (Eds.). (2014). *Projective Ecologies*. New York, NY: Actar.

[39] Klosterwill, K. (2019). The shifting position of animals in landscape theory. *Landscape Journal*, 38(1-2), 129-146. https://doi.org/10.3368/lj.38.1-2.129

[40] Robinson, A., & Davis, B. (2018). From solution space to interface. In B. Cantrell, & A. Mekies (Eds.), *Codify: Parametric and Computational Design in Landscape Architecture* (pp. 155-168). London, England: Routledge.

[41] Meyer, E. K. (2008). Sustaining beauty. The performance of appearance: A manifesto in three parts. *Journal of Landscape Architecture*, 3(1), 6-23. https://doi.org/10.1080/18626033.2008.9723392

[42] Meyer, E. K. (2017). Beyond "Sustaining Beauty": Musings on a manifesto. In M. E. Deming (Ed.), *Values in Landscape Architecture and Environmental Design: Finding Center in Theory and Practice* (pp. 30-53). Baton Rouge, LA: Louisiana State University Press.

[43] Silver, D., Schrittwieser, J., Simonyan, K., Antonoglou, I., Huang, A., Guez, A., ... Hassabis, D. (2017). Mastering the game of Go without human knowledge. *Nature*, 550(7676), 354-359. https://doi.org/10.1038/nature24270

[44] Vinyals, O., Babuschkin, I., Czarnecki, W. M., Mathieu, M., Dudzik, A., Chung, J., ... Silver, D. (2019). Grandmaster level in StarCraft II using multi-agent reinforcement learning. *Nature*, 575(7782), 350-354. https://doi.org/10.1038/s41586-019-1724-z

[45] Saliba, S. M., Bowes, B. D., Adams, S., Beling, P. A., & Goodall, J. L. (2020). Deep reinforcement learning with uncertain data for real-time stormwater system control and flood mitigation. *Water*, 12(11), 3222. https://doi.org/10.3390/w12113222

[46] Bowes, B. D., Tavakoli, A., Wang, C., Heydarian, A., Behl, M., Beling, P. A., & Goodall, J. L. (2020). Flood mitigation in coastal urban catchments using real-time stormwater infrastructure control and reinforcement learning. *Journal of Hydroinformatics*, jh2020080. https://doi.org/10.2166/hydro.2020.080

[47] *South Florida Water Management District*. (n.d.). Retrieved from https://www.sfwmd.gov/

[48] OptiRTC, Inc. (n.d.). *Optimizing Stormwater Management*. Retrieved from https://optirtc.com/

[49] *Xylem*. (n.d.). Retrieved from https://www.xylem.com/en-us/

[50] Estrada, L. (2016). Prototyping. *Towards SentienceTM: Attuning the Los Angeles River's fluvial morphology*. Retrieved from https://towardssentience.com/prototyping

[51] Estrada, L. (2018). Towards sentience. In B. Cantrell, & A. Mekies (Eds.), *Codify: Parametric and Computational Design in Landscape Architecture* (pp. 279-288). London, England: Routledge.

[52] Ramirez Gonzalez, R. J. (2016). *Design for a mind with many bodies: Cybernetic micro-interventions in the cryosphere* (Master's thesis, Massachusetts Institute of Technology). Retrieved from https://dspace.mit.edu/handle/1721.1/106370

[53] Parisi, G. I., Kemker, R., Part, J. L., Kanan, C., & Wermter, S. (2019). Continual lifelong learning with neural networks: A review. *Neural Networks*, (113), 54-71. https://doi.org/10.1016/j.neunet.2019.01.012

[54] Melenbrink, N., Rinderspacher, K., Menges, A., & Werfel, J. (2020). Autonomous anchoring for robotic construction. *Automation in Construction*, (120), 103391. https://doi.org/10.1016/j.autcon.2020.103391

[55] Great Barrier Reef Foundation. (n.d.). *RangerBot*. Retrieved from https://www.barrierreef.org/what-we-do/projects/rangerbot

[56] Brown, T. B., Mann, B., Ryder, N., Subbiah, M., Kaplan, J., Dhariwal, P., ... Amodei, D. (2020). Language models are few-shot learners. *ArXiv:2005.14165 [cs.CL]*. Retrieved from http://arxiv.org/abs/2005.14165

[57] Chen, T., Murali, A., & Gupta, A. (2019). Hardware Conditioned Policies for Multi-Robot Transfer Learning. *ArXiv:1811.09864 [cs.RO]*. Retrieved from http://arxiv.org/abs/1811.09864

[58] Barekatain, M., Yonetani, R., & Hamaya, M. (2019). MULTIPOLAR: Multi-Source Policy Aggregation for Transfer Reinforcement Learning between Diverse Environmental Dynamics. *ArXiv:1909.13111 [cs.LG]*. doi:10.24963/ijcai.2020/430. Retrieved from http://arxiv.org/abs/1909.13111

[59] *FarmBot | Open-Source CNC Farming*. (n.d.). Retrieved from https://farm.bot/

[60] Bowen, D. (2007). *Growth Rendering Device*. Retrieved from https://www.dwbowen.com/growth-rendering-device

[61] Bowen, D. (2009). *Growth Modeling Device*. Retrieved from https://www.dwbowen.com/growth-modeling-device

[62] Bowen, D. (2019). *Plant Drone*. Retrieved from https://www.dwbowen.com/plantdrone

[63] Hui, Y. (2020). Machine and Ecology. *Angelaki*, 25(4), 54-66. https://doi.org/10.1080/0969725X.2020.1790835

景观规划视角下的生态系统服务研究动态
——第十届生态系统服务伙伴全球会议综述
Research Trends of Ecosystem Services From the Perspective of Landscape Planning —Summary on the 10th Ecosystem Services Partnership World Conference

姜芊孜
山东建筑大学建筑城规学院副教授

窦月含
南方科技大学环境科学与工程学院博士后

任震*
山东建筑大学建筑城规学院副院长、副教授

JIANG Qianzi
Associate Professor of School of Architecture and Urban Planning, Shandong Jianzhu University

DOU Yuehan
Post Doctorate of School of Environmental Science and Engineering, Southern University of Science and Technology

REN Zhen
Deputy Dean and Associate Professor of School of Architecture and Urban Planning, Shandong Jianzhu University

*通讯作者
地址：山东省济南市临港南区凤鸣路1000号
邮编：250101
邮箱：arcren@163.com

摘要

生态系统服务伙伴全球会议是生态系统服务领域最高水平的学术会议之一，聚焦世界范围内生态系统服务的研究与实践，是掌握研究前沿动态的重要途径。基于部分学者已将生态系统服务评价指标及评价方法等融入景观规划设计的理论与实践之中这一现状，本文筛选出第十届会议中与景观规划相关的分论坛主题，结合各分论坛中的发言进行总结，从多类型景观的生态系统服务研究、生态系统服务在规划与管理中的应用，以及生态系统服务制图与建模三个视角对研究及实践热点进行分析和归纳。总结而言，今后将生态系统服务研究应用于景观规划领域的热点在于：1）探索面向多种景观类型的态系统服务评价；2）探索将生态系统服务融入各类景观规划的理论与实践框架；3）探索适用于景观规划与管理的生态系统服务综合建模与制图工具。

关键词

生态系统服务；景观规划；研究议题；生态系统服务伙伴全球会议；会议综述；基于自然的解决方案；生态基础设施

ABSTRACT

The Ecosystem Services Partnership (ESP) Conference is one of the highest-level global academic conferences on ecosystem service (ES) research. Focusing on the research and practice of ES worldwide, ESP Conference offers an important way to grasp the cutting-edge knowledge for scholars and professionals. Currently, ES evaluation indicators and evaluation methods have been integrated into the research and practice of landscape planning and design. This paper sorted out the break-out session themes at the 10th ESP Conference related to landscape planning and summarized the research presented in each session. It analyzed and summarized the research and practice hot spots from 3 perspectives: multiple landscape types, the application of ES in planning and management, and ES mapping and modeling. Finally, the paper offers insights on future interests of the application of ES research into landscape planning, including 1) exploring ES evaluation for multiple landscape types; 2) exploring the theoretical and practical frameworks for integrating ES Science into landscape planning; and 3) exploring integrated ES modeling and mapping tools for landscape planning and management.

KEYWORDS

Ecosystem Services; Landscape Planning; Research Interests; Ecosystem Service Partnership World Conference; Conference Summary; Nature-Based Solutions; Ecological Infrastructure

基金项目

国家自然科学基金青年基金项目“城市水系廊道生态系统服务供需均衡评价研究”（编号：51908332）
教育部人文社会科学研究青年基金项目“基于水生态系统服务供给与需求的城市绿地评价及布局优化”（编号：18YJCZH066）
山东省自然科学基金博士基金项目“基于水生态服务供给与社会需求的城市公园绿地评价及布局优化”（编号：ZR2017BEE075）
国家自然科学基金青年基金项目“生态正义对城市绿地布局的影响机制及发展预测研究——以日照市主城区为例”（编号：51808320）
山东省高等学校青创科技支持计划“区域绿色基础设施协同调控与生态安全格局构建创新团队”（编号：2020KJG004）
山东省自然科学基金培养基金项目“基于物质自循环的乡村空间格局优化研究”（编号：ZR2019PEE045）

RESEARCH FUNDS

Study on the Equilibrium Evaluation of Ecosystem Services Supply-Demand of Urban Water Corridors, National Natural Science Foundation of China (No. 51908332)
Urban Green Space Evaluation and Layout Optimization Based on the Supply and Demand of Water-Related Ecosystem Services, Liberal Arts and Social Sciences Foundation, Ministry of Education in China (No. 18YJCZH066)
Urban Park Green Space Evaluation and Layout Optimization Based on the Supply and Social Demand of Water-Related Ecosystem Services, Natural Science Foundation of Shandong Province (No. ZR2017BEE075)
Study on the Impact Mechanism and Trends of Ecological Justice Through the Layout Improvement of Urban Green Space—Taking the Central Area of Rizhao City as an Example, National Natural Science Foundation of China (No. 51808320)
Innovation Team of Regional Green Infrastructure Coordinated Regulation and Ecological Security Pattern Construction, Support Plan for Youth Entrepreneurship and Technology in Colleges and Universities of Shandong Province (No. 2020KJG004)
Optimization of Spatial Pattern of Rural Areas based on Material Self-Circular Metabolism, Natural Science Foundation of Shandong Province (No. ZR2019PEE045)

编辑 | 汪默英、田乐
翻译 | 姜芊孜、田乐、窦月含、任震
EDITED BY | WANG Moying, Tina TIAN
TRANSLATED BY | JIANG Qianzi, Tina TIAN, DOU Yuehan, REN Zhen

https://doi.org/10.15302/J-LAF-0-020012
收稿时间 RECEIVED DATE | 2020-05-27

中图分类号 | TU98, X171.1
文献标识码 | A

1 引言

生态系统服务（Ecosystem Service，简称ES）是衔接城市居民生活福祉和生境斑块自然生态过程的核心概念[1]。中国的相关研究源起于生态学[2]及地理学[3][4]领域，近些年逐渐受到城市规划[5]、景观设计[6]-[10]等领域学者的关注。部分学者已经开始尝试将ES评价指标及评价方法等融入景观规划设计的理论与实践之中。景观规划是指基于对自然和人文过程的认识，协调人与自然关系的过程；具体而言就是为某些使用目的安排最合适的地方和在特定地方安排最恰当的土地利用[11]，是融国土规划、城乡建设规划、生态保护规划和人居环境建设工程设计于一体的学科[12]。景观规划能够通过改变土地利用方式、土地覆被类型，调整景观格局结构与功能，影响ES的类型、分布及产生过程[13]。ES研究方法能够将ES的结构与功能、需求与供给等信息落到具体的环境空间之中，协调多个利益相关方，评价结果易理解，为解决空间规划问题提供了有力工具[13]。已有研究从景观规划与ES的关系入手，探讨ES研究方法如何应用于景观规划[8]-[10][14]。然而，目前景观规划领域中以会议为研究对象，对ES前沿热点进行梳理及分析的研究尚不多见。本文拟以全球ES领域最高水平的学术会议之一的"生态系统服务伙伴"全球会议（简称ESP会议）为例，通过梳理第十届会议内容，为景观规划视角下的ES研究与整合ES的景观规划实践提供借鉴。尽管会议综述具有一定时效性，但也可以从一定程度上弥补景观规划领域对ES研究与实践前沿动态关注的不足。

2 ESP全球会议对ES研究与实践的推动

ESP全球会议于2008年首次举办，现已召开了10次会议（表1）。从对ES概念的反思，到关注研究方法、解决方案，ESP全球会议一直致力于加强ES相关前沿成果的交流，呼吁研究与实践融合，推动了与生态系统保护和可持续发展相关的科学—政策—实践界面上的研究与实践发展（图1）。

第十届会议以"ES科学研究、政策与实践不断进步的十年：面向可持续未来"为主题，围绕自然保护、景观修复、可持续生态系统管理等方向展开讨论。此次会议的参会者来自65个国家和地区，参会人数超过750人。尽管ES研究已经积淀了丰富的研究成果，但是将这些科研成果融入到当前世界各地的政策与在地实践之中依然是一个巨大的挑战。

1 Introduction

Ecosystem Services (ES) is the key intermediating concept between urban residents' well-beings and the natural / ecological processes of habitat patches[1]. The associated research in China originates from the fields of Ecology[2] and Geography[3][4], and sees an increase in Urban Planning[5], Landscape Architecture[6]-[10], and other disciplines in recent years. Many scholars have integrated ES evaluation indicators and methods into the theoretical and practice exploration in landscape planning and design. Landscape planning refers to the process of coordinating the human–nature relationship through the understanding of natural evolution and socio-economic and cultural activities of the human society. Specifically, the discipline is about the appropriate organization of spatial functions and the best arrangement of land uses[11]; it covers national land planning, urban and rural construction planning, ecological protection planning, and engineering design of human settlement construction[12]. Landscape planning can impact the types, distribution, and production process of ES by altering the structure and function of landscape patterns, land use, and land-cover typologies[13]. ES research methods offer an efficient tool to address spatial planning issues by matching with and mapping the data of ES structure and function, demand and supply onto physical environments to meet the needs of various stakeholders and to develop easily-understood evaluation outcomes[13]. Existing studies focus on the relationship between landscape planning and ES and explore how ES research methods can be applied in landscape planning[8]-[10][14]. However, there are few research from the field of landscape planning systematically reviewing the ES research interests widely discussed at academic conferences. Focusing on the Ecosystem Services Partnership World Conference (hereafter ESP Conference), one of the world's highest-level academic conferences on ES, this paper, though might be deficient in timeliness, reviews and sorts out the cutting-edge ES research interests that will be beneficial for the research and practice of landscape planning.

2 ESP Conference to Promote the Research and Practice of ES Globally

The ESP Conference has held 10 conferences since 2008 (Table 1). By encouraging reflection on ES concepts and by presenting cutting-edge research methods and solutions, ESP Conference is committed to the integration of research and application, and to facilitate the development of ecosystem protection and sustainability in dimensions of scientific study, policy making, and practice (Fig. 1).

With the theme being "10 years advancing ES science, policy, and practice for a sustainable future," the 10th ESP Conference focused on the interests of nature protection, landscape restoration, and sustainable ecosystem management. The conference gathered more than 750 attendees from 65 countries and regions. Although existing ES research outcomes are fruitful, it is still challenging to apply these research results into the current policy making and local practice around the world.

表1：历届ESP全球会议主题
Table 1: Themes of ESP Conferences

会议年份 Year	会议主题 Theme	会议城市 Host city
第一届 The 1st ESP Conference (2008)	ES：关注问题的解决方案还是需要解决的问题? ES: Solution for problems or a problem that needs solution?	德国基尔 Kiel, Germany
第二届 The 2nd ESP Conference (2009)	ES建模 Modeling ES	意大利莱切 Lecce, Italy
第三届 The 3rd ESP Conference (2010)	维持自然资本和ES解决方案 Solutions for sustaining natural capital and ES	德国基尔 Kiel, Germany
第四届 The 4th ESP Conference (2011)	ES：科学研究与实践的融合 ES: Integrating science and practice	荷兰瓦赫宁根 Wageningen, the Netherlands
第五届 The 5th ESP Conference (2012)	ES时代的来临：融合人类福祉可持续性的科学研究、政策与参与 ES come of age: Linking science, policy, and participation for sustainable human well-being	美国波特兰 Portland, USA
第六届 The 6th ESP Conference (2013)	ES价值评估 Making ES count!	印度尼西亚巴厘岛 Bali, Indonesia
第七届 The 7th ESP Conference (2014)	提升公共利益的地方行动 Local action for the common good	哥斯达黎加圣何塞 San José, Costa Rica
第八届 The 8th ESP Conference (2015)	为了自然、人类与繁荣的ES ES for nature, people, and prosperity	南非斯泰伦博斯 Stellenbosch, South Africa
第九届 The 9th ESP Conference (2017)	增强ES，促进生态文明建设：借助基于自然的解决方案修复人与景观的联系 ES for eco-civilization: Restoring connections between people and landscapes through nature-based solutions	中国深圳 Shenzhen, China
第十届 The 10th ESP Conference (2019)	ES科学研究、政策与实践不断进步的十年：面向可持续未来 10 years advancing ES science, policy, and practice for a sustainable future	德国汉诺威 Hannover, Germany

注
更多会议主题信息请访问EPS全球会议官方网站。

NOTE
Please visit the official website of EPS Conference for more information about the conference themes.

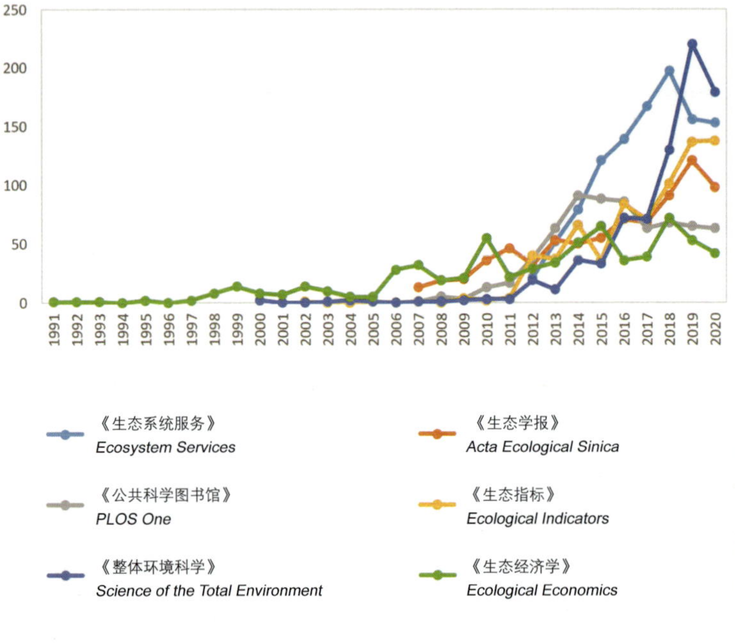

1 © 姜芊孜，窦月含，任震

1. 自2008年以来ES相关研究呈增长趋势（数据来源：Scopus数据库）

1. ES-related research has witnessed an increase in number since 2008 (Source: Scopus database)

3 Research Hotspots Related to Landscape Planning

The 10th ESP Conference consisted of biome working group sessions, thematic working group sessions, general sessions, and sectoral working group sessions, inviting 7 keynote speakers, organizing 51 break-out sessions and nearly 600 lectures, and presenting 160 posters. This paper selects 17 session topics related to landscape planning according to the official conference manual (Tables 2 ~ 4), and reviews the literature abstracts, reports, and other documents under each topic, and then sorts out the topics into 3 categories respectively focusing on 1) research object, 2) planning type, and 3) modeling and mapping method.

3.1 ES Research Among Multiple Landscape Types

ES research involves multiple landscape types such as urban landscape, ocean, river, wetland, forest, alpine area, and polar regions. In this paper, the research hotspots, difficulties, and practice applications on representative research objects, including urban landscapes, river, lake, and wetland landscapes, and forest landscapes are expanded in this paper (Table 2).

3.1.1 Urban Landscapes

By the year 2020, urban population has accounted for 56.2% of the total global population①. As one of the most important terrestrial habitat types for

表2：多类型景观的ES研究相关分会场主题
Table 2: Break-out session topics related to ES research among multiple landscape types

研究对象 Research object	研究主题 Research topic	分会场编号 Break-out session code	分会场主题 Break-out session theme
城市景观 Urban landscape	城市ES Urban ES	B10a	城市ES动态、复杂性及可持续城市发展的挑战 Urban ES: Dynamics, complexities, and challenges for sustainable urban development
	城市ES评估 Urban ES assessment	B10c	推进城市ES评估，创建更具包容性和公正性的城市 Advancing urban ES assessment for more inclusive and just cities
	城市绿色基础设施 Urban green infrastructure	B10d	影响城市生态系统正负服务的城市绿色基础设施因素 Urban green infrastructure: Factors shaping urban ES and disservices
	城市开放空间 Urban open spaces	B10e	城市和城市周边开放空间ES的治理途径 Governance approaches for ES in urban and peri-urban open spaces
	城市文化ES Urban cultural ES	T9	城市区域中的文化ES与公众健康 Cultural ES and public health in urban areas
海洋景观 Ocean landscape	珊瑚礁 Coral reef	B1b	从热带到两极：海洋文化ES评估 From the tropics to the poles: Assessing marine cultural ES
	海洋 Ocean	T6a	人类世时代海洋ES评估 Valuing marine ES in the age of Anthropocene
河湖湿地景观 River, lake, and wetland landscape	河流与湿地 Riverine and wetland	B2a	河流与湿地ES评价方法 ES assessment methods for riverine and wetland ecosystems
森林景观 Forest landscape	森林与林地 Forest and woodland	B3	半天然林和人工林：面向土地利用和气候变化的ES与权衡 Semi-natural forests and forest plantations: ES and trade-offs in the face of land use and climate change

表3：ES在景观规划与管理中的应用相关分会场主题
Table 3: Break-out session topics related to the application of ES research in landscape planning and management types

规划类型 Planning type	分会场编号 Break-out session code	分会场主题 Break-out session theme
城乡景观规划 Urban and rural landscape planning	B9-T18c	城乡协同ES治理：搭建科学研究与决策的桥梁 Governance of ES for rural-urban synergies: Bridging science and decision-making
	B10b	通过基于自然的解决方案提升城市可持续性与ES Nature-based solutions for enhancing urban sustainability and ES
	T14b	基于景观规划和管理评估景观结构对ES的影响：平衡细节和可行性 Assessing effects of landscape structure on ES for landscape planning and management: Striking a balance between level of detail and feasibility
流域景观规划 Watershed landscape planning	B2b	河流景观自然解决方案规划与实践前沿 Frontiers in planning and implementing nature-based solutions in river landscapes
	T14b	基于景观规划和管理评估景观结构对ES的影响：平衡细节和可行性 Assessing effects of landscape structure on ES for landscape planning and management: Striking a balance between level of detail and feasibility
自然保护区景观规划 Landscape planning of nature reserves	S8a	自然保护区和保护地的ES ES for nature conservation and protected areas
	T14b	为景观规划和管理评估景观结构对ES的影响：平衡细节和可行性 Assessing effects of landscape structure on ES for landscape planning and management: Striking a balance between level of detail and feasibility

3 与景观规划相关的研究热点

第十届ESP全球会议下设生物群落工作组、主题工作组、综合主题工作组及部门主题工作组，共设置7场特邀报告和51个主题分会场，包括近600场学术报告和160份墙报。本文首先根据官方会议手册中的介绍筛选出17个与景观规划相关的分会场主题（表2～4），随后采用文献研究法逐一研读各主题下的研究摘要和汇报文件，按照研究对象、规划类型和建模与制图方法分为三类。

3.1 多类型景观的ES研究

ES研究涉及城市景观、海洋、河流、湿地、森林及极地与高山区域等多种景观类型。笔者对其中较有代表性的城市景观、河湖湿地景观、森林景观的研究热点、难点及实践应用进行了详述（表2）。

3.1.1 城市景观

截至2020年，城市人口已占全球总人口的56.2%[①]。作为人类重要

① 全球城市人口数据引自世界数据图谱分析平台KnoeMa网站。

① The data of world's urban population was sourced from KnoeMa DataFinder.

表4：ES建模与制图相关研究议题
Table 4: Research topics on ES modeling and mapping

分会场编号 Break-out session code	分会场主题 Break-out session theme
T4a	时间演变：动态ES的时间维度制图 Times are changing: Temporal mapping of dynamic ES
T4b	利用社交媒体数据制图及评价文化ES Mapping cultural ES: Use of social media to assess cultural ES
T5	整合ES模型——推进建模科学与应用 Integrated ES models—Advancing modeling science and application

的陆域栖息地类型之一，城市景观也因此备受与会研究者关注，研究热点包括：

1）对城市ES动态性、复杂性的跨学科研究。如克里斯蒂安・I・伊奥亚等人评价了罗马尼亚城市蓝色基础设施的动态分布及可用性，研究了蓝色基础设施份额与城市社会经济、地理特征之间的相关性[15]。

2）环境正义视角下的城市ES评估。如弗朗西斯科・巴罗等人研究了巴塞罗那城市ES流动与需求之间潜在的不均衡对环境正义的影响[16]。

3）影响城市生态系统正负服务的城市绿色基础设施（GI）因素（如可达性、规模、设计等）。如朱莉娅・帕利沃达等人研究了德国莱比锡城市公园与棕地的植被覆盖度、物种丰富度等绿色参数对ES使用的影响[17]。

4）综合实施蓝绿基础设施以提升城市及城郊开放空间ES的治理方法。如萨布丽娜・莱等人以意大利卡利亚里三个城镇为例，通过将区域GI适宜性地图与城市总体规划叠加并进行相关性分析，识别促进区域GI提升的规划政策[18]。

5）通过文化ES研究城市自然环境对公共健康的影响。如陈先文（音译）等人总结了研究城市及郊区环境下文化ES与公众健康之间关系所面临的挑战，指出需加强文化ES在健康促进方面的研究[19]。

城市生态系统的高度复杂性和时空异质性给城市ES的测度带来了挑战。目前大部分城市ES的研究多聚焦于城市中的自然要素，因此，理解、分析和测量城市ES，特别是将ES融入城市景观规划与城市治理，是未来需要突破的研究难点[15]-[19]。就会议内容总结而言，城市景观规划与设计实践可以通过提升某一类型的服务（如文化服务或调节服务），正负服务调节，或是ES供需平衡的角度，明确GI的规模大小、形态布局、可达性等规划设计指标，进行城市GI的规划设计研究与实践。

3.1.2 河湖湿地景观

河流及河漫滩、湿地、湖泊是最复杂也最具活力的生态系统之一，它们在供应淡水、水质净化、洪水调节、生物多样性保护、粮食供应等方面发挥着关键的ES[20]。论坛的研究热点主要集中在河流、湖泊、湿地等的ES量化，以及ES研究对于跨部门、跨学科流域景观规划与管理的支持。后者的尺度从流域尺度横跨至全球，涉及的研究方法包括协同和权衡分析、情景模拟等。分论坛B2a介绍了三个重点关注的研究项

human beings, urban landscape attracted a broad attention of participants with the following interests:

1) Interdisciplinary research on the dynamics and complexity of urban ES. For example, Cristian I. Iojă et al. evaluated the dynamic distribution and availability of blue infrastructure in Romanian cities by studying the correlation between the share of blue infrastructure and urban socio-economic and geographic characteristics[15].

2) Urban ES assessment from the perspective of environmental justice. For example, Francesc Baró et al. have studied the impact of the potential imbalance between urban ES flows and demands in Barcelona on environmental justice[16].

3) Urban green infrastructure (GI) factors (e.g., accessibility, scale, design) that affect the positive and negative ES in urban settings. For example, Julia Palliwoda et al. studied the influence of green parameters such as vegetation coverage and species richness in urban parks and brownfields in Leipzig, Germany on the use of ES[17].

4) Integrated design of blue and green infrastructure to improve ES governance of urban and suburban open spaces. For example, Sabrina Lai et al. identified the planning policies that promote the improvement of regional GI by superimposing regional GI suitability maps with urban master plans of three towns in Cagliari, Italy and making correlation analysis[18].

And 5) research on the impact of urban natural environment on public health by analyzing cultural ES. For example, Chen Xianwen et al. summarized the challenges in the research of the relations between cultural ES and public health in urban and suburban environments and emphasized the research on the role of cultural ES in promoting public health[19].

The high complexity and temporal–spatial heterogeneity of urban ecosystems pose challenges to the measurement of urban ES. While most existing urban ES research concentrates on natural elements in cities, understanding, analyzing, and measuring urban ES, especially integrating ES into urban landscape planning and urban governance, are the research difficulties that need to be addressed in the future[15]-[19]. The 10th ESP Conference highlighted that urban landscape planning and design practice can be improved by enhancing a certain type of ES (such as cultural ES and regulation ES), adjusting positive and negative services or ES supply–demand equilibrium, and specifying GI planning and design indicators, such as scale, shape, layout, and accessibility.

3.1.2 River, Lake, and Wetland Landscapes

Rivers, floodplains, wetlands, and lakes are some of the most complex and dynamic ecosystems, and play key roles to freshwater water supply, water purification, flood control, biodiversity protection, and food supply[20]. Related sessions focused on the quantification of ES provided by rivers, lakes, wetlands, and the contribution of ES research to intersectoral and interdisciplinary watershed landscape planning and management. The scale of watershed landscape planning and management varies from the basin to global, and the research methods include

目：德国“河流ES指数”项目提出了针对供给、调节、文化三类ES的河流ES指数，并应用于德国多瑙河、内贝尔河等案例中，协助制定综合性的规划决策[21]；欧盟HyMoCARES项目梳理了河流修复及一般管理行动、水文形态与河流ES之间的关系，利用水文、水力及栖息地模型与现有数据量化水文形态变化对河流ES的影响，指导阿尔卑斯河流域的规划和管理[22]；简·H·詹森等人探讨了如何将气候模型和水文模型与全球湿地ES模型相整合，以探讨全球气候及土地利用变化对湿地ES的影响[23]。

研究难点包括多尺度下的数据获取、定量评价方法的选择、不同ES受益方的识别，以及相关研究方法与研究结论的跨学科应用。河流及湿地景观规划与设计一方面可借鉴上述研究的评价方法展开更加科学、有效的ES评估，另一方面可利用已有的水文形态对ES影响的研究结论，从物质空间形态入手提升河流与湿地的ES功能。

3.1.3 森林景观

森林景观的分布及其ES对全球可持续发展具有重要作用，森林的植物特性、物种与群落分布、生物量、碳储存量等均对ES具有影响[24]。分会场B3关注在土地利用和气候变化背景下，半天然林和人工林的正负ES评估及调节。研究热点聚焦在：

1）评估森林的多种ES（如气候调节、固碳、休闲娱乐及审美服务等）。如埃德加·尤尔马里斯等人绘制并评估了拉脱维亚森林中多种潜在的娱乐ES[25]。

2）土地利用、气候变化及景观管理对森林ES的影响。如克瓦德沃·K·库西等人利用InVEST模型评估了三种不同的土地利用变化情境对ES的前瞻性影响[26]；米格尔·努诺·布加略研究了可持续森林管理对于保护生物多样性和维持ES的作用[27]。

3）森林ES之间、正负服务之间，以及与其他土地利用类型之间的服务权衡。如卡拉·洛克尔克劳斯等人以智利南部外来森林种植园为例识别、绘制并量化评估了ES与生态系统负面服务[28]。其中，各种服务之间的权衡是研究的难点。例如，鉴于森林所发挥的重要ES，应增加森林面积，但森林的供给服务只有在被砍伐后才能获取，增加人工林（如种植园）的面积也会带来物种入侵等环境问题。因此，未来森林景观管

synergy and trade-off analysis, scenario simulation, etc. Session B2a introduced 3 research projects: The German River Ecosystem Service Index project proposed the “River ES Index” for the measurement of provisioning, regulatory, and cultural ES, and applied it to the cases of Danube and Nebel Rivers in Germany to assist the decision-making of overall planning[21]; the EU HyMoCARES project reviewed the relations between river restoration and general management actions, hydrological morphology with river ES, and quantified the impact of hydrological changes on river ES through hydrological, hydraulic, and habitat modeling, as well as data collection, to guide the planning and management of the Alps River Basin[22]; Jan H. Janse et al. explored how to integrate climate and hydrological models with global wetland ES models to study the impact of global climate and land-use changes on the ES provided by wetlands[23].

Difficulties in associated research include data acquisition at multiple scales, the selection of quantitative evaluation methods, the identification of different ES stakeholders, and the interdisciplinary application of related research methods and findings. The application in the planning and design of river and wetland landscapes can not only adopt ES evaluation methods to improve the scientism and effectiveness, but also learn from the existing research findings (e.g., the impact of hydrological patterns on ES) to improve the ES of rivers and wetlands through spatial forming.

3.1.3 Forest Landscapes

The distribution of forest landscapes and the ES provided plays an important role in global sustainability. The plant characteristics, species, and community distribution, biomass, carbon storage of forest greatly define its ES[24]. At the conference, Session B3 focuses on ES assessment and adjustment of semi-natural forests and plantations responding to land use and climate change. Research hotspots include:

1) Evaluation of various ES provided by forests (e.g., climate regulation, carbon sequestration, recreational and aesthetic services). For example, Edgars Jūrmalis et al. mapped and evaluated a variety of potential recreational ES of forests in Latvian[25].

2) The impact of land use, climate change, and landscape management on forest ES. For example, Kwadwo K. Kusi et al. evaluated the potential impact on ES in three land use scenarios with the InVEST model[26]; Miguel Nuno Bugalho studied the role of sustainable forest management in protecting biodiversity and maintaining ES[27].

And 3) the trade-offs among forest ES, between positive and negative services, and with other land use types. For instance, Karla Locher-Krause et al. identified, mapped, and quantified the ES and negative services of the exotic forest plantations in southern Chile[28]. Among them, the trade-off between various services poses a difficulty to such research. For example, the increase in forest area would enhance the ES by forests, but the provision service of forests can only be obtained after woodcutting, and artificial forests (such as plantations) would also

理与政策需要在多种服务间进行权衡[29]。在气候变化和土地利用变化等不同预景下，可以通过预测森林ES的变化调整景观格局，并制定针对性的森林景观管理政策。

3. 2 ES研究在景观规划与管理中的应用

景观规划可以通过调控土地覆被类型和空间格局来影响ES的类型和水平，也可以根据人类的需求通过调整服务功能特性指标促进或抑制不同ES的发挥[14]。会议上介绍的研究可应用于多种景观规划类型，包括城乡景观规划、流域景观规划、自然保护区规划等（表3）。区别于传统的工程解决方案，基于自然的解决方案（Nature-Based Solutions，简称NBS）受自然启发与支撑，是保护、恢复或可持续管理ES，同时提升生物多样性和人类福祉的行动[30]。NBS是景观规划与管理中促进ES的重要手段。

3.2.1 城乡景观规划

ES研究在城乡景观规划中的应用凸显了城乡环境中GI的关键作用及重要价值，基于ES制图，能够将城郊及乡村地区大面积的GI向城市化地区提供ES的趋势空间化。城乡景观规划中重点关注：

1）将ES纳入政策和规划，以增强ES在促进城乡协同方面的战略作用。如甘丹・萨瓦西等人识别了ES在规划过程和治理结构中的角色和作用，探究了ES连接不同规划过程和建立新的城乡协同的潜力[31]。

2）研究多种尺度下城乡景观结构对一种或多种ES功能及其供给的影响，以及政策对景观服务的影响。如安德莉亚・斯塔克裘尼等人研究了城市生态基础设施结构对洪水调节服务的影响，以及如何通过增加、保留和扩大廊道来改善网络连通性[32]；迪特尔・莫特尔曼斯等人研究了关键政策工具对城乡景观的地理要素、ES及社会生态功能的影响，为城市GI管理提供依据[33]。

3）NBS在解决城市可持续性方面发挥的作用，主要涵盖城市气候变化、人类健康及生物多样性三大主题。如托马斯・巴杜拉等人利用选择实验评估了城市居民对使用NBS适应气候变化的政策偏好[34]；大卫・杰内莱蒂等人通过评估不同受益群体的预期ES，以及在不同的时间范围内实施不同NBS的成本，实证分析了意大利北部城市空地实施NBS的潜在影响[35]。

cause environmental problems such as exotic species invasion. Therefore, future management and policy making of forest landscapes needs overall consideration on ES trade-offs[29]. Different ES scenarios on climate change and land-use change can inform the adjustment of forest landscape pattern and the formulation of specific management policies.

3.2 Application of ES Research in Landscape Planning and Management

Landscape planning can impact the types and levels of ES by adjusting land cover types and spatial patterns, and can also promote or confine the performance of certain ES types by adjusting ES functional indicators according to human needs[14]. The studies presented at the conference can be applied into a variety of landscape planning practice types, including urban and rural landscape planning, watershed landscape planning, nature reserve planning, etc. (Table 3). Different from traditional engineering solutions, Nature-Based Solutions (NBS) refers to the actions that inspired and supported by Nature to protect, restore or sustainably manage ES and enhance biodiversity and human well-beings[30]. NBS is an important means to facilitate ES performance in landscape planning and management.

3.2.1 Urban and Rural Landscape Planning

The introduction of ES science into urban and rural landscape planning highlights the key role and important value of GI to urban and rural environments. Based on ES mapping, large-scale GI in suburban and rural areas can provide ES to urban areas through spatial formation. Related research interests include:

1) Integrating ES into policy making and planning to enhance the strategic role of ES in promoting urban-rural synergy. For example, Günden Savaşçı et al. identified the roles and functions of ES in the planning process and governance structure, and explored the potential of ES to connecting different planning processes and establishing new urban-rural synergy[31].

2) The impact of urban and rural landscape structure on one or several ES functions and their delivery at multiple scales, as well as the impact of policies on landscape services. For example, Andrea Staccione et al. studied the impact of urban ecological infrastructure structure on flood regulation, and how to improve network connectivity by adding, retaining, and expanding corridors[32]. Dieter Mortelmans et al. studied the impact of key policy instruments on geographical elements, ES, and socio-ecological functions of urban and rural landscapes, so as to guide urban GI management[33].

And 3) the contribution of NBS to addressing urban sustainability, ranging urban climate change, human health to biodiversity. For example, Tomas Badura et al. evaluated urban residents' policy preference for NBS to adapt to climate change through a choice experiment[34]. By evaluating the expected ES of different beneficiary groups and the cost-effectiveness of a series of NBS in different periods of time, Davide Geneletti et al. empirically analyzed the potential impact of implementing a range of different NBS in vacant lots of a city in northern Italy[35].

3.2.2 流域景观规划

为提升流域景观的ES，会议重点关注：

1）将NBS融入流域景观规划的不同途径和范式。如克里斯蒂安·艾伯特等人提出了一个基于NBS的景观规划框架（包括确定环境和挑战、制定共同愿景、探索NBS预景、制定解决方案战略、实施方案和监测NBS效果），并将其应用于德国拉恩河景观规划中[36]；王志芳将NBS分为自然范式、本土范式、过程范式、文化范式、实验范式和绿色范式6个概念范式，提出了一个基于理论范式的NBS规划框架，并将其应用于中国山区城市河流景观规划中[37]。

2）流域景观格局或土地利用对洪水调节服务的影响。如凯尔西·麦克唐纳等人研究了美国堪萨斯城南部流域土地覆被变化对防洪ES的时空影响[38]。

3）NBS对生态、社会和经济的有效性，基于NBS的规划和设计方法及案例，以及实施NBS的治理和商业模式。如莎拉·戈特瓦尔德等人开发并测试了基于NBS的地理设计过程，并评价了其对河流景观边界管理的贡献[12]；马里奥·布里林格等人利用文献分析法对德国三个联邦州的洪水风险管理计划及其中采用的“基于自然的措施方法”（nature-based measures）进行了内容评估，并探讨了在政策准备和决策制定中采用基于自然的措施方法的潜在影响因素[39]。

3.2.3 自然保护区景观规划

1）关注自然保护区与生物多样性景观规划，同时也涉及国家公园、生物圈保护区及风景名胜区规划等。马修·米契尔等人以加拿大为例，将生态系统容量和人类需求纳入ES评估，评估了ES热点区与保护区网络的一致性，探讨了将ES纳入保护规划的途径[40]。

2）关注城市森林政策对区域ES的影响。如马蒂亚斯·里德尔等人依托“阿尔卑斯山ES的制图、维护和管理”项目，通过收集正式或非正式文书及公众对ES和人类福祉的认识资料，根据实施过程中的机会、限制以及通过ES产生的附加值，对已经实施或适合实施ES的政策工具进行评估[41]。

3）关注保护区利益相关者偏好与参与式规划。如马诺吉·巴塔利用焦点小组讨论、关键线人访谈、非正式互动及参与者观察等方法研究了尼泊尔西部保护区附近的村民从小熊猫栖息地获得的各种ES[42]；里扎·卡伦·瓦力迪阿诺等人研究了菲律宾巴拉望山脉土著居民在森林保护项目中如何理解ES的概念，并根据科学评估与地方决策者一同采取

3.2.2 Watershed Landscape Planning

In order to improve ES of watershed landscapes, the conference highlighted:

1) A series of approaches and paradigms to integrate NBS into watershed landscape planning. For example, Christian Albert et al. proposed a landscape planning framework based on NBS (including identifying context and challenges, developing a shared vision, exploring NBS scenarios, crafting solution strategies, implementing NBS, and monitoring NBS effect), and applied it to the landscape planning of the Lahn River in Germany[36]; Wang Zhifang proposed 6 paradigms of NBS, namely natural, native, progressive, cultural, experimental, and green, as well as a NBS planning framework based on these paradigms, illustrating with a case study of river landscape planning of mountainous areas in China[37].

2) The impact of watershed landscape pattern or land use on flood regulation services. For example, Kelsey McDonough et al. studied the temporal–spatial impact of land cover change on flood regulation ES in the southern basin of Kansas City, USA[38].

And 3) ecological, social, and economic effectiveness of NBS, NBS-based planning and design methods and case studies, and the governance and business models for implementing NBS. For example, Sarah Gottwald et al. developed and tested the NBS-based geodesign process and evaluated its contribution to the boundary management of river landscapes[12]. Mario Brillinger et al. used literature analysis to evaluate the flood risk management plans of three German federal states and the nature-based measures adopted, and analyzed the potential influencing factors for the adoption of NBS in policy preparation and decision making[39].

3.2.3 Landscape Planning of Nature Reserves

1) The landscape planning of nature reserves and biodiversity, as well as the planning of national parks, biosphere reserves, and scenic areas. With case studies in Canada, Matthew Mitchell et al. integrated ecosystem capacity and human needs into ES assessment, evaluated the consistency between ES hotspots and protected areas, and discussed the ways to combine ES into conservation planning[40].

2) The impact of urban forest policies on regional ES. Based on the project of “Alpine Ecosystem Services—Mapping, Maintenance, and Management,” Matthias Riedel et al. evaluated the policy tools which are implemented or suitable for implementing ES, by collecting formal or informal documents of public awareness about ES and human well-beings, according to the changes and limitations in ES implementation, and added value generated by ES[41].

And 3) stakeholders’ preferences and participatory planning of protected areas. For example, Manoj Bhatta studied various ES acquired from red panda habitats by villagers near the protected area in western Nepal through focus group discussions, key informant interviews, informal interactions, and participant observation[42]. Rizza Karen Veridiano et al. studied how indigenous people in the Palawan Mountains of the Philippines understand the concept of ES in forest conservation projects, take actions with local decision-makers based on scientific assessments, and inform the local forest management and conservation

行动，将其转化为森林管理和养护政策，为参与式规划影响规划政策提供了案例借鉴[43]。

3.2.4 小结

除了上述规划类型之外，在国土空间规划方面，费尔南多·桑托斯马丁等人以西班牙为例，通过绘制14个ES指标的空间分布图和热力图，解释了与土地利用强度梯度相关的ES协同效应和权衡，提出需要建立一个国土尺度下的新的景观规划模型[44]。

景观规划以协调人与自然关系为目标，注重规划客体的多重价值属性及空间分异，是景观管理的基本手段[45]。然而，多重价值之间在同一时空下往往相互冲突，如何把握规划客体的空间分异规律，寻求能够最大化景观多重价值、功能及潜力的空间途径，以缓解、协调价值冲突区域，是景观规划要解决的主要问题[45]。总体而言，该议题下的研究热点可总结为：

1）ES融入各类空间规划（如国土空间规划、城乡GI规划、流域景观规划、土地利用规划等）的框架、方法和途径；

2）景观结构特征及变化对ES供应及效益的影响；

3）规划或管理政策对ES的影响；

4）在景观规划设计实践中应用NBS提升各类型景观的ES。

ES将自然资源与人类福祉关联在一起，定量化的评估和可视化的表达可以使利益相关方明确价值冲突区域，从服务流动、供需、权衡等多个角度深入剖析空间潜力，借鉴景观特征影响ES的相关研究成果，可进一步优化景观格局，为多尺度、多类型的景观规划设计和管理提供科学依据。

3.3 ES建模与制图

ES建模与制图是历届ESP全球会议讨论的热点议题。第十届会议集中讨论了其在动态ES（包括价值变化、情景探索、动态可视化、实时应用、现场监测、临界点建模）②，非物质性ES评估，以及综合ES模型等方面的研究（表4）。会议上介绍的定性、定量模型可以借助机器学习等技术，构建面向用户的景观决策支持系统，提供了从理论研究向实践转化的有效途径。ES建模由通过整合物质空间数据的传统模式向满足多尺度、多用户、多需求转变；在方法上由允许数据共享与集成向鼓

② 引自第十届ESP全球会议官方网站上对T4a分会场的会议描述。

② Sourced from the "Session Description" of T4a on the official website of the 10th ESP World Conference.

policy making, which provides a case study for how participatory planning informs planning policies[43].

3.2.4 Summary

In addition to the above types of planning, in terms of national spatial planning, Fernando Santos–Martín et al. concentrated on the case studies in Spain to illustrate ES synergies and trade-offs related to land-use intensity gradient by mapping the spatial distribution and heat spots of 14 ES indicators, and put forward the need to establish a new national-scale landscape planning model[44].

Landscape planning, as a basic means to landscape management, aims at coordinating the human–nature relationship and pays attention to the multiple value attributes and spatial differentiation of planning objects[45]. However, due to the temporal–spatial conflicts among multiple values, how to understand the spatial differentiation laws of planning objects, seek spatial approaches that maximize the values, functions, and potentials of landscapes, so as to alleviate and coordinate value-conflicting areas, is a main problem to be addressed in landscape planning[45]. In general, the research hotspots in landscape planning and management can be summarized as follows:

1) The framework, methods, and approaches to the integration of ES into various spatial planning (e.g., territorial spatial planning, urban-rural GI planning, watershed landscape planning, and land use planning);

2) The impact of landscape structural characteristics and changes on ES delivery and benefits;

3) The impact of planning or management policies on ES;

And 4) applying NBS into landscape planning and design practice to improve ES of various landscape types.

ES matters and connects natural resources with human well-beings, and quantitative evaluation and visualized expression help stakeholders identify value-conflicting zones. By analyzing the spatial potentials in service flows, supply and demand, and trade-offs, and learning from the relevant research findings of the impact of landscape characteristics on ES, landscape patterns can be optimized to provide scientific bases for multi-scale and multi-type landscape planning, design, and management.

3.3 ES Modeling and Mapping

ES modeling and mapping has been a hot topic discussed at previous ESP global conferences. The 10th ESP Conference focused on the research on dynamic ES (including value change, scenario exploration, dynamic visualization, real-time application, on-site monitoring, and threshold modeling)②, immaterial ES evaluation, and integrated ES models (Table 4). The qualitative and quantitative models introduced at the conference can be used to build user-oriented landscape decision-making systems, with aid of machine learning and other technologies, facilitating associated application and practice. ES modeling is shifting from the traditional models that integrate spatial data towards the ones that respond to

励开源和机器学习改变。以"改善大西洋景观管理项目"介绍的综合建模技术为例，通过整合社会经济和气候变化情景建立生物监测空间数据库，利用模拟平台整合多个模型，可用于分析河流景观单元内自然过程及人类活动间的相互作用及多种ES评估[46]。模型还嵌入了利益相关者的参与框架，使参与性评估与模型相互补充[46]。此外，会议重点推出的ES人工智能建模平台可以实现线上快速ES评估，融合了可查找、可访问、互操作性、可重用、可定制等功能，不但可以分析ES的时空变化及受惠者流动路径，还可以使用模块化模型组件和根据上下文选择的数据自动推荐查询结果，为景观规划和政策决议提供更用户友好、更有针对性的服务[47][48]。

纵观会议研究成果，为克服ES的空间流动性和非地理定位性带来的景观规划和管理障碍，利用建模整合地理空间数据与社交媒体数据进行交互分析已经成为识别非物质ES（如文化服务、支持服务）的主流途径。T4b分论坛集中讨论了非物质性ES量化方法和制图工具进展。例如，通过识别Flickr、Twitter及Instagram等常用社交媒体中的关键词（社交媒体图片标签），以及图片中的景观特征来研究文化服务的空间分布[49][50]。除此之外，会议还指出了参与式方法对调查社会、经济、制度等影响ES服务权衡的因素的重要性[51]。

4 会议对景观规划研究与实践的启示

多尺度、多领域的景观规划可通过构建GI或生态安全格局来建立生态系统空间网络。在中国生态文明建设与国土空间规划变革的背景下，亟需通过景观规划与设计保障自然的ES，构建人与土地、人与自然的和谐关系[53][54]。本文基于第十届ESP全球会议所呈现的最新研究及应用成果，对景观规划设计专业人员提出以下建议。

4.1 探索面向多种景观类型的ES评价

从城市到乡村，从陆地到水域，从平原到山区，随着评价对象种类与尺度多样性的拓展，ES评价为卡尔·斯坦尼兹经典研究框架中的景观表述与景观评价提供了基础数据与科学依据，可直观地识别出能够提供重要ES的景观类型。一方面，应进一步加强对ES量化评估体系、测度方法与评价模型的研究，特别是关于服务需求和服务流动的量化评

different needs across scales for various stakeholders. Methodological focuses shift from data sharing and integration towards open source and machine learning. For example, in order to improve the management of Atlantic Landscapes, biodiversity and ES integrated modeling was used as a simulation platform that integrates multiple models, to analyze the interaction between natural processes and human activities in riparian landscapes, as well as the assessment of a variety of ES, by establishing a biological monitoring spatial database according to socio-economic and climate change scenarios[46]. The model also adopted a participation framework of stakeholders, and support the iteration between participatory assessment and modeling[46]. In addition, the Artificial Intelligence for ES modeling platform, which was introduced at the conference, can be used for quick online ES evaluation, supporting searching, access, interoperable, re-use, and customized functions; for analyzing temporal–spatial ES changes and the flow path of beneficiaries; and for targeted services for landscape planning and policy decision-making through modular modeling and automatic recommendations of query results[47][48].

In order to overcome the obstacles in landscape planning and management caused by spatial mobility and non-geolocation of ES, modeling integration of geospatial data and social media data for interactive analysis has become a mainstream approach to identify immaterial ES (such as cultural and supporting ES). The T4b session focused on the development of immaterial ES quantification methods and mapping tools. For example, the spatial distribution of cultural ES was studied by identifying keywords (social media picture tags) in popular social media (e.g., Flickr, Twitter, and Instagram), and analyzing the distribution of cultural ES by identifying the landscape characteristics in the pictures[49][50]. The conference also highlighted the participatory approaches to investigating the social, economic, institutional factors that influence the ES trade-off[51].

4 Conference Insights on Landscape Planning Research and Practice

Multi-scale and multi-domain landscape planning can promote the establishment of ecosystem network by building GI or ecological security pattern. In China's current ecological civilization construction and the transformation of territorial spatial planning, it urgently needs to guarantee the ES of nature through landscape planning and design, and to rebuild the harmony between human and land, and between man and nature[52][53]. Upon the latest research and application results introduced at the 10th ESP Conference, this paper offers landscape planning and design professionals with the following insights.

4.1 ES Evaluation for Multiple Landscape Types

From cities to villages, from land to water, from plains to mountainous areas, the increase in types and scales of ES evaluation objects enriches data and scientific bases for landscape representation and landscape evaluation within the Carl Steinitz's classic research framework, which helps identify the landscape types that provide critical ES. On the one hand, research on ES quantitative evaluation

估。在此基础上，深入开展对ES供需及权衡与协同关系的研究。另一方面，深入探索景观规划、景观格局与ES之间的相互作用关系，以及物质空间形态与ES评价的关联。除此之外，鉴于ES评价在表征景观空间的特征与功能方面的优势，应积极探索如何将评价结果落到具体的空间规划中，探索如何将“价值空间”转化为“空间价值”，为主体功能区划分、景观安全格局构建、生态红线划定、景观绩效评估等提供重要科学依据[54][55]，支持城市韧性与可持续发展。

4.2 探索将ES研究融入各类景观规划的理论与实践框架

正如景观设计实践与现代科研之间存在错位[56]，ES研究与规划设计实践之间也存在着较大的鸿沟。一方面，学者应加强气候变化、景观格局与特征、景观规划政策与治理措施对ES的影响机制研究，得出能够具体指导规划设计实践的格局指标和政策措施。另一方面，规划设计师应加强科学循证，充分利用ES的专业知识与科研结论转化为设计导则、空间模式和量化指标，搭建ES研究与设计实践之间的桥梁。尝试将ES理论融入各类景观的规划与设计研究框架。以景观规划设计领域较为经典的卡尔·斯坦尼兹研究框架为例：在景观表述中，对景观所提供的ES进行识别和描述；在景观过程中，理解与分析景观中的ES过程；在景观评价中，通过利用ES评价模型评估ES水平判断景观运作情况；在景观改变中，提供景观格局或结构的改变策略和预景；在景观影响中，评估景观结构或格局的变化对ES带来的影响；最终在景观决策中，基于提升ES选择最终的景观改变模型。除此之外，还需要充分考虑服务间的流动与相互关系，将ES时空格局、供需关系、权衡与协同关系纳入景观规划分析框架（图2）。

4.3 探索适用于景观规划与管理的ES综合建模与制图工具

多尺度的ES综合建模和面向用户的学习型制图技术的发展，能有效展示并预测空间格局、社会经济、保护管理等方面的变化对ES的影响。景观规划领域应积极探索ES综合建模与制图的强大功能，一方面，整合多个模型进行综合建模，搭建政府机构、大学、非政府组织和

system, measurement methods, and evaluation models—especially the quantitative evaluation on service demands and service flows—the supply and demand, and the trade-off and synergy of ES should be enhanced. On the other hand, in-depth exploration of the interaction between landscape planning, landscape pattern, and ES, as well as the relations between spatial forms and ES evaluation. In addition, in view of the advantages of ES evaluation in identifying the characteristics and functions of landscapes, future research interests might include the application of evaluation results into specific planning practices, and the promotion of the space value of sites. This will provide scientific bases for the identification of core-function areas, the construction of landscape security patterns, the delineation of ecological protection boundaries, and the evaluation of landscape performance[54][55], propelling urban resilience and sustainable development.

4.2 The Theoretical and Practical Frameworks for Integrating ES Science Into Landscape Planning

Just as there is a dislocation between research and practice in landscape design[56], there is also a big gap between ES research and associated planning and design practice. On the one hand, scholars should strengthen the research on the impact mechanism of climate change, landscape patterns and characteristics, landscape planning policies and governance measures on ES, so as to inform the development of pattern indicators and policy measures that can specifically guide planning and design practices. On the other hand, urban planners should strengthen scientific evidence-based, make full use of ES professional knowledge and scientific research conclusions into design guidelines, spatial models and quantitative indicators, and build a bridge between ES research and design practice. Meanwhile, it is necessary to try to integrate ES theory into the planning and design research framework of various landscapes. Taking the classic Carl Steinitz's research framework in the field of landscape planning and design as an example: in the landscape representation, identifying and describing the ES provided by the landscape; in the landscape process, understanding and analyzing the ES process in the landscape; In landscape evaluation, the operation of landscape is judged by using ES evaluation model to evaluate ES level; in landscape change, the strategy and prospect of landscape pattern or structure change are provided; in landscape impact, the impact of landscape structure or pattern changes on ES zone is evaluated. In the final landscape decision-making, the final landscape change model is selected based on the promotion of ES. In addition, it is also necessary to fully consider the flow and interrelationship between services, and incorporate ES spatiotemporal patterns, supply-demand relationships, trade-offs and synergy into analysis frameworks of landscape planning (Fig. 2).

4.3 Integrated ES Modeling and Mapping Tools for Landscape Planning and Management

The development of multi-scale integrated ES modeling and user-oriented learning mapping technology can effectively display and predict the impact of

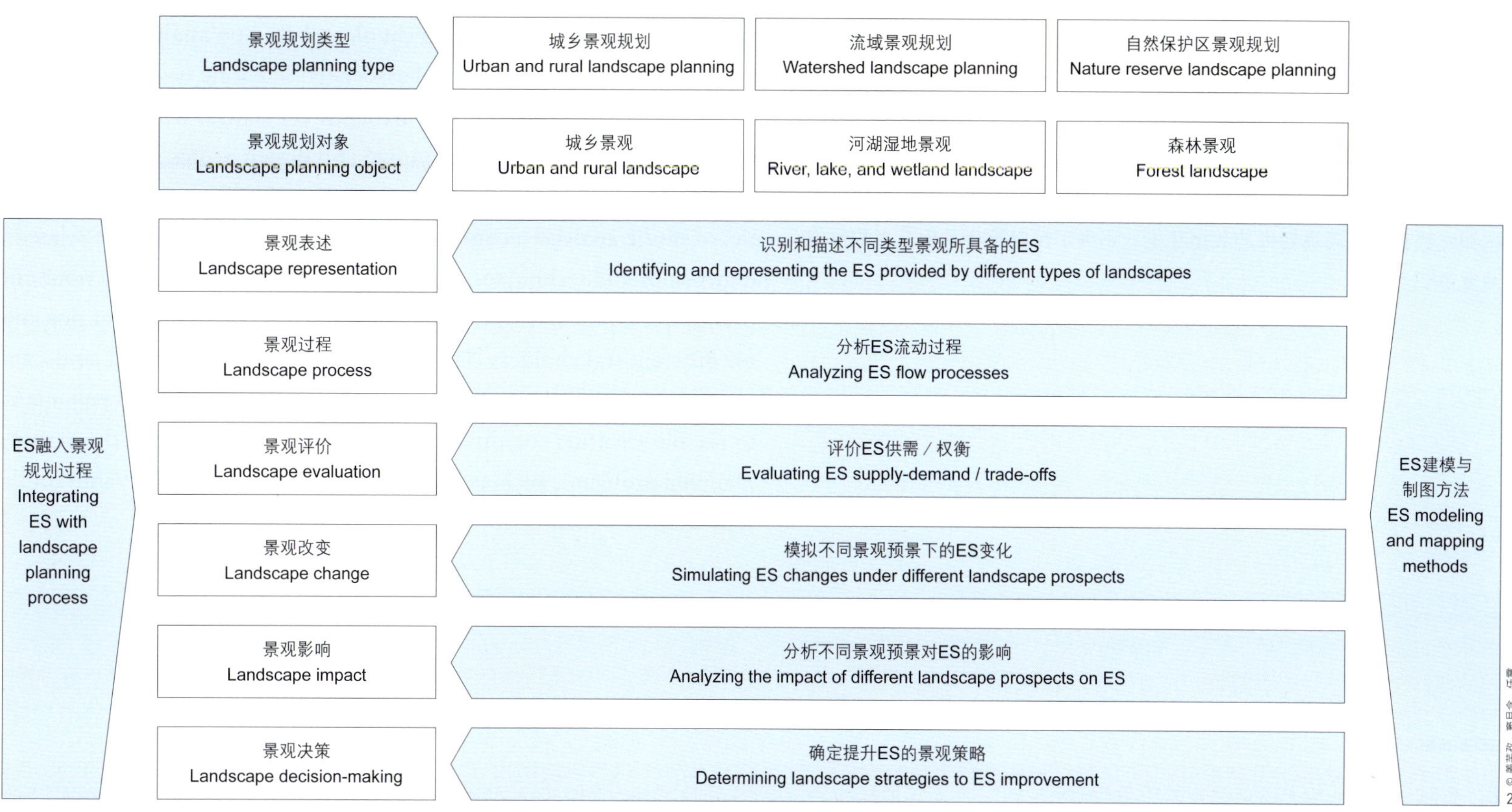

2. 融入ES的景观规划与设计研究框架

2. Landscape planning and design research framework integrated with ES

其他利益相关方的合作平台，不断纳入和学习用户上传数据，对不可见的ES进行可视化的直观展现，动态分析不同社会经济环境中多种类型ES的权衡与协同、供给与需求关系；另一方面，探索整合气候条件、地理空间、社交媒体及社会经济等多源数据融合的ES制图方法，并将其转化为适用于不同尺度景观规划的图示语言，以辅助景观分析、公众参与及多情景模拟下的景观规划方案比选。

5 结语

与生态学、地理学视角下的ES研究有所不同，景观规划视角下的ES研究以景观为载体，围绕规划设计—景观格局与功能—ES—人类福祉这一主线，将基于分析与评价的人地关系空间营建技术作为研究核心。将ES的概念和科学研究框架融入景观规划、设计和管理行动，将

changes in spatial pattern, social economy, and protection management on ES. Scholars in landscape planning field are expected to enhance the functions of integrated ES modeling and mapping. On the one hand, multiple models can be integrated for comprehensive modeling by building a cooperative platform among government agencies, universities, NGOs, and all kinds of stakeholders and continuously incorporating user-uploaded data. This can visualize the intangible benefits of ES, and support the analysis of dynamic trade-offs and synergy / supply and demand relations of multiple ES types in different social-economic contexts. On the other hand, scholars also need to explore ES mapping methods that integrate multi-source data such as climate conditions, geospatial, social media, and social economy, and improve associated graphic application in landscape planning at different scales. This method can assist landscape analysis, public participation, and decision-making of landscape planning schemes through multi-scenario simulation.

5 Conclusion

Different from the perspective of Ecology and Geography, the ES research in the field of landscape planning focuses on the interests from planning and design, landscape patterns and functions, ES, and human well-being, among which the

为以“人地关系空间营建”为核心的景观规划与设计专业带来机遇和挑战。它能加强景观规划中基于科学实证的分析技术，扩展景观规划的认知维度与技术方法，帮助分析与评价多类型景观的功能与服务，并面向不同利益相关方权衡多种规划预景和政策措施。当然，在ES融入景观规划的过程中也将面临诸多问题。例如，景观规划如何运用ES的科学认知优势克服景观规划中的数据缺失、不确定性以及利益相关方的价值冲突等[57]。**LAF**

man-land spatial construction technology based on analysis and evaluation is key. Integrating ES concepts and associated scientific research frameworks into landscape planning, design, and management actions will pose both opportunities and challenges to landscape planning and design profession that is missioned to improve human-land spatial construction. Such research can also strengthen the scientific analysis technology in landscape planning, enrich related cognitive dimensions and techniques, help analyze and evaluate the functions and services of multiple landscape types, and weigh multiple planning scenarios and policies for different stakeholders. The integration of ES research and landscape planning also faces other challenges. For example, researchers need to pay attention to how to use the scientific cognitive advantages of ES to overcome the existing landscape planning problems, such as lack of data, uncertainties, and value conflicts of stakeholders[57]. **LAF**

REFERENCES

[1] Peng, J., Yang, Y., Xie, P., & Liu, Y. X. (2017). Zoning for the construction of green space ecological networks in Guangdong Province based on the supply and demand of ecosystem services. *Acta Ecologica Sinica*, 37(13), 4562-4572. doi:10.5846/stxb201601020007

[2] Ouyang, Z., Wang, R., & Zhao, J. (1999). Ecosystem services and their economic valuation. *Chinese Journal of Applied Ecology*, 10(5), 635-640. doi:10.13287/i.1001-9332.1999.0166

[3] Xie, G., Zhen, L., Lu, C., Xiao, Y., & Chen, C. (2008). Expert Knowledge Based Valuation Method of Ecosystem Services in China. *Journal of Natural Resources*, 23(5), 911-919.

[4] Li, S., Liu, J., Zhang, C., & Zhao, Z. (2011). The Research Trends of Ecosystem Services and the Paradigm in Geography. *Acta Geographica Sinica*, 66(12), 1618-1630.

[5] Yan, W., Huang, X., & Zhou, J. (2017). Ecosystem Services Integrated Urban and Rural Land Use Planning: Conceptual Framework and Practical Approach. *Landscape Architecture*, (1), 45-51. doi:0.14085/j.fjyl.2017.01.0045.07

[6] Luo, J., Zhang, D., Liu, M., & Harald, Z. (2016). Quantitative Assessment and Mapping of Urban Ecosystem Services—The Case of Gelsenkirchen, Germany. *Landscape Architecture*, (5), 41-49. doi:10.14085/j.fjyl.2016.05.0041.09

[7] Ma, Y., Yuan, Q., & Leng, H. (2017). Review and Enlightenment of Landscape Aesthetics Service Evaluation from the Perspective of Ecosystem Service. *Chinese Landscape Architecture*, 33(6), 99-103.

[8] Wang, J., Qiu, M., Cheng, S., & Pang, L. (2017). Strategies for Physical Forms Based on Water-related Ecosystem Services Overall Capacity (WESSOC)—A Case Study of Tian'ao Water Sensitive Rural Area in Shengsi. *Landscape Architecture*, (1), 82-90. doi:10.14085/j.fjyl.2017.01.0082.09

[9] Han, Y., & Dai, F. (2018). Review of Study on Ecosystem Services Function of Urban Green Spaces: Indicators, Methods and Assessment Framework. *(Urban) Ecological System Service*, 34(10), 55-60.

[10] Wang, Y., Shen, J., Peng, Z., & Xiang, W. (2018). The Optimization of Green Infrastructure Ecosystem Services Adapted to Urban Growth. *Chinese Landscape Architecture*, 34(10), 45-49.

[11] Yu, K., & Li, D. (2016). *Landscape Architecture: The Profession and Education*. Beijing, China: China Architecture and Building Press.

[12] Gottwald, S., Brenner, J., Janssen, R., & Albert, C. (2020). Using Geodesign as a boundary management process for planning nature-based solutions in river landscapes. *Ambio*. Advance online publication. https://doi.org/10.1007/s13280-020-01435-4

[13] Xue, F., Jia, L., Zhong, L., & Wu, J. (2019). State of Art on Integrated Research of Ecosystem Services with Spatial Planning by Literature Information Analysis. *Chinese Landscape Architecture*, 35(10), 95-100. doi:10.19775/j.cla.2019.10.0095

[14] Li, F., Peng, D., & Wang, B. (2019). Application of Research on Ecosystem Services in Landscape Planning. *Landscape Architecture Frontiers*, 7(4), 56-59. https://doi.org/10.15302/J-LAF-0-020001

[15] Cristian, I. I., Denisa, L. B., Dagmar, H., Alina, C. H., & Mihai, R. N. (2021). How About Water? Urban Blue Infrastructure Management in Romania. *Cities*, (110), 1-9. https://doi.org/10.1016/j.cities.2020.103084

[16] Johannes, L., & Margarita, T. M. (2019). Who needs urban ecosystem services and who gets them? A spatial analysis of socio-environmental inequalities in Barcelona. *10th Ecosystem Services Partnership World Conference*. Hannover, Germany.

[17] Palliwoda, J., Banzhaf, E., & Priess, J. A. (2020). How do the Green Components of Urban Green Infrastructure Influence the Use of Ecosystem Services? Examples from Leipzig, Germany. *Landscape Ecology*, 35(5), 1127-1142. https://doi.org/10.1007/s10980-020-01004-w

[18] Lai, S., Leone, F., & Zoppi, C. (2019). Assessment of Municipal Masterplans Aimed at Identifying and Fostering Green Infrastructure: A Study Concerning Three Towns of the Metropolitan Area of Cagliari, Italy. *Sustainability*, 11(5), 1-17. https://doi.org/10.3390/su11051470

[19] Chen, X., de Vries, S., Assmuth, T., Dick, J., Hermans, T., Hertel, O., ... Reis, S. (2019). Research Challenges for Cultural Ecosystem Services and Public Health in (Peri-)Urban Environments. *The Science of the Total Environment*, (651), 2118-2129. https://doi.org/10.1016/j.scitotenv.2018.09.030

[20] Session description of B2a: Ecosystem services assessment methods for riverine and wetland ecosystems. (2019). *10th Ecosystem Services Partnership World Conference*. Hannover, Germany.

[21] Podschun, S. A., Hornung, L., Pusch, M., & RESI Team. (2019). Assessing the Ecosystem Service Composition in Rivers and Floodplains—The River Ecosystem Service Index (RESI). *10th Ecosystem Services Partnership World Conference*. Hannover, Germany.

[22] Carolli, M., & Pusch, M. (2019). Hydromorphology and river ecosystem services: The HyMoCARES project. *10th Ecosystem Services Partnership World Conference*. Hannover, Germany.

[23] Janse, J. H., van Dam, A. A., Hes, E. M., de Klein, J. J., Finlayson, C. M., Janssen, A. B., ... Verhoeven, J. T. (2019). Towards a global model for wetlands ecosystem services. *Current Opinion in Environmental Sustainability*, (36), 11-19. https://doi.org/10.1016/j.cosust.2018.09.002

[24] Session description of B3: Semi natural forests and forest plantations: Ecosystem services and trade-offs in the face of land use and climate change. (2019). *10th Ecosystem Services Partnership World Conference*. Hannover, Germany.

[25] Jūrmalis, E., & Lībiete, Z. (2019). Mapping the potential supply of multiple recreational services in Latvian forests. *10th Ecosystem Services Partnership World Conference*. Hannover, Germany.

[26] Kusi, K. K., Khattabi, A., Mhammdi, N., & Lahssini, S. (2020). Prospective Evaluation of the Impact of Land Use Change on Ecosystem Services in the Ourika Watershed, Morocco. *Land Use Policy*, (97), 1-19. https://doi.org/10.1016/j.landusepol.2020.104796

[27] Bugalho, M. N. (2019). The role of sustainable forest management on the conservation of biodiversity and ecosystem services. *10th Ecosystem Services Partnership World Conference*. Hannover, Germany.

[28] Locher, K. K., Lautenbach, S., & Volk, M. (2019). Ecosystem services and disservices: The case of exotic forest plantations in Southern Chile. *10th Ecosystem Services Partnership World Conference*. Hannover, Germany.

[29] Robert, A. (2019). Session B3 conclusion: An increase of forests in the future? *10th Ecosystem Services Partnership*

World Conference. Hannover, Germany.

[30] Chen, M., & Lin, G. (2019). Nature-Based Solutions: A Comprehensive Approach of Using Nature to Meet the Challenges of Sustainable Development. *Chinese Landscape Architecture*, 35(3), 81-85.

[31] Savasci, G., Lezuo, D., & Heitmann, A. (2019). Urban and Regional Planning—Integration Capability of the Ecosystem Service Approach in Governance Structures. *10th Ecosystem Services Partnership World Conference*. Hannover, Germany.

[32] Staccione, A. (2019). Green infrastructure network for floods: Spatial connectivity assessment of ecosystem services. *10th Ecosystem Services Partnership World Conference*. Hannover, Germany.

[33] Mortelmans, D., Chaurand, J., Onkelinx, T., Fickel, T., Mehring, M., Turkelboom, F., ... Roche, P. (2019). Policy coherence in green infrastructure management: Insights from six European case studies. *10th Ecosystem Services Partnership World Conference*. Hannover, Germany.

[34] Badura, T., Lorencova, E., Vackaru, D., & Ferrini, S. (2019). Using choice experiment to value preferences to support use of nature based solutions for adaptation for climate change in Prague. *10th Ecosystem Services Partnership World Conference*. Hannover, Germany.

[35] Geneletti, D., & Cortinovis, C. (2019). Nature-based solutions for urban vacant lots: A sustainable strategy? *10th Ecosystem Services Partnership World Conference*. Hannover, Germany.

[36] Albert, C., Schröter, B., Brillinger, M., Guerrero, P., Gottwald, S., Henze, J., ... Schmidt, S. (2019). Towards a Framework of Landscape Planning for Nature-based Solutions. *10th Ecosystem Services Partnership World Conference*. Hannover, Germany.

[37] Wang, Z. (2019). Using NBS planning of river landscape as a bridging procedure to mediate different interest groups in China: Case study of the Jialing river in Wushen County, Sichuan Province. *10th Ecosystem Services Partnership World Conference*. Hannover, Germany.

[38] McDonough, K., Hutchinson, S. L., Liang, J., Hefley, T., & Hutchinson, J. M. S. (2019). The Spatiotemporal Influence of Urban Development Patterns on Flood Mitigation Ecosystem Services. *10th Ecosystem Services Partnership World Conference*. Hannover, Germany.

[39] Brillinger, M., Dehnhardt, A., Schwarze, R., & Albert, C. (2020). Exploring the uptake of nature-based measures in flood risk management: Evidence from German federal states. *Environmental Science and Policy*, (110), 14-23. https://doi.org/10.1016/j.envsci.2020.05.008

[40] Mitchell, M. (2019). Quantifying and mapping nature's benefits to people for national-scale conservation planning. *10th Ecosystem Services Partnership World Conference*. Hannover, Germany.

[41] Riedel, M., Marzelli, S., & Szücs, L. (2019). Instruments for implementing ecosystem services—analysis of national instruments suitable to integrate ES in environmental governance / decision making. *10th Ecosystem Services Partnership World Conference*. Hannover, Germany.

[42] Bhatta, M. (2019). Services people recognise that they obtain from red panda habitats in western Nepal. *10th Ecosystem Services Partnership World Conference*. Hannover, Germany.

[43] Veridiano, R. K., Tumaneng, R., Pales, J. R., Monzon A. K., & de Alban, J. D. (2019). Bridging the gap from science to policy: A look on community-based forest conservation approach in the Philippines "Last Ecological Frontier." *10th Ecosystem Services Partnership World Conference*. Hannover, Germany.

[44] Santos-Martín, F., Zorrilla-Miras, P., Benayas, J., & Maes, J. (2019). Protecting nature is necessary but not sufficient for conserving ecosystem services: A comprehensive assessment along a gradient of land-use intensity in Spain. *Ecosystem Services*, (35), 43-51. https://doi.org/10.1016/j.ecoser.2018.11.006

[45] Xiao, D., & Li, X. (1998). On the Target and Principles of Landscape Planning. *Chinese Journal of Ecology*, 17(3), 46-52.

[46] Barquín, J., Álvarez-Martínez, J. M., Sitió-Calzada, A., Pérez-Silos, I., Estévez, E., Sáinz, M., & González-Ferreras, A. (2019). The ALICE Project: Improving the management of Atlantic Landscapes: Accounting for biodiversity and ecosystem services. *10th Ecosystem Services Partnership World Conference*. Hannover, Germany.

[47] Balbi, S., & the ARIES team. (2019). Philosophy of Globally Customizable ARIES models. *10th Ecosystem Services Partnership World Conference*. Hannover, Germany.

[48] Pascual, M., & Harmáčková, Z. (2019). The ARIES modelling approach: Integration and interoperability for ecosystem services science, policy and practice. *10th Ecosystem Services Partnership World Conference*. Hannover, Germany.

[49] Karasov, O., Külvik, M., Heremans, S., & Domnich, A. (2019). Mapping cultural ecosystem services in Estonia based on Flickr and VK.com social media data and topic modelling. *10th Ecosystem Services Partnership World Conference*. Hannover, Germany.

[50] Podschun, S. A., Venohr, M., Podschun, S., Mahnkopf, J., Arlinghaus, R., Hölker, F., & Wolter, C. (2019). AQUATAG-Using social media data to assess the dynamics of water-based recreational activities. *10th Ecosystem Services Partnership World Conference*. Hannover, Germany.

[51] Ballé-Béganton, J., Bailly, D., Fustec, K., Levain, A., & Philippe, M. (2019). Engaging stakeholders and scientists in participatory assessment for the development of Blue and Green Infrastructure Networks. *10th Ecosystem Services Partnership World Conference*. Hannover, Germany.

[52] Li, D. (2020). Struggles and Opportunities of the Discipline and Profession of Landscape Architecture in China's Territorial Spatial Planning Reform. *Landscape Architecture Frontiers*, 8(1), 84-91. https://doi.org/10.15302/J-LAF-1-030011

[53] Yu, K. (2019). Design in the Era of Ecological Civilization. *Frontiers*. Advance online publication. Retrieved from http://kns.cnki.net/kcms/detail/10.1050.C.20191111.1643.002.html

[54] Li, S. (2019). Reflections on Ecosystem Service Research. *Landscape Architecture Frontiers*, 7(1), 82-87. https://doi.org/10.15302/J-LAF-20190107

[55] Wang, Y., Shen, J., & Xiang, W. (2017). The Framework of Landscape Space Performance Evaluation with the Orientation of Eco-system Service. *Landscape Architecture*, (1), 35-44. doi:10.14085/j.fjyl.2017.01.0035.10

[56] Wang, Z. (2018). Bridging the Gaps between Landscape Design Practice and Scientific Research: A Graphical Interpretation. *Landscape Architecture Frontiers*, 6(5), 66-71. https://doi.org/10.15302/J-LAF-20180506

[57] von Haaren, C., Lovett, A. A., & Albert, C. (2019). *Landscape Planning with Ecosystem Services: Theories and Methods for Application in Europe*. Dordrecht: Springer Netherlands.

城市野境：比“城市荒野”更准确的措辞

Urban Wildness —A More Correct Term Than “Urban Wilderness”

万斯 · G · 马丁
Vance G. MARTIN*

世界自然保护联盟－世界保护区委员会荒野专家组创立人、联合主席，全球荒野基金会（南非）主席，荒野基金会（美国）主席
Founder and Co-chairman, Wilderness Specialist Group (IUCN / WCPA); President, Wilderness Foundation Global; President, WILD Foundation

梅拉尼 · 希尔
Melanie HILL

荒野基金会（美国）沟通与推广主管；美国科罗拉多大学波德分校传媒与公众参与学文学硕士
Director, Communication and Outreach, WILD Foundation; M.A. in Media and Public Engagement at the University of Colorado Boulder

*Corresponding Author
Address: 717 Poplar Ave, Boulder, CO 80304, USA
Email: vance@wild.org

编辑 | 冉玲于
翻译 | 嵇扬、冉玲于、田乐
EDITED BY | RAN Lingyu
TRANSLATED BY | Victor JI, RAN Lingyu, Tina TIAN

摘要

“荒野”概念具有多样化的特征与多重价值，蕴含着生物、社会-经济及象征意义。为了厘清这一概念，1992年，该术语被列入了世界自然保护联盟的“自然保护地分类”中。然而，近年来“城市荒野”一词开始流行，使那些重视自然荒野区对地球未来健康与福祉的作用并致力于保护这些区域的人士感到担忧。这种用法还很可能令（现在占全球人口大多数的）城市居民对“真正的”荒野是什么感到困惑。狭义上，城市不可能拥有严格意义上的“荒野”；但荒野的某些元素可以且应该出现在城市内及城市周边地区，从而提高人类健康和生活品质。基于此，“城市野境”或为更恰当的措辞。因此，本文主张以“城市野境”替代“城市荒野”一词，阐述替代原因的同时列举了城市野境的特征和效益；剖析了“城市野境”的成功案例；阐明野生动物（尤其是捕食者）在城市中的角色和面临的挑战；最后，结合案例说明了将城市居民与野性价值和效益联系起来的公众参与和公众教育方法论。

关键词

城市野境；城市荒野；人类与野生动物共存；生物多样性；荒野；城市自然挑战；环境教育；城市中的自然；捕食者－猎物

ABSTRACT

The concept of wilderness (荒野) has multiple characteristics and values relating to three principal areas: biological, socio-economic, and iconic. To provide clarity of concept, the term was included in the IUCN's list of Protected Area Categories in 1992. More recently, a current and fashionable expression "urban wilderness" has emerged. For those who believe in the critical importance of natural wilderness areas to the future health and well-being of our planet, and who work to protect these areas, the term "urban wilderness" causes much consternation. It is very possible that such usages will create confusion in the mind of urban dwellers—now the majority of the global population—as to what "real" wilderness is. By definition, cities cannot be "wilderness" technically. However, elements of wilderness can and should be present in and around urban areas to enhance human health and quality of life. Rather than calling this urban wilderness, however, the term should be "urban wildness (野境)." This paper presents a rationale for using "urban wildness" to replace "urban wilderness," citing some of the characteristics and benefits of urban wildness; provides case studies of urban areas that are working successfully with the concept; elucidates the role and challenges of wild animals (especially predators) in urban areas; and finally, gives an example of an engagement and educational methodology connecting urban dwellers to wild values and benefits.

KEYWORDS

Urban Wildness; Urban Wilderness; Human Wildlife Co-existence; Biodiversity; Wilderness; City Nature Challenge; Environmental Education; Nature in the City; Predator-Prey

https://doi.org/10.15302/J-LAF-1-030022
收稿时间 RECEIVED DATE | 2021-01-25
中图分类号 | R454.6, X37, X176, P578.1, S863
文献标识码 | A

1 引言

"荒野"（wilderness）一词具有多种含义。在最普遍的用法中，"荒野"往往是指"非管控的"自然区域，通常是不宜居的、未开发的偏远之地[1]。该术语在自然保护领域中还有三种更具针对性的含义：1）在生物学意义上，指"那些很少或不受人类直接影响的、自然系统相对完整的自然区域"；2）在人类社会意义上，指"未被人类开发、可提供维持生命的生态系统服务，且/或具有神圣/图腾意义，远离人类文明和人类聚居点、可于此静处"[2]的区域；3）亦指一种自然保护地类型[3]。以上4种含义皆体现出"荒野"的一个共性，即远离会对自然产生重大影响的人类聚居点。

由世界自然保护联盟（IUCN）的世界保护区委员会（WCPA）制定的《自然保护地管理分类指南》（简称《指南》）正式采用"荒野"这一术语指代自然保护地的一种类型："荒野区域"（wilderness area），分类编号为"1b"，指大规模的、未被改变或被轻微改变的，保留着自然原貌和影响力，没有永久或明显人类聚居点的地区；这类区域的自然条件需要加以保护与管理。[4]

在中国，越来越多的人呼吁将荒野视为新的国家公园体系的重要组成部分[5]，相关评判标准将荒野视为人类永久性建成环境（如城市文明）的对立面。而"荒野"一词最常见、最专业的用法均强调了荒野区域的"偏远"（remoteness）特征[6]，而中文语境下使用的"城市荒野"（urban wilderness）一词显然未体现这一点。此外，对于那些重视自然荒野区域对促进地球现在与未来健康作用的人士而言，"城市荒野"一词使他们对什么才是"真正的"荒野感到困惑。笔者认为，作为对人类福祉至关重要的资产，应当明晰荒野的概念，而非制造令人困惑的术语。

既然"偏远"是国际对荒野特征达成的重要共识，并且城市追求聚合而非远离，那么城市中就不可能存在严格意义上的荒野。但是，荒野的某些元素或品质可以出现在城市中——尤其是那些具备完善规划的理想城市。具体来说，这些元素可以是（存在于水体、森林系统、沼泽、草甸等中的）高效的自然过程、出众的自然美、标识性的野生动物（甚至是捕食者）、高质量的生物多样性和生态系统服务，有时甚至是静处（图1）。这些荒野元素可以且应该呈现在城市区域中，以提高人类健康和生活品质。基于此，"城市野境"（urban wildness）或为更恰当的

1 Introduction

The term "wilderness (荒野)" is used in varying ways. In general public use, it is often a generic descriptor referring to an area of "uncontrolled" nature, not always human-friendly, in an uncivilized and always remote place[1]. There are three ways it is used more specifically in terms of nature conservation: as a biological descriptor (areas of nature with little or no direct human impact and with natural systems as intact as possible); in relationship to human society as "an area with no human development that supplies life-supporting ecosystem services and / or to which is assigned sacred / totemic values, remote from civilization and settlements in which one can experience solitude (静处)"[2]; and as a specific type of protected area[3]. Important to note that in all the four usages of the term "wilderness," the common factor is that wilderness is remote from significant human settlements.

The usage of the term as a specific type of protected area was formally acknowledged in the Guidelines for Applying Protected Area Management Categories of the World Commission on Protected Areas (WCPA) of the International Union for the Conservation of Nature (IUCN). Protected area "Category 1b" is called "Wilderness area" and defined as: "Usually large unmodified or slightly modified areas, retaining their natural character and influence, without permanent or significant human habitation, which are protected and managed so as to preserve their natural condition."[4]

Further, in China, there is a growing call for wilderness to be regarded as an important element of the new national park system[5], further adding to the criteria that wilderness implies remoteness from established, permanent human infrastructure such as in urban civilization. Considering that the most common and professional usages of the term "wilderness" refers to the importance of remoteness for wilderness areas[6], it appears clear that the term "urban wilderness" is not consistent with its international usage. Further, for those who believe in the critical importance of natural wilderness areas to the current and future health of our planet, the term "urban wilderness" even causes consternation because it is highly possible for the term to create confusion as to what "real" wilderness is. For an asset that is so critical to human well-being as is wilderness, clarity (rather than confusion) needs to be reinforced.

Because "remoteness" is an internationally agreed-upon, important characteristic of wilderness, and because cities are characterized by proximate experience, not remote, cities, technically, cannot be or contain wilderness. However, they can easily—and preferably, for a well-planned and desirable city—exhibit elements or qualities of wilderness. For example, such elements could be high-functioning natural processes (as found in water bodies, forest systems, marshes, and meadows); superior natural beauty; representative wildlife (even predators); high-quality biodiversity and ecosystem services; and sometimes even solitude (Fig. 1). These elements can and should be present in urban areas to enhance human health and quality of life. Rather than calling this urban wilderness, however, the term should be "urban wildness (野性)." Such a clarification is also entirely consistent with the "Three

1. 美国科罗拉多州的博尔德市风貌。博尔德市及其毗邻的博尔德郡其他城镇的永久保护地面积占比达67%。这些区域受到美国联邦政府、科罗拉多州、郡和市的法律法规的保护。
2. 美洲狮经常在博尔德市出没
3. 孟买的市民环保主义者，亦是为保护野性自然而四处奔走的积极分子，通过创新公共教育来提升这个正在不断扩张的城市的公众意识。该创意地图由活动艺术家罗翰·查克拉瓦西创作，并获得市民团体“目标气候实验室”的赞助支持。

1. Boulder City (pictured here in its landscape) and surrounding Boulder County, Colorado, USA, have permanently protected areas covering 67% of the combined area of the city and county. These areas are protected under different laws and regulations the city, the county, the state of Colorado, and the US federal government.
2. Mountain lions are frequent visitors inside the city limits of Boulder.
3. Mumbai's citizen conservationists, strong and persistent activists for wild nature, increase public awareness across this sprawling city through innovative public education. The map was created by activist artist Rohan Chakravarthy and supported by another citizen collective, Purpose Climate Lab.

措辞。而这也非常符合“生物多样性保护和可持续利用的三个全球条件（3Cs）”的描述。3Cs是一个国家尺度的景观评估 / 实施工具，用来评价土地利用驱动因素与人类压力，评价对象范围从高度碎片化的景观（C1），到需要更好的保护地和连接系统的碎片化景观（C2），再到需要良好保护和管理的、偏远的大面积完整荒野区域（C3）。可见，城市野境隶属于C1[7]。近年来3Cs这一方法论已在中国得到应用。[8]

2 城市野境案例

2.1 博尔德市

美国科罗拉多州的博尔德市是一个小城市，拥有约12.5万名居民，以及就读于科罗拉多大学的约3万名学生。博尔德市恰好坐落于大平原与中落基山脉山脚的交汇处，距离州首府丹佛市的主城区仅50km。在诸如“最令人向往的小城市”“最佳居住地”，甚至是“最幸福的城市”等全国范围的调查中，博尔德市总是榜上有名。

博尔德市的地理区位和面积使得城市野境的元素较为常见：在这座城市中，猛禽（鹰和雕）、狐狸、郊狼、猞猁，甚至是黑熊和美洲狮等野生动物经常出没（图2）。这些野生动物既带来了巨大好处，也带来了明显挑战，后文将展开详细讨论。

此外，该市还有意识地制定了相关规划，通过具体行动和规划条例来增加城市野境。博尔德市是美国第一个市民通过投票（1967年）同意以征税来建立专项基金，以购买和保护城市内部及周边自然区域的城市。该市还与周边的博尔德郡的城市合作，共创造了面积占比高达67%的自然保护地（包括州和联邦自然保护地在内）。这一成就还超出了“自然需要一半”计划——这是一个全球性行动倡议，旨在为所有地球生命的存续而尽可能地保护自然——提出的目标[9]。博尔德市还是美国第一批用步行街和花园取代城市主干道的城市之一（1977年）。另外，博尔德市于1959年通过了一项命名为“蓝线”的法令，规定了城市供水海拔高度的限制，以保护自然状态和能够俯瞰城市的山麓景观。其他相

Global Conditions for Biodiversity Conservation and Sustainable Use (3Cs)," a national-scale landscape assessment / implementation tool to evaluate land-use drivers and human pressures utilizing a spectrum from highly fragmented landscapes (C1), to fragmented landscapes needing better protected area and connectivity systems (C2), to large, remote, intact wilderness areas requiring good protection and management (C3). Urban wildness is a stated condition of C1[7]. This methodology has recently been applied in China.[8]

2 Examples of Urban Wildness

2.1 Boulder City

Boulder, Colorado, USA, is a small city of some 125,000 residents plus 30,000 students at the University of Colorado. It is nestled at the exact junction of the Great Plains and the first uplift of the central Rocky Mountains, just 50 km from the major urban area of the City of Denver, the state capital. The city always

3 © Rohan Chakravarty

receives high recognition in national surveys such as "The Most Desirable Small City," "The Best Place to Live," and even "The Happiest City."

Boulder's location and size is where one would expect to easily find elements of urban wildness. Wildlife abounds in the city, with frequent sightings of raptors (hawks and eagles), foxes, coyotes, lynx, and even black bears and mountain lions (Fig. 2). Such wildlife brings numerous benefits and also obvious challenges, as discussed in the next section.

Besides, the city has also consciously planned to increase its urban wildness with specific actions and planning regulations. Boulder was the first city in the United States whose citizens voted (in 1967) to tax themselves to create a fund to purchase and preserve natural areas in and around the city. The city also works with surrounding Boulder County and, together with State and Federal protected lands, the overall county is comprised of an impressive 67% protected nature. This accomplishment exceeds the goal called for by Nature Needs Half[9], a global call-to-action to protect sufficient nature for the survival of all life on earth. Boulder was also one of the first cities in the USA to replace a main roadway with a pedestrian mall and gardens (in 1977). In addition, it passed an ordinance in 1959 called "the Blue Line" that set an elevation limit to where the city water would be supplied, thus controlling the natural condition and view-scape of the foothills that overlook the town. Numerous other planning ordinances also contributed, such as controlling the height of buildings, limiting the amount of structural growth per annum, providing affordable public transportation, and sourcing green materials for construction.[10]

关规划条例还包括控制建筑高度、限制每年的结构性增长量、提供廉价的公共交通，以及采购绿色建筑材料等方面。[10]

2.2 Mumbai

Mumbai, India, in contrast, seems not the place one would expect to find urban wildness. With a population over 20 million, the majority living in large urban slums, this financial, commercial, and entertainment capital of India is the world's 7th largest city[11]. However, despite the threats to wildness posed by such a sprawling metropolis, a range of urban wildness characteristics persist due only partially to prescient urban planning and nature management, and more so to very persistent citizen environmental activism. For just one example of many, the "Ministry for Mumbai's Magic" is a youth collective working to protect Mumbai's biodiversity, producing educational materials, and opposing development that destroys nature in the city. One of their public education projects was an innovative map (Fig. 3), with a mission to bring innovation and experimentation to solving the climate crisis through public mobilization and storytelling.

Mumbai is one of the few cities in the world that contain an entire national park within its urban boundaries. Covering an area of 87 km^2, Sanjay Ghandi National Park's (SGNP) is largely forested but with significant human recreational areas, cultural sites, and nature trails. With 2.5 million annual visitors, SGNP is one of the world's most heavily-used national parks. Its wildlife famously includes some 40 healthy free-roaming leopards (*Panthera pardus*)

2.2 孟买

相较之下，印度孟买是一座似乎很难发现城市野境的城市：孟买是印度的金融、商业和娱乐中心，也是世界第七大城市，这里的人口超过2 000万[11]，但大部分居住于城市大型贫民窟中。而现实情况恰恰相反，尽管孟买的大都市扩张式发展对野境保护构成了威胁，一系列的城市野境特征依然存在。这既得益于拥有先见之明的城市规划与自然管理对策，更是源于坚持不懈的市民环保运动。其中，"孟买魅力部"是一个致力于保护孟买的生物多样性、制作教育素材、反对破坏城市自然的开发行为的青年团体，他们开展的"创意地图"公共教育项目（图3）旨在通过公共参与和故事讲述的方式探寻解决气候危机的新方法。

孟买是当前世界上少有的、在其内部包含了一整个完整国家公园的城市之一，即桑贾伊·甘地国家公园（SGNP）。SGNP占地面积87km^2，公园内森林茂密，同时包含重要的娱乐区域、文化遗址和自然步道。

4. 火烈鸟在印度孟买东南方的塞里红树林公园中觅食。

4. Flamingos feeding in the Sewri Mangrove Park, SE Mumbai, India.

SGNP每年接待游客达250万人次，是世界上访问量最高的国家公园之一。公园中生活着大约40只健康状况良好、自由出没的花豹（*Panthera pardus*），它们以公园内丰富的小型动物为食，同时也捕食邻近社区的家养宠物与流浪动物。[12]除了种类繁多的鸟类外，还有172种蝴蝶，鳄鱼、眼镜蛇与蟒蛇等爬行动物，以及多种羚羊、鹿、豪猪、椰子猫、鬣狗、狐蝠等。[13]

孟买由7座独立的岛屿构成。每年11月至次年5月，著名的咸水涉禽大火烈鸟（*Phoenicopterus roseus*）与小火烈鸟（*Phoeniconaias minor*）都会迁徙至此，进入孟买的水道和红树林中觅食。而在2020年4月，由于新冠肺炎（COVID-19）疫情的隔离措施，导致人类活动减少，火烈鸟的数量也因此增至15万只（图4）[14]。

野境也体现在当地对自然和生物多样性进行非工业化的传统利用中。如在孟买这样的大城市中，人工捕鱼社区可以说是一种奇特的存在：该社区生活着约500万科利族人，他们的小规模捕鱼活动已有500多年的历史，这一传统在不断升级的发展压力下变得岌岌可危。这些压力包括：拟建的沿海干道、气候变化导致的水温升高、过度捕捞、严重的环境污染。[15]

2.3 北京

虽然背负着空气污染的困扰，但北京还是中国北方“最绿”的城市。从CBD中的小型公园与庭院到西部山区，这座城市拥有丰富的生物多样性与多种多样的栖息环境，包括湿地、草地、森林与大型公园。与此同时，北京恰好位于世界九大候鸟迁徙路线之一上，拥有500多种鸟类，约占全中国鸟类种类的三分之一。[16]北京的鸟类丰富度在所有G20国家的首都中排名第二[17]。

that feed on abundant small prey in the park along with domestic pets and feral animals in adjacent neighborhoods.[12] In addition to a wide range of birds are 172 species of butterflies, reptiles such as crocodile, cobra, and pythons, and many species of antelope and deer, porcupine, palm civet, hyena, langur, flying fox, and more.[13]

7 separate costal islands were eventually joined to create Mumbai. A distinct and celebrated marine-related avian feature is the greater (*Phoenicopterus roseus*) and lesser (*Phoeniconaias minor*) flamingos that migrate into Mumbai's waterways and mangroves to feed from November to May, numbering as high as 150,000 during the reduced human activity of the COVID-19 lockdown in April, 2020 (Fig. 4)[14].

Wildness can also be evident through non-industrial, traditional uses of nature and biodiversity. Unusual within such a large city as Mumbai, an artisanal fishing community still exists, at the center of which are the Koli ethnic minority numbering some 5 million people. They have practiced small-scale fishing for over 500 years and precariously persist despite the ever-escalating pressures of development. Such pressures include a proposed major coastal road; increasing water temperatures due to climate change; overfishing; and, of course, significant pollution.[15]

2.3 Beijing

Beijing, China, while it continues to reduce its sometimes high-level of air pollution, is the greenest city in northern China. From small parks and gardens in the CBD to the western mountains, the city is rich in biodiversity and diverse habitats such as wetlands, grasslands, forests, and large parks. Located on one of the 9 major migratory bird migration routes in the world, Beijing has counted more than 500 bird species, about one-third of all bird species in the entire country.[16] In a rating of major cities in all G20 countries, Beijing ranks second in bird diversity[17].

位于北京北部的奥林匹克森林公园不仅是城市休闲运动场所，也拥有可观的植被覆盖率，是公认的亚洲最大的城市绿洲。[18]占地680hm^{2}的园区中覆盖了大量的森林、草甸、人工湖，还有一处68hm^{2}的人工湿地；在公园南区共观察记录鸟类170余种。[19]而在北京市南部的南海子麋鹿自然保护区内则散养着大量的麋鹿（*Elaphurus davidianus*）——这一被《IUCN濒危物种红色名录》列为野外灭绝的物种。在中国生态修复和生态系统重建过程中，南海子的种群成功助力了将麋鹿放归至其他野外区域。[20]除此之外，北京还有很多其他野生动物，尤其是在西郊山区，包括野猪（*Sus scrofa moupinensis*）、西伯利亚狍（*Capreolus pygargus*）、猪獾（*Arctonyx collaris*）、松鼠和花栗鼠。而华北豹（*Panthera pardus japonensis*）也在北京西南山区重新开始自然繁衍。[21]

近年来，自然教育与城市生物多样性（野境元素之一）的概念在北京愈发普及。过去，普通家庭仅仅会选择去动物园和植物园观察动植物。如今，人们会倾向于选择前往更具野性的地方观察鸟类与各种野生动物，体验城市野趣。另外，有人提议北京的每个城市公园中都预留"10%的自然带"，任由植物自由生长而不被砍伐或清除，野生动植物也可以在这些地方繁衍生息。[16]也有人提出建立城市生态连接/野生动物迁徙廊道，即在六环外设置一条"野生环路"，将城市中各种陆地与河岸栖息地连接起来——这既能保障野生动物的活动，也能通过限制城市居民的游憩范围来提高他们对城市丰富的生物多样性的认识。[20]

2020年9月，位于北京城市副中心的城市绿心森林公园正式开放。园内78hm^{2}的核心区周围建造了约2m高的绿篱，作为城市中第一块允许自然修复的野性斑块。公园位于京杭大运河南岸，最终面积预计将达到11.2km^2，是纽约中央公园面积的两倍。[22]

3 捕食者的问题

人类如何与野生动物共存（特别是与捕食者的共存）是一个复杂且颇具挑战的问题，然而，在城市野境的话题中可以一谈。[23]

当人们讨论"野境"一词时，通常会联想到捕食者–猎物的关系，而这也是自然纪录片常常关注的主题——纪录片中大型动物（如狮子、熊、鹰）会捕食小型动物。这种既引人入胜又令人生畏的现象对于人类而言无异是陌生的，因为大多数人类（尤其是生活在城市中的人）不会自己宰杀食物，而是直接购买已包装好的、预加工的、随时可以烹煮的

The Olympic Forest Park in the north is not only a place for sports and recreation, but also contains significant natural coverage and is considered the largest urban green landscape in Asia.[18] Its 680-hectare area is covered by significant forests, meadows, and man-made lakes, plus a constructed wetland of 68 hm^2. In its southern section, more than 170 species of birds were recorded.[19] In the south of the city, Nanhaizi Miludeer Nature Reserve has a major population of milu deers (*Elaphurus davidianus*), a species assessed as extinct in the wild (EW) by IUCN Red List. This population was used to successfully reintroduce the species to wild areas across China in the process of restoring ecological processes and re-establishing ecosystem integrity.[20] Much other wildlife exists in Beijing especially in the mountains in the western suburbs—such as wild boar (*Sus scrofa moupinensis*), Siberian roe deer (*Capreolus pygargus*),Hog badger (*Arctonyx collaris*), squirrel, and chipmunk. The North China Leopard (*Panthera pardus japonensis*) has also begun to naturally reinhabit the mountains near the southwest area of Beijing.[21]

In recent years, nature education and the concept of urban biodiversity—an element of wildness—is flourishing in this city. In the past, ordinary families would only go to zoos and botanical gardens to view animals and plants. It is now much more common for people to go to wilder places to observe birds and various wild animals and to learn about wildness in the city. A discussion about maintaining a "10% natural zone" in each urban park in Beijing has been initiated, with the purpose of allowing plants there to grow freely without being felled or otherwise eliminated, so that wild animals and plants can thrive in these places.[16]One idea that has been raised is for an urban ecological connectivity / wildlife migration corridor, a "wild ring road" outside the Sixth Ring Road to connect various terrestrial and riparian habitats across the city. This has the potential to support wildlife and, through limited access to city dwellers for recreation, raise awareness of the city's rich biodiversity.[20]

In September 2020, the Urban Green Heart Forest Park in the sub-capital of Beijing officially opened. Within the project, fences about 2 meters high were built around the core area of 78 hectares, as the first wild patch in the city that allows for natural restoration. Located on the south bank of the Grand Canal, it will eventually cover an area of 11.2 km^2, twice the size of New York's Central Park.[22]

3 The Issue of Predators

Human–wildlife co-existence—especially with predators—is a complex and challenging issue, yet a brief summary is germane to the discussion about wildness in urban areas.[23]

When people think about "wildness" it is often related to the predator–prey relationship, frequently the subject of popular nature documentaries wherein larger animals (e.g. lions, bears, hawks) kill and consume smaller animals. This is exotic and often both fascinating and frightening because most humans (especially

© Nayan Khanolkar

5. 约40只野生花豹将孟买的SGDP作为栖息地，它们经常捕食狗和猫。

5. Approximately wild 40 leopards reside in SGNP in the center of Mumbai, often preying on dogs and cats.

食材。所以，要理解捕食者在重要自然过程方面的作用，一种方式便是从生态学角度出发。在自然界，为了生存，包括人类在内的所有生物都需要消费其他生物。这就形成了营养级联，一个不同级的生物遵循彼此之间有序的能量转换过程的系统。[24]当捕食行为减少时，自然能量的转换与生态过程的动态互动就被迫中断，导致整体生态系统健康水平的下降。

关于捕食者所带来的影响在大规模实例中体现得最为明显，如黄石国家公园重新引入狼的经典案例，既改善了生态健康，也提高了生物多样性。[25]尽管这样的例子更常见于大型荒野区域的研究中，但这也不失为城市野境话题中一个重要而有趣的元素。在关于城市中的野性自然的讨论中也不常关注捕食的话题。但事实上，如果认可野境的质量对城市区域生态健康的价值，捕食议题就应当得到重视。

在城市环境中，捕食者体型越大，对人类的威胁也就越大。如小型捕食者狐狸（*Vulpes* spp.）很容易适应城市环境，一个健康的狐狸种群能够广泛分布于大部分城市地区（如纽约和伦敦）[26]。这些捕食者并不会对人类构成直接威胁，但会对家养宠物构成威胁。而郊狼（*Canis latrans*）这种适应性极强的大型捕食者几乎见于美国本土所有州和主要城市，其城市种群对家养宠物、低龄儿童与（极少数）成人均构成更复杂的威胁[27]。最后，也是最具挑战性的问题，则与顶级捕食者有关。比如上文提到的SGNP中的花豹（图5），或是见于一些美国西部城市中的美洲狮（*Puma concolor*）等大型野生猫科动物。

简而言之，城市和城郊中的捕食者可以调节其他动物的数量（以及这些动物对土壤与植物造成的影响）——如果不加约束，这些动物往往会引发其他危害。例如，城市中的狐狸会捕食老鼠，从而有助于控制鼠群过多所造成的疾病与食物污染问题；健康的鸟类种群则对调节和辅助蚊子等昆虫的种群平衡非常重要——蚊子常常会携带疟原虫、西尼罗病毒与其他威胁人类健康的病原体；又如孟买SGNP中的花豹，流

urbanized) do not kill their food—they purchase it packaged, prepared, and ready to cook. One way to understand predators' role as an important natural process is to consider it in ecological terms. In nature, everything consumes something else in order to survive (humans are no exception). This forms a "trophic cascade," an assemblage of different levels of ecological complexity regulated in part by the orderly transfer of energy and processes between the different levels—often the consumption of prey by predators.[24] When predation is diminished, the transformation of natural energy and the dynamic interaction of ecological processes are disrupted, leading to a decline in overall ecosystem health.

Large-scale examples of the impact of predators are the easiest to comprehend, such as the highly-studied reintroduction of the wolf to Yellowstone National Park and the resulting improvement in ecological health and biodiversity.[25] While this is much easier to understand when studying a large wilderness area, it is nevertheless an important and interesting element when considering urban wildness. Predation is also a subject not often included in discourse on wild nature in cities. But the reality is that if wildness qualities are considered valuable for ecological health in urban areas, predation is important.

In urban conditions, the larger the predator, the greater the challenge. For example, a smaller predator that adapts easily to urban conditions is foxes (*Vulpes* spp.), and healthy populations can be found in most urban areas within their natural ranges, such as New York and London[26]. These predators pose no direct threat to humans, only to their household pets. Urban populations of coyotes (*Canis latrans*), a larger and highly adaptive predator found in every state and major city in the continental United States, pose a more complex threat to household pets, small children, and (very rarely) adults[27]. Finally, of course, the most challenging issue is with apex predators—those at the top of food chain. Examples are mostly larger wild cats such as the previously mentioned leopards in SGNP (Fig. 5), or mountain lions (*Puma concolor*) in some western American cities.

In very simple terms, predators in urban and suburban areas control the numbers of other animals (and their impacts on soil and flora) which, if allowed to grow unchecked, often cause other damage and issues. For example, foxes in cities prey on rats, among other things, helping control diseases and food contamination caused by overpopulation of rats. Healthy bird populations are important to control and assist the balance of insects such as mosquitos which are often vectors for plasmodium, West Nile virus, and other pathogens dangerous to humans. In the instance of the leopards in Mumbai's SGNP, a significant element of the leopard's diet is feral dogs, an over-abundance of which leads to rabies and other diseases.[28]

Some of the challenges of human–wildlife conflict are met by changing urban infrastructure. One important example is changing how highways are built, in order to accommodate wildlife movements and thus reduce wildlife

浪狗是其主要的食物来源，过多的流浪狗会增加狂犬病和其他疾病的传播风险。[28]

修建城市基础设施时也常常会面临人类与野生动物冲突的一系列挑战。为此，人类往往需要作出改变。如修建高速公路时应考虑野生动物的活动，以减少被车撞死的野生动物以及因避让野生动物而造成的交通事故伤亡数量。洛杉矶正在施工建造的“动物廊桥”便是为了方便美洲狮和其他野生动物安全穿越城市主干道而修建的[29]。

要缓解人类与野生动物的冲突，还需要人类习惯行为方面的改变。例如，美洲黑熊（*Ursus americanus*）在科罗拉多州落基山脉附近社区出没活动日益增多。为了不对其造成伤害，当地居民采用了一种经博尔德市认证的“防熊”户外垃圾箱和堆肥箱来威慑黑熊[30]。博尔德市对该措施进行了严格管理，并对未遵守的居民施以罚款。2017年，博尔德市在黑熊保护区内开具了1 376单罚单，仅对一只具有侵略性的黑熊进行了安乐死。相比之下，科罗拉多州的杜兰戈市（该市具备与博尔德市类似的垃圾箱法令，但并未强制实施）虽然记录在案的违反垃圾箱法令行为有689起、但却只开具了43张罚单，并对25只熊进行了安乐死。[31]科罗拉多大学的研究人员认为这主要是因为市政条例执行力度的不足[32]。在奖励或惩罚机制不健全的情况下，人类极少会改变自身行为；而如若人类不采用这些预防措施，野生动物就会遭殃。

另一个与城市捕食者相关的重要议题是：流浪猫对城市野境品质的负面影响。尽管这类猫科动物捕食啮齿类动物有利于人类健康，但它们对城市中的野生鸟类却构成了极大的威胁。这种威胁虽然不易量化，但其严重影响已被广大研究人员证实。例如，据美国的一项研究估计，每年平均有24亿只野生鸟类被家猫（允许在户外活动）和流浪猫捕杀，且流浪猫的捕杀率是家猫的三倍。[33]不过，经作者观察，虽然当前社会正越来越不提倡家猫在户外活动，但流浪猫的问题更为复杂。自20世纪90年代以来，“TNR”法——捕捉（Trap）、绝育（Neuter）与放归（Return）——已发展为一种能有效控制流浪猫数量的人道方式。TNR法还会为流浪猫接种狂犬病和犬瘟热疫苗。绝育后的猫会以剪去左耳一角作为标记，原地放归到一个由志愿者继续提供食物并给予照顾的“族群”中。[34]但从根本上来说，改变人类行为才是最重要的，如通过城市垃圾管理措施来阻止流浪猫觅食。

总之，人类与捕食者的福祉是息息相关的，因为人类需要健康的自然，而健康的自然又需要捕食者。捕食者对生态系统具有很强的自上而下的营养级影响。与试图达到相同效果的人工干预相比，狼群的引入轻而易举地帮助黄石国家公园修复了生态系统[35]，蟹类维持珊瑚礁平衡亦如是[36]。在城市中，捕食者能够控制害虫种群数量，减少自然植被的破坏，并通过降低动物对土壤和栖息地的不良影响而有望促进高品质的、完整的野性自然。捕食者对人类的精神层面也发挥着重要作用，是激发

roadkill and decrease deadly traffic / wildlife collisions. An example is the wildlife-crossing bridge under construction in Los Angles to facilitate movement across major highways by mountain lions and other wildlife[29].

Other challenges are met by changing human habits and behaviors. American black bears (*Ursus americanus*) are increasingly common food-foragers in communities within Colorado's Rocky Mountains. A deterrent required for use by residents are city-certified "bear-resistant" outdoor trash and compost bins[30]. Boulder has strictly managed this system with fines for residents who do not comply. In 2017, the City of Boulder levied 1,376 fines within the Bear Protection Zone and needed to euthanize only one aggressive bear. In contrast, Durango, Colorado (which has a similar garbage ordinance to Boulder, but no proactive enforcement) documented 689 trash violations, levied only 43 fines but euthanized 25 bears.[31] Researchers at the University of Colorado attribute the high number of bears euthanized to lax enforcement of municipal regulations[32]. Humans seldom change their behavior unless they are incentivized or penalized. If humans fail to comply with preventative measures, wildlife suffers.

Another important subject to note about urban predators is the negative impact of free-roaming cats on the quality of urban wildness. While such felines benefit human health by preying on rodents, they also have a highly negative impact on wild birds. Although not easy to measure, a severe impact is widely accepted by researchers. One study in the United States estimated that a median number of 2.4 billion wild birds are killed per year by both owned (and allowed to roam) and unowned (feral) cats. The unowned cats accounted for up to three times the kill rate compared to owned cats.[33] The authors observe that increasingly it is socially-discouraged for cat owners to allow their domestic pets to roam outside of the home. The matter of feral cats is more complicated. The process of Trap, Neuter, and Return, or "TNR," became popular in the 1990s as a humane way to control the population of feral cats. With TNR, the cats are also vaccinated against rabies and distemper. Their left ears are slightly clipped for identification as a sterile cat, and then they are released into a "colony" that is usually managed by volunteers.[34] But ultimately there also needs to be change in behavior, for example with how people manage their garbage in urban areas, to discourage feeding by feral cats.

In summary, the well-being of humans and predators is linked because people need healthy nature, and healthy nature needs predators. Predators exert strong top-down, trophic influences on ecosystems. In contrast to man-made interventions attempting to accomplish the same, wolves have effortlessly helped restore ecosystems in Yellowstone National Park[35] and crabs maintain equilibrium in coral reefs[36]. In urban areas, predators keep pest populations in check, limit damage to natural vegetation, and make possible higher-quality, intact wild nature by reducing animal impacts on soil and habitat. Predators are also significant to the human psyche and spirit, frequently captivating human imagination and inspiring art.[37] Predators are an essential aspect of a healthy

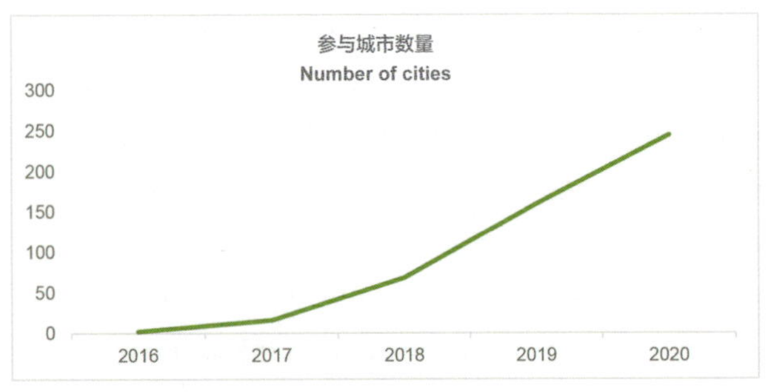

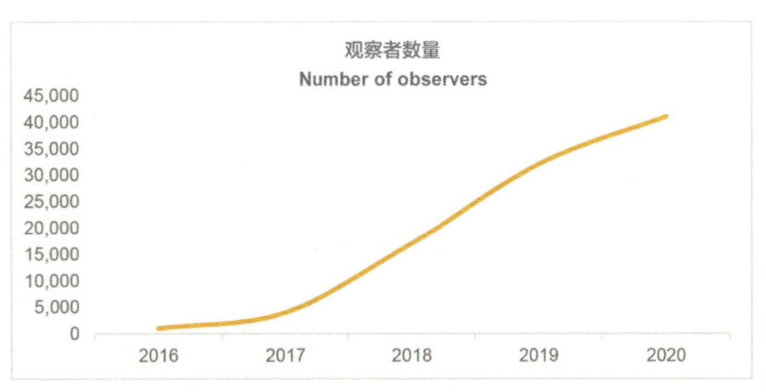

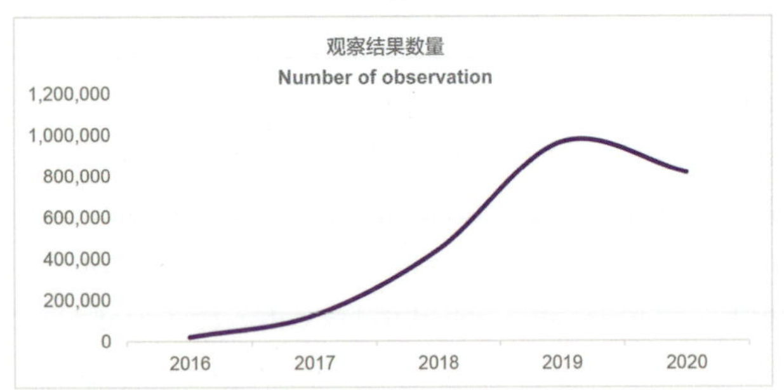

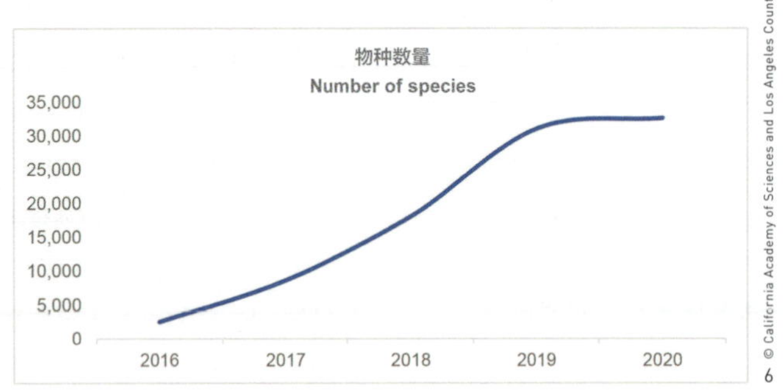

6 © California Academy of Sciences and Los Angeles County Natural History Museum

6. 2016~2020年CNC总体数据变化，包括了参与城市、观察者、观察结果，以及动植物物种总数。
7. 从参与竞赛的城市与人员数量来看，CNC是目前在全球范围内开展的最成功的城市公民科学活动。

6. Collective numbers from the CNC during years 2016 ~ 2020 include total numbers of cities, observers, observations, and species (plants and animals).
7. According to CNC metrics of number of cities and participants engaged, CNC is the most successful globally-deployed urban citizen science initiative.

想象与启迪艺术灵感的源泉。[37]捕食者是构建健康生态系统（无论是在荒野还是城市环境）的重要组分；没有它们，生态系统就会残缺，其所能提供的维持生命的生态服务也会被削弱。

4 建立城市居民与野性自然的密切联系

据联合国估计，2050年世界城市人口比例将从2020年的56.2%上升至68%（届时全球人口将达到97亿）。[38][39]随着城市人口增长，人类与自然的联系将会越来越少——这一点既体现在当前突出的人类健康问题中[40]，也是小说、音乐作品和电影故事情节等文化作品常常探讨的主

7 © Melanie Hill

ecosystem—in wilderness or in cities—and without them the system is impaired and therefore less able to provide life-supporting ecological services.

4 Engaging Urbanites With Wild Nature

By 2050, the United Nations estimates a world population of 9.7 billion, of which 68% will live in urban areas—an increase from 56.2% in 2020.[38][39] As the urban population increases, it is unsurprising that people are more disconnected from nature—a finding evident in human health issues[40] as well as in cultural products such as novels, song lyrics, and movie storylines[41]. To address this disconnection, the citizen science web platform iNaturalist used in the annual City Nature Challenge (CNC) has emerged as a leader in urban engagement with wild nature. Initiated in 2016 by the Natural History Museum of Los Angeles County and California Academy of Sciences, the first CNC was an 8-day competition between Los Angeles and San Francisco. The next year, 16 cities in the United States participated, and in 2018 the CNC comprised 68 cities internationally. By 2020 the CNC involved 244 cities and engaged 41,000 people internationally (Fig. 6).[42]

The CNC is typically a competition to determine which cities have the most "wild" nature, to engage the most people, and to document species of wild plants and animals. It occurs in two parts. The first is a 4-day "bioblitz," followed by a 6-day species identification period. Participants venture throughout their designated geographic boundary to document wild plants and animals. They upload observations to the iNaturalist platform along with their best guess at the species name, the date and location of the observation, and any other relevant

题[41]。为解决这一问题，发起一年一度“城市自然挑战赛”（CNC）的公民科学网络平台“iNaturalist”成为了建立城市与野性自然密切联系方面的领军者。2016年，第一届CNC由洛杉矶自然历史博物馆与加州科学院合作发起，这是一个在洛杉矶和旧金山之间举办的为期8天的竞赛；次年，又吸引了16个美国城市加入；2018年，参与的国内外城市达到68个；到2020年，参与的城市已达到244个，吸引了超过4万名参与者（图6）。[42]

CNC的竞赛内容包括评选出最具“野性”自然的城市、最大限度地鼓励公共参与，以及记录野生动植物物种。竞赛分为两大部分：为期4天的“生物限时寻”与为期6天的物种鉴定期。参与者需要在指定区域内探寻、记录野生动植物，然后将各自的观察结果上传至iNaturalist平台，并附上他们判断的物种名称、观察日期与地点，以及其他任何观察到的细节。iNaturalist平台的会员会对这些上传的信息提供反馈意见，以识别观察者观察到的物种。iNaturalist和CNC使不同年龄、背景和能力的人都参与到公民科学中来（图7）。[43]

2020年，CNC迎来了特殊的一年。4月，在即将开展“生物限时寻”活动的几周前，新冠肺炎疫情开始肆虐。为此，国际组织者们决定CNC将采取合作型赛制（而非竞争型），强调自然的治愈力并鼓励人们积极探索。[44]而“丹佛市—博尔德市”路线的组织者及荒野基金会都借此机会，向市民宣传如何在享受自然的同时保持安全社交距离、如何与野生动物保持适当距离、如何减轻自然步道系统人流量过大等问题。

所有需要面对面参与的团体活动均被取消了，组织者转而开发了一系列的虚拟产品和资源，包括iNaturalist在线培训会与PDF手册、物种识别虚拟派对，以及户外探险安全指南[45]。通过这些活动，参与者了解到他们自己的花园和所在社区其实是充满了野性自然的复杂生态系统。组织者表示，CNC的这些变化尤受家长和老师的欢迎，他们希望孩子们能够参与到安全的户外教育活动中。即使受到全球疫情的影响，2020年CNC的参与人数仍较往年有所增加（总数超过4.1万人，2019年为3.5万人）。2021年，鉴于情况，CNC将继续举行这种合作型赛制。

5 结论

严格来说，城市荒野并不存在，但城市野境可以且应该被视为是衡量城市区域健康、宜居程度的标准之一。在缓解气候变化、维持生物多样性、防止疫情蔓延的需求日益紧迫的今天，野性自然在应对这三大生存挑战方面展现出了史无前例的重要意义。[46]能响应气候变化与生态韧性的人类工程技术固然重要，但其在成本效益、缓解效力与生态服务方面都不及野性自然。[47]

除了以上三大生存挑战外，在城市内部与毗邻区域的野性自然还能创造出极佳的“绿意”，吸引企业入驻和市民聚居。城市野境为城市提供的健康效益已被广泛研究并不断得到证实[48]。此外，城市野境的绿意与其提供的多样的游憩机会往往还能吸引高收入的居民前来定居，从而创造更多商机、增进税收[49]。相关研究也明确指出，城市森林公园距离居民区越近，其对城市经济与福祉的贡献也就越大。[50]

details about the sighting. Once data are uploaded, other members from the iNaturalist community provide feedback on the identification, confirming the observer's guess or offering an alternative. iNaturalist and the CNC enable people of all ages, backgrounds, and abilities to participate in citizen science (Fig. 7).[43]

The 2020 CNC was unique because the COVID-19 pandemic surged in April just weeks before the “bioblitz” was scheduled. The international organizers responded by modifying the CNC into a collaborative (rather than a competitive) event that emphasized the healing power of nature and encouraged its celebration.[44] The Denver–Boulder organizers, including the WILD Foundation, used this opportunity to educate residents on: how to enjoy nature while social-distancing; how to maintain appropriate distance to wildlife; and how to reduce pressure on overcrowded nature trail systems.

All in-person group events were canceled, and a range of virtual offerings and resources have been developed, including iNaturalist training webinars and PDF guides, a virtual party for species identification, and guidelines for safely venturing outdoors[45]. Through these, participants learned that their own gardens and neighborhoods are complex ecosystems teeming with wild nature. Organizers reported that these changes in the CNC were especially popular with parents and teachers eager to have safe outdoor educational activities for children. Even under a global pandemic, the 2020 CNC had an increase in participating numbers (more than 41,000, up from just over 35,000 in 2019). For 2021, the CNC will continue with this collaborative structure until the COVID-19 pandemic is contained.

5 Conclusion

Although urban wilderness per se does not exist, urban wildness can and should be considered a valuable aspect of healthy and desirable urban areas. In modern society, with important and pressing demands to combat climate change, stop biodiversity loss, and avert further pandemics, wild nature has never been more important because it addresses all the three existential challenges.[46] Human-engineered technological response to climate change and ecological resilience is important, but it is neither as cost efficient nor as effective as the mitigating power of wild nature and its ecological services.[47]

In addition to addressing these three existential challenges, wild nature in and immediately adjacent to urban areas also creates a highly desirable “green atmosphere” that attracts businesses and people to live in such a city. The health benefits provided by wildness in urban areas have been widely researched and continually confirmed for many years[48]. In addition, a green atmosphere and the diverse recreational opportunities it provides attracts new, often higher-income residents, leading to more businesses and improved tax revenue[49]. Other studies clearly indicate that the closer urban forest parks are to residential areas, the greater their amenity value to the city's economy and well-being.[50]

中国似乎已意识到城市野境的重要性，并采取了有力措施以确保更多城市居民能够享受到这类资源的益处。除了前文所探讨的北京案例外，还有许多令人赞叹的高品质案例值得一提，其中，贵阳花溪国家城市湿地与阿哈湖国家湿地公园，都是将城市中被忽视与被污染的河岸与湿地转变为城市河流公园的经典案例。这些公园与其他公园一样，在调节与改善城市环境价值方面发挥着重要作用，尤其是在改善生物多样性、净化水体与空气、创造游憩设施，以及美化风景方面。[51][52]同样，位于六盘水市中心、占地面积90hm²的明湖湿地公园已由曾经的工业遗址转变为今天的绿洲，并在2013年被正式指定为国家湿地公园。[53]这样的城市湿地公园（UWPs）遍布全国，正成为越来越多学者的研究对象。[54]在作者看来，中国UWPs的不断增加现象具有全球代表性，即通过修复与复兴城市河岸湿地创造城市野境正受到世界各地区的广泛重视。

荒野区域远离城市，对于缓解上述地球生命所面临的生存挑战至关重要。随着城市化的不断推进，城市野境的重要性也同荒野一样与日俱增，只是城市野境与城市居民的关系更加密切。除了本文简述的诸多效益外，自然所提供的深邃之美和启智作用对维系人类精神活力与创造力而言也是至关重要的。**LAF**

China appears to understand the importance of wildness in urban areas and has taken great strides to assure that the benefits of such a resource are increasingly available to city residents. The case study of Beijing was previously discussed and, in closing, a brief mention should be made of a few other impressive examples. Many exist, and the province of Guizhou is just one example of such high standards. The Huaxi National Urban Wetland Park and Ahahu Wetland Park are two projects in Guiyang where neglected and polluted riparian and wetland areas in the city were transformed into model urban river parks. These parks and others like them play and important role in regulating and improving the environmental values of their urban area, typically such things as biodiversity, water purification, air purification, recreation, and scenic beauty.[51][52] Similarly, Liupanshui Minghu Wetland Park, a 90-hectare oasis in the middle of the city, once an industrialized site, was officially designated as a National Wetland Park in 2013.[53] Such Urban Wetland Parks (UWPs) exist across the country and are the subject of increased scientific research.[54] In the opinion of the authors, China's proliferation of UWPs could represent one of the world's most extensive national examples of restoring and reviving urban riparian and wetlands to create urban wildness.

Wilderness areas are remote from cities and are of essential importance for mitigating the previously mentioned, existential challenges to life on earth. Because our planet is increasingly urbanized and this trend will continue, urban wildness is therefore of growing importance for the same reasons as wilderness, but in a manner more targeted to city dwellers. In addition to the many benefits briefly summarized in this paper, the profound beauty and inspiration provided by nature is of supreme importance to the vitality and strength of human spirit. **LAF**

REFERENCES

[1] Nash, R. F. (1982). *Wilderness and the American mind*. New Haven, Conn: Yale University Press.

[2] Kormos, C. F. (Ed.). (2008). *A Handbook on International Wilderness Law and Policy*. Golden, CO: Fulcrum Publishing.

[3] Casson, S., Martin, V., & Watson, A. (2016). *Wilderness Protected Areas: Management guidelines for IUCN category Ib protected areas*. Gland, Switzerland: IUCN.

[4] Dudley, N. (2008). *Guidelines for Applying Protected Area Management Categories*. doi:10.2305/IUCN.CH.2008.PAPS.2.en

[5] Yang, R., Shen, X., & Ma, K. (2019). Recommendations on building up China's National-park-centric Protected Area System. *Biodiversity Science*, 27(2), 137-139. doi:10.17520/biods.2019065

[6] Hawes, M., & Dixon, G. (2020). A remoteness-oriented approach to defining, protecting and restoring wilderness. *Parks*, 26(2), 23-26. doi:10.2305/IUCN.CH.2020.PARKS-26-2MH.en

[7] Locke, H., Ellis, E. C., Venter, O., Schuster, R., Ma, K., Shen, X., ... Watson, J. E. M. (2019). Three global conditions for biodiversity conservation and sustainable use: An implementation framework. *National Science Review*, 6(6), 1080-1082. https://doi.org/10.1093/nsr/nwz136

[8] Guo, H. (2019). Applying three global conditions framework to the conservation and sustainable use of biodiversity in China. In H. Guo (Ed.), *Big Earth Data in Support of the Sustainable Development Goals* (pp. 104-106). Beijing, China: Science Press.

[9] Locke, H. (2018). The International Movement to Protect Half the World: Origins, Scientific Foundations, and Policy Implications. *Reference Module in Earth Systems and*

Environmental Sciences. Advance online publication. https://doi.org/10.1016/B978-0-12-409548-9.10868-1

[10] Camera, D. (2020, November). Green Lifestyle in Boulder. *Boulder Convention and Visitors Bureau*. Retrieved from https://www.bouldercoloradousa.com/about-boulder/green-lifestyle/

[11] United Nations. (2018). *The World's Cities in 2018*. Retrieved from https://www.un.org/en/events/citiesday/assets/pdf/the_worlds_cities_in_2018_data_booklet.pdf

[12] TNN. (2018, February 7). Sanjay Gandhi National Park census confirms 41 leopards, 27 of them new. *The Times of India*. Retrieved from https://timesofindia.indiatimes.com/city/mumbai/sgnp-census-confirms-41-leopards-27-of-them-new/articleshow/62812269.cms

[13] Wikipedia. (2019, October). *Sanjay Ghandi National Park*. Retrieved from https://en.wikipedia.org/wiki/Sanjay_Gandhi_National_Park

[14] Chatterjee, B. (2020, April 19). '25% more flamingos in MMR'. *Hindustan Times*. Retrieved from https://www.hindustantimes.com/mumbai-news/25-more-flamingos-in-mmr/story-OOBiPNb9rTsInMEAli8e2L.html

[15] Wagh, S. (2019). The Contested Coast: Impacts of Reclamation on Artisanal Fishing in Mumbai. *Sanctuary Asia*, 39(6), 26-30.

[16] Townsend, T. (2018, December 17). Beijing: Could it be the capital of biodiversity? *Birding Beijing*. Retrieved from https://birdingbeijing.com/2018/12/17/beijing-could-it-be-the-capital-of-biodiversity/

[17] Xinhua. (2020, September 21). Rare leopards reappearing in habitats near Beijing. *China Daily*. Retrieved from https://newsinfo.inquirer.net/1337907/rare-leopards-reappearing-in-habitats-near-beijing

[18] Beijing Olympic Forest Park. (n. d.). *Travel China Guide*. Retrieved from https://www.travelchinaguide.com/attraction/beijing/olympic-forest-park.htm

[19] Zhao, X., Liang, H., & Xiao, W. (2012, December). *The Checklist of Birds of Beijing Olympic Forest Park*. Retrieved from https://wenku.baidu.com/view/3c97cf56ac51f01dc281e53a580216fc710a53d1.html

[20] Townsend, T. (2020, October 26). Beijing could become the 'capital of biodiversity'. *China Dialogue*. Retrieved from https://chinadialogue.net/en/cities/beijing-the-capital-of-biodiversity/

[21] Jiang, Z. & Harris, R. B. (2016). *Elaphurus davidianus*. The IUCN Red List of Threatened Species 2016: e.T7121A22159785. https://dx.doi.org/10.2305/IUCN.UK.2016-2.RLTS.T7121A22159785.en

[22] Beijing City Sub-centre "Urban Green Heart" will open to public before National Day. (2020, August 18). *ChinaNews*. Retrieved from https://www.tellerreport.com/news/2020-08-18-beijing-city-sub-center-%22urban-green-heart%22-will-open-to-the-public-before-national-day.r1Z4woQYMw.html

[23] Mahoney, J. (2012, December 19). Why wild animals are moving into cities, and what to do about it. *Popular Science*. Retrieved from https://www.popsci.com/science/article/2012-12/why-wild-animals-are-moving-cities-and-what-do-about-it#page-2

[24] Estes, J. A., Terborgh, J., Brashares, J. S., Power, M. E., Berger, J., Bond, W. J., ... Wardle, D. A. (2011). Trophic Downgrading of Planet Earth. *Science*, 333(6040), 301-306. doi:10.1126/science.1205106

[25] Fraser, C. (2011, September 15). The Crucial Role of Predators: A New Perspective on Ecology. *Yale Environment 360*. Retrieved from https://e360.yale.edu/features/the_crucial_role_of_predators_a_new_perspective_on_ecology

[26] Hunt, E. (2020, Thursday 10). Most googled: Why are there so many foxes in London?. *TimeOut*. Retrieved from https://www.timeout.com/london/news/most-googled-why-are-there-parakeets-in-london-050219

[27] Heimbuch, J. (2017, October 3). Navigating Coexistence with Urban Coyotes. *Center for Humans and Nature*. Retrieved from https://www.humansandnature.org/navigating-coexistence-with-urban-coyotes

[28] Braczkowski, A., O'Bryan, C. J., Stringer, M., Watson, J. E. M., Possingham, H. P., & Beyer, H. L. (2018). Leopards provide public health benefits in Mumbai, India. *Frontiers in Ecology and Environment*, 16(3), 176-182. https://doi.org/10.1002/fee.1776

[29] Solly, M. (2019, August 21). California Will Build the Largest Wildlife Crossing in the World. Smithsonian Magazine. Retrieved from https://www.smithsonianmag.com/smart-news/california-will-build-largest-wildlife-crossing-world-180972947

[30] Bears and people. (n. d.). *Bear Protection Ordinance*. Retrieved from https://bearsandpeople.com/ordinance/

[31] Jonathan Romeo County & environment reporter. (2017, December 20). Death toll for bears hits record numbers in Southwest Colorado. *The Durango Herald*. Retrieved from https://durangoherald.com/articles/200407

[32] Hill, M. (2018). *Of Bears and People: A Visual Case Story of Boulder, Colorado's Efforts to Coexist with Local Bruin* (Master's thesis). Retrieved from https://bearsandpeople.com/wp-content/uploads/2018/05/MelanieHill_BearsAndPeople_Thesis.pdf

[33] Loss, S. R., Will, T., & Marra, P. P. (2013). The impact of free-ranging domestic cats on wildlife of the United States. *Nature Communications*, (4), 1396. doi:10.1038/ncomms2380

[34] LaCroix, A. E. (2006). Detailed discussion of feral cat population control. *Animal Legal and Historical Center*. Retrieved from https://www.animallaw.info/article/detailed-discussion-feral-cat-population-control

[35] Ripple, W. J., & Beschta, R. L. (2012). Trophic cascades in Yellowstone: The first 15 years after wolf reintroduction. *Biological Conservation*, 145(1), 205-213. https://doi.org/10.1016/j.biocon.2011.11.005

[36] Boaden, A. E., & Kingsford, M. J. (2015). Predators drive community structure in coral reef fish assemblages. *Ecosphere*, 6(4), 1-33. https://doi.org/10.1890/ES14-00292.1

[37] Van Horn, G. (2017). Healing the Urban Wild. *Center for Humans and Nature: Minding Nature*, 10(3), 48-54. Retrieved from https://www.humansandnature.org/healing-the-urban-wild

[38] 68% of the world population projected to live in urban areas by 2050, says UN. (2018, May 16). *United Nations*. Retrieved from www.un.org/development/desa/en/news/population/2018-revision-of-world-urbanization-prospects.html

[39] Bucholz, K. (2020, November 4). How has the world's urban population changed from 2050 to today?. *World Economic Forum*. Retrieved from https://www.wise-geek.com/how-has-the-worlds-urban-population-changed-over-time.htm

[40] Warber, S. L., Dehudy, A. A., Bialko, M. F., Marselle, M. R., & Irvine, K. N. (2015). Addressing "Nature-Deficit Disorder": A Mixed Methods Pilot Study of Young Adults Attending a Wilderness Camp. *Evidence-Based Complementary and Alternative Medicine*, Advance online publication. https://doi.org/10.1155/2015/651827

[41] Kesebir, S., & Pelin, K. (2017). A Growing Disconnection From Nature Is Evident in Cultural Products. *Perspectives on Psychological Science*, 12(2), 258-269. doi:10.1177/1745691616662473

[42] L.A. vs S.F. (n. d.). *City Nature Challenge 2021*. Retrieved from https://citynaturechallenge.org/about/

[43] Seltzer,C. (2021, February 08). What Is INaturalist? *INaturalist*. Retrieved from www.inaturalist.org/pages/what+is+it

[44] City Nature Challenge Frequently Asked Questions relating to COVID-19. (2020). *City Nature Challenge 2021*. Retrieved from www.citynaturechallenge.org/covid19

[45] Education Toolkit. (n. d.). *City Nature Challenge 2021*. Retrieved from https://citynaturechallenge.org/education-toolkit/

[46] Intergovernmental Science-Policy Platform on Biodiversity and Ecosystem Services (IPBES). (2020, October). *Workshop Report on Biodiversity and Pandemics of the Intergovernmental Platform on Biodiversity and Ecosystem Services (IPBES)* (Version 1.3). http://doi.org/10.5281/zenodo.4311798

[47] Esposito, V., Phillips, S., Boumans, R., Moulaert, A., & Boggs, J. (2011). Climate change and ecosystem services: The contribution of and impacts on federal public lands in the United States. In Watson, A., Murrieta-Saldivar, J. & McBride, B. (Eds.), *Science and Stewardship to Protect and Sustain Wilderness Values, 9th World Wilderness Congress Symposium* (pp. 155-164). Retrieved from https://www.nrs.fs.fed.us/pubs/38789

[48] Lev, E., Kahn, P. H., Chen, H., & Esperum, G. (2020). Relatively Wild Urban Parks Can Promote Human Resilience and Flourishing: A Case Study of Discovery Park, Seattle, Washington. *Frontiers in Sustainable Cities*, (2), 1-12. https://doi.org/10.3389/frsc.2020.00002

[49] Recreation Counties Attracting New Residents and Higher Incomes. (2019, January). *Headwaters Economics*. Retrieved from https://headwaterseconomics.org/economic-development/trends-performance/recreation-counties-attract

[50] Cho, S. –H., Kim, T., Roberts, R. K., Hellwinckel, C., Kim, S. G., & Wilson, B. (2014). Developing an amenity value calculator for urban forest landscapes. *Computers, Environment, and Urban Systems*, (43), 34-41. https://doi.org/10.1016/j.compenvurbsys.2013.10.005

[51] Wang, Y., He, C., Wang, L., Liu, Y., Ye, K., Yang, X., ... Su, Y. (2019). Framework for Valuating Urban Wetland Park Ecosystem Services Based on the Cascade Approach. *Polish Journal of Environmental Studies*, 28(4), 2429-2440. https://doi.org/10.15244/pjoes/91938

[52] Guiyang Municipal People's Government. (2013, March 1). Huaxi, Guiyang National Urban Wetland Park Management. *Global-Regulation*. Retrieved from https://www.global-regulation.com/translation/china/162295/huaxi%252c-guiyang-national-urban-wetland-park-management.html

[53] Turenscape. (2015, January 21). Minghu Wetland Park / Turenscape. *ArchDaily*. Retrieved from https://www.archdaily.com/590066/minghu-wetland-park-turenscape

[54] Song, S., Christian, A., & Martin, P. (2020). Exploring integrated design guidelines for urban wetland parks in China. *Urban Forestry and Urban Greening*, (53),126712. https://doi.org/10.1016/j.ufug.2020.126712

与荒野共生：城市绿地的发展前景

Working With Wilderness: A Promising Direction for Urban Green Spaces

英戈·科瓦里克
Ingo KOWARIK*

德国柏林工业大学生态系统科学 / 植物生态学教授
Professor of Ecosystem Science / Plant Ecology, Technische Universität Berlin, Germany

*Corresponding Author
Address: Technische Universität Berlin, Institute of Ecology, Rothenburgstr. 12, D 12165 Berlin, Germany
Email: Kowarik@tu-berlin.de

摘要

“荒野”（wilderness）是一个根植于人类社会的文化概念。对于当代景观设计师或是景观设计先驱来说，荒野一直以来的重要性既在于其与人工景观元素的鲜明对比可以为自然主义植物设计提供灵感，也在于如今为协调城市、城市居民与自然做出的贡献。人们习惯上将城市和荒野视为对立面，因此有必要采取新方法以便更好地应对与城市语境下荒野相关的机遇和挑战。从生态学的角度来看，城市荒野是未受明显人类干扰的、具有生态系统过程高度自我调节特性的区域。由此可以区分出两种主要的荒野类型：以许多城市中的自然遗迹为代表的“古老荒野”，以及工业城市中诞生的“新生荒野”，在设计和管理绿地时需要对不同类型的场地区别对待。古老荒野一直以来都是保护和修复的对象，以及自然主义种植的灵感来源；相对地，新生荒野长期被视为疏于管理和社会经济衰退的产物。然而，自20世纪80年代起，德国的早期先锋项目开始将城市新生荒野融入绿色基础设施，产生了将荒野与设计相结合的、前所未有的绿色空间，既可以吸引游客，又可以保护生物多样性、支持许多生态系统服务。本文旨在说明将荒野元素、过程与城市绿色基础设施相融合——以便城市适时与自然恢复联系——的机遇和挑战。

关键词

生物多样性；设计干预；自然动力学；自生植被；城市荒野；野性城市

ABSTRACT

Wilderness is a cultural construct that is deeply rooted in many societies. For landscape architects and their predecessors, wilderness has long been important as a contrast to artificial garden elements, as an inspiration for naturalistic plant designs, or today as a timely contribution to reconciling cities and their inhabitants with the natural world. Since cities and wilderness have traditionally been seen as opposites, new approaches are necessary to better address the opportunities and challenges associated with wilderness in urban regions. From an ecological perspective, urban wilderness can be defined as an area characterized by a high degree of self-regulation in ecosystem processes where direct human impact is negligible. This allows two main types of wilderness to be distinguished: "ancient wilderness" represented by natural remnants in many cities, and "novel wilderness," which arises in artificial urban-industrial sites. The two types require different approaches in designing and managing green spaces. Ancient wilderness is a traditional object of conservation and restoration, and offers inspiration for naturalistic plantings. In contrast, the emergence of novel wilderness has long been associated with neglect and socio-economic decline. Since the 1980s, however, early pioneer projects in Germany have started to integrate novel urban wilderness into the green infrastructure. The results are unprecedented green spaces that combine novel wilderness with design interventions. These places are attractive to visitors, contribute to biodiversity conservation, and support many ecosystem services. This article aims to illustrate the opportunities and challenges of integrating wilderness components and processes into the urban green infrastructure—a timely way to reconnect cities with nature.

KEYWORDS

Biodiversity; Design Interventions; Nature Dynamics; Spontaneous Vegetation; Urban Wilderness; Wild Cities

编辑 | 崔婧沄、田乐
翻译 | 崔婧沄、田乐
EDITED BY | CUI Jingyun, Tina TIAN
TRANSLATED BY | CUI Jingyun, Tina TIAN

https://doi.org/10.15302/J-LAF-1-030025
收稿时间 RECEIVED DATE | 2021-01-05

中图分类号 | S73, [TU984.11+5]
文献标识码 | B

1 引言

"荒野"（wilderness）是一个根植于人类社会的文化概念，且具有不同的象征意义[1][2]。对于当代景观设计师或是景观设计先驱来说，荒野一直以来都是一个重要的议题。早在16世纪，自然林地就作为人工景观元素的对照出现在意大利文艺复兴时期的园林中[3]。18世纪初，随着规整的文艺复兴或巴洛克园林向英国如画式园林的转变，更加自然化的公园不断涌现，荒野自此成为一个明确的设计主题[4]。克里斯蒂安·凯·洛伦兹·赫希菲尔德在其颇具影响力的《景观设计理论》一书中强调了"完全交由自然过程和无序主导"的荒野对于英国如画式园林的重要意义在于文化上的"打破和对比"[5]。

其后，景观设计师从自然植物组合中汲取灵感，开启了自然主义种植设计：从荷兰的野生动植物公园到英国的绿色概念新城镇，再到美国近年的草原或沙漠花园。[6]~[8]这些项目从自然景观中获得荒野模板，运用乡土植物，并通常包含自然过程（如植物的生命周期）。其中，诸如纽约高线公园等高度人工设计、管理的项目创造了具有象征意义、能够唤起荒野联想的新式植物配植组合。

20世纪80年代，人们向城市荒野与设计概念的融合更进一步。这一时期的德国设计项目在很大程度上依赖于城市工业区中的自生植被，建立在后工业景观之上的开创性先锋项目包括由彼得·拉茨设计的鲁尔区北杜伊斯堡公园[9]，以及柏林的相关项目[10][11]。这些前所未有的城市绿地类型是对传统荒野和植物设计观念的挑战，同时也展示了城市生物多样性保护和人与自然互动的新机遇。

在前人工作的基础上[12]，本文旨在回答：如何定义城市环境中的荒野？为什么提升城市中的荒野是有前景的？与城市荒野共生存在哪些挑战和机遇？

2 什么是城市中的荒野？

长期以来，由于解读方式各异，荒野一直是一个微妙的概念[13]。有趣的是，"荒野"一词很早就被用于描述英国如画式园林中那些或多或少设计过的小节点[4]。然而，自然保护中所指的传统荒野主要依据的是美国1964年颁布的《荒野法》中的定义——"地球及地球上生命群落中不受人类干扰"的广阔景观；欧盟《自然保护区荒野指南》中也有类似

1 Introduction

Wilderness is a cultural construct that is deeply rooted in human societies, with different symbolic meanings[1][2]. For landscape architects and their predecessors, wilderness has long been an important topic. As early as in the 16th century, wild forest patches (selvatici) were included in Italian Renaissance gardens as a contrast to artificially constructed garden elements[3]. Since the early 18th century, the transformation of formal Renaissance or Baroque gardens in Europe into English landscape gardens led to more natural parks, with wilderness as an explicit design topic[4]. In his influential *Theory of Garden Design*, Christian Kay Lorenz Hirschfeld highlighted the importance of wilderness in English landscape gardens as areas "left entirely to natural wilderness processes and free disorder," serving "as a means of interruption and contrast" to culture[5].

More recently, insights into natural plant assemblages have inspired landscape architects in the composition of naturalistic planting designs, from Heemparken in the Netherlands to green concepts for New Towns in England and to recent prairie-styled or desert gardens in the United States[6]~[8]. Inspired by wilderness templates from natural landscapes, these approaches work with native plants. They often also integrate natural processes (e.g. plants' regeneration cycles) into their projects. Some of these projects, such as the High Line in New York, are powerful in the creation of new plant assemblages that evoke associations with wilderness at a symbolic level, despite their artificial origins and ongoing maintenance.

A further step toward integrating urban wilderness into design concepts emerged in the 1980s. This new generation of design projects in Germany largely relied on the existing spontaneous vegetation of urban industrial sites. Groundbreaking pioneer projects were established in post-industrial landscapes of the Ruhr, including Peter Latz's Landscape Park Duisburg-Nord[9], and those in Berlin[10][11]. These unprecedented types of urban green spaces questioned the traditional views of wilderness and planting design. These projects also demonstrate new opportunities for urban biodiversity conservation and the interactions between people and nature.

Based on previous work[12], this article aims to provide answers to three questions: How can wilderness be defined in urban environment? Why is it promising to enhance wilderness in cities? What challenges and opportunities exist when working with urban wilderness?

2 Defining Wilderness in Cities

Wilderness has long been defined in very different ways and is therefore a subtle term[13]. Interestingly, the term "wilderness" was used early on in a green space context to describe small sections in English landscape gardens that were more or less designed[4]. Traditional wilderness concepts in nature conservation, however, largely rely on vast landscapes "where the earth and its community of life are untrammeled by man" as pronounced in the influential United States Wilderness

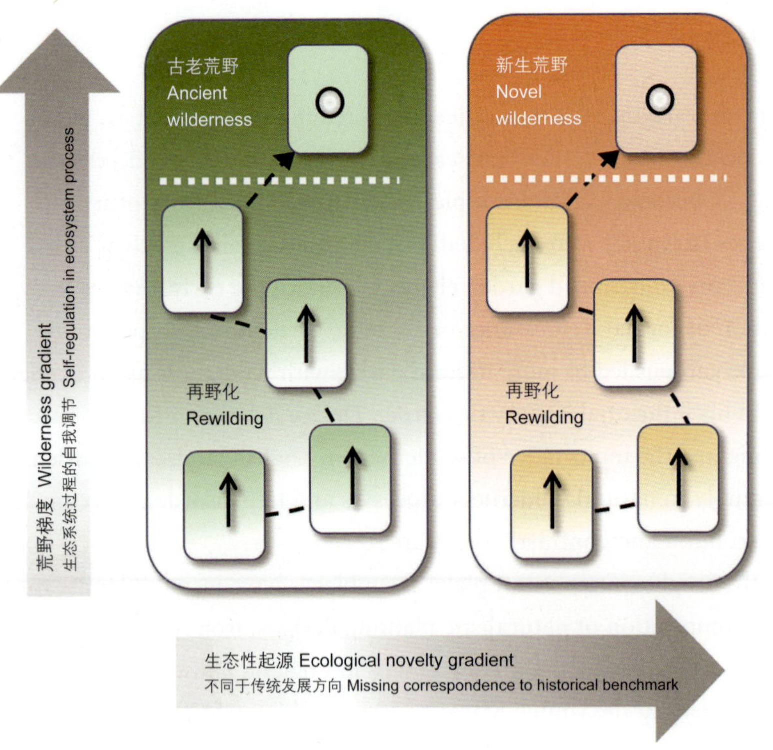

1. 城市中的两种荒野类型：古老荒野和新生荒野（以虚线上方的方块表示）。以图中虚线为界，这两种荒野类型均包含高于一般自我调节能力的生态系统过程。虚线以下，每个方块代表一个城市空间，每个空间均处在一个荒野梯度上，沿梯度越向上生态系统过程的自我调节越强。方块中的箭头表示该城市空间中绿地再野化的可能性；方块间的曲线则代表城市空间逐步转变为对应类型（古老或新生）荒野的可能性。
2. 柏林古老荒野区域中的自然森林和湿地遗迹

1. Two types of wilderness in cities: ancient wilderness and novel wilderness (boxes above dot lines). Both wilderness types share a high-level self-regulation in ecosystem processing as indicated by a position above the threshold for prevailing self-regulation (dot lines). Each box below the dot lines represents urban spaces along a wilderness gradient, which reflects an increasing role of self-regulated ecosystem processes. The arrows within the boxes illustrate rewilding opportunities within a given green space type. The curves between the boxes indicate the possibility of a step-wise transformation of urban spaces toward ancient or novel wilderness.
2. Ancient wilderness area in Berlin with remnants of natural forests and wetlands

界定。今天，在人类影响波及全球生态系统的人类世，我们似乎需要拓展对于荒野的解读：不论其规模或起源如何，荒野均应建立在未受明显人类干扰的、具有高度自我调节的生态系统过程之上[12]。在城市语境下理解这一概念将有助于应对与人类世生态系统中荒野相关的机遇和挑战。

2.1 两种荒野类型

从类型学层面来讲，根据形成方式可将城市中的荒野区域划分为两种类型：古老荒野和新生荒野（图1）。古老荒野对应自然保护中的传统荒野概念，以城市边缘留存的自然遗迹为代表，例如传统景观意义

Act of 1964, and similarly in the EU Guidelines on Wilderness in Natura 2000. Yet in the Anthropocene Epoch, with ecosystems globally being influenced by humans, a broader wilderness definition seems to be appropriate, which is based on a high-degree self-regulation of ecosystem processes, regardless of their size or origin, with direct human influences negligible[12]. Applying this concept to urban regions allows us to address both opportunities and challenges associated with wilderness in novel ecosystems.

2.1 Two Types of Wilderness

At a typological level, two types of wilderness can be defined by the origin of wilderness areas in cities: ancient wilderness and novel wilderness (Fig. 1). Ancient wilderness corresponds to the traditional wilderness concept in nature conservation and is represented in an urban context by natural remnants that exist within several city boundaries. Examples include wetlands or forests (Fig. 2) that still correspond to the historical benchmark of pristine landscapes, though they are often modulated by urban interventions[14]. In contrast, novel wilderness areas result from divergent development paths emerging in the wake of far-reaching human alterations to soils, hydrological conditions, or species communities. Thus novel ecosystems are often with unprecedented combinations of native and non-native plants[15][16]. Examples of such novel wilderness sites range from micro to landscape scale (Fig. 3) and include emerging forests in vacant lots, large derelict industrial areas, former military areas, and other types of vacant land of high biological richness[10][17]-[19].

3. 城市新生荒野具有多种尺度：从树池中（图3-1）和意大利罗马古迹附近（图3-2）的自生植被；到德国柏林墙遗址旁（图3-3）、西班牙马德里某个非正式社区花园里（图3-4）野生的臭椿（*Ailanthus altissima*）；再到德国鲁尔区盖尔森基兴的莱茵-易北雕塑公园中的后工业景观（图3-5，3-6）。

3. Novel urban wilderness ranging from the micro-site scale to the landscape scale. Spontaneous vegetation in a tree pit (Fig. 3-1) and close to antique ruins in Rome, Italy (Fig. 3-2); wild-grown *Ailanthus altissima* associated with fragments of the Berlin Wall, Germany (Fig. 3-3) and in an informal community garden in Madrid, Spain (Fig. 3-4); post-industrial landscape of the Ruhr with the "Sculpture Park Rhein-Elbe" in Gelsenkirchen, Germany (Fig. 3-5, 3-6).

© Ingo Kowarik
3-1

© Ingo Kowarik
3-3

© Ingo Kowarik
3-5

© Ingo Kowarik
3-2

© Ingo Kowarik
3-4

© Ingo Kowarik
3-6

上的湿地或森林（图2），尽管它们经常受到城市干预的影响[14]。相对地，新生荒野区域则是在人类对土壤、水文条件或物种群落的深远影响下，以不同形态或模式发展出的人类世生态系统，因此其中的乡土与非乡土植物组合通常是前所未见的[15][16]。新生荒野区域具有多种尺度（图3），也涉及多种用地类型，包括空地上的新生林地、大型废弃工业区、后军事用地和生物多样性高的其他空地类型[10][17]-[19]。

2.2 荒野的梯度

作为生态过程的产物，荒野可以反映自组织的生态系统过程的水平，不同的城市用地处于荒野梯度上的不同位置[12]，这即是罗德里克·纳什早先为非城市景观建立的荒野程度谱系[20]。如图1所示，荒野程度会随着人类影响的增加而降低，这正是城市中许多残余林地不同于亚洲寺庙林[21]或城郊游憩林[22]等纯粹荒野的原因。同样，人工设计场地的荒野程度可通过减少维护、区分空间休闲用途、利用自生植被等方式来提高。这种城市"再野化"策略类似于将衰落乡村景观发展为新生荒野区域的设计策略[23]。

人类影响（如刈草）停止后，生态系统过程便会自发开始。随着演替的推进，过往管理对群落组成和结构的影响逐渐减弱。经此形成的成熟森林相比之前的生态系统阶段更具"野性"。重要的是，荒野的类型无法转变，但同一类型的荒野元素或过程可以进行提升（如图1方框中

2.2 Wilderness as a Gradient

Since wilderness results from ecological processes, urban sites can also be assigned to a position along a wilderness gradient that reflects different levels of self-organized ecosystem processing[12]. This is the wilderness continuum which has been early established for non-urban landscapes by Roderick Nash[20]. Along this gradient, as shown in Figure 1, the level of wilderness may decrease in response to increasing cultural influences. This is why many remnant forests in cities differ from pure wilderness sites as in Asian temple forests[21] or in peri-urban recreational forests[22]. Conversely, the level of wilderness in designed areas can be increased, e.g., through less maintenance, spatially differentiated recreational use, and the acceptance of spontaneous vegetation. This is the urban analog to "rewilding" strategies that have been proposed for abandoned rural landscapes to allow for the development of novel wilderness areas[23].

Self-organized ecosystem processes start directly after the cessation of human impacts (e.g. when mowing is stopped), and, as succession proceeds, effects from previous management on community composition and structure diminish. In this way, mature forests are "wilder" than previous ecosystem stages. Importantly, there is often an option to enhance wilderness elements or processes within one type instead of shifting it to the other type as indicated by the arrows in the boxes in Figure 1. Examples are the inclusion of spontaneous vegetation in parks by reduced weeding or the allowance of decay in old trees or fallen wood in maintained green spaces. As with wilderness, ecological novelty can also be classified typologically according to the novel ecosystem concept[16], i.e. a place is novel or not.

的箭头所示）。相关举措包括降低公园内清除自生植被的频率，或在人工维护的绿地中保留枯木。与荒野一样，这些景观的生态特性也可依据人类世生态系统的概念进行分类[16]，即场所新生与否。另外，场地的生态系统也可按照从原始到高度新生的梯度来划分[24]。

2.3 不同尺度下的荒野

最后，尺度对新生荒野很重要。奥尔多·利奥波德曾表示“再小的地块也会存在荒野”[25]。事实也正如此，城市与自然景观相连时，城市荒野可以在区域尺度上存在、发展，例如巴西里约热内卢城市内部就包含部分大西洋雨林[26]；在城市尺度上，大型新生荒野区域网络也会伴随工业区转型而出现，如德国鲁尔区[27]或美国的收缩城市[28]。在斑块尺度上，以自生植被为代表的荒野可能在空地中或沿线性结构出现（如交通廊道沿线）[18][29]。在微观尺度上，一棵古树便是城市空间中古老荒野的遗存[30]；墙面、裂隙或树池中的自生植被则是新生荒野开启的标志[31]。因此，被保护或提升的城市荒野对象并不完全为大面积的区域，也包括中小型场地。

3 城市荒野支持论

全球各地的城市正逐渐将荒野提上议程[32]。许多旨在使城市变得更加野性的倡议（如“野性城市”①和“国家公园城市”②等）指出，人们对城市社会重新拥抱自然的兴趣渐增。除了人类对更自然的环境愈发青睐外，还存在如下一些关于城市荒野——特别是新生城市荒野——的重要观点：

1）保护或提升城市中古老和新生荒野有助于应对全球生物多样性危机。城市的加速发展使得许多城市内部及周边的残余古老荒野面临的压力日增，因此亟需保护或恢复当地生物多样性，尤其是乡土物种。城市中的新生荒野区域可以庇护乡土物种和濒危物种[33]。此外，在人工设计绿地内促进荒野过程可提升其动植物生境功能[34]。

2）为城市居民提供更多与自然接触的机会，有利于人类健康和福祉[35]。随着城市建成环境的增加，大部分城市居民与自然的接触愈发

① “野性城市”是由荒野基金会（美国）发起的全球性活动，旨在“为所有生灵复兴城市中的野性自然”。有关该倡议的详细信息，请访问野性城市的官方网站。
② “国家公园城市”是由国家公园城市基金会（协同其他国际组织）发起，旨在“创造人、地、自然紧密相连的城市”的倡议活动。有关该倡议的详细信息，请访问国家公园城市基金会的官方网站。

Alternatively, sites can be assigned along a novelty gradient spanning from pristine to highly novel ecosystems[24].

2.3 Wilderness at Different Scales

Finally, scale matters to novel wilderness. Aldo Leopold stated that “no tract of land is too small for the wilderness idea”[25]. Indeed, urban wilderness can exist, or develop, at a regional scale, when cities are in contact with natural landscapes. Parts of the Atlantic rainforest of Brazil, for example, are located within Rio de Janeiro[26]; At the same spatial scale, large networks of novel wilderness areas can emerge in the wake of industrial transformation as in the Ruhr of Germany[27] or in shrinking cities of the United States[28]. At the patch scale, wilderness represented by spontaneous vegetation may emerge in vacant lots or within linear structures, e.g., along transportation corridors[18][29]. At the micro scale, a single heritage tree can represent remnants of ancient wilderness in urban spaces[30]; the spontaneous revegetation on walls, and in cracks or tree pits indicates the onset of novel wilderness development[31]. Thus, approaches to protect or enhance wilderness in cities do not exclusively rely on large areas and can also include small and medium-sized sites.

3 Arguments for Urban Wilderness

Wilderness is increasingly on urban agendas around the globe[32]. The many initiatives toward making cities wilder indicate a growing interest in reconnecting urban societies to the natural world. Examples include the “WILD Cities”① and the “National Park Cities”② initiatives. Beyond a general human preference for more natural surroundings, there are some major arguments for urban wilderness in general and novel urban wilderness in particular:

1) Approaches toward conserving or enhancing ancient and novel wilderness in cities help counteract the global biodiversity crisis. Remnants of ancient wilderness within or in the vicinity of many cities are increasingly under pressure due to accelerating urban growth. This requires efforts to conserve or restore their unique biodiversity, represented by native species assemblages. Novel wilderness areas in cities can also harbor a high biodiversity, including a range of native and endangered species[33]. Moreover, allowing for or stimulating wilderness processes within the frame of designed green spaces can increase the habitat functions for plants and animals[34].

2) The creation of additional opportunities for urban residents to come into contact with natural components and processes benefits people’s health and well-being[35]. As many people have limited access to nature as cities become increasingly built up, increasing urban nature in general and wilderness in particular become an important issue of environmental justice in cities[36].

3) Integrating novel wilderness into urban green infrastructure contributes to the city’s resilience, in particular in the face of climate change. Urban wilderness supports a wealth of regulating, provisioning, cultural, and supporting ecosystem

① WILD Cities is a global campaign to regenerate and celebrate wild nature in urban areas to improve quality of life for all, initiated by WILD Foundation. For more information about this initiative, please visit the official website of WILD Cities.
② National Park Cities is a movement initiated by National Park City Foundation with many other international organizations, aiming at "making cities where people, places and nature are better connected." For more information about this initiative, please visit the official website of National Park City Foundation.

有限，城市中的环境公平需要通过增加城市自然——特别是荒野——来达成[36]。

3）新生荒野与城市绿色基础设施的融合有助于提升城市韧性，尤其是在气候变化的当下。城市荒野与一般城市绿地一样，都可以提供大量的生态系统的调节、供给、文化和支持服务[37][38]。此外，荒野中高度自我调节的生态系统还具有两个特点：第一，不同于人工建造、维护的绿地在植物生产、种植、场地整理和维护等环节中的巨大能源消耗，荒野的存在或发展没有碳足迹；第二，经特定城市条件的筛选，新生荒野中的群落组成由乡土和非乡土物种混合，依城市条件的不同可能有多种组合[15]。因此，以城市自生植被为代表的植物组合最适应特定场地条件，且无需额外的能源消耗就能适应未来环境变化。

4）新生城市荒野是自然与文化的共同产物，尤其当其与建筑遗迹交织在一起时，常能让人们理解、铭记城市用地的波澜变迁。新生荒野区域也象征着城市与自然的重新融合，因此城市居民往往会喜爱荒野[39]~[41]，并产生情感上的依赖，例如人们与柏林三角地公园中自然森林的情感联系[42]。

4 与荒野共生的机遇与挑战

对于景观设计学科来说，可共生的城市荒野包括三个类型：古老荒野场地、新生荒野场地（本文焦点），以及其他城市空间中的荒野元素和过程。在设计和管理绿地时需要对不同类型的场地区别对待。

4.1 古老荒野场地

即使是广阔的古老荒野区域（如国家公园），通常也需要必要的景观设计干预以保证自然景观内的可达性[43]。在城市地区，古老荒野一直以来都是保护和修复的对象，由于城市化进程的加快，现有的一系列成熟方法面临的挑战渐增：例如巴西的大西洋雨林，这里是全球生物多样性热点地区，虽然大部分地区已遭破坏，但一片面积约为3 300hm²的区域作为国家公园受到里约热内卢的保护。这里面临的挑战是如何防止未来林地的损失、减少来自周边城市的负面影响，及修复受损区域[26]。在城市内部，可通过修复手段（如种植乡土植物）来改善一些包含小面积残余雨林生态系统的流域[44]。

4.2 新生荒野场地

可共生的城市新生荒野场地面临的挑战众多，通常需要设计干预将之与城市绿色基础设施相融合。由于存在垃圾、涂鸦、衰败等疏于管理的迹象，人们通常对荒野存在负面认知——在象征意义上，场地的“野”亦宣告着场地的“荒”，会使人们联想到与之相关的伤痛记忆。

services as urban green spaces do in general[37][38]. Two additional benefits from the high-level self-regulation in ecosystem processing inhere in wilderness: first, wilderness sites exist or develop without a carbon footprint—in contrast to constructed and intensively maintained green spaces, which require energy inputs for plant production, plantings, site preparation, and maintenance; Second, the species composition of novel wilderness sites is filtered by the specific urban conditions, leading to novel mixtures of native and non-native species with open-ended community assembly[15]. Such plant assemblages represented by urban spontaneous vegetation are thus best adapted to the given site conditions and will adapt to future environmental dynamics without additional energy inputs.

And 4) novel urban wilderness is a co-product of nature and culture, often allowing people to understand and remember the checkered history of urban land uses that gave rise to it, especially when interwoven with built relics. Novel wilderness sites also demonstrate, at a symbolic level, the reconnection of cities to the natural world. Therefore, urban dwellers often appreciate wilderness sites[39]~[41] and may feel emotionally attached to such places—as people are to the wild forest in Berlin's Gleisdreieck Park[42].

4 Challenges and Opportunities for Working With Urban Wilderness

For the discipline of Landscape Architecture, three facets of working with wilderness in cities are particularly relevant: ancient wilderness sites, novel wilderness sites (which are the focus in this article), and wilderness elements and processes in other urban spaces. It requires different approaches in design and management.

4.1 Ancient Wilderness Sites

Even in vast ancient wilderness areas, landscape architectural interventions are usually necessary to provide access to natural wonders, e.g. in national parks[43]. In urban regions, ancient wilderness is a traditional object of conservation and restoration, with a range of well-developed approaches but also with increasing challenges due to the accelerating urbanization. An example is the Atlantic rainforest of Brazil, a biodiversity hotspot. Most parts have been destroyed, but a large area of 3,300 hectares is being protected as a national park in Rio de Janeiro. Here, the challenge is to prevent future losses of forest areas, reduce negative impacts from adjacent urban areas, and restore damaged parts[26]. Within the city, some watersheds contain smaller remnants of Atlantic rainforest ecosystems, which can be enhanced through restoration efforts, e.g. plantings of native species[44].

4.2 Novel Wilderness Sites

Diverse challenges exist when working with novel wilderness in cities. Design interventions are often needed to integrate such areas into the urban green infrastructure. Many times, wilderness places are laden with negative connotations due to signs of neglect, such as littering, graffiti, and general decay. On a symbolic

© Ingo Kowarik
4-1

© Ingo Kowarik
4-2

© Ingo Kowarik
4-3

© Ingo Kowarik
4-4

4. 柏林南部自然公园中未经干扰的森林动态（图4-1），不定期放牧的空地（图4-2），以及设计干预后的废弃铁轨（图4-3，4-4）。

4. Natur-Park Südgelände in Berlin. Undisturbed forest dynamics (Fig. 4-1), occasionally grazed clearings (Fig. 4-2), and design interventions on a former freight yard (Fig. 4-3, 4-4).

例如，美国底特律地区和德国鲁尔区，新生荒野因工业的衰落得以在前工业用地上发展，使人在情感上回忆起场地曾经的社会经济繁荣一去不再[45]；在柏林，许多新生荒野是伴随着二战造成的破坏及其后柏林墙对城市的割裂（1961~1989）发展起来的[46]。

人们对于新生荒野的负面认知可通过景观设计干预来改善（图4），其中景观感知的关键点在于通过提供正面感知元素来体现“管护的迹象”[47]。这些干预产生了荒野和人工绿地的混合体，而挑战在于如何保留场地过去“非正式”的独特性[48]，并将自生植被的组成、结构和功能在演替中的自然变化纳入考量。

通过增设正式入口、园路和其他绿地要素，可提升荒野对公众的吸引力[49]。信息系统是一种有效手段，包括谛听漫步等创新性形式[50]。通过结合艺术作品，可实现与充满野性的自然的对比，例如柏林南部的自然公园[51]或鲁尔工业森林中的许多地区[27]。建在曾经将城市一分为二的柏林墙遗址上的柏林绿带，通过将现代设计方法引入新生城市荒野，将饱含历史伤痛的遗迹融入新的绿地之中[46]。

这些项目的一大挑战是如何应对自然界的无序动态变化。在大多数没有人类的干预情况下，经过几年的自然演替，场地会被茂密的木本植被覆盖。一方面，演替过程中物种的更迭很好地反映了自然对新兴城市

level, people's perceptions of novel wilderness may reflect the painful events that led to ruptures with the former land-use history, thereby enabling the natural dynamics in the first place. For example, in the Detroit region of the United States or in the Ruhr area of Germany, industry decline has allowed the development of novel wilderness on previously industrial land, and the wilderness is now linked, emotionally, with preceding traumatic socio-economic effects[45]. In Berlin, many novel wilderness sites developed in the wake of destructions due to World War II and the subsequent division of the city by the Berlin Wall from 1961 to 1989[46].

Negative connotations of novel wilderness can be ameliorated by landscape architectural interventions (Fig. 4) by offering positively perceived signs as "cues to care"—a key issue in landscape perception[47]. Such interventions result in hybrids between wilderness and designed green spaces. The challenge here is to preserve the distinctiveness of the site, to leave room for informal uses that existed before[48], and to take the nature dynamics into account since the composition, structure, and function of spontaneous vegetation usually change during successional processes.

Formalizing access by establishing official entrances, paths, and other elements of green spaces usually increases the attractiveness of wilderness areas for a broader public[49]. Information systems are useful, including innovative approaches such as sound walks[50]. With the integration of artworks, contrasts to wild nature can be achieved, as in Berlin's Natur-Park Südgelände[51] or in many areas of the Industriewald Ruhr[27]. The Berlin Green Belt, being created where the Berlin Wall once divided the city into two, is an example of integrating remnants of the painful past into new green spaces by combining modern design approaches with novel urban wilderness[46].

环境的适应。新生林地体现了在城市中几乎不可见的、未加控制的生态系统过程，可作为新生荒野保育区加以保护。另一方面，林木茂盛的荒野也存在两个缺陷：首先，环境心理学研究表明，相比茂密的林地，人们更喜欢开放或半开放空间[52]——阿普尔顿的“视界—遮蔽”理论[53]将其解释为人们一般希望“看的同时不被看”，如用一棵树或树丛遮蔽自己，并瞭望开阔区域。其次，尽管以乡土或引进树种建群的城市新生森林可供多样的动植物栖息[54]，但这些林地并不适宜那些习惯生活于阳光充足、开敞环境的濒危动植物栖息。柏林的新生草原比新生林地庇护了更多的濒危植物物种[55]。因此，荒野中不同结构的生境镶嵌也有利于生物多样性保护。

应对这些挑战的方法是调节部分地区的植被动态，以在更大区域内实现不同演替阶段的持续共存。为此，柏林会在部分已经作为公园或自然保育区保护起来的新生荒野中仅进行不定期的刈草或放牧，其余则不加管控。由此形成的林地和开敞栖息地镶嵌不仅可以吸引游客，也吸引了多种动植物来此安家。这其中的一些区域可用于游憩活动，而其他区域为了保护物种丰富的草原群落或保证野生植被的萌发免受干扰，只能沿路而游。对许多动植物来说不可或缺的先锋地块，可以像柏林北站公园那样，通过整合现有的不透水地面或不定期移除表土来维持（图5-3）。在德国法兰克福波那梅斯前军用机场的项目中，部分混凝土跑道被破开，不仅在结构上产生了生动有趣的效果，也十分利于林地重建（图5-1，5-4）。当地下水重新渗出或后工业场地构筑物中的雨水得以收集时，新生湿地便可建立——这取决于场地的原用地性质（图6）。

In these projects, a particular challenge is how to deal with the wild dynamics of nature. In most cases without human intervention, dense woody vegetation will result from natural succession after a few years. On the one hand, the alteration of species during succession perfectly reflects nature's adaptation to novel urban conditions. Emerging novel forests well manifest the uncontrolled ecosystem processes, which are rarely experienced in cities. Such areas can be protected as novel wilderness reserves. On the other hand, densely forested wilderness areas see two disadvantages. First, studies from environmental psychology have shown that dense forest stands are less appreciated than open or semi-open spaces[52]. This preference is often explained in terms of Appleton's prospect-refuge theory[53], according to which people generally have a need for "seeing without being seen," e.g., with a tree or group of trees as the refuge and the open area for prospect. Second, although emerging urban forests dominated by either native or introduced trees can host diverse plant and animal assemblages[54], they are less important in providing habitat for endangered plant and animal species that are often specialists of sunny, open sites. Novel grassland in Berlin thus harbors more endangered plant species than novel forests[55]. Maintaining differently structured habitat mosaics in wilderness areas is thus also beneficial for biodiversity conservation.

The solution to these challenges is to modulate vegetation dynamics in some places so that different succession stages continuously coexist in a larger area. To this end, parts of novel wilderness areas in Berlin, which have been conserved as parks or nature reserves, are mown or grazed occasionally, while in other parts

5. 与荒野共生。同一块场地中起始阶段（上行）与充分生长的自生植被（下行）的对比。法兰克福波那梅斯的废弃飞机跑道被破碎成块（左列）；柏林三角地公园中自然森林生长在铁路道渣上和设计过的道渣床两侧（中列）；柏林北站公园里部分移除表土的场地和部分修剪的草地（右列）。

5. Working with urban wilderness. Pioneer stages (row above) are contrasted with more mature spontaneous vegetation in the same sites (row below). Former airstrip partly broken into clods in Bonames, Frankfurt (left); wild forest on rail ballast and designed rail ballast bed in "Gleisdreieck-Park," Berlin (middle), partially removed topsoil and partially mown grassland in "Park auf dem Nordbahnhof," Berlin (right).

© Ingo Kowarik
5-1

© Ingo Kowarik
5-2

© Ingo Kowarik
5-3

© Ingo Kowarik
5-4

© Ingo Kowarik
5-5

© Ingo Kowarik
5-6

6-1 © Ingo Kowarik

6-2 © Ingo Kowarik

6-3 © Ingo Kowarik

6. 世界文化遗产德国弗尔克林根钢铁厂中共存的工业遗迹和处于演替中段的新生荒野（包括新生湿地）。
7. 意大利罗马前斯尼亚湖的工业遗迹中偶然出现的一片湖（图7-1），自然林地斑块（图7-2），非定期修剪的社交草坪（图7-3），以及提供遮荫的野生臭椿（图7-4）。

6. World Cultural Heritage Site Völklingen Ironworks, Germany. Coexistence of industrial remnants and novel wilderness with intermediate succession stages and novel wetlands.
7. Lago Ex-SNIA in Rome, Italy. Industrial remains, an unintentionally emerging lake (Fig. 7-1), wild forest patches (Fig. 7-2), and occasionally mown areas (Fig. 7-3) for social activities. Wild trees of *Ailanthus altissima* provide shades (Fig. 7-4).

nature dynamics are allowed to proceed. The resulting mosaics of forested and open habitats are attractive to visitors as well as to many animal and plant species. Some of these areas are accessible for recreational activities, others can only be experienced following paths to conserve species-rich grassland communities or to allow for the emergence of less disturbed ruderal vegetation. Pioneer sites, which are indispensable for many plants and animals, can be maintained by integrating existing impervious surfaces or by occasionally removing topsoil, as what has been done in the Park auf dem Nordbahnhof (Fig. 5-3). In the project for the former Bonames airfield in Frankfurt, Germany, some of the concrete of a former airstrip was broken up into clods, which achieved an interesting structural effect, but also strongly favored reforestation (Fig. 5-1, 5-4). Novel types of wetlands can develop, for example, when groundwater begins to infiltrate or rainwater to collect in built structures of post-industrial sites, this often in association with artifacts from the previous land use (Fig. 6). A prominent example is the post-industrial site "Lago Ex-SNIA" in Rome, Italy, where the ruins of a former textile factory seem to emerge from a lake (Fig. 7). As a result of construction work, groundwater was no longer pumped out when the industrial use ceased here. This small area harbors a considerable biodiversity[56] and demonstrates that different components can be well combined when working with novel urban wilderness. In this case as in many others[11][19], the engagement of local initiatives or grassroot movements is key in preventing the destruction of novel wilderness areas that are often located in the neighborhoods with limited access to green areas.

4.3 Wilderness Elements Within Traditional Green Spaces

In addition to working with novel wilderness areas at a larger scale, wilderness components can be fostered within a range of urban spaces as part of urban rewilding. Working with spontaneous vegetation has been a topic in planting design for a while, with multi-faceted approaches to integrating wild-grown plant communities in green spaces or to modulating such plant assemblages by adding aesthetically attractive species[57]. Non-native species can be accepted as typical components of urban spontaneous vegetation unless they spread into adjacent endangered ecosystems.

Converting frequently mown lawns to less intensively maintained meadows increases opportunities for natural processes and is often accepted when the ecological benefits are explained[58]. Other approaches to enhancing wilderness processes in green spaces include the retention of decaying or fallen trees. These are not only important habitat elements for many animals and fungi but also can inspire feelings to an unpredictable environment and evoke a sense of mystery[59]. Such structures obviously contrast with the traditional appearance of green spaces but are usually accepted by the public when information about their ecological value is provided.

Finally, unusual wilderness concepts for green spaces are also conceivable. An outstanding example comes from the French landscape architect Gilles

其中的典型案例是意大利罗马的后工业遗址“前斯尼亚湖”，纺织厂的废墟犹如自湖中诞生（图7）。工业活动停止后，先前构筑工程中不再抽取地下水，这一小块区域内蕴藏着可观的生物多样性[56]，并证明了在新生城市荒野中不同的部分可以得到有机结合。与其他许多案例一样[11][19]，地方倡议和基层运动的参与是防止那些绿地有限的社区中新生荒野遭破坏的关键。

4.3 传统绿地中的荒野元素

除研究更大尺度的新生荒野外，提升城市空间中的荒野元素以助城市再野化也是可行之道。利用自生植物的种植设计已经成为业内话题之一，包括运用多种方法整合野生植物群落野和绿地、在植物组团中增加景观效果良好的物种[57]。在不会扩散至周边濒危生态系统的情况下，非乡土物种也可用作城市自生植被。

将定期修剪的草坪转变为低维护的草甸，以促进场地的自然过程，而在向公众说明其生态效益后也常能得到大众认可[58]。促进绿地中荒野过程的其他方法包括保留朽木和倒木，因为它们不仅可以作为许多动物和真菌的重要栖息地元素，也可激发人们对不可预料的环境的神秘感[59]。这种群落结构显然与传统绿地的外观不同，但当公众了解了其生态价值后，通常便会认可。

最后，绿地中也可以营建不同寻常的荒野。一个很好的例子是由吉尔·克雷蒙设计的法国里尔的新亨利—马蒂斯公园，其设计概念包括在传统绿地中央建设一个高约7m、只进行了基本种植工作的高地，游客不可进入，自然就不会受到干扰。[60]

5 结语

城市环境中的荒野设计是景观设计行业的时下热点，也具有发展前景。荒野在其起源或生态性（古老或新生）、规模（从小地块到大区域），以及自然过程决定生态系统状态的程度（从初始阶段到成熟森林）等方面存在很大差异。因此，认识到场地的具体特征和机遇是其未来发展的关键。除保留完全未受干扰的荒野外，适当的设计干预也是可行的。当地社区参与保护、开发或调节城市荒野区域也是行之有效的方法。最终，在城市绿色基础设施中提升荒野有望将人们与自然世界重新联系在一起，并保护城市生物多样性。**LAF**

致谢

感谢匿名同行评议审稿人一针见血的意见，以及克莱恩・拉夫丁女士对本文英文写作的帮助。

© Ingo Kowarik

7-1

© Ingo Kowarik

7-2

© Ingo Kowarik

7-3

© Ingo Kowarik

7-4

Clément. His concept for the new Parc Henri Matisse in Lille, France included a plateau about 7 meters high, inaccessible to visitors, in the middle of a traditionally designed green space, where nature stay undisturbed after only a few initial plantings.[60]

5 Conclusion

Working with wilderness in urban regions is a timely and promising field for landscape architecture. Wilderness varies greatly in terms of its origin or ecological novelty (ancient or novel), its scale (from small patches to large areas), and the extent to which natural processes determine the state of the ecosystem (from initial stages to mature forests). Recognizing the specific characteristics and opportunities of a site is therefore key to its future development. Design interventions are often appropriate, as is the inclusion of completely undisturbed areas. Involving the local neighborhood has often proven successful for preserving, developing, or mediating urban wilderness areas. Ultimately, enhancing wilderness within urban green infrastructure is a promising to reconnecting people with the natural world and for urban biodiversity conservation. **LAF**

ACKNOWLEDGEMENTS

The author is grateful to the anonymous reviewers for their clairvoyant comments and to Mrs. Kelaine Ravdin for improving the English writing.

REFERENCES

[1] Nash, R. F. (2014). *Wilderness and the American mind*. New Haven, CT: Yale University Press.

[2] Kirchhoff, T.,& Vicenzotti, V. (2014). A Historical and Systematic Survey of European Perceptions of Wilderness. *Environmental Values*, 23(4), 443–464. https://doi.org/10.3197/096327114X13947900181590

[3] Gothein, M. L. (1926). *Geschichte der Gartenkunst* [History of Garden Art]. Jena, Germany: Eugen Diederichs.

[4] Hunt, J. D., & Willis, P. (Eds.). (1988). *The Genius of the Place: The English Landscape Garden, 1620-1820*. Cambridge, MA: MIT Press.

[5] Hirschfeld, C. C. L. (1780). *Theorie der Gartenkunst (Vol. 2)* [Theory of Garden Art (Vol.2)]. Leipzig, Germany: G. Weidmanns Erben und Reich.

[6] Kühn, N. (2011). *Neue Staudenverwendung*. Stuttgart, Germany: Ulmer.

[7] Dunnett, N., & Hitchmough, J. (Eds.). (2008). *The Dynamic Landscape: Design, Ecology and Management of Naturalistic Urban Planting*. London, England: Taylor & Francis.

[8] Cai, T. Z. (2020). Ecological or Naturalistic: A Brief Review and Several Thoughts on Contemporary Planting Design. *Landscape Architecture Frontiers*, 8(3), 102-114. https://doi.org/10.15302/J-LAF-1-030017

[9] Latz, P. (2003). Landscape Park Duisburg-Nord: The Metamorphosis of an Industrial Site. In N. Kirkwood (Eds.), *Manufactured Sites* (pp. 163-17). London, England: Taylor & Francis.

[10] Kowarik, I., & Körner, S. (Eds.). (2005). *Wild Urban Woodlands: New Perspectives for Urban Forestry*. Berlin, Germany: Springer.

[11] Lachmund, J. (2013). *Greening Berlin: The Co-Production of Science, Politics, and Urban Nature*. Cambridge, MA: MIT Press.

[12] Kowarik, I. (2018). Urban Wilderness: Supply, Demand, and Access. *Urban Forestry and Urban Greening*, (29), 336-347. https://doi.org/10.1016/j.ufug.2017.05.017

[13] Cronon, W. (1996). The Trouble With Wilderness: Or, Getting Back to the Wrong Nature. *Environmental History*, 1(1), 7-28. https://doi.org/10.2307/3985059

[14] Jim, C.Y. (2017). Conservation and Creation of Urban Woodlands. In P. Y. Tan, & C. Y. Jim (Eds.), *Greening Cities* (pp. 307–330). Singapore: Springer.

[15] Kowarik, I. (2011). Novel Urban Ecosystems, Biodiversity, and Conservation. *Environmental Pollution*, 159(8-9), 1974-1983. https://doi.org/10.1016/j.envpol.2011.02.022

[16] Hobbs, R. J., Higgs, E. S., & Hall, C. (Eds.). (2013). *Novel Ecosystems: Intervening in the New Ecological World Order*. Hoboken, NJ: John Wiley & Sons.

[17] Bonthoux, S., Brun, M., Di Pietro, F., Greulich, S., & Bouché-Pillon, S. (2014). How Can Wastelands Promote Biodiversity in Cities? A Review. *Landscape and Urban Planning*, (132), 79-88. https://doi.org/10.1016/j.landurbplan.2014.08.010

[18] Anderson, E. C., & Minor, E. S. (2017). Vacant Lots: An Underexplored Resource for Ecological and Social Benefits in Cities. *Urban Forestry and Urban Greening*, (21), 146-152. https://doi.org/10.1016/j.ufug.2016.11.015

[19] Trentanovi, G., Campagnaro, T., Kowarik, I., Munafò, M., Semenzato, P., & Sitzia, T. (2021). Integrating Spontaneous Urban Woodlands Into the Green Infrastructure: Unexploited Opportunities for Urban Regeneration. *Land Use Policy*, (102), 105221. https://doi.org/10.1016/j.landusepol.2020.105221

[20] Lesslie, R. (2016). The Wilderness Continuum Concept and Its Application in Australia: Lessons for Modern Conservation. In S. J. Carver, & S. Fritz (Eds.), *Mapping Wilderness* (pp. 17-33). Dordrecht, the Netherlands: Springer.

[21] Gao, H., Ouyang, Z., Chen, S., & Van Koppen, C. S. A. (2013). Role of Culturally Protected Forests in Biodiversity Conservation in Southeast China. *Biodiversity and Conservation*, 22(2), 531-544. https://doi.org/10.1007/s10531-012-0427-7

[22] De Meulder, B., Shannon, K., & Nguyen, M. Q. (2019). Forest Urbanisms: Urban and Ecological Strategies and Tools for the Sonian Forest in Belgium. *Landscape Architecture Frontiers*, 7(1), 18-33. https://doi.org/10.15302/J-LAF-20190103

[23] Navarro, L. M., & Pereira, H. M. (2012). Rewilding Abandoned Landscapes in Europe. *Ecosystems*, 15 (6), 900–912. https://doi.org/10.1007/s10021-012-9558-7

[24] Heger, T., Bernard-Verdier, M., Gessler, A., Greenwood, A. D., Grossart, H. -P., Hilker, M., ... Jeschke, J. M. (2019). Towards an Integrative, Eco-Evolutionary Understanding of Ecological Novelty: Studying and Communicating Interlinked Effects of Global Change. *BioScience*, 69(11), 888-899. https://doi.org/10.1093/biosci/biz095

[25] Diemer, M., Held, M., & Hofmeister, S. (2003). Urban Wilderness in Central Europe: Rewilding at the Urban Fringe. *International Journal of Wilderness*, 9(3), 7-11.

[26] Matos, D. M. S., Santos, C. J. F., & Chevalier, D. D. R. (2002). Fire and Restoration of the Largest Urban Forest of the World in Rio De Janeiro City, Brazil. *Urban Ecosystems*, 6(3), 151-161. https://doi.org/10.1023/A:1026164427792

[27] Dettmar, J., (2005). Forest for Shrinking Cities? The Project "Industrial Forest of the Ruhr". In I. Kowarik, & S. Körner (Eds.), *Wild Urban Woodlands: New Perspectives for Urban Forestry* (pp. 263–277). Berlin, Germany: Springer.

[28] Riley, C. B., Perry, K. I., Ard, K., & Gardiner, M. M. (2018). Asset or Liability? Ecological and Sociological Tradeoffs of Urban Spontaneous Vegetation on Vacant Land in Shrinking Cities. *Sustainability*, 10(7), 2139. https://doi.org/10.3390/su10072139

[29] Bonthoux, S., Voisin, L., Bouché-Pillon, S., & Chollet, S. (2019). More Than Weeds: Spontaneous Vegetation in Streets as a Neglected Element of Urban Biodiversity. *Landscape and Urban Planning*, (185), 163-172. https://doi.org/10.1016/j.landurbplan.2019.02.009

[30] Jin, C., Zheng, M., Huang, L., Qian, S., Jim, C. Y., Lin, D., ... Yang, Y. (2020). Co-existence Between Humans and Nature: Heritage Trees in China's Yangtze River Region. *Urban Forestry and Urban Greening*, (54), 126748. https://doi.org/10.1016/j.ufug.2020.126748

[31] Huang, L., Qian, S., Li, T., Jim, C. Y., Jin, C., Zhao, L., ... Yang, Y. (2019). Masonry Walls as Sieve of Urban Plant Assemblages and Refugia of Native Species in Chongqing, China. *Landscape and Urban Planning*, (191), 103620. https://doi.org/10.1016/j.landurbplan.2019.103620

[32] McKinney, M. L., Kowarik, I., & Kendal, D. (2018). The Contribution of Wild Urban Ecosystems to Liveable Cities. *Urban Forestry and Urban Greening*, (29), 334-

335. https://doi.org/10.1016/j.ufug.2017.09.004
[33] Kowarik, I., & von der Lippe, M. (2018). Plant Population Success Across Urban Ecosystems: A Framework to Inform Biodiversity Conservation in Cities. *Journal of Applied Ecology*, 55(5), 2354-2361. https://doi.org/10.1111/1365-2664.13144
[34] Müller, A., Bøcher, P. K., Fischer, C., & Svenning, J. C. (2018). 'Wild' in the City Context: Do Relative Wild Areas Offer Opportunities for Urban Biodiversity? *Landscape and Urban Planning*, (170), 256-265. https://doi.org/10.1016/j.landurbplan.2017.09.027
[35] Myers, Z. (2020). *Wildness and Wellbeing: Nature, Neuroscience, and Urban Design*. Singapore: Springer Nature.
[36] Sikorska, D., Łaszkiewicz, E., Krauze, K., & Sikorski, P. (2020). The Role of Informal Green Spaces in Reducing Inequalities in Urban Green Space Availability to Children and Seniors. *Environmental Science and Policy*, (108), 144-154. https://doi.org/10.1016/j.envsci.2020.03.007
[37] Chen, W. Y. (2017). Urban Nature and Urban Ecosystem Services. In P. Y. Tan, & C. Y. Jim (Eds.), *Greening Cities* (pp. 181–199). Singapore: Springer.
[38] Pueffel, C., Haase, D., & Priess, J. A. (2018). Mapping Ecosystem Services on Brownfields in Leipzig, Germany. *Ecosystem Services*, (30), 73-85. https://doi.org/10.1016/j.ecoser.2018.01.011
[39] Hwang, Y. H., Yue, Z. E. J., Ling, S. K., & Tan, H. H. V. (2019). It's Ok to Be Wilder: Preference for Natural Growth in Urban Green Spaces in a Tropical City. *Urban Forestry and Urban Greening*, (38), 165-176. https://doi.org/10.1016/j.ufug.2018.12.005
[40] Mathey, J., Arndt, T., Banse, J., & Rink, D. (2018). Public Perception of Spontaneous Vegetation on Brownfields in Urban Areas—Results From Surveys in Dresden and Leipzig (Germany). *Urban Forestry and Urban Greening*, (29), 384-392. https://doi.org/10.1016/j.ufug.2016.10.007
[41] Li, X., Fan, S., Kühn, N., Dong, L., & Hao, P. (2019). Residents' Ecological and Aesthetical Perceptions Toward Spontaneous Vegetation in Urban Parks in China. *Urban Forestry and Urban Greening*, (44), 126397. https://doi.org/10.1016/j.ufug.2019.126397
[42] Lichtenstein, A., & Mameli, F. A. (Eds.). (2015). *Gleisdreieck / Parklife Berlin*. Berlin, Germany: Transcript Verlag.
[43] Carr, E. (1999). *Wilderness by Design: Landscape Architecture and the National Park Service*. Lincoln, NE: University of Nebraska Press.
[44] Herzog, C. P. (2016). A Multifunctional Green Infrastructure Design to Protect and Improve Native Biodiversity in Rio De Janeiro. *Landscape and Ecological Engineering*, 12(1), 141-150. https://doi.org/10.1007/s11355-013-0233-8
[45] Draus, P., Haase, D., Napieralski, J., Roddy, J., & Qureshi, S. (2019). Wounds, Ghosts and Gardens: Historical Trauma and Green Reparations in Berlin and Detroit. *Cities*, (93), 153-163. https://doi.org/10.1016/j.cities.2019.05.002
[46] Kowarik, I. (2019). The "Green Belt Berlin": Establishing a Greenway Where the Berlin Wall Once Stood by Integrating Ecological, Social and Cultural Approaches. *Landscape and Urban Planning*, (184), 12-22. https://doi.org/10.1016/j.landurbplan.2018.12.008
[47] Nassauer, J. I., (1995). Messy Ecosystems, Orderly Frames. *Landscape Journal*, 14(2), 161–170. doi:10.3368/lj.14.2.161
[48] Rupprecht, C. D. D., Byrne, J. A., Ueda, H., & Lo, A. Y. (2015). 'It's Real, Not Fake Like a Park': Residents' Perception and Use of Informal Urban Green-Space in Brisbane, Australia and Sapporo, Japan. *Landscape and Urban Planning*, (143), 205-218. https://doi.org/10.1016/j.landurbplan.2015.07.003
[49] Unt, A. -L., & Bell, S. (2014). The Impact of Small-Scale Design Interventions on the Behaviour Patterns of the Users of an Urban Wasteland. *Urban Forestry and Urban Greening*, 13(1), 121-135. https://doi.org/10.1016/j.ufug.2013.10.008
[50] Del Tredici, P., & Rueb, T. (2017). Other Order: Sound Walk for an Urban Wild. *Arnoldia*, 75(1), 14-25.
[51] Kowarik, I., & Langer, A. (2005). Natur-Park Südgelände: Linking Conservation and Recreation in an Abandoned Railyard in Berlin. In I. Kowarik, & S. Körner (Eds.), *Wild Urban Woodlands: New Perspectives for Urban Forestry* (pp. 287–299). Berlin, Germany: Springer.
[52] Brun, M., Di Pietro, F., & Bonthoux, S. (2018). Residents' Perceptions and Valuations of Urban Wastelands are Influenced by Vegetation Structure. *Urban forestry and Urban Greening*, (29), 393-403. https://doi.org/10.1016/j.ufug.2017.01.005
[53] Appleton, J. (1975). *The Experience of Landscape*. London, England: Wiley-Blackwell.
[54] Kowarik, I., Hiller, A., Planchuelo, G., Seitz, B., von der Lippe, M., & Buchholz, S. (2019). Emerging Urban Forests: Opportunities for Promoting the Wild Side of the Urban Green Infrastructure. *Sustainability*, 11(22), 6318. https://doi.org/10.3390/su11226318
[55] Planchuelo, G., von der Lippe, M., & Kowarik, I. (2019). Untangling the Role of Urban Ecosystems as Habitats for Endangered Plant Species. *Landscape and Urban Planning*, (189), 320-334. https://doi.org/10.1016/j.landurbplan.2019.05.007
[56] Battisti, C., Dodaro, G., & Fanelli, G. (2017). Paradoxical Environmental Conservation: Failure of an Unplanned Urban Development as a Driver of Passive Ecological Restoration. *Environmental Development*, (24), 179-186. https://doi.org/10.1016/j.envdev.2017.05.003
[57] Kühn, N. (2006). Intentions for the Unintentional: Spontaneous Vegetation as the Basis for Innovative Planting Design in Urban Areas. *Journal of Landscape Architecture*, 1(2), 46–53. https://doi.org/10.1080/18626033.2006.9723372
[58] Fischer, L. K., Neuenkamp, L., Lampinen, J., Tuomi, M., Alday, J. G., Bucharova, A., ... Klaus, V. H. (2020). Public Attitudes Toward Biodiversity-Friendly Green space Management in Europe. *Conservation Letters*, 13(4), e12718. https://doi.org/10.1111/conl.12718
[59] Gundersen, V., Stange, E. E., Kaltenborn, B. P., & Vistad, O. I. (2017). Public Visual Preferences for Dead Wood in Natural Boreal Forests: The Effects of Added Information. *Landscape and Urban Planning*, (158), 12–24. https://doi.org/10.1016/j.landurbplan.2016.09.020
[60] Gandy, M. (2013). Entropy by Design: Gilles Clément, Parc Henri Matisse and the Limits to Avant-Garde Urbanism. *International Journal of Urban and Regional Research*, 37(1), 259-278. https://doi.org/10.1111/j.1468-2427.2012.01164.x

从瓦砾堆到自然保护区
——加拿大多伦多汤米－汤普森公园
From Rubble to Refuge
—Tommy Thompson Park in Toronto, Canada

沃尔特·科姆
Walter KEHM

LANDinc工作室高级主管；哈佛大学景观设计学硕士
Senior Principle at LANDinc; MLA of Harvard University

彼得·德尔·特雷迪奇
Peter DEL TREDICI*

哈佛大学阿诺德植物园荣誉退休高级研究员；波士顿大学生物学博士
Senior Research Scientist Emeritus, Arnold Arboretum of Harvard University; PhD in Biology, Boston University

*Corresponding Author
Address: Arnold Arboretum, 1300 Centre St., Boston, MA 02130, USA
Email: ptredici@oeb.harvard.edu

编辑 | 王颖、崔婧沄
翻译 | 王颖、李慧彦
EDITED BY | WANG Ying, CUI Jingyun
TRANSLATED BY | WANG Ying, LI Huiyan

摘要

加拿大多伦多市的汤米－汤普森公园建于一处大型垃圾填埋场上，由安大略湖湖滨向内延伸5km。自20世纪50年代到70年代末，项目利用建筑瓦砾和港口淤泥实施填湖工程，而后因经济形势变化被迫停工。项目搁置后，来自世界各地的众多植物在这里扎根，数百种候鸟在此筑巢觅食，原本的垃圾填埋场自发演变成为了“自然保护区”。20世纪90年代，多伦多市政府通过精心规划设计与施工，将其改造为一座公园——汤米－汤普森公园。通过提高公众可达性、野生动植物和栖息地的多样性，以及生态功能性，汤米－汤普森公园成为了探究自然演变与设计干预之间动态交互的理想案例，我们可以从中探知这两个看似矛盾的过程如何随时间推移而和谐相融。

关键词

莱斯利街岬角；人类世生态系统；生态设计；广布植物区系；野生动植物保护区；城市荒野

ABSTRACT

Tommy Thompson Park in the city of Toronto, Canada was originally a massive landfilling project that extended 5 kilometers out into Lake Ontario. It was constructed from construction rubble and harbor dredge from the 1950s through the late 1970s, when the project was halted due to changing economic conditions. Left to its own devices, the landfill spontaneously evolved into a "nature preserve" when innumerable plants from around the world established themselves and hundreds of migrating bird species descended on the site for nesting and feeding. In the 1990s, the city of Toronto took control of the site and transformed it into a park—Tommy Thompson Park—after a carefully planned design and construction process. The design interventions enhanced public accessibility, wildlife and habitat diversity, and ecological functionality. Tommy Thompson Park is an ideal case study for examining the dynamic interaction between spontaneity and design and for how, over time, these seemingly contradictory processes can come together harmoniously.

KEYWORDS

Leslie Street Spit; Novel Ecosystem; Ecological Design; Cosmopolitan Flora; Wildlife Refuge; Urban Wilderness

https://doi.org/10.15302/J-LAF-1-030024
收稿时间 RECEIVED DATE | 2020-12-09
中图分类号 | TU986.2
文献标识码 | B

1 © The Toronto Regional Conservation Authority

1. 2013年汤米－汤普森公园鸟瞰图

1. Aerial view of Tommy Thompson Park in 2013

1 引言

“变化”是城市永恒的主题。城市结构随着城市愿景的不断发展更新而改变，老旧基础设施和废弃建筑纷纷被拆除，场地上堆积着有待处理的挖方土壤。这样的场景也曾在多伦多市汤米－汤普森公园（当地居民称之为“莱斯利街岬角”或“岬角”）上演（图1）。20世纪50年代，圣劳伦斯航道建成后，多伦多港口委员会做出了一项颇具远见的决定——在外港码头新建一处船舶进坞设施来扩建多伦多的内港。计划要求建造一条长达5km的防波堤，直抵安大略湖。新近出版的《偶然的荒野：多伦多汤米－汤普森公园的起源与生态》①一书记录了这一码头扩建计划的历史渊源及其演变为今日汤米－汤普森公园的全过程。

新码头的建设需经历大规模的填湖工程，分三个阶段实施，历时多年。第一阶段起始于20世纪50年代末，首先利用原场地拆除后遗留的大量砖块、混凝土砌块、电线杆、人行道铺装、路缘石、钢筋、彩色厨房地砖和各种骨料等材料铺筑了一条通往湖中央的道路。第二阶段主要对多伦多港外围的泥沙实施疏浚，以开辟一条新航道；疏浚出的泥沙堆积在新建防波堤的西缘，形成了许多湖湾和湖滨空间。到第三阶段，随着泥沙倾倒作业的持续推进，场地的东半侧逐渐围挡出三个湖水充盈的储水空间。在施工高峰期，每天约有三四百辆卡车将混有淤泥和黏土的建筑瓦砾倾倒在岬角东侧。[1]

1 Introduction

The only thing constant about cities is change. Old infrastructure is removed, buildings are demolished, and excavated soil has to be disposed of as new urban design visions reorder the structure of the city. Such is the case of Toronto's Tommy Thompson Park, or as local residents call it, “the Leslie Street Spit” or simply the Spit (Fig. 1). When the St. Lawrence Seaway was completed in the 1950s, the Toronto Harbor Commissioners made a visionary decision to expand Toronto's inner harbor by creating a new outer harbor port docking facility. The plan entailed the construction of a breakwater extending 5 kilometers into Lake Ontario. The historical origins of this port expansion plan and its evolution into today's Tommy Thompson Park is the subject of the newly published book, *Accidental Wilderness: The Origins and Ecology of Toronto's Tommy Thompson Park*①.

The construction of the new port facilities required a massive three-phase lake filling process over many years. In phase one, beginning in the late 1950s, an access road was constructed into the lake using demolition site rubble containing bricks, concrete blocks, utility poles, sidewalks, curb stones, rebar, multi-colored kitchen floor tiles, and a variety of aggregates. During the second phase, sand from the outer Toronto harbor was dredged to create a new ship channel and deposited against the western edge of the new breakwater road, creating a number of embayments and new beaches. The third phase saw continued dumping that filled the eastern half of the site and enclosing three large cells filled with lake water. At the peak of construction, 300 ~ 400 trucks a day deposited construction rubble mixed with silt and clay soil along the east side of the Spit.[1]

① 该书由沃尔特·科姆所著、罗伯特·波利摄影，收录了有关场地历史和生态情况的详尽信息。

① This book written by Walter Kehm with photography by Robert Burley is very comprehensive in its treatment of the site and readers can consult it to form more detailed information about its history and ecology.

年复一年，填湖工程势头未减，最终在湖中形成了一处连通各方的地形，宛如城市中的喀拉喀托火山。场地的最终面积达324hm^2，甚至超过了纽约中央公园。依据扩建计划，场地中约一半的区域会被改造为一系列封闭的矩形直壁储水空间，以备将来储存从唐河河口疏浚出的沉积物（可能包含石油副产品、重金属和制药废料等有毒物质）。项目原本计划在填满这些空间后，在其上方铺设防渗层，后覆盖土壤和草皮，将其变身为公园、娱乐或潜在商业用地。20世纪70年代末，受当地水运航线调整的影响，这一宏大的岬角扩建计划因资金中断而被迫搁置。

多年来，重启岬角项目的提案层出不穷，但悉数被否，其中反对声最大的是一个名为“岬角之友”的社会团体。然而，项目的悬而未决倒给了大自然母亲出手的机会：海鸥和燕鸥纷纷在平坦的瓦砾堆上筑巢；丛生的杂草也吸引了成千上万只加拿大雁（*Branta canadensis*）迁徙至此。但鸟类的迅速繁殖已对居民的生活造成了干扰，人们不得不通过在鸟蛋上涂油的方式来加以控制。20世纪90年代，双冠鸬鹚（*Phalacrocorax auritus*）开始在高大的美洲黑杨（*Populus deltoides*）上筑巢并迅速繁殖（图2）。直至今日，这片岬角仍然是这些物种在北美地区最大的繁殖地。

在实施改造前，场地只通过一条光秃秃的道路与外界相连，道路两侧皆是排水沟。20世纪70年代末，沃尔特·科姆（本文第一作者）初次到访岬角，第一印象是“仿佛行驶在法国的乡间小路上”：十米高的美洲黑杨在潮湿的排水沟中自然生长，笔直成列，如同人工栽植的一般齐整，令人惊叹（图3）。这份来自大自然的“种植设计”作品或许在启示我们，景观设计师应该让自然自由发展，并通过不断优化地形坡度和排水策略来提升场地的生态功能性和生物多样性。

每次到访，汤米–汤普森公园总会发人深省，它仿佛在提醒我们：多伦多——乃至所有其他城市——都不过是自然演绎的结果。人们将粘土烧成砖，将石灰石制成水泥，从乡间冰川沉积中开采骨料制作混凝土

Year after year, work continued unabated and eventually produced a highly branched landform that emerged from the lake like an urban Krakatoa. The final build out covered more than 324 hectares—a parcel of land larger than Central Park in New York City. As part of the plan, approximately half of the area was left as enclosed water cells which were engineered as rectangular straight wall structures with the capacity to receive a large quantity of sediments dredged from the Don River containing potentially toxic substances such as petroleum by-products, heavy metals, and pharmaceutical waste at some point in the future. The original idea was to slowly fill the cells to capacity, at which point they would be capped with an impervious layer and then covered with soil and grass so that they could be used for park, recreation or possibly commercial activities. The ambitious port expansion plan for the Spit came to an abrupt halt in the late 1970s when shifts in regional shipping routes destroyed the economic underpinnings of the project.

Over the years, various schemes were proposed for redeveloping the unfinished Spit and one by one they were rejected as a result of the opposition expressed by a variety of individuals and, most significantly, a community group known as the "Friends of the Spit." It was during this period of indecision that Mother Nature took matters into her own hands as gulls and terns found the level rubble to be a safe place for building nests. Once grasses started growing, the Canada Geese (*Branta canadensis*) arrived and before too long, thousands of them had migrated to the Spit. They formed huge breeding colonies to the extent that they were seen as nuisances that had to be controlled by oiling their eggs. In the 1990s, Double-Crested Cormorants (*Phalacrocorax auritus*) began nesting in the tall Eastern Cottonwoods (*Populus deltoides*) and rapidly multiplied (Fig. 2). Today, the Spit contains the largest breeding colony of this species in North America.

Access to the site at this time was provided by the barren, linear access road with drainage ditches running parallel to it for its entire length. The senior author's (Walter Kehm) first impression of the Spit in the late 1970s was one of driving along a French countryside lane. Straight lines of Eastern Cottonwood had seeded themselves in the wet ditch bottoms. At 10 meters in height, they created a formidable, straight allee that felt like it had been intentionally planted (Fig. 3). The realization that nature was creating its own planting plan suggested

© Peter Del Tredici 2

© Peter Del Tredici 3

2. 在多伦多市中心附近筑巢的双冠鸬鹚
3. 自行车道两旁的美洲黑杨笔直成列

2. Double-Crested Cormorants nesting close to downtown Toronto
3. Bike path lined with Eastern Cottonwood trees

4-1

4-2

5

砌块、人行道铺装和路缘石；再用铁矿石加工钢筋、钢梁，用石英砂制造玻璃。堆积在岬角上的建筑瓦砾和其他各类碎片经过波浪冲击等风化作用后变为了小颗粒，不仅为植物生长提供了基质，也为野生动物提供了栖息地（图4）。原本笔直矗立的建筑化身为瓦砾，成为了一方沃土——汤米–汤普森公园中发生的自然过程仿佛令这座城市看到了重生的机遇（图5）。

2 来自公众的支持

20世纪80年代，多伦多及地区保育局受托为这一废弃的岬角制定未来规划[2]，但各类提案都遭到了公众的反对。正如上文所述，“岬角之友”在抵制场地中的一切大规模建筑或商业开发计划中展现了其重要影响力。

在这个漫长的公众参与过程中，生态演替也在场地中稳步进行。春夏时节，新形成的浅滩成为了鸟类和哺乳动物的栖息地，鱼类种群也迅速增长。同时，借助风和鸟类的传播，来自全球各地的温带植物也纷纷扎根于此（图6，7）。[3]不论源自何方，这些植物都已预先适应了这种由湖中瓦砾构成的生长环境。从这层意义上说，这些植物虽不同于欧洲殖民前在湖岸占主导地位的历史植物群，却也称得上是岬角的乡土物种。

为了回答“未来在哪里”这一长久以来困扰岬角发展的问题，科姆受聘为首席景观设计师，与EDA规划及景观咨询公司共同制定方案并召

4-1. 公园东侧堤坝上的美洲山杨（*Populus tremuloides*）及金属废弃物（摄于2019年）
4-2. 公园东侧堤坝上的建筑瓦砾与植物（摄于2019年）
5. 从公园最南端的灯塔角看多伦多的天际线（摄于2019年）

4-1. Quaking Aspen (*Populus tremuloides*) trees with metal parts along the east side dike in the park, 2019.
4-2. Plants growing from the rubble in the shoreline of the east side dike, 2019.
5. View of the Toronto skyline from the southernmost Lighthouse Point in the park, 2019.

that the role of landscape architects should be to let nature evolve without interference and to enhance ecological functionality and biodiversity through the design of new topographic grading and drainage strategies.

Visiting Tommy Thompson Park is always a humbling experience because it reminds the visitor that Toronto, like every other city, is really just a rearrangement of elemental nature. Clay became bricks, limestone became cement, and aggregate quarried from glacial depositions in the countryside formed into concrete blocks, sidewalks, and curbs. Steel rebar and beams are made from iron ore and glass comes from silica sand. Through wave action and weathering, the construction rubble and other miscellaneous debris that were deposited on the Spit were pulverized into small particles that provide the substrate for plants to grow on and, by extension, habitat for wildlife (Fig. 4). As a result of these natural processes, Tommy Thompson Park has emerged as a reincarnation of the city (Fig. 5), albeit in a horizontal rather than a vertical mode.

2 Public Advocacy

In the 1980s, the Toronto and Region Conservation Authority was given the responsibility to develop plans for the future of the abandoned Spit[2]. However, various concepts were proposed and rejected by the public. As noted above, the Friends of the Spit group was particularly effective in facilitating the defeat of any plans that called for large-scale buildings or commercial development.

Through this long public engagement process, ecological succession proceeded at its own steady pace. New species of birds and mammals arrived in spring or summer and in the newly formed shallows, fish populations have expanded dramatically. Simultaneously, plant species from all parts of the temperate world became established, transported there by birds or the incessant wind (Fig. 6, 7).[3] Regardless of where they might have originated, the cosmopolitan array of plants that now grow on the Spit are pre-adapted to the conditions created by dumping rubble in the lake. In this sense then, these plants—as opposed to the historic flora that dominated the lake shore before European settlement—are the Spit's native species.

To address the impasse question "What is the future of the Spit?", the senior author was retained as the principal landscape architect with the firm of EDA

开公众会议开展评估。科姆经常在这里骑行，对场地十分熟悉，他也一直在思考如何才能将生态融入公园设计中。当前的景观设计课程会教授学生如何在景观上叠加形态，这一专业也因此被视为一门“在所有地理空间层次上赋予景观以形态并提升其功能性的艺术和科学”。依据这种说法，景观设计就是要不加掩饰地实施人工干预，并将设计师个人主观感受融入设计过程之中。但景观设计课程中极少充分探讨如何营造可以让动植物自由演化、让以人为核心的元素退居配角的环境。汤米–汤普森公园的设计过程即体现了这种不同以往的理念——首先关注野生动植物的栖息需求，而后才是人的需求。

1985年，项目进行了为期一年的公众意见收集活动，公众的支持与参与是该规划设计的一个关键流程。其中景观设计师主要负责组织和举办公众集会，听取各方对公园未来的愿景，同时推动不同利益群体间达成共识。意见收集过程中召开了多次会议，每次会议可容纳约100人，分为10组，每组分别开展圆桌会议。在景观设计师简要介绍后，人们可利用场地基础平面图、白纸和彩笔，自由画出他们理想中的公园景观，最后各组派一位代表对本组方案进行详细说明。这种方式使与会人员达成共识：应保留场地的自然风貌，就像未曾规划设计过一样——这一愿景为后续总体规划的制定奠定了基础。

3 生态设计

进入正式设计阶段后，项目团队首先围绕湖泊气候展开了详细的场地分析，包括风向、潜在种源地、场地水文、土壤、野生动物迁徙模式和植被动力学等；而后了解了可能在场地中出现的植物、鱼类、鸟类和哺乳动物的栖息地需求，将其纳入设计考量。最终，由科姆制定的“保护性设计”总体规划将整个场地划定为城市野生自然保护区，以保护生

Collaborative to prepare plans and hold public meetings for their evaluation. He was very familiar with the area as he often frequented there for bicycle riding and had long been intrigued by the question of how ecology can be incorporated into the park design process. Landscape architects are taught in design studio to superimpose form on the landscape. The profession's definition is seen as "the art and science of giving form and enhancing function to the landscape at all geo-spatial levels." This statement implies overt intervention and allows for the inclusion of the designer's subjective feelings. What is not taught sufficiently is how to create environments where plants and animals are allowed to evolve on their own and the human-centric elements play a supporting rather than a leading role. The design process for Tommy Thompson Park was unusual in that it focused primarily on the understanding of the habitat needs of wildlife, and secondarily on the human needs.

Public advocacy and participation was a critical piece of the planning and design process during the one-year time period, in 1985, that was allocated for citizen involvement. It was the responsibility of the landscape architect to organize and host public gatherings to obtain input from the public on the park's future and to reach consensus among conflicting stakeholders. The public process involved several meetings in a room accommodating 10 round tables with seating for 10 people at each table. A site base plan, blank paper, and colored pens were provided for each table. After the landscape architect's introduction, the people were asked to freely draw their ideal views of the park. The intuitive drawings from each table were collected and a spokesperson from each table gave a short presentation on their plan. The diagrams and sketches resulted in the participants reaching a consensus that kept the site natural and seemingly unplanned—a vision that later became instrumental in the development of the master plan.

3 Ecological Design

The formal design process began with a careful site analysis of the lake climate, including wind directions, the location of potential seed sources, site hydrology, soils, wildlife migration patterns, and vegetation dynamics. In addition, research was conducted to understand potential plant, fish, bird, and mammal habitat requirements that could be incorporated into the design. The master plan prepared

© Robert Burley
6

© Robert Burley
7

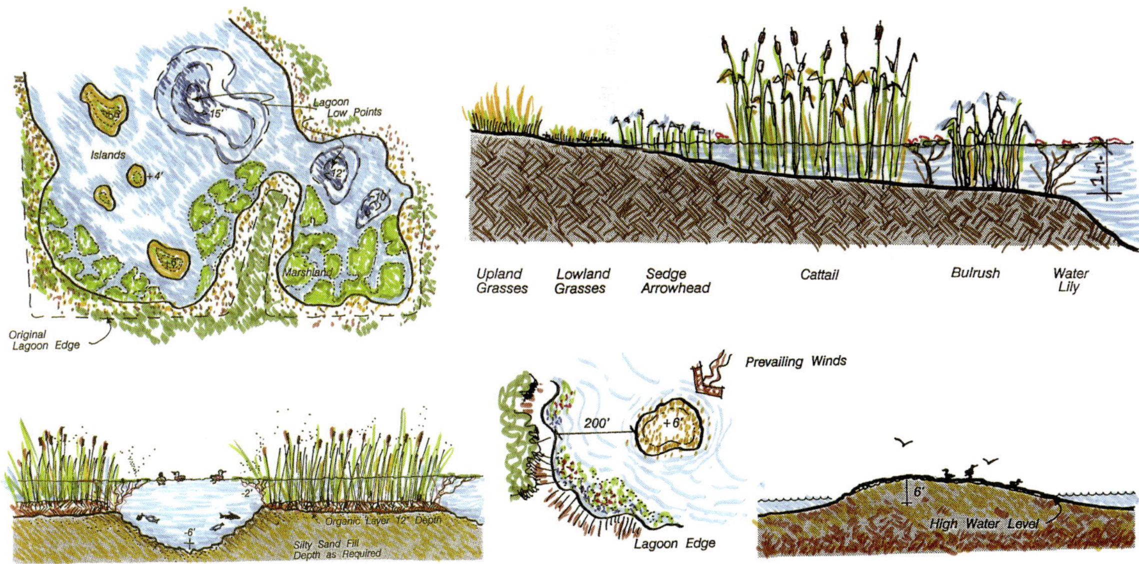

© Walter Kehm

8

6. 公园低沼泽区中的野花（摄于2014年）
7. 二号储水空间及湿地（摄于2020年）
8. 湿地设计草图示例

6. Wildflowers in the Flats in the park, 2014.
7. The Wetlands, Cell 2, 2020.
8. Samples of wetland sketches

物多样性、促进城市居民的身心健康。[4]依据总体规划，场地需禁止机动车通行，并设置多条步道和自行车专用道，方便游客到访。

项目采取了多项人工干预措施来推动生态进程、营建多样化的栖息地。其中最重要的一项举措是打破原有的直壁储水空间，将其改造为具有不同水深且边缘起伏的湿地，并建立水生植被（图8）。[5]在后来的湿地规划方案中，这些空间用于疏浚物填埋，并在水下1~1.5m处封顶。20世纪90年代，一号储水空间中的首片湿地建设启动，建成后就成为了鸟类、鱼类和两栖动物的重要栖息地。其他储水空间的改造目前也正在实施或规划中。

汤米—汤普森公园的景观形态融合了坡地和排水设计考虑，为生态修复提供了基础。在地形设计过程中，风是首要考虑因素之一（设计需要考虑当地的盛行风向），而后需逐步确定地形高程、朝向和日照，划定陡坡和缓坡、低湿洼地和离水区域、冷热坡面、低压潜在种子沉积区等，并绘制相应的剖面图和坡度断面图（图9）。

地形设计细致地考虑了场地的排水需求。一般而言，场地中的水会在滞蓄区就地收集，而溢流则可依地势在湿地间流灌。时至今日，这项设计的效果已经显现：湿生植物——尤其是红枝山茱萸（*Cornus sericea*）——生长旺盛，而美洲山杨（*Populus tremuloides*）、美洲黑杨和刺槐（*Robinia pseudoacacia*）等先锋树种则取代了原本在湿地离水边缘扎根的繁茂灌丛。这些植被吸引来了更多的野生动物，包括郊狼、河

by the senior author was entitled “Conservation by Design,” which recommended that the entire site would be designated as an urban wild refuge area and serve as a sanctuary to protect natural biodiversity while simultaneously enhancing human mental well-being and physical health.[4] The site should be car free and contain numerous hiking trails and designated bicycle pathways to enhance accessibility.

To foster ecological processes and create diverse habitats, several design interventions were implemented. The most important of them was the elimination of the engineered straight walled retention cells by converting them into wetlands with varying water depths and undulating topographic edges that allowed for the establishment of aquatic vegetation (Fig. 8).[5] This plan was abandoned and replaced with a wetland proposal in which filling with dredge material would be capped at approximately 1 ~ 1.5 meters below the surface of the water. The construction of the first wetland in Cell 1 started in the 1990s and upon completion it has become an important habitat for birds, fish, and amphibians. The remaining cells are in varying stages of construction or planning.

The ecological regeneration plan for Tommy Thompson Park was based on the design of grading and drainage into landscape topographic forms. Wind became one of the most important considerations, as the prevailing breezes would provide guidance for landform design. Landform height, aspect and solar exposure, steep and shallow slopes, wet depressions and dry areas, hot and cool slopes, and low pressure potential seed deposition zones were selected and developed with cross-section sketches and grading plans (Fig. 9).

The design of the landforms was guided by the creation of sensitive drainage plans. Water was to be captured on site in detention and retention areas with overflows that allow for decanting from one wet area to another. On site today, the significance of this design intervention is evident: plants needing wet conditions, notably the shrubby Red-Osier Dogwood (*Cornus sericea*), are getting what they need while at the drier edge a dense thicket of shrubs took root and eventually gave way to pioneer trees including Quaking Aspen (*Populus tremuloides*), Eastern

9. “保护性设计”总体规划中的典型剖面示例
10. 公园中的灯塔角（摄于2020年）
11. 公园中随处可见简易的砖块雕塑
12. 2020年2月更新后的汤米–汤普森公园总平面图

9. Typical Cross Section of the Conservation by Design
10. Lighthouse Point in the park, 2020.
11. Sculptures that can be found throughout the park
12. Tommy Thompson Park site plan, updated in February 2020.

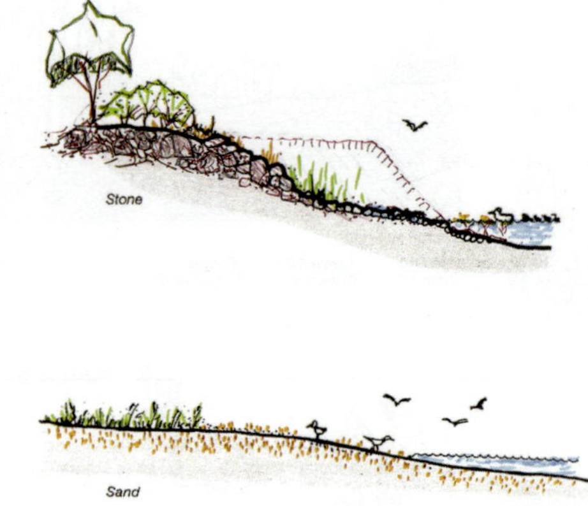

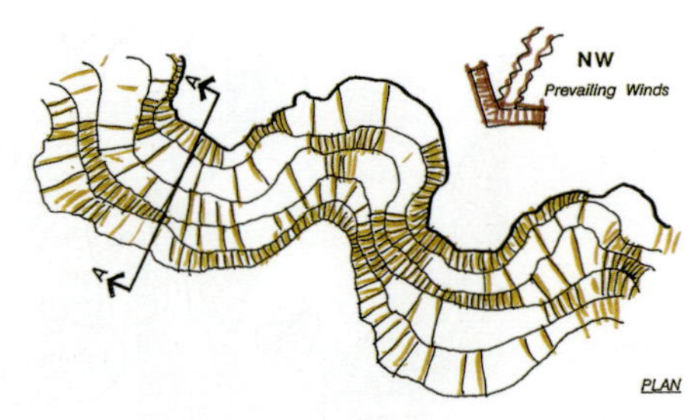

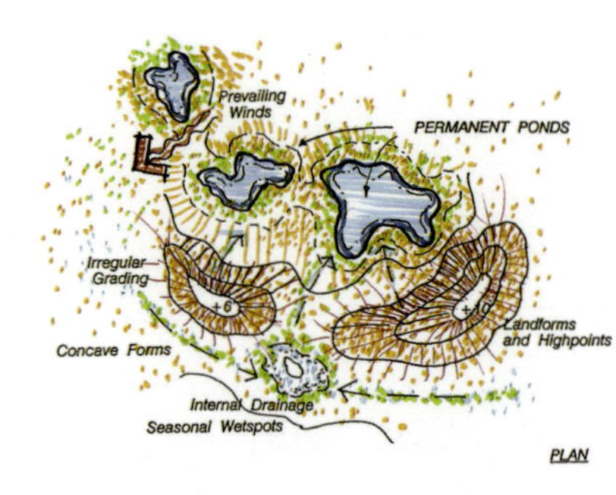

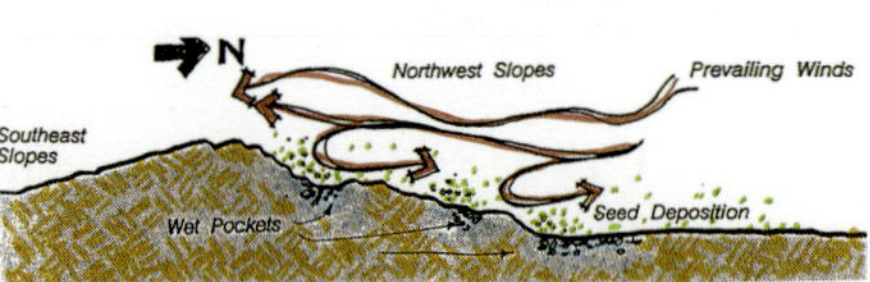

© Walter Kehm
9

狸、水獭、鼬、蛇、乌龟、老鼠和田鼠。大量鸟类的光临也使这里成为了观鸟胜地。

随着步道设施的不断完善，这座公园如今已化身为一处都市秘境。在这里，人们可以暂时忘却城市的喧嚣，拥抱荒野，看一抹斜阳掠过城市中的湿地湖湾，看成群的飞鸟空中翱翔（图10）。河滩上成堆的红砖黄砾、混凝土砌块、条形地砖和钢筋成为了艺术创作的源泉，砖块雕塑在公园中随处可见（图11）。人们还利用这些材料搭建了温馨的休息区，可以眺望广阔无垠的水域。汤米–汤普森公园的经验或许可以为规划设计工作带来启示：人们青睐那些能够参与其中、与之互动的环境，同时也享受动植物不受人类干扰、自由生长的自然环境。简言之，人们更希望融入自然，而非与自然对立。如今新冠肺炎（COVID-19）疫情肆虐，诸如汤米–汤普森公园一类的场所可以为人们提供大自然的庇护，场地中小型草地或沼泽地居多，虽然不适宜聚集性活动，但湖滨的碎石堆为人们提供了休憩和缓解精神压力的私密空间（图12）。疫情之下，公园的游客量大涨，但即使游客密度增加，地形开阔的汤米–汤普森公园仍未给人拥挤之感——这种安全的社交距离正是出于自然的设计。

4 人类世生态系统

汤米–汤普森公园的成功有目共睹，但它同时也给了我们一个重要启示：大自然做功并非一朝一夕之事，与生态系统相关的问题也不是设计师一张图纸就可以解决的；相反，它们会随着外界的变化缓慢而自由地发展。工程师和景观设计师们为汤米–汤普森公园的生态演变创建了良好条件，让大自然这位主人可以打开大门迎接各位“宾客”的到来。如今，已有约350种鸟类来此栖息，这也为公园赢得了全国“重点鸟类保护区”的美誉。

当然，汤米–汤普森公园的自然生态群落并非适合所有生物。自20世纪90年代起，14 000多对双冠鸬鹚来此安家，产生的鸟粪不仅臭气熏天，还导致美洲黑杨这一优势种的大量死亡，并由能够在高氮土壤环

Cottonwood, and Black Locust (*Robinia pseudoacacia*). As these vegetation processes have unfolded, wildlife has become more abundant in the park, including coyotes, beaver, otter, mink, snakes, turtles, mice, and voles. The abundance of avian life makes it a favorite destination for birdwatchers.

Because of enhanced pedestrian accessibility, the park has become an urban sanctuary where the residents of Toronto’s densely populated inner city can connect directly with an urban wildness. They can watch brilliant sunsets illuminating the city over wetland embayments or see huge flocks of birds soaring overhead (Fig. 10). The piles of bricks (both red and yellow), concrete blocks, kitchen tiles, and rebar that cover the beaches have become a source for people’s artistic expression as evidenced by the sculptures found throughout the park (Fig. 11). People also use these materials to create intimate sitting areas looking out over an infinite expanse of water. The lesson for park planning and design is that people enjoy visiting places where they can manipulate the environment to create a personal connection to the site and where nature is allowed to follow its own trajectory with a minimum of human intervention. In short, these are places where people feel they are part of nature, not a threat to it. Today, with the COVID-19 pandemic raging, a place like Tommy Thompson Park is important because it allows people to find a safe refuge in nature. The natural conditions of the site provide a series of small meadows or glades like spaces that discourage large gatherings and the water edge with piles of rubble become private sitting areas where people come to rest and relieve mental stress (Fig. 12). Site visitations have never been higher, but even with this increased density Tommy Thompson Park still feels uncrowded because of its wide open topography. Nature has spontaneously provided a design for self-distancing.

4 A Novel Ecosystem

For all its success, however, Tommy Thompson Park does come with one important caveat—it takes time for nature to do its work. Ecosystems are not

境中生存的繁茂底层草本植被逐步取代——虽然枯木的枝丫仍可供鸟类筑巢。随着时间的推移，不论是陆地上还是水中残留的鸟粪，都将促进一个外观上截然不同的生态系统的形成。

这处延伸至安大略湖中由垃圾填埋而成的场地本不存在任何原生物种——可以说，汤米—汤普森公园不同于任何“自然”生物集群，而是生态学家所谓的“人类世生态系统”的一个完美实例。在这里，人们得以探究在城市化、全球化和气候变化的相互影响下，可适应环境急速变化的韧性生态系统的构建过程[6]。地球生态系统的未来无从预知，但汤米—汤普森公园的成功足以让我们更加乐观地展望未来——不论人类对地球造成何种困扰，我们都可以借助大自然的力量解决难题。**LAF**

REFERENCES

[1] Kehm, W., & Burley, R. (2020). *Accidental Wilderness: The Origins and Ecology of Toronto's Tommy Thompson Park*. Toronto, Canada: University of Toronto Press.

[2] Metropolitan Toronto and Region Conservation Authority (MTRCA). (1982). *Aquatic Park Environmental Study*. Toronto, Canada: MTRCA.

[3] Friends of the Spit. (1990). *Checklist: Plants of the Leslie Street Spit, Toronto*. Retrieved from http://friendsofthespit.ca/wp-content/uploads/2016/09/FOS-Checklist-Plants-of-the-Leslie-Street-Spit.pdf

[4] *Tommy Thompson Park Concept Plan Potential Site Uses*. (1986). Toronto, Canada: Metropolitan Toronto and Region Conservation Authority.

[5] *Wetland Concept Plan—Tommy Thompson Park Disposal Cell 1*. (1994). Toronto, Canada: Metropolitan Toronto and Region Conservation Authority.

[6] Del Tredici, P. (2014). The Flora of the Future. In C. Reed, & N. -M. Lister (Eds.), *Projective Ecologies* (pp. 198-217). New York, NY: Actar Press and Harvard Graduate School of Design.

designed in an air-conditioned downtown office, rather they develop slowly and unpredictably in response to real world conditions. Engineers and landscape architects set the table for ecological change in Tommy Thompson Park, but nature controlled the ever-expanding guest list that now consists of some 350 species of birds—a huge number that has earned the park national recognition as an "Important Bird Area."

This is not to say that the spontaneous ecological community in Tommy Thompson Park is to everyone's liking. The 14,000-plus pairs of Double-Crested Cormorants that began arriving in the 1990s produce copious amounts of smelly excrement that has killed many of the large Eastern Cottonwoods that once dominated the site. While the skeletons of the dead trees still serve as nesting sites for the birds, a thick under-story of herbaceous species that can tolerate the high levels of soil nitrogen has replaced them. Over time, the legacy of guano, both on the land and in the water, is facilitating the development of an ecosystem that will look very different from the one that is there today.

Given that nothing is native to a landfill jutting out into Lake Ontario, Tommy Thompson Park is a perfect example of what ecologists refer to as a "novel" ecosystem that has no analog with any "natural" assemblage of organisms. As such, the park presents a unique opportunity to study the processes whereby the forces of urbanization, globalization, and climate change interact to produce a resilient ecosystem that can track rapidly changing environmental conditions[6]. While the ecological future of planet Earth is uncertain, the existence of Tommy Thompson Park offers a reason for optimism because it shows that nature can be a willing partner in helping clean up the mess people have made of the planet. **LAF**

© Robert Burley

10

© Robert Burley

11

© Walter Kehm

12

生态种植势在必行：创建功能性的系统，而非程式化的生态

Ecological Planting Imperative: Functional Systems, Not Stylized Ecologies

托马斯·雷纳
Thomas RAINER*

Phyto Studio设计工作室负责人
Principal of Phyto Studio

*Corresponding Author
Address: 2901 5th Street S, Arlington, VA 22204, USA
Email: thomas@phytostudio.com

摘要

通过创建由植物构成的人工生态系统，景观设计项目得以缓解气候变化的严峻影响。尽管人们普遍认识到了生态学对于景观塑造的重要性，但景观设计专业人士却普遍缺乏构建稳定植物系统的知识和实践技能，因此迫切需要探索种植设计的新方法和新工具。本文概述了城市环境下高生物多样性植物系统的设计原理和方法，着重介绍了可提升物种丰富度、功能多样性和空间复杂性，有助于构造更具韧性的植物景观的设计方法。种植设计中选择那些对胁迫、干扰和竞争表现出相似适应性状的物种，以及构建由多样化植物形态构成的多层次组合，将有助于建构具有兼容性、长期稳定的植物组合。为平衡多种植物组合带来的视觉复杂性，本文结合美国华盛顿特区Phyto设计工作室的案例与研究和实践经验，探讨了提升景观效果的种植设计策略。这些方法总结于作者探讨如何创建人工植物群落的著作——《后荒野世界的种植设计》一书。

关键词

生态种植；种植设计；植物群落；生物多样性；多样植物系统；种植策略体系

ABSTRACT

The ability of landscape architectural projects to mitigate the worst effects of climate change will depend upon designed ecological systems. These systems will be built with plants. Despite the recognition of ecology as an essential driver of landscapes, the professionals of landscape architecture too often lack the knowledge and practical skills to create robust vegetative systems. New approaches and tools are required. This article outlines principles and methods for designing biodiverse plant systems for urban sites. Planting methods that increase species richness, functional diversity, and spatial complexity are emphasized as a way of developing more resilient plantings. Selecting species with similar evolutionary adaptions to stress, disturbance, and competition—as well as creating multi-layered compositions of diverse plant morphologies—allows designers to create compatible, long-lived plant mixes. To balance the increased visual complexity of diverse plant mixes, the article explores design techniques to make plantings more appealing to the public. The strategies explored here are based on the projects, experience, and research of Phyto Studio, a Washington, D.C. based studio. The methods build on work described in the author's book, *Planting in a Post-Wild World*, an exploration of how to create designed plant communities.

KEYWORDS

Ecological Planting; Planting Design; Plant Community; Biodiversity; Diverse Plant Systems; Planting Strategy Systems

编辑 | 田乐
翻译 | 田乐、李思佳
EDITED BY | Tina TIAN
TRANSLATED BY | Tina TIAN, LI Sijia

https://doi.org/10.15302/J-LAF-1-030023
收稿时间 RECEIVED DATE | 2020-12-10

中图分类号 | TU986
文献标识码 | B

1 基于生态学的种植设计需求

景观设计领域能否为应对气候变化作出贡献，取决于人工生态系统成功与否。这类生态系统由诸多元素构成，包括土地、水、石头、构筑物、管网等；但在生态层面而言，植物或为其中最重要的元素。植物群落整体上作为一个动态系统，对于陆地生态系统的功能发挥举足轻重：植物可驱动碳、氧循环，辅助成土，调节水循环，并滋养万物。尽管人们普遍认识到了生态学对于景观塑造的重要性，但景观设计专业人士却普遍缺乏构建稳定植物群落的知识和技能。传统的种植方法仍然在行业中占主导地位，以致人工设计的环境难以具备自然环境的复杂性和功能性，因而亟需探索植物设计的新方法与新工具。本文结合美国华盛顿特区Phyto设计工作室的研究和实践经验，对城市环境下的多样化城市植物群落设计原理与方法进行了阐述。

通过种植设计来改善景观生态功能潜力巨大。生态思维的谨慎运用可以为应对更宏大的环境问题（如干旱、洪水、水土流失和物种入侵）提供创新型解决方案。此外，生态思维的运用还可以帮助解决持续存在的城市问题，如抑制杂草、避免植被管理中对化学品的过度依赖，以及高效利用维护资源。

为了提升景观设计项目的生态健康水平，设计师需要重新理解种植设计的功能性，而非形式上的美学特性——这并非否认美学在种植设计中的重要性；实际上，令公众意识到植物景观的有序乃至赏心悦目，才是自然种植设计成功的关键。然而，植物物种的筛选、布置与管理不能仅仅出于形式考虑；种植设计应依据当代生态科学和恢复生态学的生态学原理进行。

作者认为，人工植物群落的生态功能取决于其所提供的生态系统服务。天然存在的植物群落具有众多已被广泛证实的生态系统服务[1]，这些服务对于土壤微生物的生长繁殖、养分循环、无脊椎动物和其他动物的生命支持，以及大气环境中的碳封存、雨水渗透和存储、废物处理和旱涝灾害的缓解至关重要[2]。可以提升植物群落的生态系统服务的特征包括物种丰富度（物种总数）、功能多样性（不同物种在群落中发挥的功能作用）和空间复杂度（物种的空间分布与栖息方式）。简而言之，物种多样性的提升可优化植物群落的功能服务[3]——即使在某一群落中两个物种可能发挥着相似的功能，但由于环境条件的变化，它们在不同

1 The Need for Ecologically Informed Planting Design

If the profession of landscape architecture is to have a meaningful impact on climate change, it will depend upon the success of designed ecosystems. These systems will be composed of many elements: earth, water, stone, structures, and pipes; but perhaps the most consequential element to their ecology is plants. Plants working together as dynamic systems have an outsized role in the function of terrestrial ecosystems. They drive the carbon and oxygen cycles, build soil, regulate hydrologic cycles, and feed the world. Despite the recognition of ecology as an essential driver of landscapes, the professionals of landscape architecture too often lack the knowledge and skills to create robust vegetative systems. Conventional planting approaches still dominate the profession, resulting in designed environments that lack the complexity and functionality of their natural counterparts. New approaches and tools for the design of plants are needed. This article outlines the principles and methods for designing diverse plant systems for urban sites. The strategies explored here are based on the projects, experience, and research of Phyto Studio, a Washington, D.C. based studio.

The potential for improving a landscape's ecological function through planting design is immense. A more rigorous application of ecological thinking can create innovations, mitigating bigger environmental issues such as drought, flooding, erosion control, and invasive species. It can also help address persistent urban issues like weed control, overreliance on chemical inputs to manage vegetation, and insufficient maintenance resources.

To achieve a greater level of ecological health in landscape architectural projects, a renewed focus on planting's functionality, as opposed to its formal aesthetic qualities, is required. This is not to say the aesthetics of plantings do not matter; in fact, the need for the public to perceive a naturalistic planting as ordered and even beautiful is critical to its success. However, formalistic concerns cannot drive their selection, arrangement, and management. Instead, ecological principles derived from contemporary ecological sciences and restoration ecology must be the primary drivers of planting design.

Ecological function, in this article, is defined by how well a designed plant community provides ecosystem services. Naturally occurring plant communities provide a wide range of well-documented ecosystem services[1] that are essential for soil microbiology, nutrient cycling, support of invertebrates and other fauna, sequestration of atmospheric carbon, stormwater infiltration and storage, detoxification of wastes, and mitigation of floods and droughts[2]. There are several characteristics which can increase the ecosystem services of a planting. Species richness (the total number of species), functional diversity (the functional roles that different species play in a planting), and spatial complexity (where and how species inhabit) are some of the main drivers of ecosystem services. Simply put, increased diversity increases the functional services of the planting[3]. Even when two species appear to perform the same function within a community, one may outperform another in different years as environmental conditions change[4]. This kind of

发展阶段的表现也会出现优劣差异[4]。植物群落中的这种功能性交叠使其能够更好地应对气候变化的影响。

2 超越单一物种集群：当前景观设计中种植设计手法评述

一项针对中国、北美和欧洲景观设计获奖项目的非正式调查显示，当前的种植方法主要通过模式化的植物配置来表达设计思想。当然也有一些特例，但上述项目大多更加注重植物群落的视觉构成，而非构建动态的群落功能或生态特性。

这并非一个全新的议题。单一物种种植“组团”或“集群”是形式主义设计传统的一种典型特征，融合了植物材料运用的大多数经验智慧。虽然具体模式随时间而改变，但植物在单一物种集群或组团中的排布方式并没有发生变化。自安德烈·勒诺特或意大利文艺复兴时期的欧洲古典园林以来，植物就已被排布成各种图案以表现规整、对称的几何形状——即便是在其他自然主义运动中，如英国的如画式造园运动（或美国弗雷德里克·劳·奥姆斯特德的园林作品），尽管植物集群的形状是自然且不规则的，但植物材料仍以单一物种群体的形式排布。

按植物物种分组是一种实用的植物群落建构方式。这种排布方法使植物配置模式更加清晰可辨，并传达出一种有别于野生植物群落的秩序感与人工管理理念。从生态角度来看，这种方法的问题在于单一物种组团的排他性使用。单一物种组团种植有如下缺点：首先，相同物种的种植会产生相同的形态、特性和生长习性，这意味着这些植物不能有效地覆盖地表，即使是密集集群，植物之间或植物基部也经常出现间隙。此外，在植物休眠期间，植物之间也会产生间隙。这些空间或时间上的空隙给了杂草和外来物种侵入的机会。在阳光照射下，植物之间暴露的土壤中微生物的功能会被削弱，将碳释放到大气中，并降低土壤的渗水能力。这一问题的常见解决方法是厚铺护根覆盖物或使用芽前除草剂（在北美地区十分常见），但这些方法都会加剧环境问题。其次，单一物种组团的过度运用导致大型项目中的生物多样性极低。在传统的植物间隔下，植株密度为3 ~ 6株/m^2，而生态种植手法可将植株密度提升至9 ~ 15株/m^2。

3 种植设计新理念：构建多样的植物系统

一种新的种植理念是用由彼此兼容的植物物种构成的多种植物组合来代替单一物种种群（图1）。植物组合可以实现单一物种种植的美学效果——如果某组植物的高度相同且远观质地一致，那么它就可以表现

functional redundancy within a planting enables it to better withstand the impacts of climate change.

2 Beyond Monocultural Massing: A Critique of Current Landscape Architectural Planting Approaches

A casual survey of award-winning landscape architectural projects in China, North America, and Europe reveals that planting approaches primarily focus on arranging plants in patterns to express design ideas. There are notable exceptions, of course, but in most of these projects, a planting's visual and compositional qualities are prioritized—as opposed to functional or ecological dynamics.

This is not new. The use of monocultural "blocks" or "masses"—the defining feature of formalistic design tradition—has united most of the history of planting design. While the patterns have changed over time, the arrangement of plants in monocultural groups or blocks has not. Since the classical European gardens of André Le Nôtre or the Italian Renaissance, plants have been arranged in patterns to express formal, symmetrical geometries—Even during more naturalistic movements like the British picturesque (or the American counterpart in Frederick Law Olmsted's work), while the shapes of plant masses were natural and amorphous, plants were nonetheless arranged in monocultural groups.

Arranging plants in groups of the same species is a useful compositional tool. This method of arrangement makes patterns more legible and conveys a sense of intentionality and care that distinguishes it from wild vegetation. From an ecological perspective, the problem is the exclusive use of monocultural blocks. Monocultural blocks have several disadvantages. First, the plantings of same species have the same shape, behavior, and temporal sequence. That means they rarely cover ground effectively—Even in a dense grouping, there are often gaps created between or below the plants. Gaps are also created during dormancy. These gaps in space or time are where weeds and invasive species establish. The exposure of open soil between plants to sunlight degrades soil microbiology, releases carbon into the atmosphere, and reduces the soil's ability to infiltrate water. Deep bark mulches or pre-emergent herbicides (prevalent in North America) are often used to deal with this issue—each of which results in negative environmental consequences. Second, the reliance on monocultural blocks results in large-scale projects with minimum biodiversity. Traditional plant spacing gets 3 to 6 plants per square meter, whereas more ecological approaches can get anywhere from 9 to 15 plants in the same space.

3 An Alternative: Diverse Plant Systems

An alternative is to replace monocultural groupings with diverse mixes of compatible species (Fig. 1). Aesthetically, a group of plants can function like a monoculture. If the height of the mix is the same, and its texture from a distance appears consistent, it can convey the same sense of pattern and legibility as a single

传统的组团式种植方法
Traditional plant massing

7HM
35PV
30AH+
15AO
16CA
25DC
12SA

多层次种植方法
Multi-layered planting

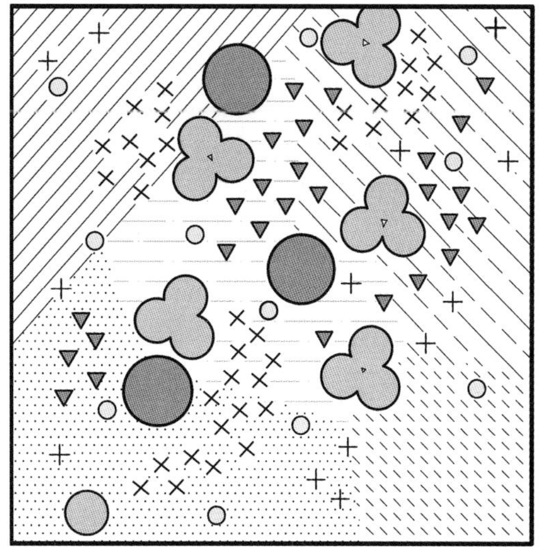

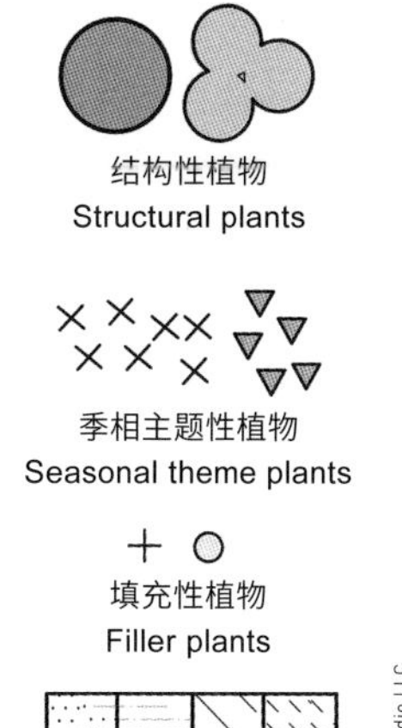

1

1. 图中显示了传统的组团式种植（左）与多层次种植（右）之间的区别。

1. Diagrams show the difference between traditional plant massing (left) and the kind of multi-layered planting (right).

出与单一物种种植相同的视觉效果。同时，多样化的植物组合也具有独特的美学优势（如多个花期、季相变化丰富、与硬质景观相衬的繁茂植物效果），其中以草本植物为主的组合最为突出。这一方法的关键在于理解如何构建稳定的植物群落。

其核心理念是以植物群落为单位进行种植设计。天然存在的植物群落是不同种群的集合，它们都可适应特定的场地环境条件。数千年来的共同演化使植物与环境及植物物种彼此都高度适配，这些野生植物群落经常为景观设计师带来灵感。而新理念的不同之处在于，不仅要将野生植物群落作为物种选择的参考来源（一种相对常规的做法），还要将它们视为功能性系统的模板。

这一区别非常关键。如果设计师仅将野生植物群落作为选用植物的参考来源而忽略了它们作为一个整体的功能性构成，那么设计出的植物群落将需要人工养护来维持。种植设计的目标是增加物种多样性，同时为不同物种间的稳定共存提供条件。当一个群落中的植物在空间和时间上占据不同的生态位时，就会产生稳定性。例如，耐荫的草本植物会在较冷的季节中生长并覆盖地面；而在夏季，这些物种中的大多数处于休眠状态，其上方为植株较高且喜阳的植物。这种生态位的差异化可提升生态系统服务，并维持植物组合的长期稳定。稳定性本身并不能使植物群落更具功能性。实际上，无论是稳定的植物群落还是不停变化的植物群落，都可以提供生态系统服务，但稳定性能够有效减少对人工景观的维护。不同的物种必须彼此兼容——每个物种就像拼图一样相互嵌合，

species grouping. Diverse mixes of plants—particularly herbaceous dominated ones—offer unique aesthetic advantages such as multiple flowering events, dynamic seasonal changes, and a lush counterpoint to hardscape. Understanding how to assemble plants into stable communities is the key.

The central idea is planting as a community. Naturally occurring plant communities are assemblages of different populations, all adapted to tolerate specific environmental conditions. Thousands of years of co-evolution results in plants with a high degree of fitness both to its environment and between each other. These wild plant communities are often claimed by landscape architects as inspiration. The difference is not just using plant communities as an inspiration for species selection (a more conventional approach), but instead using them as templates for functional systems.

The distinction here is critical. If a designer merely uses a wild plant community as an inspiration for a plant list, but ignores their functional role as an assembly, the result will be a planting that requires labor and maintenance to persist. The goal is to increase diversity while providing the conditions for stability between different species. Stability is created when plants within a community inhabit different niches in space and time. For example, shade-tolerant herbaceous species actively cover the ground during cooler months. In summer many of these species go dormant while taller, sun tolerant species grow above them. This kind of niche differentiation increases ecosystem services while providing stable, long-term combinations. Stability, by itself, does not make a planting more functional. In fact, both stable and highly dynamic plant communities can provide ecosystem services. However, stability is important for reducing maintenance in designed landscapes. Species must be compatible with each other—each interlocking together like a puzzle, and their dynamic qualities should balance each other. For example, if one species

2 © Claudia West

2. 由Phyto设计工作室设计师克劳迪娅·韦斯特设计的生物截留雨水花园。图片展现了人工植物群落一年四季的动态混合变化，在整个生长季节都有地表覆盖、花期不断。
3. 用于植物选择的各种生态与美学筛选机制

2. Bioretention planters designed by Claudia West of Phyto Studio. The images show how dynamic mixes change through the season, offering both ground cover and flowering events throughout the growing season.
3. Plant selection should be passed through various ecological and aesthetic filters.

它们的动态特性也应相互平衡。例如，若一个物种的花期是初夏，另一个的花期是仲夏，那么它们就是兼容互补的。

互补物种的选择需要跳脱出传统园艺的种植设计思路。最重要的是，所选物种必须对同样的环境压力具有耐受性，这就需要首先考虑场地中影响植物生长的外部因素。植物对各种压力（如光照、水分或养分不足）的耐受力将在很大程度上影响其在场地中的分布。英国生态学家约翰·菲利普·格莱姆提出的“植物生存策略”概念[5]（C—S—R理论）为设计者提供了有效参考。他认为植物在野外环境中面临三种限制因素：1）位于水分、光照和土壤肥力充足地区时，与其他物种间的激烈竞争（竞争者）；2）高压条件，如干旱、土壤肥力较低或极端温度（胁迫耐受者）；3）高度外部干扰（杂草型植物）。这一理论强调针对不同的城市环境条件需要创建不同的植物系统。干扰性较高和土壤湿度较大的城市绿色基础设施适合杂草型植物和竞争者植物生长，而土壤浅薄且高温的绿色屋顶则适宜引入胁迫耐受者植物。格莱姆还强调某些物种是不相容的，即便它们来自同一生物群系。例如，北美草原植物可能备受设计师青睐，但若将胁迫耐受者植物淡紫松果菊（*Echinacea pallida*）与竞争性植物美国薄荷（*Monarda didyma*）或紫苞泽兰（*Eutrochium purpureum*）混合种植于肥沃的土壤中，将导致淡紫

blooms in early summer, another will bloom in mid-summer. In this way, they are complementary.

Selecting complementary species requires thinking about planting in ways that are often ignored in traditional horticulture. Above all, species must tolerate the same environmental stresses. The key concept is to define a site by the external factors that limit plants' growth. A plant's tolerance to different kinds of stress—low light, water or nutrients—will to a large degree influence its distribution on site. British ecologist John Philip Grime's concepts of plant survival strategies[5] (C–S–R theory) are a useful shorthand for designers. He describes three limitations that plants face in the wild: 1) strong competition from other species found in sites with abundant moisture, sun, and soil fertility (Competitors or "C"); 2) highly stressful conditions like drought, limited fertility, or temperature extremes (Stress-tolerators or "S"); and 3) high levels of external disturbance (Ruderals or "R"). Grime's strategies highlight different systems that might be applied to different urban conditions. Urban green infrastructure with its high disturbance and moist soils favors ruderals and competitors, whereas a green roof with its shallow soils and high temperatures favors stress-tolerators. It also shows that some species—even those from the same biome—are incompatible. For example, North American prairie species might be the focus of a designer's plant list. Mixing a stress-tolerator like *Echinacea pallida* with a competitive *Monarda didyma* and *Eutrochium purpureum* together in rich soils,

3 © Phyto Studio LLC

松果菊的死亡。因此重要的一点是，不要将对压力具有不同适应性状的植物混合种植。

4 多层次地表覆盖

构建多样植物组合的关键在于通过植物分层，对地表进行密集覆盖。地表覆盖对建立功能性植物群落来说最为重要。除了个别极端条件地区或受干扰的地区外，大多数温带气候地区的土壤裸露情况是暂时性的，每个裸露的地方都是潜在的生态位。野外环境中的所有地表都覆盖着植物，这就为景观设计师提供了一个简单但尚未得到充分实践的设计原则：植物本身可以起到“护根物”的覆盖作用[6]。

为了有效覆盖地表，人工设计的植物组合具有不同的垂直层次，每一层在全年中扮演着不同的角色。人工植物群落的构建需要两个基本层：由地被植物组成的近地面的基底层，与由较高的直立植物组成的第二（上）层，这一层的植物通常占据视觉主导作用。

基底层是指由耐荫植物构成的低矮圆丘状组合。良好的基底层中，植物的传播方式各异，其中许多物种为无性繁殖，它们在水平方向上分布在较高植物——如草莓属（*Fragaria* spp.）、路边青属（*Geum* spp.）、淫羊藿属（*Epimedium* spp.）、筋骨草属（*Ajuga* spp.）、金千里光属（*Packera* spp.）、老鹳草属（*Geranium* spp.）、蝶须属（*Antennaria* spp.）和细辛属（*Asarum* spp.）——的基部周围。基底层物种也包括种子自播、成簇生长的植物，例如薹草属（*Carex* spp.）、重楼属（*Paris* spp.）、矾根属（*Heuchera* spp.）、报春花属（*Primula* spp.）和蓝禾属（*Sesleria* spp.）。可在春季形成短暂而绚丽景观效果的马裤花属（*Dicentra* spp.）、报春花属，以及水仙（*Narcissus* spp.）等隐芽植物，与可在冬季形成稳定景观效果的薹草属和矾根属等，即为一种可行的植物组合。

上层多采用传统景观设计中的常见植物，包括观赏草、直立阔叶草本植物和亚灌木。上层植物应成簇状、不分散且寿命长。就基底层

will result in the death of the *Echinacea*. It is important not to mix species with different evolutionary adaptations to stress.

4 Covering the Ground With Multiple Layers

The key to assembling diverse plant mixes is to densely cover the ground by layering plants. Covering ground is the most important concept of creating a functioning plant community. In most temperate climates, except for extreme or disturbed sites, bare soil is almost always a temporary condition. Every bare spot is an available niche, and in the wild, all niches are filled with plants. This fact prompts a simple, yet underutilized design principle for landscape architects: plants themselves can function as mulches[6].

To effectively cover the ground, plant mixes are designed at different vertical layers, each performing different roles throughout the year. Start with two basic layers: the base layer composed of low ground-covering species, and a second (upper) layer composed of tall, upright species that tend to be more visually dominant species.

The base layer describes a mix of low, hummocky plants which are shade tolerant. Good base layers are a combination of plants with different spreading behaviors. Many are clonal species that spread horizontally around the base of taller species (such as species in the genus of *Fragaria*, *Geum*, *Epimedium*, *Ajuga*, *Packera*, *Geranium*, *Antennaria*, and *Asarum*). Other base layer species may be clump-forming plants that more often spread by seed (*Carex*, *Paris*, *Heuchera*, *Primula*, *Sesleria*, etc.). Mixing species allows the designer to balance species that are showy in spring but ephemeral (*Dicentra*, *Primula*, and geophytes like *Narcissus*) with species that are stable and winter present (*Carex* and *Heuchera*).

The upper layer is composed of plants more traditionally associated with landscape architectural plantings, including ornamental grasses, upright forbs, and shrub-like mounding perennials. Upper layer plants should be clump-forming, non-

和上层的比例而言，基底层的物种多样性和生物量应该更高；上层植物应间隔更大、植株密度更低，随着时间的推移，上层植物不会导致基底层因少光而死亡，植物群落的稳定性会更高。花葶直立无叶的物种是良好的上层植物材料，如百子莲属（*Agapanthus* spp.）、葱属（*Allium* spp.）、独尾草属（*Eremurus* spp.）、夏风信子属（*Galtonia* spp.）、火把莲属（*Kniphofia* spp.）和丝兰属（*Yucca* spp.）。花朵长于直立茎顶端的夏季开花植物，如松果菊属（*Echinacea* spp.）、刺芹属（*Eryngium* spp.）、钓钟柳属（*Penstemon* spp.）、狼尾草属（*Pennisetum* spp.）和一枝黄花属（*Solidago* spp.）的许多物种均为理想的上层植物材料。

植物的生态特性——植物与环境及植物彼此间的相互作用——对物种选择至关重要，这意味着各种生态和设计层面的筛选机制尤为关键（图3）。一开始，可能会有众多植物材料进入设计师的视野，但设计师可通过层层考量，筛选出那些更具韧性的物种。这个筛选过程不同于传统的园艺方法，后者的选择更多出于美学考虑，包括花朵的色彩、高度或质感对比等。

5 利用设计框架使高生物多样性的植物组合更加特色鲜明

随着植物群落变得更加动态和自然化，公众也可能认为其景观效果与杂草无异，或毫无美感可言。随着人们对于美的社会共识不断扩大，生态美学有望逐步为公众所接纳。这意味着最终落在景观设计师肩上的“将生态功能转化为美学形式”的责任将更重。本文在此提出几项策略。

首要策略是在植物群落周围使用几何框架。“有序框架”（orderly frame）概念由琼·艾弗森·纳索尔[7]首先提出，在公众眼中，这代表着秩序感和人工管理。在Phyto设计工作室的实践中，相对于路缘、矮墙、铺路、草坪、树篱或其他结构元素，草本植物组合的边界感更加模糊、多变，设计师可以加强这种鲜明对比。

spreading, and long-lived. In terms of proportions of the two layers, the base layer should have more diversity of species and biomass. The upper layer species are spaced farther apart and at lower densities, creating more stability in the plantings over time as the taller species are less likely to shade out the ground layer. Good upper layer plants include emergent vegetation with leafless upper stems such as *Agapanthus*, *Allium*, *Eremurus*, *Galtonia*, *Kniphofia*, and *Yucca*. Summer flowering species whose flowers rise above their foliage are quite useful in this layer. Many species of *Echinacea*, *Eryngium*, *Penstemon*, *Pennisetum*, and *Solidago* may work well.

Plants' ecology—their interaction with their environment and each other—is critical to species selection. In developing plant lists, a systematic process that considers various ecological and design filters is important (Fig. 3). While a plant list may be initially broad, purging the list of species that do not pass each filter is important for developing the most resilient selections. This filtering process differs from traditional horticultural approaches that focus on aesthetic considerations like flower color, height, or textural contrast.

5 Using Design Frames to Make Biodiverse Plant Mixes Legible

As planting becomes more dynamic and naturalistic, it may also be perceived by the public as messy or unattractive. As much as one may hope the social conventions for beauty would broaden to embrace a more ecological aesthetic, ultimately the burden rests on landscape architects to translate ecological function into an aesthetic form. Several strategies can be considered.

The primary strategy is to use geometric frameworks around the planting. These "orderly frames"—a concept first articulated by Joan Iverson Nassauer[7]—signal to the public an intentionality and care. In Phyto Studio's practice, herbaceous plant mixes are often conceptualized as a liquid that is poured into a mold. Designers may use curbs, low walls, paving, turf, hedges, or other constructed elements that provide a sharp contrast.

低矮草类植物群落
Short grassy plant community

低矮阔叶植物群落
Short broadleaf (forby) plant community

© Phyto Studio LLC
4

另一个策略是限制植物组合的高度。与肩齐平的高度会让许多人感到威胁，而与膝盖齐高的植物组合，即使物种繁多也不会让人们感到眼花缭乱。低矮的植物群落常需要将土壤肥力维持在较低水平，高肥力的土壤往往会加强植物的竞争而导致群落的衰败；土壤表层15 ~ 20cm可使用砾石或粗砂，以降低土壤肥力并抑制杂草。

另一个策略是限制植物组合的视觉复杂性。由外观相似的物种组成的植物组合远观可形成相同的质感。例如，当低矮的草类组合中混有类草状的阔叶草本植物（通常为单子叶植物），其外观则与单一集群相似。相反，全部由阔叶草本植物组成的组合则可能表现为单一的叶片质感。植物组合中不同物种的反差程度决定了其视觉复杂性。

最后一个策略是设计出具有强烈开花效果的植物组合。一项由谢菲尔德大学开展的研究显示，在色彩丰富的植物群落中，当花朵面积不低于27%（临界阈值）时，观赏者的审美感知最佳[8]。多个花期是多样植物组合的优势。因此，拥有不同花期的兼容性物种的比例是其中关键的设计因素。这就要求采用足够多的开花效果强烈的单个物种，但也需要在组合中为其他花期较晚的物种留出充足空间。生命周期极短的阔叶草本植物，尤其是隐芽植物或报春花等早春开花的植物，即为适宜的植物材料。

本文中讨论的策略融合了园艺学与生态学原理。在植物群落的复杂性或功能性方面，人工设计的植物组合可能永远无法和真正的自然生态系统相媲美，但本文中提出的方法和策略或能够为景观设计师提供参考，促使他们通过种植设计来提升植物群落的多样性和功能性。当景观设计师掌握了植物的生态特性以后，便可提高设计品质，创造出常规种植无法具有的景观效果和生态绩效。**LAF**

Another strategy is to restrain the height of a mixed planting. A mix that is shoulder-height will feel intimidating to many people, whereas even a visually diverse mix at knee-height can feel calm and restrained. Shorter plantings often require low fertility soils to be sustained. Highly productive soils often produce competitive vegetation that flops. Using gravel or coarse sand in the top 15 ~ 20 centimeters can help reduce fertility and weed pressure.

Limiting the visual complexity of a mix is another strategy to consider. Mixes composed of similar looking species may all appear as one consistent texture from a distance. For example, a low grass matrix filled with grass-like forbs (typically monocots) will appear similar to a monocultural grouping. Or in contrast, a mix composed of all broadleaf forbs may appear as a single leafy texture. The degree of internal contrast between the species in a mix will determine its visual complexity.

A final strategy is to design mixes to have strong flowering events. In studies conducted by the University of Sheffield, colorful planting with flower-cover above a critical threshold (27%) was associated with the highest level of aesthetic preference[8]. Multi-flowering-season is an advantage of diverse mixes. To achieve this, proportion of compatible species that bloom during different weeks is a critical design factor. It is important to have enough of a single species to create a strong flowering event yet leave enough space in the mix for subsequent waves of flowers. Ephemeral forbs are particularly useful, especially geophytes or early season blooming plants like *Primula*.

The strategies discussed here represent a hybrid of horticulture and ecology. Designed mixes may never have the complexity or functionality of true wild ecosystems. However, these approaches can be valuable tools for landscape architects to embed more diversity and functionality in plantings. Armed with the knowledge of how plants behave ecologically, they can elevate their work, creating effects not possible with conventional planting. **LAF**

4. 图中所示两个植物组合的植株高度和质感相同，组合中的所有物种都具有相似的形态和质感（都是草类与阔叶植物的组合）。通过这种方式，既可以实现物种多样性，也可以避免造成眼花缭乱的视觉效果。

4. Two examples of plant mixes where both height and texture are restrained. All species within the mix have similar forms and textures (grassy vs. broadleaf). In this way, diversity is achieved without visual complexity.

REFERENCES

[1] Storkey, J., Döring, T., Baddeley, J., Collins, R., Roderick, S., Jones, H., & Watson, C. (2015). Engineering a plant community to deliver multiple ecosystem services. *Ecological Applications: Ecological Society of America*, 25(4), 1034-1043. doi:10.1890/14-1605.1

[2] Daily, G. C. (Ed.). (1997). *Nature's Services: Societal Dependence on Natural Ecosystems*. Washington, D.C.: Island Press.

[3] Eisenhauer, N., Schielzeth, H., Barnes, A. D., Barry, K., Bonn, A., Brose, U., ... Jochum, M. (2019). A multitrophic perspective on biodiversity-ecosystem functioning research. *Advances in Ecological Research*, (61), 1-54. https://doi.org/10.1016/bs.aecr.2019.06.001

[4] Isbell, F., Calcagno, V., Hector, A., Connolly, J., Harpole, W. S., Reich, P. B., ... Loreau, M. (2011). High plant diversity is needed to maintain ecosystem services. *Nature*, 477(7363), 199-202. doi:10.1038/nature10282

[5] Grime, P., & Pierce, S. (2012). *The Evolutionary Strategies that Shape Ecosystems*. Chichester, UK: Wiley-Blackwell.

[6] Rainer, T., & West, C. (2015). *Planting in a Post-Wild World*. Portland, OR: Timber Press.

[7] Nassauer, J. (1995). Messy ecosystems, orderly frames. *Landscape Journal*, 14(2), 161-170.

[8] Hoyle, H., Hitchmough, J., & Jorgensen, A. (2017). All about the 'wow factor'? The relationships between aesthetics, restorative effect and perceived biodiversity in designed urban planting. *Landscape and Urban Planning*, (164), 109-123.

城市荒野景观营造：以上海乡土生态科普示范基地为例

Urban Wilderness Construction: An Example of Shanghai Urban Biodiversity Education Base

郭陶然*
城市荒野工作室创始人

山冰沁
城市中国研究中心研究员，联合国可持续发展解决方案网络项目专员

GUO Taoran
Founder of Forest City Studio

SHAN Bingqin
Research Assistant at Urban China Research Center; Local Pathways Fellow at the United Nations Sustainable Development Solutions Network

*通讯作者
地址：上海市闵行区沈杜公路5919弄16号
邮编：201112
邮箱：taoranguo@163.com

编辑 | 崔婧沄、王颖
翻译 | 山冰沁、罗伯特·格雷厄姆、崔婧沄
EDITED BY | CUI Jingyun, WANG Ying
TRANSLATED BY | SHAN Bingqin, Robert GRAHAM, CUI Jingyun

摘要

恢复受损的城市生态系统是城市荒野景观的核心价值之一。通过城市荒野景观的营造，可在城市破碎化生境中恢复该地区原有生物群落的结构和功能，并在低人工干预的情况下，使乡土生物群落稳定地存在与演替。本文介绍了以生物多样性恢复为主要目的的"上海乡土生态科普示范基地"项目，项目探讨和研究了主动型城市再野化过程中应采取的设计原则与技术路径，并围绕这一目标进行了生境类型划分、乡土生物引种、生物群落构建、生态效益评估等一系列工作，以期丰富城市荒野景观营造及城市环境下基于自然的解决方案的技术积累与理论研究。在项目实施的一年半时间内，项目地共记录乡土植物260种、昆虫255种、两栖爬行动物7种、鸟类71种及哺乳动物6种，其生物多样性和动物的种群密度均远高于周边未改造的人工林地，并且植物群落已开始进行自发的正向演替，取得了较为理想的效果。该项目的技术方案在城市郊野公园、野生动物栖息地、生态廊道、科普教育基地等项目中有着广阔的应用前景。

关键词

城市荒野景观；乡土物种；群落演替；城市生物多样性；生态修复；基于自然的解决方案

ABSTRACT

One of the core values of urban wilderness construction is to restore the structures and functions of biological communities in fragmented urban habitats, and enable the stability and ecological succession of native communities with low human intervention. The paper discusses the design principles and technical methodologies in active urban rewilding by the example of Shanghai Urban Biodiversity Education Base project. Aiming to restore urban biodiversity and enrich the technical and theoretical research of urban wilderness construction and Nature-based Solutions, this project conducted habitat division, native species introduction, natural community construction, ecological benefit assessment, etc. In a year and a half, 260 native plant species, 255 insect species, 7 amphibian and reptile species, 71 bird species, and 6 mammal species were recorded within the 1.7 hm^2 project site, showing higher biodiversity and density of animal populations than unrestored consructed forests surrounding. Along with the spontaneous progressive succession of the plant communities, the project has achieved good results. The technical approaches proposed in the project can be broadly applied in design and construction of country parks, wildlife habitats, ecological corridors / networks, and environmental education bases.

KEYWORDS

Urban Wilderness; Native Species; Community Succession; Urban Biodiversity; Ecosystem Restoration; Nature-based Solutions

https://doi.org/10.15302/J-LAF-1-040022
收稿时间 RECEIVED DATE | 2020-12-10

中图分类号 | TU986.2, TU986.5+2, X176, Q145+.2, Q16
文献标识码 | B

1 引言

根据联合国《生物多样性公约》，生物多样性是指地球上各个生态系统中所有具有生命的生物的多样性，包括生态系统多样性、物种多样性和遗传多样性三个层次[1]。目前对于生物多样性的保护与恢复措施大多集中在自然保护地，对于非自然保护地（尤其是城市地区）生态系统修复与保护的认识与关注尚显不足，将城市作为“生态系统”进行研究亟待更多理论与实践的积累[2]~[6]。已有研究表明，城市的生物多样性具有重要作用，且城市生态系统可支撑较高的生物多样性，其中涉及许多濒危物种与受胁物种[4][7][8]。更重要的是，城市生物多样性恢复与保护工作具有现实的迫切需求。城市地区承载了全球一半以上的人口[9]，而许多城市化进程发生在生物多样性的热点地区[10]，对生物多样性产生了深刻而不可逆的负面影响：直接表现为城市地表覆盖的改变导致自然生境的破坏、退化与破碎化，间接表现为加剧了气候变化，这些都造成了城市生物多样性的破坏与衰退[11]~[13]。

现有研究归纳了多种城市生物多样性保护的方法与策略[6]，如城市绿地管理中划定保护区[14][15]，协调城市土地利用与生物多样性保护[16]，将生物多样性融入城市设计[17]，以及促进城市荒野的发展[18][19]等。其中，城市荒野（urban wilderness）通常指城市中残留的自然保护地、修复过的自然生态系统、废弃荒地，以及人工设计的荒野景观[19]~[21]，其最突出的特征在于，虽处于人类活动密集区域中，却不受或较少受到人类干预、保留自然原貌并发生自然演替[22]~[24]。也有研究认为在城市范畴下，“城市野境”（urban wildscape）这一术语更适合描述城市中仍在进行自然演替且生态过程占主导的荒野景观，如城市内部或周边的自然林地、未利用或被遗弃的场地、河流廊道、棕地等[24]~[26]。曹越等人的研究将此语境下对城市荒野的保护与营造途径分为4种，即保护（在城市保护地中保护野性自然）、修复（再野化部分城市区域）、设计（在城市公园中营造类荒野景观）、融合（在城市空间中系统性融入野性自然）[24]。除了划定城市中及其边缘地带的自然保护地外，城市生物多样性的保护与恢复主要依赖于场地修复：一类是自然发生的被动型城市再野化，即城市废弃荒地经过自然演替形成野生动物栖息地；另一类是由人类介入引导的主动型城市再野化，即人类根据生态演替的规律对场地进行系统性生态修复。

由于被动型城市再野化历时长，对场地周围自然连通性要求高，虽在国外有成功案例，但在国内大型城市中较难实现。我国城市建成区面积与人口规模远大于大多数国外城市，人类干扰更为频繁，且大多数城市的园林绿化并没有使用足够数量和种类的乡土物种，导致较难通过物种自然扩散的方式恢复生态系统结构和功能。在这种条件下，采取人为规划及引导的主动型城市再野化更具现实意义。目前，中国主动型城市再野化的成功案例尚不多见，仍处于研究探索阶段。本文以城市荒野工作室的“上海乡土生态科普示范基地”项目为例，介绍了以城市生物多样性恢复与保护为目的的主动型城市再野化技术路径与场地实践经验，以期丰富城市荒野景观营造及城市环境下基于自然的解决方案的理论研究与技术积累。

2 场地背景与修复设计

2.1 场地情况

该项目位于上海浦江郊野公园内。总面积1.7hm^2，为国有林地；场地较为平整，无明显的地势变化；外围三面环水，内部无水系。在2019年7月实施改造前，工作室对现场进行了土质检测和植被调查。结果显示，场地内土壤较为粘重，有机物含量低，偏碱性（pH≥7.8）；种有香樟（*Cinnamomum camphora*）、女贞（*Ligustrum lucidum*）、意大利214杨（以下简称“意杨”，*Populus × canadensis* ‘I-214’）、梧桐（*Firmiana simplex*）等乔木和部分园艺品种的地被植物，植物种类较为单一。受土质与地形影响，排水不畅，植物生长状况不理想，女贞、梧桐等乔木已陆续出现死亡情况。外来物种入侵情况严重，在降雨多、气温高的6月，地表约60%的面积被喜旱莲子草（*Alternanthera philoxeroides*）与白车轴草（*Trifolium repens*）覆盖，约5%的面积被春飞蓬（*Erigeron philadelphicus*）、钻叶紫菀（*Symphyotrichum subulatum*）、加拿大一枝黄花（*Solidago canadensis*）等菊科入侵物种覆盖（图1），乡土草本植物的生长受到明显抑制。

2.2 设计原则

项目旨在探索城市生物多样性恢复的技术路径，同时保育因城市发展而丧失栖息地的乡土生物。围绕生物多样性恢复的主要目标，工作室制定了如下设计原则：

1）使用长三角地区乡土植物的苗木，在场地条件受限、苗木短缺及无法满足生态功能的情况下，可酌情选择少量具有相似生态功能的非乡土物种进行替换，但其比例不得超过植物总量的5%；

2）以接近自然群落的结构进行植物配置，推动自然演替；

3）根据场地条件营造多样的生境类型，各生境类型之间借由植物种类的变化自然过渡，杜绝人工构筑物或绿篱分隔，以保证野生动物的活动不受限制；

4）确定重点研究和保育的生物种类，并以特定野生动物的取食及栖息特点选择植物、营造生境；

5）道路、护栏、解说牌、警示牌等设施以灰褐色、绿色为主色调，杜绝使用过于鲜艳的颜色，以免使野生动物受惊。

根据以上设计原则，工作室对场地进行了初步设计，而后在实际施工过程中结合场地实际条件，进一步优化了地形、水系和植物等的设计。

2.3 技术流程

根据场地现状和项目目标，工作室结合群落演替规律制定了技术流程（图2）。

2.4 功能分区规划

该项目为生物多样性恢复技术的研究和展示基地，因此需要在有限的空间内营造尽可能多样的生境，最大限度提高可容纳物种的上限，方便未来的研

1. 改造前喜旱莲子草与白车轴草混生的草地，后方为死亡的女贞。

1. Before restoration, *Alternanthera philoxeroides* and *Trifolium repens* covered the site with dead *Ligustrum lucidum* behind.

© 郭海然

1

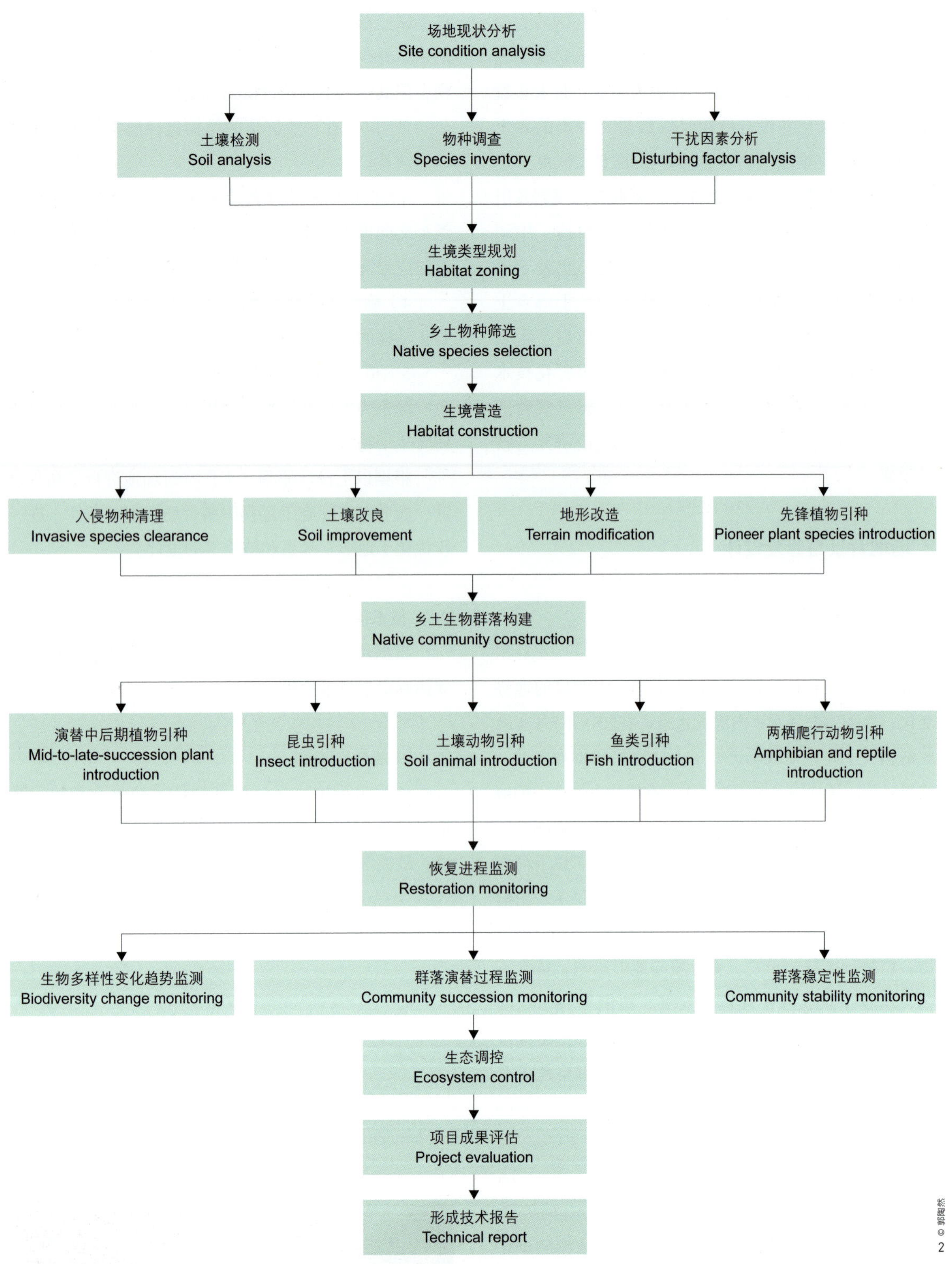

2. 技术流程示意图
3-1. 基于生物群落差异的生态功能分区
3-2. 改造后场地航拍图（摄于2020年6月）

2. Diagram of the technical roadmap
3-1. Ecological zoning based on community differences
3-2. Aerial photography of the optimized site (June, 2020)

究和教学。工作室根据现有场地条件，将其划分为7个不同的生态功能区：乡土蝶类招引区、乡土灌木展示区、乡土水生生物保育区、乡土常绿树种区、科普活动区、乡土常绿／落叶树种混交区，以及乡土落叶树种区（图3–1）。

3 项目实施

3.1 基础环境改造

在施工阶段，工作室遇到了以下难点：1）场地内部缺少水系，难以为水生生物和两栖动物提供栖息环境；2）土质较差、排水不畅导致树木不断死亡；3）入侵物种数量较多，无法通过人工拔除有效控制；4）现有林地不能移栽或砍伐，地形无法完全按要求改造。

针对以上问题，工作室首先进行了地形调整和水系营造：在场地中央空旷处挖掘小型池塘，使用水泵抽取场地北侧外部河道水进入内部水系，流经池塘后沿人工小溪流入南侧外部河道；将场地内的排水沟与池塘连通，增强雨季排水能力。挖出的土方则在东侧落叶林中堆高形成缓坡，用于种植不耐水湿的乡土乔木（图3–2）。

地形改造完成后，采用人工和机械结合的方式对场地进行了整体翻耕，同时施加腐熟的园林垃圾，增加土壤有机质。根据工作室以往项目的经验，翻耕可以打破入侵物种目前的优势，给土壤种子库中的乡土植物种子创造萌发的机会，从而形成禾本科先锋植物与入侵物种相竞争的局面，辅以人工调控，逐渐扩大禾本科植物的竞争优势。这一方法能够显著降低入侵物种的盖度与发芽率，为接下来乡土植物的群落构建打下基础。此外，为满足未来科研需求，工作室在场地中增设了电路、无线网络、灌溉系统和监控系统。

3.2 乡土生物群落构建

有别于人为干预强度较大的景观营造方式，城市荒野景观需要使用乡土物种构建合理的群落结构，使其自发演替。在土壤翻耕后，除原有乔木外，场地上的其他植物已经被人工清除（可将此时的场地视为生态学意义上的“次生裸地”），当新的植物开始生长，漫长的次生演替过程就此发生：喜光、耐贫瘠、种子萌发率高且生长迅速的先锋物种（如部分禾本科植物和由鸟类传播的速生木本植物）会最先出现，在演替初期覆盖地表的大部分面积。随着先锋物种的生长，树荫面积不断扩大，喜光的禾本科植物逐渐被耐阴植物取代；林下湿度增加，顶级群落建群种的幼苗开始萌发，经年累月逐渐取代先锋树种成为这片林地的优势种。在土壤种子库足够丰富的前提下，这一过程中会出现大量的演替中期植物，但总体趋势不变。

该项目中的每一个功能分区实质上就相当于一种乡土生物群落，也都遵循着上述演替过程。物种的引入不是一蹴而就的，而是需要在3～5年的时间里，不断根据环境的变化引入不同的物种，在不违背演替规律的情况下增加群落内的生物多样性。除了增加植物的多样性外，对于具有重要生态功能但无法自然迁移至项目地的动物（如鱼类、两栖动物及扩散能力较差的昆虫等），还需在生境营造满足其生存需求后进行人为引种。下文将以乡土水生生物保育区、科普活动区、乡土常绿树种区和乡土落叶树种区为例，介绍对应生物群落的营造过程。

水生生物保育区位于项目的中轴线，其中心为一个人工挖掘的小型水塘（图4），水塘面积约100m²，最深处约1.5m，未进行防渗处理。水塘内种植刺苦草（*Vallisneria spinulosa*）、眼子菜（*Potamogeton distinctus*）等沉水植物（图5），并投放方形环棱螺（*Bellamya quadrata*）、圆顶珠蚌（*Unio douglasiae*）等底栖生物。二者均有助于水质净化，为其他生物的引入创造了条件。一个月后，逐渐引入高体鳑鲏（*Rhodeus ocellatus*）、青鳉（*Oryzias latipes*）等十余种乡土鱼类。由于水塘面积较小，为保证水塘生态系统的平衡与稳定，不得引入乌鳢（*Channa argus*）等捕食能力过强的鱼类。2019年9月至2020年8月，陆续引种乡土水生、湿生植物30种，进一步增加了该区域的生物多样性，国家二级保护植物粗梗水蕨（*Ceratopteris pteridoides*）已在水塘西北侧的浅滩上建立了稳定的种群。

位于水塘西侧的是科普活动区的草地，种有糠稷（*Panicum bisulcatum*）、荩草（*Arthraxon hispidus*）、狗牙根（*Cynodon dactylon*）、竹叶茅（*Microstegium nudum*）等乡土草本植物（图6）。由于禾本科植物较多，短额负蝗（*Atractomorpha sinensis*）、中华稻蝗（*Oxya chinensis*）、迷卡斗蟋（*Velarifictorus micado*）等直翅目昆虫数量丰富，为蛙类提供了充足的食物。工作室观测到金线侧褶蛙（*Pelophylax plancyi*）、泽陆蛙（*Fejervarya multistriata*）、黑斑侧褶蛙（*Pelophylax nigromaculatus*）、饰纹姬蛙（*Microhyla ornata*）、中华蟾蜍（*Bufo gargarizans*）在此活动（图7）。

规划的常绿树种区原本为一片樟树林。由于郁闭度过高，喜阳植物无法存活，因此工作室在林下栽种了菜蕨（*Diplazium esculentum*）、双穗求米草（*Oplismenus undulatifolius var. binatus*）、紫金牛（*Ardisia japonica*）、朱砂根（*Ardisia crenata*）等本土阴生植物。在春夏季，斑驳的阳光照在林下低矮的阴生植物上，景观效果出色（图8）。此外由于林下光照较弱，适宜作为陆生萤火虫黄脉翅萤（*Curtos costipennis*）的栖息地。经过一年的引种和复育工作，已有少量萤火虫出现（图9）。

意杨林所在的落叶树种区位于场地东侧。由于意杨并非上海的乡土植物，且生长过速、病虫害较多、林木稀疏，工作室计划用乡土落叶树种逐渐取而代之。区域内已有较多构树（*Broussonetia papyrifera*）、桑（*Morus alba*）等先锋树种个体借助鸟类传播自发生长。在不进行疏伐的情况下栽种榔榆（*Ulmus parvifolia*）、朴（*Celtis sinensis*）、楝（*Melia azedarach*）、椿叶花椒（*Zanthoxylum ailanthoides*）、枳椇（*Hovenia acerba*）等十余种乡土落叶树种。随着意杨因病虫害、台风等自然因素死亡，该区域可逐渐恢复为以乡土落叶树种为主的群落。

4 生态效益评估

4.1 生态恢复进程监测

城市荒野景观产生的生态价值是高度人工化的园林所不可替代的，但尚未形成有效、合理的评估标准。在该项目的整个营造过程中，城市荒野工作室及华东师范大学生态与环境科学学院共同对植物、昆虫、两栖动物、鸟类和哺乳动物进行了持续监测，以初步评估该项目的生态价值。

植物调查通过普查整理植物名录，并结合样方法采集不同生境类型中的植物及林下环境数据。昆虫调查针对不同物种分别采用网捕法、巴氏罐诱法、灯诱法、扫集法、振落法和搜捕法，记录场地内昆虫物种及数量。两栖动物调查采用样线法，观察记录水边或周围草丛中的两栖动物种类及数量。鸟类调查同样采用样线法，记录其种类和数量。哺乳动物调查采用红外相机监测法，统计兽类活动时间、出现频率等数据。

自开始施工至2020年11月，场地内共记录到乡土植物260种、昆虫255种、两栖爬行动物7种、鸟类71种及哺乳动物6种，其多样性和动物的种群密度均远高于周边未改造的人工林地。昆虫的多样性对于病虫害防控十分重要，工作室还特别开展了对城市传粉昆虫种类及与植物对应关系的监测和研究（图10）。

在植物和昆虫的多样性足够高的情况下，鸟类会被食物吸引而来，监测中还发现鸟类在场地内的筑巢数量较多。2019年冬季，小太平鸟（*Bombycilla japonica*）等较为罕见的鸟类在这里成群越冬（图11）。在哺乳动物方面，经过一年以上的红外相机调查，可确定场地内东北刺猬（*Erinaceus amurensis*）、

1 乡土蝶类招引区
Native Butterfly Attracting Zone
2 乡土灌木展示区
Native Shrub Zone
3 乡土水生生物保育区
Native Aquatic Species Conservation Zone
4 乡土常绿树种区
Native Evergreen Tree Zone
5 科普活动区
Environmental Education Activity Zone
6 乡土常绿／落叶树种混交区
Mixed Native Evergreen / Deciduous Tree Zone
7 乡土落叶树种区
Native Deciduous Tree Zone

3-1

3-2

© 郭陶然
4

© 郭陶然
5

© 郭陶然
6

© 郭陶然
7

黄鼬（*Mustela sibirica*）、黑线姬鼠（*Apodemus agrarius*）均有稳定的种群；并且自2020年9月开始，监测到有华南兔（*Lepus sinensis*）在场地内长期停留（图12，13）。但同时也发现，流浪猫对黑线姬鼠和鸟类的捕食情况十分严重，未来需要加强监测和管理。

理论上，本项目应在施工前一年内对项目地的生物多样性开展调查，以便客观对比、评估改造前后的生物多样性变化情况。但由于施工前预留时间过短，改造前并未对场地进行充分调研。未来或可考虑通过以附近未改造林地为参照的方式来研究其生物多样性的变化趋势。

4.2 生态调控

一般而言，城市荒野景观具有较高的生物多样性，并且以自然演替为主，人为干预为辅，因此养护工作量较小，但技术难度较高，需严禁使用任何化学杀虫剂，否则会对生物多样性造成显著负面影响。就实际情况而言，项目场地内螳螂、瓢虫、寄生蜂和蜘蛛等捕食性昆虫和节肢动物数量较多，对维持昆虫种群的平衡起到了显著作用，因此该项目从未也无需使用任何杀虫剂，就能保证植物健康生长（图14）。

此外，项目未对自然死亡的树木和枯枝落叶等园林垃圾进行外运处理。死亡树木锯成数段后堆放在林下，任其自然腐朽（图15）。随着真菌对树木的分解，拟步甲、锹甲等甲虫会在朽木中产卵，其幼虫以朽木为食，可加速分解过程。通常在3~5年内，大部分朽木会被分解为松软的有机质，可用于改善土壤。草本和树叶则任其自然凋落，在冬季形成落叶层，为土壤动物提供理想的栖息环境。

养护过程中最大的工作量在于对外来入侵植物的防控。在项目实施前，场地内喜旱莲子草、春飞蓬、加拿大一枝黄花等入侵植物的数量十分庞大，若单纯依靠人工清理，工作量巨大，且效果不理想。项目大量应用乡土植物中糠稷、荩草、狗牙根等先锋草本植物，迅速挤占了入侵植物的生长空间，入侵植物的覆盖率在一年内从65%降低到5%。剩余入侵物种需要在开花前人工拔除以防再次扩散。这一步骤的工作量主要取决于场地内原有入侵物种数量，而入侵物种会随着乡土植物群落结构的稳定逐渐减少。相关案例可见工作室于2016年实施的建设项目，经过4年的自然演替和人工防控，截至2020年，入侵物种已无法构成威胁（图16）[27]。

除上述内容外，其他养护工作主要为道路保洁、设备维护，以及处理台风等自然灾害带来的植物折断、死亡问题，养护成本远低于常规绿地。

5 城市荒野景观的科普功能

由于场地内生境类型多样、乡土生物群落结构较为完整，相比于常规的公园绿地，可开展的科普活动种类更加丰富，效果也更好。自2020年5月对外开放以来，场地中共开设自然教育课程18门，累计4 500人次参加；其中亲子夜间生物观察活动累计已有1 500人次参加，以项目生态修复过程为主题开展的职业体验课程"小小城市生态修复师"获评全国科普日优秀活动。随着场地中生物多样性的不断提升，未来将设计更具有本土特色的课程体系。为了配合课程的开展，项目还设计了一套基于生态学的解说系统。有别于常规的植物解说牌，解说内容并不着重于植物结构和分类的介绍，而是用通俗易懂的语言从生态学的角度阐释物种间的关系，更具有故事性和趣味性，解说牌的所有物种图均为手绘图，以便展示生物最典型的结构和形态（图17，18）。

6 结语

过去，主动型城市再野化的实践中常常存在以下误区：1）忽视群落结构与功能，将"生物多样性"简单地理解为"更多物种"，设计施工中欠缺参照本地生态系统生态演替规律进行设计与调控的思维；2）把重点仅放在"造林"上，将"生物多样性"简单地理解为"植物多样性"，或认为只要提高场地的植物多样性，动物多样性就"自然而然"地恢复，因而忽视动植物之间生态过程的综合影响，无法使城市荒野的植物设计真正满足动物的需求；3）忽视植物的遗传多样性，将"生物多样性"局限于"物种多样性"，施工中并未对选用苗木的产地和繁育方式加以区别（相比扦插和组织培养，实生苗具有更高的遗传多样性），所营造的城市荒野缺乏完善的生物多样性优化功能；4）对于城市荒野的功能界定模糊，将城市再野化项目等同于类荒野景观的营造，在审美、游憩需求与生物多样性保护功能（如栖息地营造、生态廊道/生态网络构建）之间难以平衡，场地设计目的不明。而受限于前述设计施工的误区，后期运营上的更多功能（如相关科学研究监测以及生态科普教育活动等）难以实现。

生物多样性的恢复与维持是城市荒野景观的重要目的与功能之一。为实现其价值，设计施工应遵循生态学规律，充分考虑不同生物类群对栖息地和食物的需求，以乡土物种构建可自然演替的生物群落。本项目探讨和研究了主动型城市再野化过程中应采取的生物多样性恢复技术手段，并围绕这一目标进行了生境类型划分、乡土生物引种、生物群落构建、生态效益评估等一系列工作，取得了较为理想的效果。但作为一个半封闭状态的实验性项目，该项目并未对市民的游憩和景观审美需求做出积极回应。生物多样性恢复与人类活动需求有机结合是城市荒野景观营造期望实现的目标，但二者存在天然的矛盾，工作室仍在探索解决这一问题的适宜技术和设计方法。

目前，中国的城市荒野景观营造还处于探索阶段，其设计理念、技术路径、苗木采购乃至养护管理均缺乏可供借鉴的成熟案例，还需要进行大量的基础研究才能推广应用，因此短期内实现难度较大。但随着生态文明建设的不断推进，城市荒野景观的生态功能将会受到前所未有的重视，在郊野公园、野生动物栖息地、生态廊道、科普教育基地等项目中有着广阔的应用前景。此外，低廉的维护成本也是促进其发展的一大优势。随着人力成本不断上升，养护要求不高的部分城市林地更加适宜采用这一方式进行营造。**LAF**

项目信息

项目地址： 中国上海市浦江郊野公园内
项目面积： 1.7hm^2
景观设计： 城市荒野工作室
首席设计师： 郭陶然
项目团队： 谢惊华、山冰沁、魏羚峰、董佳、蒲川、马泽豪
设计时间： 2019年7月至今

4. 2020年8月的池塘
5. 水生生物保育区种的龙舌草（*Ottelia alismoides*）
6. 场地中的小溪及草地
7. 场地中出现的金线侧褶蛙
8. 林下阴生植物群落
9. 场地中出现的黄脉翅萤

4. Pond in August, 2020
5. *Ottelia alismoide* in the Aquatic Species Conservation Zone
6. The creek and grassland on the site
7. *Pelophylax plancyi* on the site
8. Understory shade-tolerant plant communities
9. The *Curtos costipennis* on the site

© 郭陶然
8

© 郭陶然
9

1 Introduction

According to the United Nations Convention on Biological Diversity, "biological diversity" means the "variability among living organisms from all sources including, *inter alia*, terrestrial, marine, and other aquatic ecosystems and the ecological complexes of which they are part; this includes diversity within species, between species, and of ecosystems"[1]. Currently, most of the measures for biodiversity conservation and restoration are implemented in protected areas, while those outside of protected areas, especially in urban areas, are still insufficient, indicating that studying urban areas as an "ecosystem" needs more theoretical and practical support[2]~[6]. Previous studies show that urban ecosystems are able to harbor relatively high urban biodiversity, including many endangered and threatened species[4][7][8]. More critically, the conservation and restoration of urban biodiversity are urgent at present, since over half of the global human population lives in urban areas[9]. However, urbanization sometimes occurs in biodiversity hotspots[10], causing profound and irreversible negative effects on biodiversity: destruction, degradation, and fragmentation of natural habitats directly led by urban surface change, and indirect exacerbation of climate change, all of which have resulted in urban biodiversity loss[11]~[13].

Previous studies conclude several approaches and strategies for urban biodiversity conservation[6], including the designation of protected areas that are increasingly complemented by integrative approaches arguing for a biodiversity-friendly management of green spaces[14][15], a reconciliation of urban land use and biodiversity conservation[16], the integration of biodiversity in urban design[17], and / or the promotion of urban wilderness[18][19]. Here, urban wilderness refers to remaining natural protected areas, restored natural ecosystems, abandoned wilderness areas, and wilderness landscape designed by humans[19]~[21], with its feature of being intact in ecological succession and free from human interventions though located in human settlements[22]~[24]. Other studies suggest that in the context of "urban areas," the term "urban wilderness" suits better to describe urban wildscapes where succession occurs and ecological processes dominate in cities, such as natural forests, unused land, river corridors, abandoned sites, or brownfields inside or around the city[24]~[26]. In such context, Cao Yue et al. categorized the protection and construction of "urban wilderness" into 4 approaches: protection (of wild nature in urban protected areas), restoration (by rewilding specific urban areas), design (of wildscapes in urban parks), and integration (of wild nature into urban areas systematically)[24]. Besides identifying natural protected areas within cities and suburbs, conservation and restoration of urban biodiversity depend mainly on ecosystem restoration for certain sites through two paths: one is the natural succession from urban wastelands to wildlife habitats, i.e. the passive urban rewilding; and the other is the active urban rewilding guided by human intervention, meaning that humans conduct systematic ecosystem restoration based on the natural laws of ecological succession.

Although with successful cases abroad, passive urban rewilding is difficult to achieve in large Chinese cities as it takes a long time and requires high connectivity to nature around the sites. Due to the large built area and population size, human interference is more frequent in most Chinese cities. In addition, there are insufficient native species used in landscape architecture practices, resulting in obstacles in restoring the ecosystem structures and functions through the natural spread of native species. Thus, it is more practical to take an active urban rewilding approach with proper planning and guidance. Currently, with rare successful cases, active urban rewilding in China still needs more research and practices. This paper, taking Shanghai Urban Biodiversity Education Base project started in 2019 by Forest City Studio as an example, introduces the field practices and technical methodologies in active urban rewilding to enrich the technical and theoretical research on urban wilderness construction and Nature-based Solutions in urban environments.

2 Site Background and Design

2.1 Site Conditions

The project site is located in Shanghai Pujiang Country Park, occupying a state-owned forest of 1.7 hm^2, where there was a flat terrain without obvious topographical shifts. The site was surrounded by water on three sides, with no internal water system. Before the restoration by the project in July 2019, the project team conducted soil analyses and vegetation surveys. The results show that soils on the site were sticky and alkaline ($pH \geq 7.8$) with low organic content, and plant species were limited, including merely *Cinnamomum camphora*, *Ligustrum lucidum*, *Populus × canadensis* 'I-214', and *Firmiana simplex* trees, and some horticultural ground covers. Trees such as *Ligustrum lucidum* and *Firmiana simplex* suffered mortality due to the poor drainage under certain soil texture and terrain conditions, while native herbaceous plant species were suppressed by invasive species—in humid and hot June, 60% of the site surface was covered by *Alternanthera philoxeroides* and *Trifolium repens*, and 5% by Asteraceae species such as *Erigeron philadelphicus*, *Symphyotrichum subulatum*, and *Solidago canadensis* (Fig. 1).

2.2 Principles of Design

Aiming to explore the technical methodologies of urban biodiversity restoration and conserve native species losing habitats due to urban development, the project team established following 5 principles:

1) Use native nursery stocks of the Yangtze River Delta. In case that site conditions are

limited or stocks are insufficient that cannot satisfy the ecological functions, no more than 5% of the total plant species could be replaced with non-native species that have similar ecological functions;

2) Design quasi-natural plant communities to foster ecological succession;

3) Based on site conditions, create a variety of habitats where they transit naturally to others via the change of plant species composition, and eliminate any artificial structures or hedges to guarantee wildlife activities;

4) Identify significant species for research and conservation, and select plant species and / or create habitats based on the foraging and / or perching features of certain wild animals;

5) Set facilities of roads, guardrails, commentary signs, and warning signs mainly in gray, brown, or green tones, and eliminate the use of particularly bright colors that may frighten wild animals.

Based on the design principles above, the team made a preliminary design plan for the site, and further optimized the terrain, water system, and plant design considering the actual site conditions.

2.3 Technical Roadmap

In accordance with the site conditions and project goals, the team formulated the technical roadmap, shown in Figure 2, based on the law of community succession.

2.4 Function Zoning

As to providing a base for biodiversity restoration technology research and exhibition, it is necessary to create habitats as diverse as possible within the limited space, harboring maximal species to facilitate future research and public education. According to existing conditions, the site was divided into 7 ecological function zones, including Native Butterfly Attracting Zone, Native Shrub Zone, Native Aquatic Species Conservation Zone, Native Evergreen Tree Zone, Environmental Education Activity Zone, Mixed Native Evergreen / Deciduous Tree Zone, as well as Native Deciduous Tree Zone (Fig. 3-1).

3 Project Implementation

3.1 Basic Environmental Optimization

During the construction process, the project team confronted the following difficulties: 1) The site lacked an internal water system, failing to provide habitats for aquatic and amphibian species; 2) Increasing number of trees died due to the poor soil quality and drainage; 3) Too many invasive species to effectively control by manual pulling; 4) The state-owned forests were not allowed to move or cut, which restricted the terrain modification.

To address the above issues, the project team first carried out topographic modification and water system construction. Small ponds were dug in open space in the center of the site, filled with water pumped from the outside river on the north side of the site, forming an internal water system that flows along the constructed creek into the outside river on the south. In addition, ditches were connected with the outside rivers to enhance drainage during the rainy season. All excavated soils formed a pile with gentle slopes in the eastern forests, where wet-intolerant native trees were planted (Fig. 3-2).

After modifying the terrain, the project team adopted a combination of manual and mechanical methods to conduct an overall plowing for the site and fertilized it with decomposed garden wastes to increase soil organic matter. The team's previous experiences have proved that plowing helps break the dominance of invasive species so that the native plants in the soil seed bank can germinate. In this manner, the pioneer species of Poaceae could gradually outcompete invasive species with proper human intervention and then dominate. This approach will significantly reduce the coverage and germination rates of invasive species, providing vantage for native plant community construction. Additionally, electric circuits, Wi-Fi, irrigation systems, and monitoring systems were set to support future research.

3.2 Native Community Construction

Different from intensively managed

© 郭陶然
10-1

© 郭陶然
10-2

© 马涞豪
10-3

© 马涞豪
10-4

10. 独居蜂大多属于传粉昆虫，对植物多样性的维持具有重要意义。而和营社会性生活的蜜蜂（*Apis* spp.）不同，独居蜂营独居生活，偏好在植物空茎、树洞、石缝内营巢。本项目为研究独居蜂对筑巢生境和传粉植物的偏好，在7种生境类型中各搭设一组人工蜂巢（图10-1，内部为供独居蜂筑巢用的芦苇秆），成功吸引到切叶蜂（Megachilidae spp.，图10-2为切割过的叶片）在此筑巢（图10-3，10-4）。

10. Most solitary bees, vital pollinators to maintain plant diversity, prefer nesting in hollow stems, tree holes, or gaps between rocks, rather than living socially in colonies as honeybees (*Apis* spp.) do. To investigate the preference of solitary bees regarding nesting habitat and plants, 7 bee hotels are set one per habitat (Fig. 10-1, the reed stalks for solitary bees to nest), successfully attracting Megachilidae spp. (Fig. 10-2 showing leaves that are cut) to nest (Fig. 10-3, 10-4).

11. 小太平鸟（摄于2019年12月）
12. 红外相机拍摄到的黄鼬
13. 红外相机拍到的华南兔

11. *Bombycilla japonica* (December, 2019)
12. *Mustela sibirica* recorded by camera trap
13. *Lepus sinensis* recorded by camera trap

landscapes, urban wilderness is constructed with reasonable community structures by utilizing native species to guarantee spontaneous succession. After plowing, all plants except trees are cleared manually, creating a "secondary bare area" in an ecological context, and an endless secondary succession takes place when new plants grow. At the beginning stage, most areas of the site will be covered by sun-loving, robust, highly-germinated, and fast-growing pioneer plant species such as some Poaceae plants and woody plants spread by birds, who will bring expanding shade and increasing humidity under the canopy. Then the sun-loving grasses will be replaced by shade-tolerant plants while the climax species are germinating, gradually replacing the pioneer species and dominating the forests. If the soil seed bank is sufficiently abundant, a large number of mid-successional plants will appear in this process, but finally, they will reach similar climax communities.

Each function zone in this project is essentially a native community, following the above succession processes. Species will be introduced constantly during 3 to 5 years according to the changes in the environment and natural laws of succession to increase biodiversity. Animals with important ecological functions who cannot migrate to the site (e.g. fish, amphibians, and insects with poor dispersal ability) will also be introduced to the site after creating habitats that meet their survival needs. The following examples of the Native Aquatic Species Conservation Zone, Environmental Education Activity Zone, Native Evergreen Tree Zone, and Native Deciduous Tree Zone demonstrate the processes of community construction.

The Native Aquatic Species Conservation Zone is located at the central axis of the site with a 100-square-meter man-made pond in the middle (Fig. 4), whose deepest depth is about 1.5 meters without anti-seepage treatment. Submerged plants such as *Vallisneria spinulosa* and *Potamogeton distinctus* (Fig. 5), and benthos such as *Bellamya quadrata* and *Unio douglasiae* were introduced into the pond. A month after introduction when they began to help purify the water, a dozen of fish species such as *Rhodeus ocellatus* and *Oryzias latipes* were introduced gradually. Considering the limited pond size, the introduction of predators such as *Channa argus* will be restricted to maintain ecological equilibrium and ecosystem stability. From September 2019 to August 2020, 30 native aquatic plant species were introduced to the site and further increased the biodiversity there: *Ceratopteris pteridoides*, a second-class protected plant species in China, has established a stable population on the northwest shoal of the pond.

The grassland west to the pond, i.e. the Environmental Education Activity Zone, is the place for native herbs such as *Panicum bisulcatum*, *Arthraxon hispidus*, *Cynodon dactylon*, and *Microstegium nudum* to grow (Fig. 6). Feeding on plentiful Poaceae plants, Orthoptera insect species , e.g. *Atractomorpha sinensis*, *Oxya chinensis*, and *Velarifictorus micado*, became abundant, thus attracting frogs including *Pelophylax plancyi*, *Fejervarya multistriata*, *Pelophylax nigromaculatus*, *Microhyla ornata*, and *Bufo gargarizans* to the grassland (Fig. 7).

The *Cinnamomum camphora* forest was restored as the Native Evergreen Tree Zone by planting native shade-tolerant plants, such as *Diplazium esculentum*, *Oplismenus undulatifolius* var. *binatus*, *Ardisia japonica*, and *Ardisia crenata*, under the forest due to high canopy density. In spring and summer, sunlight passes through the tree foliage, sparkling on the underbrush, which produces excellent landscape effects (Fig. 8). This weak light condition in the understory is also suitable for the terrestrial firefly *Curtos costipennis*. After one year of introduction and breeding, a small number of fireflies have appeared in this zone (Fig. 9).

The forest of *Populus × canadensis* 'I-214' in the Native Deciduous Tree Zone on the east side of the site was planned to be replaced by native deciduous trees due to their non-native origin, fast-growing, pests and diseases, and poor quality. Before restoration, pioneer trees spread by birds such as *Broussonetia papyrifera* and *Morus alba* have been growing spontaneously in the zone. A dozen of native deciduous trees including *Ulmus parvifolia*, *Celtis sinensis*, *Melia azedarach*, *Zanthoxylum ailanthoides*, and *Hovenia acerba* were planted without thinning

Populus × *canadensis* 'I-214' who will die out due to (a)biotic factors e.g. pests or typhoons. The zone then will gradually get restored with native deciduous tree domination.

4 Ecological Benefit Assessment

4.1 Monitoring of Ecosystem Restoration Process

The ecosystem services and their value provided by urban wilderness are irreplaceable by artificial gardens. However, effective or reasonable assessment criteria have not been developed yet. During the restoration of the site, the project team and the School of Ecological and Environmental Sciences at East China Normal University have cooperated to conduct continuous monitoring of plants, insects, amphibians, birds, and mammals to assess the ecosystem services of the project.

Plant surveys including general investigation and relevés were adopted to inventory the flora and (a)biotic data in various habitats. Insect surveys utilized aerial nets, Barber pitfall traps, light traps, sweep nets, beating sheets, and / or observation worksheets to collect insects and record their species and individual numbers on the site. Both richness and abundance of amphibians were observed and recorded via the line-transect method, i.e. walking along the designed routes surrounding the water and tussocks. Birds were surveyed by the same method but along different routes.. Mammals are monitored by camera traps to record data, e.g., the time and frequency of animal activities.

Till November 2020, the project team has recorded 260 native plant species, 255 insect species, 7 amphibian and reptile species, 71 bird species, and 6 mammal species within the project site since restoration, showing higher biodiversity and animal population density than unrestored artificial forests surrounding. As insect diversity plays an important role in pest and disease control, monitoring and researching the particular linkage between urban pollinator insects and plant species were conducted (Fig. 10).

When plants and insects diversity are high enough, birds will be attracted by food. A high frequency of birds was found nesting on the site. In the winter of 2019, some rare bird species, e.g. *Bombycilla japonica*, migrated to the site for the winter (Fig. 11). Stable populations of mammals, such as *Erinaceus amurensis*, *Mustela sibirica*, and *Apodemus agrarius*, are found on the site after over-one-year monitoring. Meanwhile, the team also recorded *Lepus sinensis* staying on the site since September 2020 (Fig. 12, 13). However, the threat to *Apodemus agrarius* and birds from stray cats is severe, which needs further monitoring and management in the future.

Theoretically, biodiversity surveys should be conducted within one year before the restoration to better compare and evaluate the changes of biodiversity before and after restoration. However, limited by the short preparation period of the project, biodiversity data before restoration are insufficient. In the future, a comparison between the project site and unrestored forests surrounding may be doable to reflect the trend of biodiversity changes on the project site.

4.2 Ecosystem Control

Generally, urban wilderness with high biodiversity is mainly under natural succession and supplemented by human intervention, thus requiring relatively lower but more technical maintenance. No chemical pesticides on the site are allowed so as to minimize negative impacts on biodiversity. In fact, the abundance of carnivorous arthropods such as mantises, ladybugs, parasitoid wasps, and spiders can help maintain the equilibrium of insect populations. Therefore, the project enabled the healthy growth of plants without any pesticide (Fig. 14).

Additionally, all green wastes, including leaf

14. 场地中出现的一种寄生性青蜂（Chrysididae sp.）
15. 场地中被真菌分解的朽木
16. 建成于2016年的上海宜嘉苑生态保育区，这里生长有乡土植物260种，已形成稳定的群落结构。

14. A Chrysididae sp. on the site
15. Wood decayed by fungi on the site
16. Shanghai Yijiayuan Protected Area built in 2016, where 260 native plant species are recorded and stable communities have been formed.

© 马泽豪
14

© 郭陶然
15

© 郭陶然
16

17. 隐藏在朽木中的解说牌，介绍了天牛蛀食导致树木死亡的过程。
18. 乡土蝶类招引区长廊中的蝴蝶解说牌，便于儿童在活动过程中识别蝴蝶。

17. Information board hidden in decayed wood, introducing the process of longhorn beetles feeding on tree tissue and causing the death of a tree.
18. Tour guide signs in the gallery of the Native Butterfly Attracting Zone help children identify butterflies during educational activities.

litter or naturally dead trees sawn and piled in the understory for natural decay, remain on the site (Fig. 15). As fungi decompose the wood, darkling beetles and stag beetles will lay eggs where decayed and their larvae feeding on the rotten part will accelerate the decomposition. Within 3 to 5 years, most wood will decompose into organic matter, which can be used to improve soil quality. Without human intervention, herbs and leaves wither naturally, creating a layer of litter in winter, which provides suitable habitats for soil animals.

The heaviest maintenance workload is invasive plant control as a large number of invasive plants such as *Alternanthera philoxeroides*, *Erigeron philadelphicus*, and *Solidago canadensis* existed on the site before restoration. Manual clearance is too heavy to be feasible or efficient. Therefore, a large number of pioneer plant species, such as *Panicum bisulcatum*, *Arthraxon hispidus*, *Cynodon dactylon*, are grown, which quickly occupied the space, and as a result, the coverage of invasive plants was reduced from 65% to 5% within one year. The remaining needs to be manually removed before they flower to prevent further expansion. The workload at this step mainly depends on the abundance of invasive species that gradually decrease as the native plant community becomes stable. Another similar project completed by the project team started in 2016, where invasive species were no longer a threat after 4 years of ecological succession and manual control by 2020 (Fig. 16)[27].

In addition to the above, other maintenance work mainly includes road cleaning, equipment maintenance, and management of plant breaking or death caused by natural disasters such as typhoons. The cost of maintenance is much lower than that of traditional green spaces.

5 Environmental Education Function of Urban Wilderness

Compared to traditional green spaces, the site has more diverse habitats and a relatively complete community structure, for which a larger variety of environmental education activities with better feedback can be organized. Since the open of the site in May 2020, 18 environmental education courses have been offered, with 4,500 participants attending, among which a parent-child activity about nocturnal species observation has attracted 1,500 person-times; a course about experiencing professional ecosystem restoration, called "Little Restoration Specialist," was awarded the "Outstanding Activity on National Science Popularization Day." The team plans to develop a curriculum system with more local characteristics in the future as the biodiversity of the site is being optimized. In addition, a set of explanatory signs based on ecological knowledge was designed to cooperate with the courses, which explain the relationships between species with easy-to-understand and interesting words, instead of introducing plant structure or taxonomy. All species pictures are hand-drawn to better illustrate the most typical morphology of a creature (Fig. 17, 18).

6 Conclusion

Previous practices of active urban rewilding often have the following issues. First, they simply understood "biodiversity" as "more species," resulting in ignorance of the community structures and functions, and fewer concerns on the law of ecological succession learning from the native ecosystems in designing and managing practices. Second, they often focused only on "tree planting," understanding "biodiversity" as "plant diversity," or deemed that animal diversity would be optimized "naturally" as long as plant diversity was increased, and therefore ignored the comprehensive interaction of ecological processes between animals and plants. As a result, those urban wilderness practices could not truly meet the needs of native animals. Third, they limited "biodiversity" to "species diversity," ignoring genetic diversity, for which they did not distinguish the origins and breeding methods of the nursery stocks (plants growing from seed usually have higher genetic diversity than those by cuttings or tissue culture), resulting in urban wilderness without the capacity for biodiversity improvement. Fourth, they ambiguously defined the urban wilderness construction as equivalent to wildscape design, without the clarification of urban wilderness functions, thus hardly balancing the aesthetic and recreational functions against biodiversity conservation (e.g., habitat creation and ecological corridor / network construction). Moreover, these issues further limited the future site management and operation (e.g., related scientific research, monitoring, and environmental education activities).

The restoration and maintenance of biodiversity are some of the important objectives and functions of urban wilderness. Thus, in both design and construction processes, the needs of different biological groups should be the main focus so as to create native communities with natural succession following ecological laws. The project explored the technical methodologies of biodiversity restoration in active urban rewilding by conducting habitat division, native species introduction, natural community construction, ecological benefit assessment, etc., and has achieved positive results. However, citizens' recreational and aesthetic needs were to some extent ignored in this semi-enclosed experimental project. For future urban wilderness construction, integrating the seemingly contradictory biodiversity restoration and human activity needs should be an emphasis. Thus, the project team will continue exploring appropriate technology and design solutions to the problem.

Currently, urban wilderness construction in China still needs further research. Although mature design concepts, technical methodologies, seedling procurement, and even maintenance and management cannot be achieved overnight, the ecological functions of urban wilderness are promising along with continuous and extensive basic research and advance of Ecological Civilization Construction in China. There are many application possibilities in country parks, wildlife habitats, ecological corridors, and environmental education bases. In addition, the low maintenance cost is a major advantage of urban wilderness which will be appreciated by urban forests requiring low maintenance, as labor costs continue to increase. **LAF**

PROJECT INFORMATION

LOCATION: Pujiang Country Park, Shanghai, China
AREA (SIZE): 1.7 hm^2
LANDSCAPE DESIGN: Forest City Studio
CHIEF DESIGNER: Guo Taoran
PROJECT TEAM: Xie Jinghua, Shan Bingqin, Wei Lingfeng, Dong Jia, Pu Chuan, Ma Zehao
DESIGN PERIOD: July, 2019, on going

REFERENCES

[1] Secretariat of the convention on biological diversity. (2005). Handbook of the Convention on Biological Diversity. Retrieved from https://www.cbd.int/handbook

[2] Ricketts, T., & Imhoff, M. (2003). Biodiversity, urban areas, and agriculture: Locating priority ecoregions for conservation. *Conservation Ecology*. Advance online publication. https://doi.org/10.5751/ES-00593-080201

[3] McKinney, M, L. (2002). Urbanization, biodiversity, and conservation. *BioScience*, 52(10), 883-890. https://doi.org/10.1641/0006-3568(2002)052[0883:UBAC]2.0.CO;2

[4] Nilon, C. H., Aronson, M. F. J., Cilliers, S. S., Dobbs, C., Frazee, L. J., Goddard, M. A., ... Yocom, K. P. (2017). Planning for the future of urban biodiversity: A global review of city-scale initiatives. *BioScience*, 67(4), 331-341. https://doi.org/10.1093/biosci/bix012

[5] Parris, K. M., Amati, M., Bekessy, S. A., Dagenais, D., Fryd, O., Hahs, A. K., ... Williams, N. S. G. (2018). The seven lamps of planning for biodiversity in the city. *Cities*, (83), 44-53. https://doi.org/10.1016/j.cities.2018.06.007

[6] Planchuelo, G., Kowarik, I., & von der Lippe, M. (2020). Plant traits, biotopes and urbanization dynamics explain the survival of endangered urban plant populations. *Journal of Applied Ecology*, 57(8), 1581-1592. https://doi.org/10.1111/1365-2664.13661

[7] Aronson, M. F. J., Sorte, F. L. A., Nilson, C. H., Katti, M., Goddard, M. A., Lepczyk, C. A. ... Winter, M. (2014). A global analysis of the impacts of urbanization on bird and plant diversity reveals key anthropogenic drivers. *Proceedings of the Royal Society B*, 281(1780), 20133330. https://doi.org/10.1098/rspb.2013.3330

[8] Shwartz, A., Turbé, A., Julliard, A., Simon, L., & Prévot, A. (2014). Outstanding challenges for urban conservation research and action. *Global Environmental Change*, (28), 39-49. https://doi.org/10.1016/j.gloenvcha.2014.06.002

[9] Urban areas. (n.d.). UN Decade on Ecosystem Restoration. Retrieved from https://www.decadeonrestoration.org/types-ecosystem-restoration/urban-areas.

[10] Seto, K. C., Güneralp, B., & Hutyra, L. R. (2012). Global forecasts of urban expansion to 2030 and direct impacts on biodiversity and carbon pools. *Proceedings of the National Academy of Sciences*, 109(40), 16083-16088. https://doi.org/10.1073/pnas.1211658109

[11] Forman, R. T. T. (1990). Ecologically sustainable landscapes: The role of spatial configuration. In I. S. Zonneveld, & R. T. T. Forman (Eds.), *Changing landscapes: An ecological perspective* (pp. 299-309). New York, NY: Springer Verlag.

[12] Luck. G. W. (2007). A review of the relationships between human population density and biodiversity. *Biological Reviews*, 82(4), 607-645. https://doi.org/10.1111/j.1469-185X.2007.00028.x

[13] Grimm, N. B., Faeth. S. H., Golubiewski, N. E., Redman, C. L., Wu, J., Bai, X., & Briggs, J. M. (2008). Global change and the ecology of cities. *Science*, 319(5864), 756-760. https://doi.org/10.1126/science.1150195

[14] Aronson, M. F. J., Lepczyk, A. L., Evans, K. L., Goddard, M. A., Lerman, S. B., MacIvor, J. S., ... Vargo, T. (2017). Biodiversity in the city: Key challenges for urban green space management. *Frontiers in Ecology and the Environment*, 15(4), 189-196. https://doi.org/10.1002/fee.1480

[15] Chollet, S., Bradant, C., Tessier, S., & Jung, V. (2018). From urban lawns to urban meadows: Reduction of mowing frequency increases plant taxonomic, functional and phylogenetic diversity. *Landscape and Urban Planning*, (180), 121-124. https://doi.org/10.1016/j.landurbplan.2018.08.009

[16] Elmqvist, T., Fragkias, M., Goodness, J., Güneralp, B., Marcotullio, P. J., McDonald, R. I., ... Wilkinson, C. (2013). *Urbanization, biodiversity and ecosystem services: Challenges and opportunities—A global assessment*. Dordrecht, the Netherlands: Springer.

[17] Garrard, G. E., Williams, N. S. G., Mata, L., Thomas, J., & Bekessy, S. A. (2018). Biodiversity sensitive urban design. *Conservation Letters*, 11(2), 12411. https://doi.org/10.1111/conl.12411

[18] Hwang, Y. H., Yue, Z. E. J., Ling, S. K., & Tan, H. H. V. (2019). It's ok to be wilder: Preference for natural growth in urban green spaces in a tropical city. *Urban Forestry & Urban Greening*, (38), 165-176. https://doi.org/10.1016/j.ufug.2018.12.005

[19] McKinney, M. L., Kowarik, I., & Kendal, D. (2018). The contribution of wild urban ecosystems to liveable cities. *Urban Forestry & Urban Greening*, (29), 334-335. https://doi.org/10.1016/j.ufug.2017.09.004

[20] Kowarik, I. (2018). Urban wilderness: supply, demand, and access. *Urban Forestry & Urban Greening*, (29), 336-347. https://doi.org/10.1016/j.ufug.2017.05.017

[21] Threlfall, C. G., & Kendal, D. (2018). The distinct ecological and social roles that wild spaces play in urban ecosystems. *Urban Forestry & Urban Greening*, (29), 348-356. https://doi.org/10.1016/j.ufug.2017.05.012

[22] Diemer, M., Held, M. & Hofmeister, S. (2003). Urban wilderness in central Europe—Rewilding at the urban fringe. *International Journal of Wilderness*, 9(3), 7-11.

[23] Wang, X., & Wang, X. (2017). Urban wildness based on the view of landscape architecture. *Chinese Landscape Architecture*, 33(8), 40-47.

[24] Cao, Y., Martin, G. V., & Yang, R. (2019). Urban wildness: Protection and creation of wild nature in urban areas. *Landscape Architecture*, 26(8), 41-45.

[25] Wang, X. (2019). Urban wildness and urban habitat. *Landscape Architecture*, 26(1), 4-5.

[26] Auyeung, D. S. N., Campbell, L. K., Johnson, M., Sonti, N. F., & Svendsen, E. (2016). Reading the landscape: Citywide social assessment of New York City parks and natural Areas in 2013-2014. *Social assessment white paper No. 2. New York, NY: New York Department of Parks and Recreation* (p.69). Retrieved from https://www.nrs.fs.fed.us/pubs/50617

[27] Qdaily. (2018, March 9). Restoring the ecosystem within the concrete jungle: What did Urban Wilderness Studio do in Shanghai? Retrieved from https://baijiahao.baidu.com/s?id=1594444675416019849 &wfr=spider &for=pc

培育城市荒野

专栏编辑
蔡哲铭
加拿大多伦多大学约翰·H·丹尼尔斯建筑、景观与设计学院博士研究生

荒野唤起了人们对城市化影响之外原始自然的集体想象。尽管在北美地区，“荒野”（wilderness）概念的出现被视作殖民主义的产物①[1]，但这并不影响“荒野”一词的流行——作为一种语义工具，它已然具备了某种象征意义。同样地，“城市荒野”（urban wilderness）一词将矛盾的“城市”与“荒野”并置组合，对景观设计师而言既是机遇也是挑战。一方面，城市荒野表达了公众对城市中非人工景观的惊叹——常被忽视的乡土物种及其生态绩效为人们所见，促使公众认知和欣赏丰富而富有韧性的城市生态环境形象。另一方面，唯有重整人们对城市景观的认知论，才能更加深入地理解城市荒野这个颇具挑战性的自然概念——如果我们仅仅将城市景观看作单纯的绿色背景或人类对自然的掌控，那么就很难真正成为城市生态系统的一份子。

城市荒野既存在于人们的想象之中，也兼具现实成效。身处气候变化和环境危机的背景下，我们需要通过“野性”来明确城市的生态绩效。在生态修复领域，野性可以理解为非人类生命的自主性[2]。这种自主性意味着生态过程是自然发生的，而不以人的意志为转移。吉尔·克莱芒曾提出“第三类景观”（le tiers paysage）概念，认为这种自主性体现了一种“生物智能”，即“不断重塑的能力”[3]。然而，这种自主性的内涵却很难在城市中实现：人造景观加剧了人类与自然的二元对立。如何才能通过景观设计体现并演绎城市生态系统的社会性价值？本期的两篇文章基于各自的实践提供了另一种思路：通过公众参与和切身体验来展示（城市荒野的）社会和生态价值。

在《日本大阪城市边缘的艺术与生态》一文中，帕特里克·M·莱登和姜受希分享了城市自然工作室的两个将自然与社区相融合的艺术项目。城市自然工作室致力于探索生态艺术与传播，同时促进人们对自然的认识与尊重。工作室开展了一系列工作坊和艺术节活动，专注于推动建立人与生态系统的密切关系。相关活动包括土壤工作坊、寻觅野生草本植物、以“水”为主题的跨学科艺术节等。这些活动不仅将社区居民凝聚在一起，也让人们有机会观察自然现象和过程并与之互动。参与活动的过程让更多人意识到，人类是自然的产物，是生态系统的一部分。莱登和姜受希的实践准确传达了一种具身性体验；这种具身性极大推动了“心灵的再野化”和人与自然关系的建立。

在《呼唤野性》一文中，南希·西顿分享了位于纽约市布鲁克林区的景观设计公司未来绿色工作室的作品，展示了他们对城市自生植物的研究成果，以及该研究在设计实践中的关键作用。这些项目立足于城市生态学研究，提供了全新的研究模式。相关的调查方法包括街头漫走观察、物种识别、物种记录和表现传达（如人行道上的喷绘标识和社交媒体应用程序的使用）；更具交互性的研究模式可以让非专业人士也参与其中。工作室的研究促进了参与者了解植物生境及其在极端城市条件下的生态绩效；而这些极端条件普遍作为场地限制存在于城市景观设计项目中，由此看来，研究也间接提高了景观设计的绩效表现。此外，工作室研究与设计相结合的实践模式也将体验并理解城市生态的过程渗透学科内外。

上述两个各具特色的实践为人们从社会层面理解城市生态和生态绩效提供了新的思路：不依赖于单纯的文本和图像学习，而是积极参与到互动式学习和实践中。同时，这两个实践也强调了在培育未来韧性城市过程中专注力与具身性的重要价值——培育城市景观的过程亦是人类向景观寻求滋养的过程。**LAF**

① 很多文化都对“荒野”内涵有所探讨。本文中特指美洲语境下的“荒野”，它对日后的环境保育政策产生了重要影响。移民美洲的欧洲人提出“荒野”概念，将荒野理解为可以驯化开发的处女地（即北美大陆），他们将土地所有权合法化，却无视原住民的利益（来源：参考文献[1]）。

① The notion of wilderness can be found in multiple cultures, however, it is referring to the American concept here as it became instrumental for environmental and conservation policies. The American wilderness, led by Euro-Americans, understood as virginal land to be domesticated, legitimizing the land ownership while neglecting the indigenous people (Source: Ref. [1]).

https://doi.org/10.15302/J-LAF-1-050030
收稿时间 RECEIVED DATE | 2021-02-22
中图分类号 | TU984
文献标识码 | C

Cultivating the Urban Wilderness

COLUMN HOST
Taro Zheming CAI
PhD Student, John H. Daniels Faculty of Architecture, Landscape, and Design at University of Toronto

Wilderness evokes a collective imagination of the pristine nature independently of urbanization activities. The emergence of the idea in North America is considered an artifact of colonialism①[1]. Nonetheless, the term "wilderness" has become a useful and popular semantic tool evoking symbolic meanings. As such, "urban wilderness," a term of paradoxical juxtaposition, demonstrates both opportunities and challenges for landscape architects. On the one hand, urban wilderness illustrates the public awe of the uncultivated landscape in the city—promoting a particular image and appreciation of the rich and resilient urban ecology—shedding light on often overlooked native species and their ecological performance. On the other hand, the urban wilderness is a challenging conception of nature and requires an epistemological reorientation toward urban landscape—it is hard to be part of the urban ecosystem when considering urban landscape a mere green backdrop or mastery of nature.

Urban wilderness is both imaginary and performative. In the context of climate change and environmental crisis, we need to articulate the performative aspect of urban ecology by acknowledging wildness. In the realm of ecological restoration, wildness can be defined through nonhuman autonomy[2]. Such autonomy implies ecological processes that are not willed in an anthropocentric sense but occur spontaneously. Similarly, in his concept of the "third landscape" (le tiers paysage), Gilles Clément articulates this autonomy as a "biological intelligence," which has an "aptitude for constant reinvention"[3]. However, this notion of autonomy is conceptually tricky in the urban realm: the binary of human and nature seems even more distinguished in the designed urban landscape. How can landscape design visualize and represent urban ecology on a social level? The following two articles provide alternative approaches through the practice that embraces public participation and embodied experiences, demonstrating social and ecological values.

In Art and Ecology at the Edge of Osaka, Japan, Patrick M. Lydon and Suhee Kang share two projects from their ecological art and media studio, City as Nature, exhibiting art projects that bring together nature and the community. City as Nature promotes the public's awareness and respect of nature. Through a series of workshops and festivals, it focuses on cultivating positive human relationships with the ecosystem. Programs from City as Nature, including the soil workshop, weed foraging, and an interdisciplinary festival on water, not only bring the community together but also make the natural phenomena and processes legible and interactive. These programs help participants recognize humans as ecological beings and part of the ecosystem. There is an excellent sense of embodiment in Lydon and Kang's practice, and the embodiment is essential in the process of "rewilding minds" and building relationships with nature.

In Invoking the Wild, Nancy Seaton shares work from Future Green Studio, a landscape firm based in Brooklyn, New York, revealing their studies on spontaneous urban plants (SUP) and the critical role of research in their design practice. Situated in urban ecology studies, these SUP projects offer a different mode of research. The research investigation, including walks of observation, identification, species documentation, and representation (such as the spray-paint frames on the sidewalk and the use of social media applications), is an interactive process that engages participants beyond the office. The research facilitates knowledge of plants' habitats and their ecological performative benefits in extreme urban conditions which often are common site constraints for urban landscape projects, advancing the performance of designed landscape. Additionally, Future Green Studio's research–design practice suggests an active process of experiencing and understanding urban ecology in the discipline and beyond.

Two distinct practices demonstrate alternative approaches in cultivating a social understanding of urban ecology and ecological performance through an interactive act of learning and doing, instead of mere texts and images. Both practices propose attentiveness and embodiment in cultivating a resilient urban future—cultivating the urban landscape is to ask the landscape to cultivate us. **LAF**

REFERENCES

[1] Callicott, J., & Nelson, M. (1998). *The Great New Wilderness Debate* (pp. 97-102, 652-690). Athens, GA: University of Georgia Press.

[2] Woods, M. (2005). Ecological Restoration and the Renewal of Wildness and Freedom. In T. Heyd (Ed.), *Recognizing the Autonomy of Nature: Theory and Practice* (pp. 170-188). New York, NY: Columbia University Press.

[3] Clément, G. (2015). *The Planetary Garden and Other Writings* (p. x). Philadelphia, PA: University of Pennsylvania Press.

日本大阪城市边缘处的艺术与生态
Art and Ecology at the Edge of Osaka, Japan

帕特里克·M·莱登
城市自然工作室生态艺术家、负责人

姜受希
城市自然工作室草药师、社区协调人

Patrick M. LYDON*
Ecological Artist and Director, City as Nature

Suhee KANG
Herbalist and Community Coordinator, City as Nature

*Corresponding Author
Address: 2-8-20 Kitakagaya, Osaka, 559-0011, Japan
Email: patrick@cityasnature.org

摘要

城市自然工作室坐落于日本大阪市郊区的北加贺屋街区（原造船厂所在地），致力于探索生态艺术与传播。工作室与来自不同学科、领域、国家和地区的从业人员及公私营组织合作，开展了多项生态艺术项目，借此重建人、过程、场所与人类赖以生存的生态系统之间的联系。本文呈现了在北加贺屋开展的两个项目研究。在大阪分部项目中，工作室利用从当地回收的物料，对一处拥有80年历史的老旧市场中的典型土木结构排屋进行了改造，改造后的实体生态空间包括一处自然花园和一系列众筹项目，兼具居住和生态艺术功能。另一个项目城市自然节是在当地多个公共或私有空间中举行的一项生态艺术表演活动，旨在通过不同从业人员、公众及城市空间本身之间的艺术对话，探索城市与自然的关系。借由上述项目，工作室期望进一步探寻能够培养设计师、管理者、市政领导、市民，以及城市内外生态系统各群体之间独特而意义非凡关系的方法。通过持续、真诚地与环境对话，人们或许能够发现一种众生平等下的新城市形态。

关键词

生态艺术；跨学科合作；人类再野化；社区参与；日本

ABSTRACT

City as Nature is an ecological art and media studio based primarily in Kitakagaya, a former shipbuilding district on the outskirts of Osaka, Japan. Working with local and international practitioners, and public and private organizations across multiple disciplines and sectors, they produce ecological art projects that re-connect people, process, and place with the ecosystems in which we dwell. Two narrative project studies in Kitakagaya are presented here: 1) The Branch Osaka, a physical ecological space built inside a typical wood-and-earth row house in an 80-year-old marketplace—rebuilt by City as Nature, using locally recycled materials, it now serves as a residence and ecological art space, with a natural garden and donation-based programming; 2) City as Nature Festival, an ecological neighborhood "happening," taking place in multiple local public and privately-owned spaces. The festival explores urban relationships with the nature through art-driven dialogs between practitioners, the general public, and the urban space itself. From these projects, City as Nature hopes to explore approaches to cultivating relationships—individual, meaningful relationships between designers, executives, civic leaders, citizens, and the communities of ecosystems in and around our cities. Through an ongoing, truthful dialog with the environment, people might just discover the possible city, an equitable place for all beings.

KEYWORDS

Ecological Art; Interdisciplinary Collaboration; Human Rewilding; Community Engagement; Japan

翻译 | 王颖、崔婧沄、蔡哲铭
TRANSLATED BY | WANG Ying, CUI Jingyun, Taro Zheming CAI

https://doi.org/10.15302/J-LAF-1-050029
收稿时间 RECEIVED DATE | 2021-02-05

中图分类号 | TU984, B845.65
文献标识码 | B

1. 绘有住吉高灯笼的精美木版画，由长谷川贞信（初代）作于1860年左右。
2. 如今位于大阪市住之江区的住吉高灯笼

1. A beautiful block print of the Sumiyoshi Tall Lantern by Hasegawa Sadanobu I (c. 1860)
2. Present day Sumiyoshi Tall Lantern in Suminoe-Ku, Osaka.

1

1 引言

在一幅表现12世纪难波（大阪的旧称）住吉高灯笼美丽图景的木版画中，挺拔秀美的日本黑松林旁耸立着一座灯塔，远处海上风光一览无余（图1）。这座灯塔奇迹般地保留至今（图2），但历经9个世纪的沧桑后，海岸线早已远退，须穿过公寓楼、地铁站、购物街、高速公路和赛艇体育场馆才能抵达5km开外的渡轮码头和大阪湾水域。

分隔海岸与灯塔的是一项历时400余年的填海项目，位于大阪市郊区的北加贺屋街区（原造船厂所在地）即为这一项目首批改造的场地。北加贺屋见证了人类的壮举与工程奇迹，但如今的景观却平平无奇，了无与水相关的历史痕迹，人们也日渐发觉与环境脱节。鉴于此，致力于探索生态艺术与传播的城市自然工作室期望通过行动重建人与水及自然的联系。

2 重建联系的点滴行动

北加贺屋并非如想象的那般缺少特色或生活气息。恰恰相反，这里位于河口湾，造船厂众多，随处可见仓库、工厂、花园、小型住宅、个体商户和艺术工作室（图3，4）。漫步街区之中，人类智慧所创造的美丽与多元扑面而来。

然而，同日本乃至全球的许多城市一样，街区结构和公共形象背后隐藏着严峻的社会及生态问题。人们深知，人为地将自身、自身所从事的工作，以及城市从我们所属的生态系统中分离，是引发上述问题的重要原因[1]。更重要的是，人类所有的心理效应反过来也会作用于生态系统[2]；那些与城市环境内外的自然联系甚少的人们，时常表现出一些加剧与自然隔阂、破坏环境的生活习惯——即使他们是出于好意。

最本质的脱离在于
我们早已忘记自己是自然的产物
城市的形态和功能
仅在梦中永续
这也是无数设计师、科学家与哲学家
无法触及的梦想

唯有从根本上认识到人类是自然的产物，我们才能够逐步构建生态城市。秉持这一理念，城市自然工作室开始着手重建自然与栖居城市的人类个体的关系。工作室坚信，这一实践将为真正意义上的可持续城市提供自然发展的基础。

2

3. 在名村造船厂废弃场地上为艺术表演做准备。
4. 北加贺屋街区中大阪分部和口袋农场所在的小巷

3. Preparation for an art performance at the former Namura Shipbuilding yards
4. Alley where the Branch Osaka and Pocket Farm are located in Kitakagya

3 大阪分部空间

3.1 工作坊

"大阪分部"是城市自然工作室的首个长期面向公众的项目。这里原先是一处拥有80年历史的鱼店，以日本传统街市风格建造，下店上宅。空间结构由简单的木、土、瓦等材料建造，但租用时已无法居住。工作室历时三个月，采用大量回收材料人工重建了这一空间（图5）。

这些回收材料由千岛土地公司捐赠，工作室人员用自行车慢慢地将它们从一家旧仓库搬运到大阪分部（图6）。此外，其他人也伸出援手：当地旅馆的居民帮助铺沙、刷墙，邻居捐赠了植物，远方的朋友捐款，当地都市农业协会"MinnaNouen"（大家的农园）负责人为我们确定了"#kkgreen"（即"绿色北加贺屋"）的社区标语和标签。所有这些过程凸显了一种社会生态系统，其中，社区支持、人际网络，以及共同参与发挥了重要作用。

在大阪分部及其口袋农场中开展的所有工作坊和活动均致力于帮助人们认识到自身是自然的产物。然而大约10年前——在工作室尚无固定办公地点时——工作坊最初的尝试充满了艰辛。我们时常反问自己，城市居民与景观生态疏离已久，是否真的能够通过简简单单的方式恢复人们与自然的关系？

工作室开展的第一批工作坊为参与者提供了简单易学的指导。首先是引导参与者认识土壤的生物学特征，让他们了解每寸土壤中都生活着数以百万计的生物；而后开展了利用土壤和植物色素制作季节色卡（图7）、冥想感受（图8）、寻觅野生草本植物（图9）等一系列活动。所有活动的参与规则都很朴素：练习观察与敬畏土壤中的生命；向它们传达你的善意；通过这些活动过程发现土壤（生态系统）的美。

人们对于工作坊的反馈渐渐帮助工作室打消了疑虑。一位老人站在她的花园中，惊喜地感叹："我在这里种了大半辈子花，却从来没有从这样（土壤）的角度认识它。"后来，在大阪分部的花园中，一位年轻女性微笑着抚摸她手中的土壤色卡："直到今天我才知道土壤竟如此美丽。"

在与不同专业背景的人士共同开展了上百场活动之后，城市自然工作室能够信心满满地肯定许多生态心理学家和宇宙学家数十年以来的观点：人类与环境培养深刻、有意义且广博关系的能力与生俱来，只需勤加练习[3]。此外，这些关系的形成亦可以从根本上改变人类如何工作，以及如何看待、设计、开展自己的生活的方式。

这种思考和行为方式在日本广为存在——可见于神社和佛寺，以及渗透于城市和乡村的自然农法中。人类对自身与环境关系的看法一直在改变，而将这一改变推广至其他城市文脉和地域却要比我们想象得容易。只需满足场所和容许两大需求就可实现[3]——"场所"即可供自然繁荣发展的地域；"容许"来自于社会层面，即要允许和接纳乍看略显奇异的人与自然的关系，包括与树木对话、与野草为友，或向土壤中的微生物致谢。尽管这些举措对于某些社会而言再正常不过，但在高度工业化社会背景下的确较难被接受。

以艺术构想为灵感的实践或可为如何处理这种社会容许提供借鉴——艺术家能够坦然接纳不同的观察视角，而他们的古灵精怪从不须经过"社会许可"。在这一观念的引导下，或许我们都能如约瑟夫·博伊斯所说，发现存在于我们内心的艺术气质[5]。

3.2 口袋农场

口袋农场以帕特里克·格迪斯和福冈正信的作品为灵感，是一处为践行"与自然建立关系"理念而专门设立的空间，用以提升场地的社会和生态价值。在这里，价值的衡量标准不是金钱，而是更为有趣的依据——在行走途中为一朵昨日未曾留意的花而驻足的次数、农场中野草的丰富度，以及分给附近居民的野生草本茶的数量（图10）。

访客常常惊讶于野生草本茶是由口袋农场中茂盛生长的野草制作而成的——通常情况下，野草是被修剪和拔除的对象。在口袋农场，人们很少会因蒲公英（*Taraxacum* spp.）、艾草（*Artemisia* spp.）、鱼腥草（*Houttuynia cordata*）或其他植物的不请自来而烦扰（图11），而是以感恩的心态接纳。如今，野草化身为沙拉食材，或干燥后作为注册草药师姜受希随时制成混合花草茶的原料，免费赠予访客（图12）。

与大自然更亲密的联系、不可估量的感官愉

悦，令我们深刻体会到人类所栖身的生态系统之丰饶，这些都是金钱难以衡量的城市空间价值。它教会了人们感恩自然，放慢脚步关注身边城市环境中出乎意料的丰富动植物世界（图13），用新的方式感知和品味世界。

这些生命形式潜力无穷，可以帮助人们找到前进的道路，而口袋农场的使命之一就是与他人分享这种潜力。我们并非要向人们宣扬“正确对待自然的方法”；相反，我们期望鼓励人们与自然构建更多元的关系，而这种关系完全取决于个人意志、特质，以及对周边生命的理解。

4 城市自然节

真诚的观察
是无憾的观察
是所谓的真见
需无视名谓
由求知欲
寻觅名谓掩盖下的缝隙

城市自然节是一项持续一周的生态艺术即兴表演活动，在北加贺屋周边的多处公共及私有空间举办（图14）。这里的工作以“自由”为核心，并辅以有意义的“限制”——以某次活动为例，艺术家和所有参与者需回答一个问题：你与水是什么关系？

这个问题意味着一种思维轨迹——可以由“水”这个话题向其他任何话题延展：在当下的场所里，人类与水的关系是怎样的？构成这一场所的恩惠于水的生命形式与我们关系如何？这里的动植物、土壤中的微生物、真菌、菌丝体，以及我们无法用肉眼看到、却维持着我们目所能及的世界的一切生命，又与我们关系如何？我们与看不见的水有怎样的关系？当我们意识到并开始维护这种关系时，又会是怎样的？

在城市自然节期间，植松琢磨在人类与树木及彼此之间空气交换的关系中发现了水；已为人母的花本幸乃画出了羊水，提醒我们人类都曾是子宫中的“水生生物”；川中政宏缓慢而有条不紊地将机油与海水混合，凸显了工业主题下的水。与此同时，近百年前由船工建造的展厅建筑本身在筑山有城的艺术作品中呈现出一个向一侧缓缓下沉的结构，陷入下方的土壤和水中。

跨学科的艺术节活动旨在消除学科之间、人与人之间，特别是物种之间的等级差异。罗宾·拉瑟和玛格丽特·佩雷曾通过《水的信号：多物种迁移与代替》项目践行了上述目标——参与者改变了航海旗的旗语，尝试与共生于地球上的水生生物交流。当地与国际参与者共制作了50多面独特的旗帜，描述他们各自与水的对话（图15）。街道上开展了以多物种交流为主题的游行，反响热烈。数百名当地民众——手工匠人、农民、厨师、建筑师、儿童、家长、教师、大学生，以及各行各业的从业人员都参与其中。他们与来自7个国家的30位创意工作者合作，共同发掘了人类、城市与水相互交织的时刻和地点。

我们所做的工作正是找寻人类在这一关系中的意义所在——这是一次探索之旅、颂扬之旅。如果我们秉承这种精神来完成城市中的所有工作，将会如何？在这些“旅程”中，我们总能够找到许多有关设计、生产等可持续性问题的答案。

5 与城市自然建立联系

城市的再野化
始于
心灵的再野化
野化梦与想象

人类倾向于将河流和植物视为自然，将人工环境视为自然之外或之上。但当人们将自身视为自然的一员时，这种观点就不准确了：如果人类属于自然，那么城市亦是自然的一部分。

如果人们认可了这种物质性状态，并以这种视角来建造、使用及停用某种城市结构，城市会变成什么样？如果自然将这种过程诠释为一种出生、生长、死亡，以及腐朽的循环往复，人类将如何在这样的世界里促使某一物质良性循环下去？

我们很难在空调房中找到以上问题的答案，但或许可以在培养设计师、管理者、市政领导、市民，以及城市内外生态系统各群体之间独特而意义非凡关系的过程中进一步探寻。通过持续、真诚地与环境对话，人们或许能够发现一种众生平等下的新城市形态。**LAF**

© Suhee Kang
5

© Patrick M. Lydon
6

5. 莱登与邻居讨论营建口袋农场的想法。
6. 姜受希用自行车将建筑材料从仓库搬到大阪分部。

5. Lydon talking with a neighbor about ideas for Pocket Farm
6. Suhee Kang moving construction materials from a warehouse to the Branch Osaka by bicycle

© Suhee Kang 7

1 Introduction

There is a beautiful block print of the 12th century Sumiyoshi Tall Lantern in Naniwa (present day Osaka) where the lighthouse stands beside a picturesque grove of Japanese black pines (Fig. 1). It has a commanding view of the ocean. Miraculously, the lighthouse still exists today (Fig. 2). The ocean, however, has moved so far away during these 9 centuries that you must now walk 5 km—heading past apartments, subway stations, shopping streets, freeways, and a boat race stadium—before arriving at the present-day ferry terminal, and the waters of Osaka Bay.

The ground in between these two points is the result of some 400 years of gradual land reclamation projects, and the neighborhood of Kitakagaya, a former shipbuilding district on the outskirts of Osaka, Japan, occupies the frontier of this reclamation. Kitakagaya is an amazing feat of engineering and human power. Yet standing in this uniform landscape, with curiously few hints of the area's watery past, one is also left feeling somehow disconnected from the environment. City as Nature, an ecological art and media studio, wonders in this situation, how one might reclaim our relationship with the water and more generally, the nature.

2 Small Acts of Re-connection

It is not as if this neighborhood called Kitakagaya lacks character or a sense of livability. It is bursting with it. Standing at the shipyards, where city meets estuary, the neighborhood comes across as a dense combination of warehouses, factories, gardens, tiny homes, independent businesses, and artist studios (Fig. 3, 4). A walk around the neighborhood gives the impression of the beauty and diversity of creative human enterprise.

Yet as with so many urban areas—both in Japan and globally—there are major social and ecological issues beneath the structures and public personas encountered on the street. People know that the artificial separation of themselves, their jobs, and cities from the ecosystem that they are part of plays a large role in creating these issues[1]. More so, all the psychological effects loop directly back into the ecological ones[2]; humans who are not well-connected to nature in and around their urban environments exhibit habits that—even when well-intended—often further the separation from and abuse of the environment.

There is a fundamental disconnect
we have forgotten that we are ecological beings
form and function of cities
sustainable only in dreams
intangible hopes of the countless
designers, scientists, philosophers

Because we cannot shape ecological cities without this fundamental understanding that

© Suhee Kang 8

© Patrick M. Lydon 9

7. 一位工作坊参与者正在用土壤和植物色素制作色卡。
8. 工作坊参与者聚集在12种可食植物周围冥想感受。
9. 由姜受希主持的“寻觅野生草本植物”工作坊在北加贺屋公园的梅园中举行。

7. A workshop participant recording a soil and plant color palette, using direct pigments from the soils plants.
8. Participants gathering around a mandala of 12 edible plants, to take part in a sensing workshop.
9. Herb foraging workshop by Kang in the plum orchard at Kitakagaya Koen

we are ecological beings, the work of City as Nature, begins with the cultivation of these relationships, between nature and individual urban-dwelling human beings. City as Nature believes that this practice offers a reasonable foundation on which a truly sustainable city can grow, naturally.

3 The Branch Osaka

3.1 The Workshop

City as Nature's first non-transient, public-facing space is the Branch Osaka. This space was actually an 80-year-old fish shop, built in the traditional Japanese market street fashion: tiny shop on ground floor, tiny sleeping room above. The structure is a marvelous simple work of wood, earth, and tile, but was uninhabitable when City as Nature began renting it. For three months the studio rebuilt the space by hand (Fig. 5), using mostly reclaimed materials.

The materials—donated by Chishima Land Company—were slowly transported from an old warehouse, using bicycles (Fig. 6). Countless hands helped; residents from a local guesthouse sanded and painted, neighbors donated plants, faraway friends donated funds, and the director of MinnaNouen, the local urban farming association, declared #kkgreen (Kitakagaya Green) as our neighborhood motto and hashtag. The process highlights a social ecosystem; in this ecology, community support, relationships, and co-involvement are essential.

All workshops and events at the Branch Osaka and its Pocket Farm are rooted in the practice of understanding human existence as ecological beings. Yet the first attempts at these workshops some 10 years ago—before City as Nature had a space—were filled with an uneasiness. Could urban dwellers, exceedingly disconnected from the ecology of their landscapes, really reclaim this relationship with nature so easily?

Instructions for these first workshops were simple. City as Nature first made participants aware of the basic biology of the soil, and the millions of creatures living in each square centimeter. Then there were actions—seasonal palette with soil and plant pigments (Fig. 7), sensing meditation (Fig. 8), and weed foraging (Fig. 9). All actions are framed by simple rules of engagement: practice awareness and respect for the lives in the soil; let these lives know your intention; and work together to discover the beauty in this relationship.

Responses to these workshops help quell our skepticism. An elderly woman stood in her own garden and spoke with wonderment: "I have worked in this garden my whole life, and I have never seen it this way." Later, in the Branch Osaka garden, a young woman smiled, touching the textures of her soil color palette, "Until today, I never knew that soil could be beautiful".

After hundreds of events with people from all kinds of professional backgrounds, City as Nature says confidently what many ecopsychologists and cosmologists have claimed for decades: we human beings have an innate ability to cultivate deep, meaningful, informative relationships with the environment, and all it takes is practice[3]. Further, cultivating these relationships can radically change the way we approach our jobs, how we see, how we design, and how we go about our lives.

This way of thinking and doing already exists throughout Japan, in the Shinto shrines and Buddhist temples, and on the natural farms dotting both city and countryside.This change—in how we view ourselves in relation to the environment to happen in broader contexts and geographies is simpler than we might think. Humans generally require only place and permission[4]: place where nature is allowed to thrive, and permission from society, to engage in relationships that might seem strange at first. Strange, as in talking to a tree, or befriending weeds, or giving thanks to the microbes in the soil. These acts are normal for some societies, yet difficult for most industrialized ones.

© Patrick M. Lydon

10. 精选当地野草和草药，晾干保存于大阪分部的走廊中，可用于制作野生草本茶和药酒。

10. A selection of local weeds and herbs are dried and kept in the Branch Osaka gallery space, for making teas and tinctures.

An art-based practice offers an effective way to approach the "social permission" aspect of this work—artists embrace alternative ways of seeing and do not generally ask permission from society to do strange things. In this way, perhaps we might all embrace, as Joseph Beuys said, the artist that exists inside each of us[5].

3.2 Pocket Farm

Inspired by the work of Patrick Geddes and Masanobu Fukuoka, Pocket Farm is a space dedicated to taking this concept of building relationships with the nature into practice, and is used to produce social and ecological value within the neighborhood. This is not the value measured in monetary terms. It is measured in far more interesting ways: the number of times people stop in their tracks just to enjoy a new flower they did not notice the day before, the diversity of weeds resident in this farm, the cups of tea made from these weeds and then shared with neighbors (Fig. 10).

This tea—and the status given to weeds in the Pocket Farm in particular—is a surprise to most visitors. Normally, such plants are attacked, cut, and rooted out. At Pocket Farm,

11. 口袋农场东入口处开花的野生草本植物
12. 大阪分部中正在准备晾干的香叶天竺葵（*Pelargonium graveolens*）、鱼腥草、迷迭香（*Rosmarinus officinalis*）和各种薄荷的叶子。
13. 姜受希和莱登坐在口袋农场中的豆藤下

11. Flowering weeds at the east entrance to Pocket Farm
12. Leaves of geranium (*Pelargonium graveolens*), chameleon plants, rosemary (*Rosmarinus officinalis*), and various mints are prepared for drying at the Branch Osaka.
13. Kang and Lydon sitting in the shade of Kagawamame beans at Pocket Farm

people rarely bother the dandelions (*Taraxacum* spp.), mugworts (*Artemisia* spp.), chameleon plants (*Houttuynia cordata*), or other self-appointed plant denizens (Fig. 11). When we do, a nod of gratitude is given. Instead of discarding these plants, they are added to a salad, or dried for mixing into the numerous blends of herb tea that Suhee Kang, a licensed herbalist, produces throughout the year and serves freely to visitors (Fig. 12).

Attempting to value urban spaces in non-monetary ways—through meaningful relationships and invaluable moments of sensory delight—teaches us much about the fullness of the ecology we are part of. It teaches us to be thankful. It teaches us to be slowly attentive to a surprisingly rich world of plants and animals that live within our urban neighborhoods (Fig. 13). It teaches us to smell and taste that world in new ways.

These plant lives have an unbelievable potential to help human beings find a way forward, and one of the jobs of this Pocket Farm is to share that potential with others. The motivation of this work is not about dictating how someone should treat nature, so much as it is about creating the possibility for relationships. What this relationship is like for you, is entirely up to your own determination, character, and understanding of the lives around you.

4 City as Nature Festival

Truthfully seeing what is
unapologetically seeing what is
what is truthfully seeing
but disregarding the name of a thing
as curiosity finds the ways
in and around the cracks that names conceal

The City as Nature Festival is a week-long ecological art happening, taking place in multiple public and privately-owned spaces around Kitakagaya (Fig. 14). The work here is based on a combination of freedom, along with a meaningful constraint. In this particular time and place, the constraint is a question, to artists and all participants: what is your relationship with water?

This question implies a trajectory of thinking; it flows from water, into all forms. How is the human relationship with water in this place? How is our relationship with all of

the life forms touched by water that makes up this place; the plants, the animals, the microbes in the soil, the fungal life forms, the mycelium, and with all of these lives that we do not see, yet that support all that we do see? How is our relationship with the invisible water, and what does it look like when we recognize and cultivate that relationship?

During the festival, Takuma Uematsu found water in the relationship between humans and trees, and the atmosphere that we both exchange. Pittore Felice, a mother of two young girls, painted the amniotic fluid, reminding us that we are aquatic species in the womb. A slow and methodical act of mixing of machine oil and sea water highlighted the industrial theme of Masahiro Kawanaka's work. Meanwhile the exhibition building itself, built by former shipwrights nearly a century ago, was revealed by Yuki Tsukiyama's artwork, as a structure slowly sinking sideways, back into the soil and water below.

An interdisciplinary festival suggests the removal of hierarchy between disciplines, between people, and here especially, between species. Robin Lasser and Marguerite Perret achieved this in their project "Signaling Water: Multi-Species Migration and Displacement," where participants altered the language of maritime flags, communicating messages to the aquatic species that we co-inhabit this world with. Over 50 unique flags were produced by local and international participants, describing their personal dialogs with water (Fig. 15). A multi-species communication parade, with fifes and drums and flags, broke out into the streets. Hundreds of local people joined—craftspeople, farmers, chefs, architects, children, parents, teachers, students from local high schools and universities, and various other practitioners. They connected with 30 creative practitioners from 7 countries, and together people uncovered the moments and places where humans and their cities are intertwined with water.

This is a work of determination to find our place here as human beings. It is a discovery. It is a celebration. What if all of our work in cities could be done with this spirit? Somewhere here, we surmise, could be the answer to many questions of sustainability in design, production, and otherwise.

5 Building a Relationship With Urban Nature

The rewilding of a city
begins in the sense
the rewilding of the minds
of dreams and imaginations

Humans have a sense that discerns rivers and plants as nature, and the built environment as something outside of or above nature. When we see ourselves as ecological beings however, this view turns out to be inaccurate. If we are ecological beings, all parts of the city are parts of this ecology, too.

What would cities look like if people approached the materiality, and the process of construction, use, and decommissioning of the urban structures with such a view? If nature treats this process as one birth, growth, death, and decay—where the last step gives back to the first—how might people also embrace an urban world where the birth and decay of material form contributes to a more virtuous cycle?

The answers to such questions are less likely to be discovered in a climate-controlled office than they are to be found in cultivating relationships—individual, meaningful relationships between designers, executives, civic leaders, citizens, and the communities of ecosystems in and around our cities. Through an ongoing, truthful dialog with the environment, people might just discover the possible city, an equitable place for all beings. **LAF**

© Patrick M. Lydon
14

© Patrick M. Lydon
15

14. 千鸟文化的中庭是“城市自然节”的展示空间之一。
15. 工作室负责人之一花本幸乃为《水的信号：多物种迁移与代替》项目的游行做准备。

14. One of several display spaces during the City as Nature Festival was the central atrium at Chidori Bunka.
15. Workshop co-leader Pittore Felice preparing her flag for the "Signaling Water: Multi-Species Migration and Displacement" parade.

REFERENCES

[1] Roszak, T. (1992). *The Voice of the Earth* (p. 14). New York, NY: Simon & Schuster.

[2] Ives, C. (2015, October). A New Reconnection Agenda for People and Nature. *The Nature of Cities*. Retrieved from https://www.thenatureofcities.com/?p=11160

[3] Sewall, L. (1995). The Skill of Ecological Perception. In T. Roszak, M. Gomes, & A. Kanner (Eds.), *Ecopsychology: Restoring the Earth, Healing the Mind*. Berkeley and London: University of California Press, Sierra Club.

[4] Lydon, P. (2020). Urban Ecology: Art and the Cultivation of Ecological Mindsets. In I. Douglas, P. Anderson, D. Goode, M. Houck, D. Maddox, H. Nagendra, & P. Y. Tan (Eds.), *The Routledge Handbook of Urban Ecology* (2nd ed.). London, England: Routledge.

[5] Beuys, J. (1979). Introduction. In C. Tisdall, *Joseph Beuys* (p. 7). New York, NY: Solomon R. Guggenheim Museum.

呼唤野性
Invoking the Wild

南希·西顿
未来绿色工作室高级助理设计师

Nancy SEATON*
Senior Associate Designer, Future Green Studio

*Corresponding Author
Address: 18 Bay Street, Brooklyn, NY 11231, USA
Email: info@futuregreenstudio.com

摘要

在人类的印象中，荒野植物是随遇而安、坚韧又脆弱的——人类亦如是。城市环境中充斥着的植物，诗意地扎根于工业基础设施遗迹之上——无论是顺着路沿和铁丝网、于路面裂缝之间，还是在空地、碎石堆和公路分隔带中。

未来绿色工作室通过一系列城市漫走、演讲、公民科学的活动对城市自生植物进行调查，并将成果集结为《城市自生植物：纽约城野草》一书，希望借此促使人们与周边的街道、墙壁、土地和树池等环境互动。这项工作也不断为工作室的众多景观设计项目提供种植理念支撑，力图展现出城市荒野强健且富有魅力的一面。在进行种植设计时，工作室会从项目所在地的植物群落（如橡树林和灌木丛）中选择能够耐受目标生境环境的物种；项目地的植物和生态总能为设计师提供源源不断的灵感。野生植物不再被视为破坏城市环境的幽灵；反之，它们是保证人类与其他地球居民健康和福祉的无形资产，展现了城市促进未来生态演进发展的能力。

关键词
城市自生植物；野性；野生植物；可持续性；景观设计；生态学

翻译 | 崔婧沄、王颖、王琰
TRANSLATED BY | CUI Jingyun, WANG Ying, WANG Yan

ABSTRACT

Wild places remind us of the adaptability, resilience, and fragility of plants and humans alike. The urban environment is awash in plant life, often taking root in remnants of industrial infrastructure in poetic ways—along roadsides and chain-link fences, between cracks of pavement, and within vacant lots, rubble dumps, and highway medians.

Future Green Studio's investigations into spontaneous urban plants have aspired to engage people with their neighborhood environments—streets, walls, lots, and tree pits—through a series of walks, talks, citizen science participation, and the publication of a book, *SUP: Weeds in NYC*. This work continues to feed planting concepts behind many of the studio's designed landscapes, which seek to capture the rugged vision of urban wilderness. Species for the studio's projects are selected for their ability to tolerate the proposed habitats created on sites and are often drawn from local plant communities, such as oak barrens and shrublands; the plants and ecologies of project sites are a frequent source of inspiration. The studio does not see uncultivated plant growth as the specter of disinvestment, but as an asset to the performance, health, and well-being of its inhabitants, human or otherwise, which demonstrates the ability of the city to support the evolving ecologies of the future.

KEYWORDS
Spontaneous Urban Plants; Wildness; Wild Plants; Sustainability; Landscape Design; Ecology

https://doi.org/10.15302/J-LAF-1-050028
收稿时间 RECEIVED DATE | 2021-01-29

中图分类号 | TU984
文献标识码 | B

1 引言

或许，在人工设计的城市的衬托下，人们才能更好地欣赏自然的野性之美——它与包裹着城市的光滑如镜的、没有任何感情色彩的混凝土和玻璃截然相反。城市环境充满了这种野性，野生的植物扎根于城市的各种缝隙中——顺着路沿和铁丝网，于路面裂缝之间，以及空地、碎石堆和公路分隔带内。尽管许多人将这些城市自生植物等同于荒废或无序，但另一部分人却惊叹于这些无畏的物种能在糟糕的立地条件下繁衍生息，哪怕再微弱、再渺小（图1）。

人们对于野生植被盘踞于建筑遗迹之上的迷恋并非始于后工业时代[1]，早在18世纪，乔凡尼·巴蒂斯塔·皮拉内西关于罗马古迹的风景画中就有所体现（图2）：这些版画展现了遗迹的诗意本质，是对稍纵即逝的人类生活和文明的注释——“毋忘你终有一死”（Memento mori）①。尽管这些作品的核心是体现崇高的（常常是幻想的）建筑和工程技艺，但它们也体现了博物学家在记录欧洲和北美城市中的植物生命方面的共同兴趣②。这种“探索”罗马遗迹的热潮在皮拉内西完成研究一个世纪之后依然强劲：1855年，一本介绍罗马斗兽场中生长的420种野生植物的旅游指南得以出版，其中包括每种植物的特性、实际用途，以及相关的文学作品和神话。[2]

自19世纪初到20世纪末，植物学家不断划分和细化植物区系，并将重点放在缺少文献记载或“未开发”的地区。但直到20世纪70年代，当科学家发现全球各地城市中均存在广布植物区系，城市生态学才被视为一个独立的研究领域[3]。在美国，研究机构

对记录这一植物区系中物种的兴趣日益浓厚。早在1974年，哈佛大学就发行了一期《阿诺德亚》研究报告，专门介绍“城市野生植物”（wild plants in the city）——而非“杂草”（weeds）——的野外识别。[4]

纽约市的两所植物园为该市植物区系的长期研究项目提供了赞助。1990年，布鲁克林植物园发起了一项对纽约市约80km半径范围内所有植物的研究，即“纽约大都会植物志计划”。这项工作大大丰富了关于该市植物区系的数据资料，并为植物标本库提供了新的标本，记录了乡土物种数量减少及非乡土植物数量增加的迹象[5]，并以一系列对比图的形式加以呈现。2018年，纽约植物园发起了“纽约市生态植物志计划”，旨在鼓励公民科学家参与保存、保护乡土植物，同时为政策决策补充最新数据资料。2018年出版的《城市植物状况》提出了纽约市植物保护的多元策略，包括吸纳志愿者协助纽约植物园的研究工作。[6]

长达数十年间，关于入侵植物和非乡土植物负面影响的讨论十分广泛，上述两个项目也都有所涉及。但植物没有主观意愿——这些物种的繁荣或衰退完全取决于人类行为。

除大量非乡土植物外，城市植物群中只有最强健的乡土植物才能存活，因此常被认为毫无价值或纯粹是“有害的”。是否有可能扭转人们的印象，让他们认识到这些无需人类栽培的植物对城市有诸多裨益？

这绝非存心引发争论——世界上超过一半的地区已经历城市化；随着生物和非生物系统的不可逆转的改变，城市逐渐不再适合原有物种生存，转而演化出了新的生态系统。[7][8]彼得·德尔·特雷迪奇在《东北部城市野生植物：野外手册》中强调了城市野生植物在当代城市生态中的重要作用：并非是要用其取代复杂的乡土植物群落，而是为普罗大众详述当代现实和科学趋势。[9]

2 城市自生植物探索

在上述话题的持续热议的背景下，未来绿色工作室（Future Green Studio，以下简称FGS工作室）围绕城市环境中的野生植物（或城市自生植物）主题开展了一系列项目。项目的第一阶段始于2011年，主要内容包括在工作室附近的街头漫走、观察记录和常见物种的识别。在这一阶段，工作室标记了自身办公场所附近第三大街人行道中的城市自生植物：用黄色颜料圈画标记自生植物，促使人们关注这些无处不在又常被忽视的植物（图3）。设计这个标记的意图之一是鼓励社区居民更仔细地观察周围环境，关注共同居住于这座城市的植物，并通过细微的环境改变来一改人们对杂草的消极认知。之后，工作室启动了一项艺术研究，并利用社交应用程序“Instagram”（标签为“#spontanenousurbanplants”）来吸引更多市民与当地环境互动。在应用程序的推广下，人们积极参与新一轮的植物探索浪潮，在各个角落寻找典型和不常见的城市物种，并通过一幅幅精美的照片记录下城市中的野草奇观（图4）。

从2013年到2016年，FGS工作室还参与了一系列城市漫走活动：包括全天候探索活动，以及利用午休时间在红钩区（工作室所在地、布鲁克林废弃滨水工业区）开展的漫走活动（图5）。在这期间，FGS工作室开始根据实地观察和文化用途及起源研究，编绘植物物种档案。任由野生植被在夹缝中生长，对城市来说是一种财富——人行道上和树池中的植被垫层能够缓冲雨水，减弱大型风暴的环境累积效应，进而减少水土流失；非人工栽植的树木可以为高温的铺装地面遮阴，降低城市热岛效应（图6）。工作室创始人大卫·赛特这样描述城市自生植物项目（图7）：“城市自生植物令人惊叹之处在于，它们不需要人工辅助就能在极端的、不稳定的城市环境中生存并自我维护，同时还能提供与传统景观植物和行道树相同的生态效益。我们不应试图除掉它们，而应抓住机会，享受其恩惠，并向更多人介绍它们。”[10]

① “Memento mori”，拉丁语意为“毋忘你终有一死”，引申义为“提醒死亡必然性的事物”。

② 欧美早期城市植物志主要包括：《巴黎植物志》（塞巴斯蒂安·瓦扬，1722）；《植物种志》（卡尔·林奈，1753）；《伦敦植物志》（威廉·柯蒂斯，1777）；《费城植物概要》（威廉·巴顿，1818）；《纽约周边植物日志》（约翰·托里，1818–1820）；以及《波士顿植物志》（雅各布·毕格罗，1840）。

1. 纽约市曼哈顿晨边高地地区岩石缝隙中生长出的欧洲千里光（*Senecio vulgaris*）
2. 《蒂沃利哈德良别墅的雕塑展廊废墟》（出自《罗马风景画》，皮拉内西作于1748～1774年）

1. *Senecio vulgaris* emerging from crevice in Morningside Heights, Manhattan, New York City.
2. *Rovine d'una Galleria di Statue nella Villa Adriana a Tivoli*, from *Vedute di Roma*, Piranesi, 1748 ~ 1774.

3 野性作品

城市植物具有极强的适应力，能够在各种恶劣环境中生存。受此启发，FGS工作室将在城市景观中遇到的极端环境条件视作机遇，而非限制因素。工作室早期的项目——建成于2013年的纽约市曼哈顿肉库区345号（图8-1）便是一例。该社区历史悠久的负载雨篷及附近的高线公园为建设第十四大街居民楼植物密集的入口雨篷提供了借鉴。建造的景观沿立面自发生长，有着各种城市自生植物生长地的狂野气质和体量。极浅的生长介质（约15~51cm，由工作室铺撒）支撑着火炬树（*Rhus typhina*）、草本植被和沿着混凝土雨篷边缘生长的垂吊植物（图8-2）。该项目在许多方面体现了城市自生植物的精神：飘落的种子偶然“发现”了这里，因而雨篷这种不寻常的地方才会出现悬空的植物景观。肉库区345号的鬼斧神工为工作室的其他项目带来了许多灵感，例如庞德街41号（图9）和22号（图10）的立面种植。

FGS工作室的大部分设计对象为城市构筑物、屋顶和驳岸，常受到荷载和活动类型的限制。鉴于每个场地独特的植被、原生土壤、地形、水文和地质条件，FGS工作室认真研究每块场地的自然史。在生长介质厚度受限的情况下，选取能够产生最大体量感的各类植物，以创造出具有野性之美、质感分明、季相鲜明的景观。于2016年完工的布鲁克林丹波区帝国商店绿植屋顶（面积超4 650m²）即为其中一个案例（图11）。

FGS工作室从项目地的植物和生态中汲取灵感，依据建成环境创造的特定生境来进行物种选择。在观察到野生植物在极端恶劣的条件下都能繁荣生长后，工作室惊叹于自生植物极强的适应力。工作室在城市中观察到的植物并非都是入侵种，其中许多是乡土的滨海植物，能够适应干旱、高温、贫瘠的土壤和盐雾。在进行种植设计时，工作室会从项目所在地的植物群落（如橡树林和灌木丛）中选择能够耐受目标生境环境的物种（图12）。该策略已在近期多个项目中使用，包括2019年设计的位于亚特兰大的乔治亚电力公司项目，该项目选用了皮埃蒙特地区和海滨平原的植物。另一个进行中的项目位于曼哈顿，是原圣约翰火车总站所在地。建筑设计团队创建了一处穿过废弃工业铁路的“剖断面”，后续这里很快会栽种乡土植物（图13）：这处种植设计看似轻松、自然，充满野性，但却不乏工程巧思。工作室综合考虑了实地观测到的能够适应城市环境的物种、曼哈顿的历史生态[11]，以及纽约市公园与娱乐管理局自然资源小组发布的植物列表[12]，总结出植物清单。工作室的许多设计与新型建筑结构融合，在有限的条件下为原本缺乏活力的空间创造出了未来的生态发展可能。尽管既不致力于、也不可能重现当地现存生态的复杂性，工作室的目的是将场地置于具体环境中，再现本土景观风貌（图14）。

总体而言，FGS工作室未来仍有较多工作要做：量化绿色屋顶和城市绿色空间的优势；了解植物的表现，以及对传粉者、昆虫、鸟类和其他野生动物（工作室一直致力于吸引它们进入场地）的供给能力（图15）；另一个工作重点是与城市生态学家、土壤科学家、学生和热心志愿者合作，对这些场地进行监测。野性意味着未知——它充满活力、与众不同，未囿于整齐划一，能够随时间而发展变化，却又易于掌控。

4 结语

FGS工作室通过一系列城市漫走、演讲、市民科普活动对城市自生植物进行调查，并将成果集结为《城市自生植物：纽约城野草》一书，希望借此促使人们与周边的街道、墙壁、土地和树池等环境互动。这项工作同时为FGS工作室的许多设计贡献了种植理念：探索与沉浸。城市荒野野性、强健且富有魅力的一面激发了工作室创作灵感，野生植物不再被视为破坏城市环境的幽灵；反之，它们是保证人类与其他地球居民健康和福祉的无形资产，展现了城市促进未来生态演进发展的能力。自然过程发生于世界的任何角落，无关政治边界或生物分类。城市各种角落中萌发的栽培或野生植物，时刻提醒着我们——所有生命彼此联系、彼此适应，坚韧而又脆弱。**LAF**

© Future Green Studio 3

© Future Green Studio 4

© Nancy Seaton 5

3. 纽约市布鲁克林第三大街上用黄色颜料标记的城市自生植物
4. 布鲁克林红钩区瓦楞板围墙边的城市自生植物
5. 午休漫走和植物识别

3. SUP highlighted on 3rd Street, Brooklyn, New York City
4. SUP along a corrugated fence in Red Hook, Brooklyn
5. Lunchtime stroll and botanical identification

1 Introduction

Wildness is perhaps best appreciated in contrast to the designed urbanity of cities, a counterpoint to the smooth neutrality of concrete and glass with which they are clad. The urban environment is full of such wildness, as uncultivated plants take root in the interstitial fabric—along roadsides and chain-link fences, between cracks of pavement, and within vacant lots, rubble dumps and highway medians. While many perceive these spontaneous urban plants (SUP) as a sign of dereliction or entropy, others marvel at the intrepid species' ability to thrive in the unlikely places where they are found, however small the moment of botanical revolt (Fig. 1).

The fascination with wild vegetation taking hold of architectural remnants is hardly a new, post-industrial phenomenon[1], and can be seen in Piranesi's 18th-century view of Roman antiquities (Fig. 2). These prints showcased the poetic nature of ruins that served as memento mori①—a commentary on the transience of human life and civilizations. While the forms of sublime, often fantastical, architecture and feats of engineering were at the core of these views, they also speak to the parallel interest of documenting plant life encountered by naturalists in European and North American growing within cities②. The popularity of "discovering" the ruins of Rome was still strong a century after Piranesi produced his studies, and a tourist guide to the 420 wild plants that could be found growing on the Colosseum of Rome was printed in 1855, which included the properties of each species, practical uses, and references in literature and mythology.[2]

Botanists continued to catalog and refine floras throughout the 19th and 20th centuries, with an emphasis on territories that had not been documented, or that were perceived as pristine. It was not until the 1970s that urban ecology was recognized as its own field of studywith scientists identifying a cosmopolitan flora that was common between cities around the globe[3]. In the United States, institutions became increasingly interested in documenting the species that composed this group of plants. As early as 1974, Harvard University

6 © Future Green Studio

7 © K. Taro Hashimura for FGS

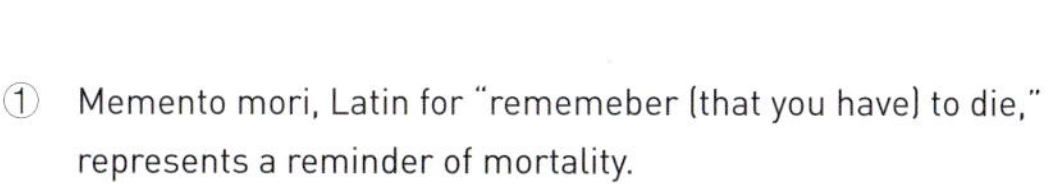

① Memento mori, Latin for "rememeber (that you have) to die," represents a reminder of mortality.

② An incomplete snapshot of early Euro-American urban floras includes *Botanicon Parisiense* (Sébastien Vaillant, 1722); *Species Plantarum* (Carl Linnaeus, 1753); *Flora Londinensis* (William Curtis, 1777); *Compendium Florae Philadelphia* (William Barton, 1818); *Calendarium Florae for the Vicinity of New York* (John Torrey, 1818–1820) ; and *Florula Bostoniensis* (Jacob Bigelow, 1840).

6. 自发生长的合欢（*Albizia julibrissin*）可为人行道提供遮阴
7. 纽约市皇后区如今酒吧外部的荒野，其中无益的城市自生植物已被清除。

6. *Albizia julibrissin*, as SUP, providing shade to pavement.
7. Managed wilderness (i.e. removing unwanted SUP) at Nowadays, Queens, New York City.

published an issue of *Arnoldia* dedicated to field identification of what they called "wild plants in the city," significantly not calling them weeds.[4]

In New York City, two of the botanic gardens have sponsored long-term research projects about the city's flora. Brooklyn Botanic Garden initiated a study of all plants within a fifty-mile radius of New York City in 1990—New York Metropolitan Flora Project. The work significantly increased data of the city's flora, filling herbaria with new specimens that documented the shrinking populations of indigenous species and the expansion of non-native plants, represented in a series of comparative maps.[5] In 2018, The New York Botanical Garden (NYBG) established the New York City EcoFlora Program, which seeks to engage citizen scientists with the preservation and protection of native plants, while also supplementing current data to inform policy decisions. The 2018 publication, "The State of the City's Plants" projects a multivalent strategy for plant conservation in New York City that includes volunteer participation, alongside the work of NYBG researchers.[6]

Both projects are embedded in a decades-old, expansive conversation about the detrimental effects of invasive and non-native plants, but plants have no volition—humans have created the conditions in which species thrive or decline and continue to make them.

The urban flora, composed of primarily non-native species and only the most vigorous natives, is commonly dismissed as valueless or simply "bad." Is it possible to challenge the negative perception of these plants that grow without human cultivation and evaluate positive contributions?

This is not just a provocation—more than half of the world is urbanized; the ability of cities to support historic genera falters as the biotic and abiotic systems are irrevocably altered, becoming novel ecosystems.[7][8] Peter Del Tredici's *Wild Urban Plants of the Northeast: A Field Guide* emphasizes the significant role this group of plants plays in contemporary urban ecology, not promoting them as a replacement of complex native plant communities, but detailing contemporary realities and scientific trends for a broad public readership.[9]

2 SUP Explorations

Situated within this continuum of discourse, Future Green Studio (FGS) launched what would become a series of projects around the theme of wild plants found in the urban environment or SUP. Begun in 2011, the first phase of the project included office walks, recorded observations, and identification of the commonly found species. This phase highlighted SUP along a section of the 3rd Street sidewalk near the office. Yellow circles were painted around SUP to draw attention to the ubiquitous, but generally overlooked plants (Fig. 3). One of the intentions of framing these plants was to invite neighborhood residents to look more closely—to start actively noticing the plants that they cohabit in the city with—to upend the perception of weeds as a nuisance by subtly changing the context. In the next steps, the office initiated an art and research project, and engaged a broader audience to interact with their local environments through the application, Instagram #spontanenousurbanplants. The Instagram allowed people to participate in a

© DDG Partners

8-1

© Izabela Riano-Lev

8-2

new wave of botanical exploration, searching out typical and unusual species in all corners of the city, creating a spectacle of weeds through artful photography (Fig. 4).

The office participated in an additional series of walks (2013 ~ 2016), some full-day explorations, others lunch-time rambles around Red Hook, Brooklyn, a formerly industrial, waterfront neighborhood where the office is situated (Fig. 5). FGS began to compile plant profiles and charts of species grounded in field observations and research into cultural uses and nativity. The appearance of wild vegetation can be an asset, if left to grow in the interstices in between places: mats of vegetation in the sidewalk and tree pits contribute to erosion control—slowing stormwater, reducing the cumulative impact of major storm events; uncultivated trees offer shade to otherwise hot, paved surfaces, lowering the urban heat island effect (Fig. 6). In describing the SUP project, founding principal, David Seiter, states the following (Fig. 7), "[w]hat's remarkable about all spontaneous urban plants is the fact that they require no human assistance to assert and maintain themselves in extreme, often volatile urban conditions, while providing the same ecologically performative benefits of traditional landscape plants and street trees. Rather than seek to discard and eradicate them, we now have an opportunity to harness their benefits and tell their histories."[10]

3 Wild Works

Inspired by the plant adaptations that allow urban flora to survive in a variety of harsh habitats, FGS sees opportunities rather than limitations in the extreme environmental conditions found in urban landscapes. An early project in the office remains a foundational one: 345 Meatpacking, Manhattan, New York City, built in 2013 (Fig. 8-1). The historic loading canopies of the neighborhood along with the nearby High Line provided precedents for the creation of a dense entrance marquee at the residential building on 14th Street. The constructed landscape has the appearance of one that spontaneously erupted along the facade, bearing the wild demeanor and volume that any number of SUP sites exhibit. The extremely shallow growing media provided, 6 ~ 20 inches, supports clusters of staghorn sumacs (*Rhus typhina*), an herbaceous mix, and cascading plants that spill through the openings and over the edges of the concrete canopy (Fig. 8-2). This project embodies the spirit of SUP in many ways, as the awning is not a site where plants are typically seen, passersby "find" the suspended landscape by accident. Whimsical and idiosyncratic, 345 Meatpacking has introduced many to the office's work, along with the facade planting at 41 Bond Street (Fig. 9) and 22 Bond Street (Fig. 10).

Most of the studio's design work has been in cities, on structure, rooftops, and bulkheads, with weight and program restrictions. To bring a sense of identity to sites that have long been stripped of vegetation, native soils, topography, hydrology, and geology—paved over and built upon—FGS looks to the natural history of each site. Plant palettes are assembled to provide maximum volume for the often-limited depth of growing media, to create landscapes that provide a wild beauty, full of contrasting textures and seasonal markers, as in our work at Empire Stores in Dumbo, Brooklyn, with over 4,650 square meters of planted green roof, completed in 2016 (Fig. 11).

FGS embraces the plants and ecologies of project sites for inspiration, using specific habitats created by the built environment to inform species selection. The studio draws on lessons of plant adaptation learned through observing uncultivated plants thriving despite exposed conditions. Not all the SUP encountered by the studio were invasive species; many plants discovered on walks were native, seaside plants

9 © Future Green Studio

10 © Future Green Studio

8. 曼哈顿肉库区345号及其生长着植物的雨篷
9. 2011年竣工的曼哈顿庞德街41号立面种植
10. 曼哈顿庞德街22号种植效果图

8. 345 Meatpacking, Manhattan and its vegetated marquee.
9. Facade planting at 41 Bond Street, Manhattan, completed in 2011.
10. Rendering of 22 Bond Street, Manhattan.

© K. Taro Hashimura for FGS
11

© K. Taro Hashimura for FGS
12

© Cook + Fox
13

© Future Green Studio
14

able to withstand drought, heat, lean soils, and salt spray. Species for the studio's projects are selected for their ability to tolerate the proposed habitats created on sites and are often drawn from local plant communities, such as oak barrens and shrublands (Fig. 12). This strategy has been employed on several recent projects, including Georgia Power in Atlanta (designed, 2019), which incorporated plants from the Piedmont and the coastal plain. Another current project is in the site of the former St. John's Terminal in Manhattan. Here, the architectural team has created a sectional cut through the former industrial rail, which will soon support a cultivated ecology of native plants (Fig. 13). The planting is designed to appear effortless, naturalistic, wild—but is a highly engineered orchestration. The palette was assembled considering field-observations of urban-adapted species, historic ecologies detailed in Manhattan[11], and plant lists issued by the Natural Resources Group of the New York City Department of Parks and Recreation.[12] Many of the places FGS designs are incorporated into new construction, composing future ecologies for spaces that would otherwise be inert, for conditions that have never existed. While it is neither possible nor the goal to reproduce the complexity of an extant, native ecology, it is the intention to evoke scenes of local landscapes, to situate places within specific contexts (Fig. 14).

There is much work to be done in quantifying the benefit of green roofs and urban green spaces in general, to understand which plants are performing well, and are best able to support a rich array of pollinators, insects, birds, and other wildlife—which the studio regularly tries to attract (Fig. 15); monitoring these sites is high on the list of next steps in the studio's practice, in partnership with urban ecologists, soil scientists, students, and

11. 布鲁克林帝国商店的屋顶花园
12. 布鲁克林儿童博物馆的乡土植物花园
13. 工作室设计的曼哈顿圣约翰火车总站效果图
14. 布鲁克林海军上将排屋前停车场上的乡土植物混种

11. Greenroof at Empire Stores, Brooklyn
12. Native garden at Brooklyn Children's Museum, Brooklyn
13. Rendering of proposed St. John's Terminal, Lower Manhattan
14. Native mix at Admiral's Row Parking Lot, Brooklyn

传粉者和昆虫
Pollinators and insects

15

enthusiastic volunteers. Wildness is an invitation to the unexpected, which embraces vigor and heterogeneity over manicured monocultures, engagement with time, and often, a light hand in control.

4 Conclusion

FGS's investigations into spontaneous urban plants have aspired to engage people with their neighborhood environments—streets, walls, lots, and tree pits—through a series of walks, talks, citizen science participation, and the publication of a book, *SUP: Weeds in NYC*. This work continues to feed planting concepts behind many of the FGS's designed landscapes, which foster a sense of discovery and immersion. The rugged vision of urban wilderness the studio is inspired by does not see uncultivated plant growth as the specter of disinvestment, but as an asset to the performance, health, and well-being of its inhabitants, human or otherwise, which demonstrates the ability of the city to support the evolving ecologies of the future.

Natural process is not something that happens elsewhere but can be observed in whatever context we may find ourselves; there are no political boundaries or classifications that divide the biotic. Cultivated and uncultivated plants sprouting from all manner of surfaces within cities serve to remind us of the interconnectedness, adaptability, resilience, and fragility of all life. **LAF**

REFERENCES

[1] Arnold, S. (2015). Urban Decay Photography and Film: Fetishism and the Apocalyptic Imagination. *Journal of Urban History*, 41(2), 326-339.

[2] Deakin, R. (1855). *Flora of the Colosseum of Rome*. London, England: Groombridge and Sons.

[3] Kowarik, I., & Körner, S. (Eds.). (2005). *Wild Urban Woodlands: New Perspectives for Urban Forestry*. Berlin, Germany: Springer-Verlag.

[4] Paqe, N. M., & Weaver, R. E., Jr. (1974). Wild Plants in the City. *Arnoldia*, 32(4). Retrieved from http://arnoldia.arboretum.harvard.edu/issues/100

[5] Moore, G., Steward, A., Clemants, S., Glenn, S., & Ma, J. (2002). An Overview of the New York Metropolitan Flora Project. *Urban Habitats*. Retrieved from http://www.urbanhabitats.org/v01n01/nymf_full.html

[6] Atha, D., & Boom, B. (2018). State of New York City's Plants 2018. Retrieved from https://www.nybg.org/content/uploads/2018/08/SCI_State-of-the-Citys-Plants-2018_Final-8.2_Low.pdf

[7] Hobbs, R. J., Arico, S., Aronson, J., Baron, J. S., Bridgewater, P., Cramer, V. A., ... Zobel, M. (2006). Novel Ecosystems: Theoretical and Management Aspects of the New Ecological World Order. *Global Ecology and Biogeography*, 15(1), 1-7. doi:10.1111/j.1466-822X.2006.00212.x

[8] Morse, N. B., Pellissier, P. A., Cianciola, E. N., Brereton, R. L., Sullivan, M. M., Shonka, N. K., ... McDowell, W. H. (2014). Novel Ecosystems in the Anthropocene: A Revision of the Novel Ecosystem Concept for Pragmatic Applications. *Ecology and Society*, 19(2), 12. doi:10.5751/ES-06192-190212

[9] Del Tredici, P. (2010). *Wild Urban Plants of the Northeast: A Field Guide*. New York, NY: Cornel University Press.

[10] Seiter, D. (2011). Profiles of Spontaneous Urban Plants. The Architectural League's Urban Omnibus. Retrieved from https://urbanomnibus.net/2011/12/profiles-of-spontaneous-urban-plants/

[11] Sanderson, E. (2009). *Manhattan: A Natural History of New York City*. New York, NY: Abrams Books.

[12] Natural Resources Group, & NYC Department Parks and Recreation. (2019). *Native Plant Guide* (3rd ed.). Retrieved from https://www.nycgovparks.org/greening/natural-resources-group/publication

15.《百老汇购物中心协会恢复和维护方案》中计划监测的城市野生动植物

15. Urban wildlife to be monitored in the future, Broadway Mall Association Restoration and Maintenance Plan.

LAURENT
CREATIVE
LAURENT
CREATIVE
联系电话 | 13816172953（范工）
邮箱 |lr@laurent-creative.com
地址 | 上海市杨浦区杨树浦路2866号国际时尚中心13号楼3层
广告 / AD

关于《园林》杂志

《园林》创刊于1984年，为月刊，主编：张浪。国内统一刊号：CN31-1118/S，国际刊号：ISSN1000-0283。上海市绿化和市容管理局主管，上海市园林科学规划研究院和中国风景园林学会联合主办，面向国内外发行的综合性学术刊物。曾获全国“双效”期刊和上海市优秀科技期刊称号。是一本集风景园林规划与设计、理论研究、学科综述、专题论述、科学研究与技术研发报告、典型案例解析等于一体的学术刊物。

办刊宗旨

本刊为风景园林学综合性学术期刊，刊载风景园林学及相关交叉学科的新理论、新技术、新进展，提供学术交流平台，服务我国风景园林行业发展。旨在以专业的角度，探索学科热点，推动行业科技进步，兼备学术性、实用性和人文性。

期刊收录

刊载文章被科学引文数据库（SCD）、中国学术期刊网络出版总库（CNKI）、万方-中国学术期刊数据库（CSPD）等数据库收录。

栏目设置

主要设有热点专题、园林规划设计、园林空间、园林植物、园林艺术、园林管理、应用研究等栏目。

投稿要求

1.稿件须为Word文档，字数以6000～7000字为宜（含图及表），要求5号宋体，语言简练，论点明确，数据可靠。来稿结构顺序为：中英文题（中文20字以内）、中英文摘要（第三人称书写，中文300字以内，独立成文）、中英文关键词（3～5个）、文章主体、参考文献等。

2.正文标题序号用1，1.1，1.1.1……均左顶格书写，标题层次以4级为限。文中涉及的人名、地名、学名、公式、符号应核实无误；外文字母的文种、正斜体、大小写、上下标等清楚注明；计量单位、符号、数字用法、专业名词术语一律采用相应的国家标准；植物种或品种应标注准确拉丁学名。

全年专题

为紧贴时代脉搏，突显时代主题，集中展示中国风景园林标志事件和新时代重大规划，2021年《园林》拟推出如下专题（所列专题顺序，不作为最终发刊专题顺序）：

（1）人民城市理念下的风景园林；（2）山地景观；（3）园艺博览会；（4）江南园林传承；（5）行业技术标准研究；（6）城市绿地空间生态安全格局；（7）疫情下的康养景观；（8）公平性视角下的城市景观；（9）公园城市；（10）美丽乡村景观；（11）城市双修；（12）城市生态廊道。

《园林》专题文章采用专家约稿与作者自由来稿相结合的方式。同时，诚邀各专题相关领域优秀学科带头人自荐或推荐符合本刊甄选标准的优质稿件，协助编辑部组稿。

《园林》优先发表国际合作项目、国家级、省部级攻关项目或重点科研项目所产生的重要论文，并在本刊相关平台不定期滚动展示。投稿邮箱：garden899@vip.163.com，联系电话：（021）54353667。欢迎投稿！

北京怡然文轩

专注景观、建筑、规划、室内等设计领域书籍与期刊发行

序	期刊名称	类型	期数	定价（元）	年定价（元）
1	建筑创作	双月刊	6	120	720
2	建筑学报	月刊	12	46	552
3	世界建筑	月刊	12	45	540
4	建筑技艺	月刊	12	32	384
5	城市建筑	月刊	12	35	420
6	城市建筑	上旬建筑设计	12	35	420
7	城市建筑	下旬景观规划	12	35	420
8	建筑实践	月刊	12	86	1032
9	DOMUS（中文版）	月刊	12	138	1656
10	时代楼盘	月刊	12	50	600
11	建筑细部	双月刊	6	68	408
12	中国建筑装饰装修	月刊	12	60	720
13	世界建筑导报	双月刊	6	39	234
14	建筑师	双月刊	6	45	270
15	新建筑（中文版）	双月刊	6	38	228
16	设计新潮	季刊	4	40	160
17	城市环境设计	双月刊	6	176	1056
18	建筑与文化	月刊	12	45	540
19	景观设计学	双月刊	6	68	408
20	景观设计	双月刊	6	88	528
21	风景园林	月刊	12	42	504
22	国际新景观	双月刊	4	87	348
23	雕塑	双月刊	6	32	192
24	国际城市规划	双月刊	6	38	228
25	城市规划	月刊	12	32	384
26	规划师	月刊	24	40	960
27	北京规划建设	双月刊	6	30	180
28	城市规划学刊	双月刊	6	38	228
29	住区	双月刊	6	36	216
30	设计	月刊	12	35	420
31	城市住宅	月刊	12	23	276
32	室内设计与装修（ID+C）	月刊	12	35	420
33	设计世界（原装饰装修天地）	月刊	12	38	456
34	现代装饰（现代装饰与家居版合）	月刊	12	49	588
35	室内（中国台湾）	月刊	12	100	1200
36	室内设计师	季刊	4	60	240
37	照明设计	双月刊	4	38	152
38	设计家	双月刊	6	40	240
39	设计新潮	季刊	4	40	160
40	装潢世界 & 软装饰界	10 月刊	10	60	600
41	hinge（中国香港）	11 月刊	11	150	1650
42	城市中国	季刊	4	40	160
43	缤纷	双月刊	6	68	408
44	a+u（日本）	月刊	12	350	4200
45	domus（意大利）	11 期	11	260	2860
46	商店建筑（日本）	月刊	12	320	3840
47	新建筑住宅特集（日本）	月刊	12	330	3960
48	idea（日本）	季刊	4	350	1400
49	INTERIOR DESIGN（美国）	月刊	12	150	1800
50	ARCHITECTURAL RECORD（美国）	月刊	12	220	2640
51	ARCHITECTURAL REVIEW（英国）	月刊	12	200	2400
52	landscape architecture（美国）	月刊	12	200	2400
53	ddn（意大利）	9 期	9	230	2070
54	area（意大利）	6 期	6	390	2340
55	L'ARCA（意大利）	双月刊	6	260	1560
56	INTERNI（意大利）	10 期	10	300	3000
57	THE PLAN（意大利）	8 期	8	320	2560
58	CASABELLA（意大利）	11 月刊	11	320	3520
59	ELLE DECOR（意大利）	10 期	10	180	1800
60	AD（意大利）	月刊	12	220	2640
61	JA（日本）	季刊	4	380	1520
62	AD（美国）	月刊	12	160	1920
63	AIT（德国）	10 期	10	220	2200
64	icon（英国）	月刊	12	210	2520
65	Wallpaper（英国）	月刊	12	200	2400
66	HOMES & GARDENS（英国）	月刊	12	150	1800
67	MARK（荷兰）	双月刊	6	280	1680
68	FRAME（荷兰）	双月刊	6	280	1680

注：2021 年定价陆续调整中，以最终正式售价为准

联系人：黄小姐　联系电话：010-6321 1517 / 6616 8107 / 6611 9249

（图片：深圳福田记忆公园实景）

土人学社
TURENSCAPE ACADEMY
TURENSCAPE ACADEMY
TURENSCAPE'S MISSION OF PRESERVING ECO-SYSTEMS AND CULTURAL HERITAGE IS FURTHER ENHANCED BY THE ESTABLISHMENT OF ITS EDUCATIONAL ARM, TURENSCAPE ACADEMY (TA). TA IS AN INTERNATIONAL INSTITUTION FOCUSING ON SUSTAINABLE DESIGN TRAINING IN ARCHITECTURE, LANDSCAPE ARCHITECTURE, URBANISM, AND ART & DESIGN. ESTABLISHED IN 2015, TA IS SPEARHEADED BY DR. KONGJIAN YU (HARVARD GSD), FOUNDER OF TURENSCAPE, FOUNDING DEAN OF THE PEKING UNIVERSITY COLLEGE OF ARCHITECTURE AND LANDSCAPE ARCHITECTURE, PROFESSOR AND HONORARY FOREIGN FELLOW OF THE AMERICAN ACADEMY OF ARTS AND SCIENCES. ITS CORE VALUES INCLUDE THE EXPLORATION OF ENVIRONMENTAL, SOCIAL, AND CULTURAL SUSTAINABILITY FOR THE DESIGN OF BETTER BUILDINGS, LANDSCAPES, AND CITIES IN A RAPIDLY URBANIZING WORLD.
土人学社注重人与环境的共融和谐、注重城市可持续发展、注重设计人才的挖掘和培养，为规划/建筑/景观等业界精英、专业人士、新入行的设计人员、在校学生以及关注绿色生态发展的人士等，提供国际性、高层次的专业培训。
北京总部：北京市海淀区中关村北大街127-1北大科技园303-3
西溪南教学基地：安徽省黄山市徽州区西溪南镇西溪南村小学路36号